JERSEY OCCUP

*German:* "Oeufs, canards, lapins? Pour Officers là."
*Farmer's wife:* "Non, non."

# JERSEY OCCUPATION DIARY

Her Story of the
German Occupation
1940-1945

*Nan Le Ruez
with Best Wishes*

Nan Le Ruez

Illustrations by Joyce Le Ruez

**SEAFLOWER BOOKS**

Published in 1994 by
SEAFLOWER BOOKS
16½ New St John's Road
St. Helier
Jersey

Seaflower Books is an imprint of Ex Libris Press,
to whom all enquiries and correspondence should be addressed:

EX LIBRIS PRESS
1 The Shambles
Bradford on Avon
Wiltshire
BA15 1JS

Typeset in 10 point Palatino

Design and typesetting by Ex Libris Press
Cover design by Jeanette Litterick
Cover printed by Shires Press, Trowbridge, Wiltshire
Printed and bound in Britain by
Cromwell Press, Broughton Gifford, Wiltshire

ISBN 0 948578 61 0

*This book is dedicated to my dear sons David, Christopher, Peter and John,
and in memory of their father who waited seven long years for his bride.*

# CONTENTS

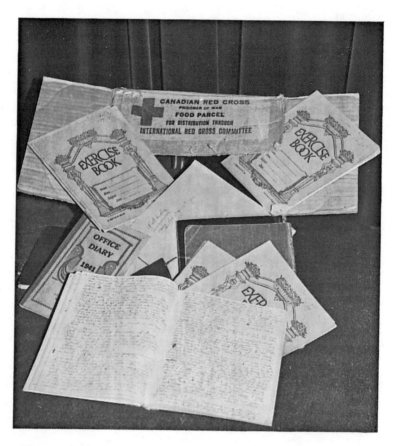

*The exercise books in which Nan Le Ruez wrote her diary during the Occupation years; they were packed away in a Canadian Red Cross box when Liberation came and have been kept there ever since.*

# Publisher's Preface

It was Nan Le Ruez herself who, during 1993, transcribed her diary from a number of hand-scripted exercise books via a word-processor on to floppy disk. In doing so, she omitted about one third of the material at her disposal. To me fell the task of editing the remainder, consisting in the main of correcting typographical errors and general tidying up. I have made no substantive changes though I have made a number of quite minor cuts, usually in order to avoid unnecessary repetition. What I have also done is to fill out names where the author had made do with abbreviations – obvious to her but perhaps not always so to the reader. In general I have tried to maintain consistency of style though the diary is written in good clear prose which contributes greatly to its readability.

This is perhaps all the more remarkable when one remembers that English was not the natural spoken language in the Le Ruez household, nor between the Le Ruez and many of their Jersey friends and neighbours. Their first language was and remains Jersey Norman-French, an archaic tongue which, even during the German Occupation, was in decline. The fact that it was a tongue peculiar to the country-dwelling islanders and was incomprehensible to the Germans rendered it a useful, secret means of communication during those years.

English, however, was the author's preferred written medium. On first reading the diary, I was struck by certain odd-sounding expressions. For example, the author always refers to having read something on the *Evening Post* rather than *in* the *Evening Post*. When I queried this with her she recalled that, in Jersey-French, she would say, 'J'ai liu chenna sus l'Evening Post', which, literally translated, would read, 'I read that on the *Evening Post*.' It seemed a real loss to edit out these authentic touches of a Jersey-French speaker so I decided to leave them in.

On the other hand, the author's use of capital letters seemed a touch quirky. Capital letters are always ascribed to flowers, such as Hydrangeas, Carnations, etc. As you read, you will quickly realise how flowers are valued as an inspiration and thing of beauty. I have, there-fore, maintained capitals for flowers. The few instances where I have felt it necessary to include a note or elaboration, perhaps to explain the meaning of a Jersey-French word, I have done so by inserting it in sqaure brackets. Otherwise, the diary is exactly as the author transcribed it during 1993, as she selected and keyed in text from her original writings.

When I published my first Channel Island book under the Seaflower imprint in 1992, I promised myself that I would avoid publishing anything concerned with the Occupation years – I considered there was quite enough already available. However, when this diary came my way, I realised after reading a few pages that I would love to publish it. I believe it is a unique document which appeals in so many different ways. I feel it has helped me understand the impact of those dark years and its effect on the local people, not least my Jersey cousins. I hope you are moved and enlightened as much as I was in reading it.

An attractive addition to the diaries are the pencil drawings by Nan's sister, Joyce, who, throughout the Occupation, kept a sketch book in which she recorded her observations. Many of the incidents and characters which prompted Nan to take up her pen prompted Joyce to take up her pencil. The drawings are executed in the same simple and unselfconcious style which characterise the text and provide the perfect complement.

In preparing the book for printing, it occurred to me that it would be a good thing to share a part of the proceeds with the Red Cross, whose work was so important in maintaining communication, albeit imperfect, between loved ones during the war, and in bringing much needed food and supplies during the final, difficult months. We hardly need reminding of the unfolding tragedies of Bosnia and Rwanda and the desperate need that still exists for the relief work carried out by the Red Cross. I am therefore happy that the Red Cross agreed to accept a donation based on sales of this book.

*Roger Jones*
*July 1994*

# Acknowledgements

That I got started at all, is entirely due to my friends, Janet and Trevor Rose, Margaret and Peter Lapes, and especially to the author Geoffrey Trease. who made me realise that my personal record of those Occupation years should not be wasted. Without the push they gave me, my Diary would never have been published. I felt compelled to act upon their advice and encouragement. My gratitude to them is unbounded, as it is to those who helped me with the next step – to find a publisher. These were my cousins in Jersey, Richard and Mary Le Brocq, and Philip and Sally Le Brocq, also the authors K C Renault and Sonia Hillsdon. It was the latter who recommended that I approach Roger Jones.

I cannot speak highly enough of my publisher Roger Jones, who has taken such a personal interest in me and my work. He has shown a great deal of patience with a complete amateur such as myself, especially in correcting my many computer errors, and he has painstakingly gone through far more material than either of us realised there would be when I started on the job.

I could never have coped with the intricacies and quirks of a word processor without the continued help of my sons David, Christopher and Peter; also Graham Brooks and Paul Cooper, who also came to my aid. My sons and their wives have given tremendous support to me all along and Christopher, John and Diana have taken pictures for me. To them all I am so grateful.

I also wish to thank all those, who, when I asked, were willing for me to publish what I had written about them, all those years ago, or about their relations. It was not possible to get in touch with everyone, but I hope that I will not have upset anyone by anything I wrote.

I am grateful to my husband's sister, Elsie, especially, and to all other friends who have kept giving me the encouragement I needed. It is of great regret to me that my dear friend Joyce Walker has not lived to see the publication of my book; she was so looking forward to it.

Finally, I have had many qualms about making public something so very personal, but I have done so in the firm belief that it was something God wanted me to do. To Him be the Glory.

*Nan Le Ruez and Alfred Du Feu; just engaged, April 1938.*

# INTRODUCTION

My parents were Henry Prouings Le Ruez and Adèle Marie, née Le Brocq. They had ten children, of whom the two youngest died in infancy. I was their second child, born on July 21st, 1915 in a farm called Westfield in St. Mary's, Jersey, my father's family home. I was christened Annie Margaret, but have never been called by any other name than 'Nan'.

When I was seven-years-old, we moved to Homestead, St. Peter, which was my Mother's family home, where her parents and a great-aunt were still living. Grandpa Le Brocq had been Constable of St. Peter's and was well-known as a breeder and exporter of Jersey pedigree cattle, and my brothers have carried on the tradition.

By the time the Occupation came, my Mother's parents and aunt had long since died, also my Mother's last two precious babies, and my father's parents from Westfield had come to live with us, so that we were twelve living at Homestead. We were all working on the farm except the youngest girl, Joyce, who had a job at solicitor Oliver Mourant's office in St. Helier. We had all left school by the age of 16, or earlier, as we were needed on the farm. With such a large family to bring up and grandparents to care for, further education was completely out of the question for us. We all worked equally hard during the Occupation to help keep ourselves and others. Everything took longer to do than was normally the case. For example, all the hot water that was needed for cooking, washing-up, baths, etc. had to be heated in a large cauldron on an open wood fire for which wood was scarce and often not dry. Tears of frustration were sometimes shed, which did not help the fire to burn! The water for washing the clothes was heated in the copper in the wash-house, part of a cottage situated in the farmyard. Whatever water was needed for boiling, washing or rinsing had to be carried in in buckets from outside.

In December 1937 I had met Alfred Du Feu at a party. He was home for Christmas from Handsworth College, Birmingham, where he was training for the Methodist ministry. We became engaged three months later, when he returned for his Easter vacation. In those days, a Methodist minister was not allowed to marry until the end of his probation, i.e. seven years from the day he entered Training College. My fiancé still had four years probation to do, so we knew we could not get married until 1942. We would also have to be separated most of the time, as he was due to go to Nigeria as a missionary. He sailed from Liverpool in September 1938, and he was to come home for six months' furlough in April 1940. How I dreaded the thought of having to part from him again then. Little did I realise that worse than that was in store for us!

When 1940 came, the war was on, and Alfred was asked by the Missionary Society to stay in Africa a little longer. And when France capitulated to the Germans and we were thrown into a panic, I was waiting to know when he was coming home. My first thought was to get away as soon as possible and with others in the family I queued for a whole day to register for a place on a boat. Then I had second thoughts – England was being bombed and we were not. In his last letter my fiancé had said that he had been told that his boat might have to be diverted to America (because the Germans were expected to invade England). Rather than go off in a panic and maybe jump from the frying-pan into the fire, was it not more sensible to wait another day or two, when I hoped to get a letter with definite news. And that is what I did, having prayed earnestly for guidance. That letter was on the way, with instructions for me, but I never got it until the war was over. Jersey was bombed and occupied by the Germans before it had time to reach me! Then began a great ordeal for both of us – a test of our love for one another and of our Christian faith.

Since my school-days, I had, on and off, kept a diary, mostly about gardening and Church activities, and during the German Occupation I continued to do so. But that what I wrote at that time would ever be published, or be worth publishing, never entered my head. At the end of the war I put those diaries in an empty Red Cross parcel box and there they remained, unread, for nearly fifty years. Every time we moved, the box travelled with us, and though I did sometimes mention to friends that I had written these diaries, no one ever saw them, and I myself had forgotten a great deal of what I had written. For various reasons, I have not included the whole of what I wrote, but the entries in this book, apart from minor editing undertaken by my publisher, are exactly as I wrote them. It may well be that writing things down acted as a means of relieving some of the tension of those difficult days, otherwise I cannot explain why I wrote at such length.

The Methodist Church in Jersey was, at the time of the Occupation, divided into four sections, each with its own set of ministers and lay preachers. The section to which I belonged was known as the French Circuit and consisted of 17 chapels, the main one (known as the Circuit chapel) was Grove Place in St. Helier. This area was shared between three ministers and two probationers. There were 33 Local (Lay) preachers and five 'on trial'. The Rev. W J Ward, Superintendent, was in overall charge. He prepared the plan of preaching appointments, and we all went where we were sent. Our ministers had been appointed to Jersey by the Methodist Conference.

Apart from one or two exceptions there are, unfortunately, no photographs taken during the Occupation, as we were not permitted the use of cameras. Therefore I am very grateful to my sister, Joyce, for allowing me to use the sketches which she drew during those days and which illustrate, in a remarkable way, some of the things I wrote. Those, like my diary, had to be kept hidden!

*Nan Du Feu*
*July 1994*

# PEOPLE IN THE DIARY

*The Le Ruez family at Homestead, St. Peter's:*
>Grandpa ('Papa') and Granny;
>Dad and Mother;
>*Their eight children, in descending order of age:* Francis, Nan, Kathleen, Laurence, Christine, John, Joyce, Herbert.

*The Le Ruez family at Westfield, St. Mary's:*
>Uncle Ernest (Dad's brother) and Auntie Edith;
>Leslie and Margaret.

*The Le Brocq family at Les Potirons, St. Mary's:*
>Uncle John (Dad's uncle, brother to Granny Le Ruez);
>Eunice and Lucille, his daughters;
>Aunt Elize, his sister; Evie (her daughter);
>Emmeline, wife of Uncle John's son, Jack.

*At Grève d'Azette:*
>Auntie Lulu, Mother's sister; Uncle Gordon.

*In Birmingham:*
>Auntie Janet (Mother's sister); Uncle Bert;
>Adèle, Florence and Marion (their daughters).

*Other close relations:*
>Uncle Edward (Mother's brother); Auntie Hazel (his wife, evacuated during the Occupation);
>Cousin Henry, his eldest son, in India; Cousin Doris, Henry's sister;
>Peter, another son, in the RAF (killed early in war);
>Uncle Fred (Mother's brother) in America; Auntie Lucy, his wife.
>Cousins Henri and Laurence Picot in Queensland (Mother's nephews)
>Uncle Philip Le Brocq (Granny's brother); Auntie Julia, his wife.

*Grandpa's relations at St. Ouen's:*
*His nieces:*    Alice Amy and Hilda;
>Florrie and her husband, John Pirouet and son, John;
>Lizzie and her husband, Jack Malzard and daughter, Betty;
>Ellen Amy.

*Others related to us, near or far:*

> Cousin Sylvia Le Brocq and Oliver Mourant (solicitor); her brother-in-law and Peter, his son;
> Cousin Olive Crill, wife of Constable Syd Crill and Peter, their son;
> Cousin Frank Le Gros; Cousin Eunice du Val, wife of Constable du Val;
> Mrs Cecil Hamon; Mrs Dorey; Le Brocq family from The Stores, St. Peter's;
> Priscilla Du Heaume; Eunice and Gwen Germain; Irene; Mrs Amy (baker).

*Alfred's relations:*

> *At Montpelier, Beach Road, St. Helier:*
> George and Alice Du Feu, his parents (referred to in the diary as Father and Mother – not my own Dad and Mother) and Elsie, his sister.
> *At St. Martin:*
> *The Le Seelleur family from Cloverly (where Alfred and I met):*
> Mr and Mrs Le Seelleur and their daughters, Bunty and Muriel.
> Miss Linda Le Seelleur and her sister, Mrs Captain Ahier, from Springside.
> Others: Margaret Du Feu; Mr and Mrs Slade.

*Friends at Les Nièmes Farm, St. Peter's:*

> Mr and Mrs Vibert and their children, Raymond, Phyllis and Beryl who later, all married into our Homestead family.

*Friends at La Pompe, St. Mary:*

> Mr and Mrs John S Arthur and their daughters, Miss Ethel and Miss Winnie; Miss Clara, their aunt.

Joy (Miss Joyce Deverell Walker), my special friend, and her Mother;
Emily Hamon, her friend;
Mr Curwood, Emily's uncle;
Mrs Captain Syvret and Joan, her daughter;
Phyllis Le Brun.

In addition to the above family and friends, many other friends and acquaintances are mentioned in the diary.

Because the Methodist Church played such a central part in my life, many preachers are mentioned by name; these are as follows:

*Ministers:*    Rev. W J Ward (Methodist superintendent); Rev. Clark; Rev. Dr. Leslie Church; Rev. W C H Fell; Rev. Foss; Pastor Hanks; Rev. Killen; Rev. C N Mylne; Rev. Norman; Rev. J W J Scott; Rev. A T Skyrme; Rev. R E South; Rev. Stuart; Rev. F B Struthers; Rev. Bernard Titmus (Alfred's friend, in England).
*Local preachers (Lay preachers):*    E P Ahier; Philip E Brée; A De B Breton; Mr Bull; Irene De La Perrelle; Elsie Du Feu; Francis Du Feu; Lilian Du Feu; Philip Huelin; R. Howells; Reg. Jeune; Edward Le Feuvre; Enid Le Feuvre; John B Le Quesne; Philip Le Ruez; Philip Noel; Arthur Querée; Walter Querée; P J Sarre; E Siouville; Mr Watson.

*The Le Ruez children;*
*Above, from left to right:*
*Nan, Kathleen, Christine*
*and Joyce (photo taken after*
*the Occupation);*
*Left, from left to right:*
*Francis, Herbert, John*
*and Laurence (photo taken*
*before the Occupation).*

*Above left:*
*Dad and Mother,*
*photographed in 1966,*
*both aged 81 years;*
*Above right:*
*Uncle Edward Le Brocq;*
*Below right:*
*Granpa ('Papa')*
*and Granny.*

*Above: Alfred's parents, George and Alice Du Feu;*
*Below, from left to right: Miss Winnie Arthur,*
*Kathleen Le Ruez, Miss Clara Arthur, Mother*
*and Miss Ethel Arthur, at La Pompe, St. Mary.*

*Above: Homestead, St. Peter's, our home during the Occupation;*
*Below: Westfield, St. Mary's, my birthplace and home of Uncle Ernest,*
*Auntie Edith, Leslie and Margaret.*

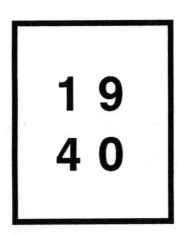

**1 9 4 0**

*July 1st.*     Auntie Lulu phoned about 10am and told us that planes had dropped Nazi flags and letters to the Bailiff. We soon found that it was only too true; we discovered a Proclamation stuck near the public pump here at the corner, ordering us to put up white flags of surrender before 7am tomorrow. Failure to obey will mean heavy bombardment.

*July 2nd.*     First German planes landed at about 7pm at our Airport yesterday, when they roared low over our house. Today plenty German planes came and went. Soldiers were posted in different places in town. No-one is allowed to listen to any broadcast except German. The hardest part of this is that we cannot communicate with anyone outside Jersey, nor get any news at all. I feel like crying when I think of how worried my dear Alfred will be.

*July 3rd.*     It feels so strange as we put the clocks forward last night, two hours ahead of the proper time. It was quite daylight at 10pm. Mother made redcurrant jelly; I squeezed it. Afternoon I thinned the grapes in the greenhouse. I feel so down especially when I think of Alfred.

*July 5th.*     I went to town with Mother this afternoon. We had not yet seen any Germans but when we got to the Town Hall there was one on guard, with his tin helmet and rifle. I saw two young soldiers leaning out of a window smoking cigarettes and others walking about town, whistling. They all look very healthy and strong. Went to get the bus at the Weighbridge and saw the damage done by the bombs. I received a note from Lilian in which she said: 'This is an opportunity to practise what we have preached!'

*July 7th. SUNDAY.* We are thankful to be able to worship as usual. We all went to Philadelphie tonight. Mr Siouville preached a very good sermon: 'My grace is sufficient for thee.' What a fine and good man he is.

*July 21st.* My Birthday. Mother gave me a silver tea-ball. I wrote to Alfred, even though the letter cannot be posted, but, on this, my birthday, I am thinking so much about him.

*July 26th.* Stayed in bed all day. Bother! Knitted some of Alfred's socks and began reading the *Life of Samuel Chadwick*. Mother came to my room tonight, so very upset because Mrs Le Brocq told her that the Germans are taking away the men of military age. I hope it is not true. We could not bear this. I pray to God, but sometimes it is no comfort – it is so difficult.

*July 30th.* I helped Mother indoors whilst the girls were in the potato field. Now that we cannot have much meat, meals take longer to prepare as we must do so many vegetables. Evie and Aunt Elize came this afternoon. Evie wheeled her Mother in a bath-chair!

*August 4th. SUNDAY.* Went to Bethlehem morning. Rev. Skyrme preached. He arrived in a landau drawn by two horses. We met it carrying Rev. Ward back from St. Ouen's. How comfortable he looked, sitting there in the back!

*August 5th.* Girls in field. Joyce had a holiday, so she helped with the potatoes also. I helped indoors, did some gardening and scraped the gravel. There is a rumour that the English have raided an outpost in Guernsey and captured ten prisoners.

*August 6th.* Lots of planes today. Some passed so low and at such speed that we were very frightened. Poor Mother is so upset. She called me to come indoors. I don't know why Mother should have to suffer so.

*August 7th.* Herbert and I went to La Pompe to see Miss Winnie's puppies. We did no digging today; boys weeded roots. No fishing (except by rod) from yesterday. Rumour says that it is because German bodies have been found by fishermen. A lot of air activity yesterday and today.

*August 8th.* Afternoon, we saw about sixty German planes heading for England, some having taken off from the Airport here. How awful it is to know that they are on a raid to England. Tonight I feel very anxious about Alfred. It is so dangerous on the sea, and he may be leaving Africa. How I wish I knew about him. News that over a thousand planes visited England yesterday. How anxious we feel about people in England, especially about Auntie Janet, when we hear about raids in the Midlands.

*August 19th.* Picked lovely bunch of Sweet Peas. How flowers help to cheer us! Constable du Val came with five Germans to see heifers. Francis went down to field at St. Ouen's with them, but, fortunately, they did not find the heifers good enough!

*August 23rd.* New Proclamation today to say that we must not spread propaganda; penalty – 15 years imprisonment.

*August 25th. SUNDAY.* About 4am I was awakened by sound of planes and a bomb falling, followed by anti-aircraft fire. It seemed terribly near and I trembled in my bed. It was German guns shooting at British planes bombing the Airport. It was first time we heard anti-aircraft fire and it was not pleasant. Tonight, at chapel, I was silly and broke down and cried when we were singing Hymn 916: *Holy Father, in Thy mercy, Hear our anxious prayer, Keep our loved ones, now far distant, 'neath Thy care.* It was when I thought of my dear Alfred.

*August 31st.* Very warm and fine. All day we have heard continuous gunfire. We don't think it was bombing which has made the house shake. We think it was British warships bombarding the coast of France from Cherbourg to St. Malo.

*September 7th.* After the News this morning, we were thrilled to hear 'Beautiful Jersey' played by Edward O'Henry at the BBC Theatre organ.

*September 8th.* Very heavy German raids over London last night. It is awful. Nevertheless, our brave King and Queen went with the Princesses to worship at Windsor this morning. Today has been appointed by the King as a National Day of Prayer. Tonight, we listened in to the Archbishop of Canterbury preaching. After, we heard an appeal on behalf of evacuated Channel Islanders by Lord Justice du Parcq – tears came to my eyes.

*September 12th.* How I long for Alfred. It is hard to think that I must face another winter without him. I wonder how he is, and where he is.

*September 13th.* Real rain at last. Rained all morning. It cleared this afternoon and Mother and Kath went to town. News that a deliberate attack has been made on Buckingham Palace; Royal Chapel destroyed. Our dear King and Queen were in residence, but were unhurt, thank God.

*September 16th.*     Rained again, but cleared later. Strong gale blowing. Cycled to First Tower and had lunch with Joy who had invited Elsie as a surprise for me. Mrs Walker then came and I was so pleased to see her. I went to town to see Rev. Ward and offered to take the services for which Alfred had been planned. He was glad and gave me his blessing.

*Sept. 17th.*     Strong gale blowing. Washed my hair and dried it in the sun and wind outside my bedroom window.

*Sept. 22nd. SUNDAY.*     Left Montpelier at 9.30am with Elsie and Irene de la Perrelle. We cycled to St. Martin's chapel and arrived at 10.05. Went into vestry where Mr and Mrs Le Seelleur made us welcome. Service began just after 10.30. I felt very much at home there and not nervous. I announced the hymns, took first prayer, the 2nd lesson, and gave the sermon. My text was St. John XI v. 5 and 6. Irene took the other parts of the service.

*Sept. 24th.*     We have been so excited. RAF planes dropped leaflets for us during the night! 'News from England' with a message form our dear King and Queen; also, picture of them standing in the ruins where Buckingham Palace had been bombed. Mr Bisson, our neighbour, brought us a leaflet to read, then John brought bits which he had found in the yard at Westfield. How wonderful it is to realise that they are thinking of us in England. God bless them all.

*Sept. 29th. SUNDAY.*     Went to Bethlehem morning. Spoke to the children on 'the Harvest truly is plenteous, but the labourers are few.' Rev. Skyrme here for dinner and tea. Lilian came for tea and we took the service together at Bethlehem tonight. Alfred had been planned, so I preached the sermon and conducted the service. It was so much better than I expected. Lilian took second Reading and second Prayer. All went well. There were about 60 people present. I know that many friends were praying for me, and I feel so happy to have done this for my dear Alfred, and for God.

*October 1st.* Mrs du Feu phoned to say that Father had been knocked down by a car driven by two Germans who took him to hospital. I hope he is not too bad, especially for Alfred's sake.

*Oct. 2nd.*     Went to Montpelier. Dined alone with Elsie, as Mother had gone to hospital to meet Father. They came back in a cab! I am thankful that Father is not looking too bad. A small bone is broken in the leg so it must be in plaster for a month. Bought coat at Brownes. Shops are closing for ten days. (new Proclamation came out this morning) so town overflowing with people.

*Oct. 4th.*     Bichards, our grocer sent us some *biscottes* from France. They look like pieces of bread toasted and are lovely and crisp like rusks. I feel so lonely of Alfred. How long will it be before I see him again?

*Oct. 6th, SUNDAY.*     We began services in the afternoon as we are not allowed any heating or lighting at all. Service at 3pm. Philip Le Ruez, who was planned, did not turn up so Uncle John read a sermon. We heard later that sirens had sounded by mistake in the Eastern parishes so Philip thought there was an air-raid.

*Oct. 8th.*     Raymond Vibert found a leaflet, written in French. He was so excited! Cycled to town; it rained all the way. Went to Filleul's to help to choose prizes for Sunday School. Went to Montpelier and stayed to sleep. Lilian called to see me about our preaching appointment at Tabor. Father is looking quite well. German soldiers have called twice to see him and brought him a box of cigars!

*Oct. 10th.*     It was announced on the *Evening Post* last night that one could send enquiries about relatives in England, so Father will try to send a message to Alfred through the Mission House in London.

*Oct. 15th.*     Stayed in bed all day. How I hate those horrid colds! All very upset as Dad was told that all young men (18 to 35 years) must register. One cannot tell what it means.

*Oct. 18th.*     Mrs Le Sueur came to see Mother, and she prayed with her. It is so sweet of her. She too is anxious about her son. We've been upset because Leslie and Margaret have been taken to Overdale Hospital as they both have scarlet fever. Uncle went as far in the ambulance and he thinks they will be quite happy there. Another boy from St. Ouen's was also taken today; it has been so sudden.

*Oct. 22nd.*     Began planting Wallflowers in the Avenue. We were so excited to hear a programme broadcast on the Channel Islands. Heard some Islanders speak in our *patois* but we did not know who they were. (*Salut, Salut, Jerriais, a bétôt, et que Dieu vos garde*). Some evacuated children also spoke and sent messages to their people here. We were disappointed not to hear anyone we knew. How one longs for some personal news.

*Oct. 30th.*     This morning I scrubbed potatoes for flour. This afternoon we began scraping them in a large tin. Evie helped Mother and the four of us girls all the afternoon. Aunt Elize was upstairs with Granny.

*Oct. 31st.* Stormy and rainy. Alice Amy here; she helped us to finish scraping potatoes. Afternoon we were threshing. We had tea early so as to give the men theirs afterwards. We made them a big stew, and broccoli. What a busy day with so many people to feed.

*November 1st.* Cycled to town as 'St.Ouen' rumoured that there was baking powder at the Drug Stores. I did not get any as it was already sold out. However, I bought two sieves to sieve our potato flour.

*Nov. 3rd. SUNDAY.* Pouring rain and wind. Left at 9.45am and cycled to Tabor Chapel. Got soaked but had brought hat, shoes and stockings to change. Caretaker of chapel lent me a towel to wipe my legs and feet. Lilian and I were to take the service together, but, I had to do it alone as she arrived too late. The weather was so bad that she had to walk part of the way. I felt so sorry, as she had prepared a children's address. Joy and Emily came to hear me! Léa Le Rossignol had asked me to dinner, but I came home and got soaked again!

*Nov. 7th.* Alice Amy here. Afternoon, seven people turned up! I had invited Léa to tea, but before she arrived Cousin Frank Le Gros came awhile, then Miss C Arthur and Mrs Arthur to see Granny and, later, Rev. and Mrs Scott. What an afternoon! We are glad to see that Mr and Mrs Scott don't seem too upset at having been turned out of the Manse by the Germans. As Mr Scott said: "Now I shall have a story to tell to the nations."

*Nov. 11th.* We began peeling apples for black butter [a traditional Jersey dish]. Heard that a troop-carrier had crashed on the Island and 23 Germans killed. J B Le Quesne is supposed to be making all the coffins but one can never know the truth about anything these days. Rev. Scott is still looking for a place in which to live.

*Nov. 12th.* We peeled more apples and Mother boiled cider ready for making black butter. Notice on *Evening Post* tonight that all wireless sets are going to be confiscated; reason given is that there has been espionage in Guernsey! We feel very upset for it will be terrible to be altogether without news. We are cut off from everyone and everything.

*Nov. 14th.* Cyclone last night – supposed to be the worst in living memory in Jersey. No one injured but hundreds of trees down and roofs blown off houses. We had five trees down and chutes off cottage. Three chimney-pots fell off the Manse at Croix-au-Lion, but it is the Germans who are there so Rev Scott did not care! Roof blown off ward at Overdale – room where Leslie and Margaret are. They were unhurt.

*Nov. 15th.* Went to Mr Bauche's orchard to see all the trees that had been blown down – lots of apple trees and two pine trees. Heard that Coventry had been heavily bombed last night – about a thousand casualties and much damage. How terrible it is; one can hardly bear to think these days.

*Nov. 18th.* Father started to go to the office again after seven weeks at home. His leg was taken out of plaster on Saturday.

*Nov. 19th.* Leslie and Margaret came back from Overdale Hospital yesterday. Went to see them at Westfield this afternoon. Leslie looks very pale and thin, but Margaret about as plump as usual! Uncle angry because there were no nurses at night with the children, and except that a woman patient rushed into the ward and pulled Margaret out of bed, she could have been killed when the roof fell in during the storm.

*Nov. 24th.* Went to Bethlehem morning and afternoon. After afternoon service we presented a clock to Eunice Dallain on the occasion of her marriage to John Richardson (September 28th) from the Sunday School staff.

*Nov. 25th.* Mother and I did shopping together in town. Bought quilt for Granny's bed and small eiderdown and blankets because soon there will be none as the Germans are buying all they can. I bought a pair of blue shoes for £1.1s.9d. at Beghins – had to wait ages as the shop was crowded.

*Nov. 27th.* I planted border at back of house with Wallflower and Forget-me-nots.

*December 25th. CHRISTMAS DAY.* Cold, but fine. Dad, Joyce and Herbert went to the service at Bethlehem. I was afraid I'd break down, so I stayed home. It is so difficult these days. There was plenty to do, cleaning, etc. Evie and Lucille called. Mr Oliver Mourant was here for dinner and tea. At 4 o'clock we listened to the King speaking to his people. How lucky we are to have our wireless still. Uncle John, Uncle Philip Le Brocq, Uncle Ernest, Leslie and Margaret came this afternoon. After tea I went to see Miss Bauche. Tonight we played games and read but when Mother began to play Carols I longed so much for Alfred that I had to go out of the room so that no one would see me cry! Later, when everyone had gone to bed I came downstairs and wrote him a few lines.

**1 9 4 1**

*January 4th*        Everything still covered with snow, and showers have fallen at intervals all day. Spent day as usual on Saturdays – after washing up, swept bedrooms, stairs, etc. Did 'my' washing. We spend much time making fire to boil potatoes for the pigs – 5 or 6 *chaudièthes* [a Jersey-French word meaning cauldron] a day, and more on Saturdays. Prepared Sunday School lesson tonight and chose hymns. Bed and prayers about 10.30 to 11pm.

*Jan. 5th. SUNDAY.* This afternoon, at Bethlehem, the preacher failed to come, so Uncle John read a sermon from the *Christian Herald* and chose some hymns. He asked me to preach the sermon but I had no notes with me so I had to refuse. I felt very sorry, as I could have helped and Uncle John does not read very clearly, so we didn't obtain much benefit from the *Christian Herald* sermon. We all sat by a nice fire in the sitting-room this evening. Raymond Vibert was with us. We listened to a broadcast service by the Bishop of Lichfield. It was broadcast from an air-raid shelter somewhere in England, and those brave people were singing hymns so beautifully and someone was playing a piano. The tears came to my eyes; it brought it all so near – what the people are going through every night. They are so splendid. Could I have sung hymns like that if I had been in their place, I wondered?
I long for Alfred. Sometimes I feel downhearted. We so wanted to marry and set up a Christian home together and to serve God together in the Methodist ministry, and sometimes I am afraid it may not be.

*Jan. 12th. SUNDAY.*        At Bethlehem, Mr G. preached. He is one of the young men who had come over from England for the potato season and who belongs to Rev. Stuart's class of young workers at Wesley chapel. There is a lot of fuss over these young men; they are suspected of being Hitler's fifth colum-nists etc. It is so difficult these days, but I feel that one must be charitable rather than suspicious.

*Jan. 13th.*     After taking up Grandpa's breakfast and washing-up, I began scrubbing potatoes for flour and continued until 6.15pm except for dinner and dishes, also about an hour in the afternoon, when I pruned the Hydrangeas along the Avenue. It was so mild and sunny, it seemed a pity to miss the opportunity of pruning. Mother was at the wash-house today. Tonight we did sewing and reading.

*Jan. 15th.*     This morning the postman brought us a Red Cross Enquiry from Uncle Bert Cox in Birmingham, but there was not a word of news and the Enquiry was dated August 6th! We could send 25 words in answer, so I wrote out this message: *All of us at home safe and very well, also relatives. Anxious about you. Tell Alfred Nan is fine Love to all.* How we pray that they will get it soon. We are so anxious about our loved ones away.

*Jan. 20th.*     Rainy day, not cold. Got up at 8.20am. Washed supper dishes. Had breakfast, then took up Granny's and Grandpa's. Devotional reading and prayers in my bedroom a few minutes, then about 10am washed all the dishes, made my bed. Changed water in both tins of potato pulp. Cup of coffee at 11.15, then all rest of morning I washed apples. After dinner washed dishes, saucepans, sinks. Peeled apples for black butter all afternoon. At 6 o'clock prepared Granny's tea and took it up. Set table for us. Had tea, washed up. Changed water in tins of potato pulp again. By then it was 8.30pm. I typed out part of a sermon until 9.40pm. Then sat by the fire and read a light book until 10 o'clock. Had a good wash. Devotional reading and prayers. Now writing this in bed at 11.30. Will think of Alfred and then – sleep!

*Jan. 22nd.*     Alice Amy came. Dear Auntie Alice, she is so fond of us, and she always manages to bring us things from Joyce Hamon's shop at St. Ouen; there are so many things one cannot get now. It was a great joy when she brought me two tins of Brasso last week and a packet of Statice seeds today! What little things bring pleasure now. One learns to be thankful for them.

*Jan. 26th SUNDAY.*     I preached at Bethesda afternoon. Herbert cycled with me to the top of Jubilee Hill, then I went on alone. Lovely view of the sea – sun came out just as I got to the bottom of the hill. Got off my bicycle and stopped to look at the beauty around me, Corbière Lighthouse in the distance. Also looked at the place near the wall where Alfred and I made it up after we had misunderstood each other that Friday afternoon. Now I feel how stupid we both were!

*Jan. 29th.*     Mother and I went shopping in town. Went to Summerland factory to try to get wool but could get nothing! Town full of Germans buying up. There is now almost nothing left in the shops. We saw carpets at Le Gallais ready packed for Germany and the money the Germans pay is of no value to us. We are being robbed of everything. Evidently, there is little clothing to be had in Germany. I went on to Montpelier to tea and stayed to sleep. I had not been for three weeks.

*February 2nd.*     Wrote a little to Alfred, but my letter is getting very long, having got started last July! Mrs Leon Raimbault's brother, Henry, was shot dead by a German patrol last Saturday – he was walking in the Military Zone near the Five Mile Road after 8pm which is against orders.

*Feb. 6th.*     Joyce Walker, Elsie and Léa came afternoon and we played games in the drawing-room and had tea by the fire. I feel so sad tonight to think of how people are lacking food, especially milk and butter. It almost made one want to cry to see the weeny pat of butter that Joyce brought as her ration. Mother felt so sorry that she put more butter in her bag, buttermilk and a little potato flour. Joyce had brought us a two-pound loaf, which was very thoughtful of her.

*Where the cooking was done at Homestead – the* Chaudièthe *is in the centre, the bread oven in the wall on the right*

*Feb. 7th.*     Went to see Miss Bauche. She gave me a lovely large Concordance of the Old and New Testaments and wrote my name in it with the text: *The Lord bless thee and keep thee* from the Book of Numbers. How good she is, dear Miss Bauche! She has been knitting long socks for the boys and wishes she could do more, as she says she is so fond of us.

28

*Feb. 8th.*     In the greenhouse I mixed some ground and sowed about a hundred Sweet Pea seeds in pots and boxes – some of Dobbie's left over from last year, and some I had saved. There is an Order on the *Evening Post:* from tonight. It is forbidden to use electric light from 11pm to 7am.

*Feb. 12th.*     At last, news of Alfred. Elsie phoned to say that Father had had a Red Cross message from Alfred: *I am very well and living at Auntie Janet's.* It is wonderful to know that he is safe and I feel him near to me. But it has been a shock to hear that he is in England. I kept on thinking that probably he had stayed in Nigeria. Oh, my thoughts and feelings are so mixed.

*Feb. 13th.*     This morning the postman brought two Red Cross messages for me from Alfred. He was spending a few days with Peggy and Arthur. How thoughtful of him to tell me, for now I know that they are also safe. I was so anxious for them. I went this afternoon to Einnim at First Tower and showed Elsie and Joy and the Brigade girls who were there my Red Cross messages. I celebrated the occasion by giving each of them a chocolate out of a box Emily had given me last July! Mrs Le Rossignol phoned; she had also heard. What a difference this bit of news has made to us all – we are full of new hope and courage now and don't feel so dreadfully cut off.

*Feb. 15th.*     Cycled to town this morning. Bought overalls and last pair of breeches for the boys at the Vier Soudard. One cannot buy trousers anywhere. Met Joy so we had lunch together at Gaudins, which was an unexpected pleasure! Got back in time to wash dinner dishes, swept stairs and hall, then went and sowed Sweet Peas and Love-in-the-mist in garden. Auntie Lulu phoned to say she had to go to hospital for a week and would I go and keep house for Uncle Gordon.

*Feb. 16th. SUNDAY.*     It has been a wonderful week because at last I've had news of Alfred. But I feel sort of bewildered for somehow I did not think he had come back to England. How it makes me long for him when I know that he is nearer. And how hard it is for him. I hope he is not angry that I did not go to England, but it was so difficult to know what to do during those three days of panic. I felt that God had guided me to stay here. I wish I knew how long Alfred has been in England and oh, must he go back to Africa?

*Feb. 17th.*     Mother went to see Dr. Lewis to find out about Auntie Lulu – she did not expect to hear the bad news which he told. He gave Mother no hope at all for her recovery. He cannot understand how she came to wait so long before going to him. Now it is too late. What a shock it is to all of us.

*Feb. 21st.*     Snowed quite heavily but it did not stay long on the ground.

Finished scraping potatoes afternoon. Auntie Lulu phoned to say she is not going to hospital before Monday; the Germans have taken over another ward, so everything is upset. Auntie is upset as she is rapidly getting worse and is very anxious at another delay. Poor Auntie does not know the truth, but she is beginning to realise that she is bad.

*Feb. 24th.* Cycled to Beaufort Square, Grève d'Azette. Found Miss Gilbert doing the washing. Uncle had gone to take Auntie Lulu to hospital. About noon they both came back, as there was no room yet at hospital. It is awful – poor Auntie Lulu looked yet worse today. I am terribly afraid for her. She said that Uncle had broken down and cried this morning, and I must take great care of him when she is away.

*Feb. 26th.* Cycled to town. Had tea at Montpelier. Elsie came as far as Beaufort Square with me. Auntie had gone to hospital about 6pm. She had received a Red Cross message from Auntie Janet. Uncle and I wrote out a reply tonight. I have come up to bed about 9.45. Said my prayers, etc. Trying not to feel lonely. I wish I was not alone in this big room.

*March 2nd. SUNDAY.* Went to Montpelier for tea. Elsie and I went to Grove Place this evening; Rev. Ward was preaching. It did me so much good to go. We had a lovely service and God seemed near. I prayed much for Alfred. Elsie came back with me here to sleep. We spoke to Uncle for about an hour then went to bed about 10pm. I feel as if I had been months away from home! It has been such a strange week. How I long to be back at our lovely home. Being here has made me realise what a happy and lovely home I have. It is so lonely here, and Uncle has no religion.

*March 7th.* Did cooking for Uncle all morning. Afternoon met Mother in town. Tried on a few hats at De Gruchy's but none fitted, and of course they have very few now. Mother went on to see Auntie Lulu in hospital whilst I did shopping with Joy. She asked my advice about buying a rabbit which was in the Market. They asked £1 for it. I told her it was too much for such a miserable-looking creature!

*March 9th. SUNDAY.* Went home afternoon. Spoke with Dad and Mother by the fireside for a while. Had tea then went to Bethlehem for 6pm service. Mr P. preached and was rather long as I was wanting to get back! Called home and saw Granny a few minutes, then had to cycle back here. I found it hard to leave home when they were all settling down for a nice quiet evening by the fire! It is such a long journey back to Grève d'Azette. Arrived in town about 8.40pm. Had supper at Montpelier. Elsie and I came along here to sleep. Uncle was just back from the neighbours where he goes after he has been to hospital;

this he does so as not to have to light his own fire!

*March 12th.* Spent all morning turning out Auntie's bedroom and putting that and other things tidy for her return. Did a little cooking and we had dinner early. Uncle got a taxi for Auntie and they returned from hospital at 2pm. I made a cup of tea for Auntie, but she seemed in a great hurry for me to be going as soon as possible. Seeing this, I took my baggage, fixed it on the bike and departed! So glad to be back after a fortnight away! Alice here. We scrubbed potatoes all afternoon.

*March 15th.* Lovely day, sunny and warm. Swept bedrooms as usual, then gardening. Planted Wallflowers in empty spaces, and put manure around all the Rose bushes. William Laffoley called to see how we made potato flour. He also looked at my Rose bushes and showed me the mistakes I had made in pruning. I was glad to learn!

*March 16th. SUNDAY.* Went to Bethlehem. Nice to be at Sunday School again! We had very good services with Rev. Scott and Rev. South today. It was our Overseas Missionary Sunday. How I thought of Alfred and imagined him doing Missionary Deputation work in England, for I hope he is still in England. This week the Germans have gone away from our Manse, also from other places they had occupied in this area. At St. Ouen's, John P. was forced to pull their guns for them with his tractor.

*March 21st.* Girls helping to plant potatoes.

*March 23rd. SUNDAY.* It has been wonderful to get news from Alfred again this week, though afterwards it always unsettles me – it seems so impossible that we should even see one another for many many months yet, as things are now. A poor young Frenchman, aged 21, was shot at St. Ouen's Manor by the Germans last Monday. I think he had tried to escape from France and get to England.

*March 26th.* Did housework, washed flower-pots in greenhouse and scrubbed potatoes. Uncle Ernest came to see Granny. She is not at all well, and full of strange ideas which terrify her. We can't do much to help her.

*March 29th.* Mother's Birthday. We gave her a Flower-bowl. I filled it with Polyanthus, Hyacinths and Japonica, and put it on the breakfast table. The Misses Arthur had sent Mother a loaf, and Auntie Edith, a pot of jam and some chocolate spread. What a treat, so acceptable in these days. Some food for sick children and babies has been received through the Red Cross. We don't know who sent it, but it is wonderful to know that someone has remembered poor little Jersey! God bless them!

*April 1st.*    Went to see Auntie Lulu. Found her looking very downhearted. I felt so sad. She gave me a lovely supper cloth that she had worked for me.

*April 3rd.*    This afternoon cycled with Phyllis and Beryl Vibert to Grove Place, where we had a Girls' League rally. We were about thirty and it was a very good meeting... it seemed to me to be a preparation for Easter. Lilian gave a short talk, and I read Matt. 28 and made the prayer. Then we had discussion groups, then our tea (which we had all brought). Afterwards Enid summed the group findings, then we all cycled back home, about 7pm.

*April 5th.*    The postman brought me a Red Cross 'note' requesting me to call at the Post Office, so I cycled to town and found a message from Alfred but all written in German. They told me he asked how I was getting on. I had to answer there and then, and a girl took down what I said – it was all so unsatisfactory.

*April 11th. GOOD FRIDAY.*    All day long I've been thinking of Alfred and have been filled with doubts and fears. Perhaps I did wrong to stay in Jersey. It is all my fault that we are not together now. I can't bear to think of him having come back to England and not found me waiting to welcome him. And he is in danger – last night Birmingham was heavily bombed, and he is there. I think all these thoughts come and make me so unhappy and feeling like crying. It was at Easter-time that Alfred returned from Handsworth College for ten days vacation, three years ago, when we became engaged. All that happy time comes back to me now. Will such happy days ever come again, I wonder?

*April 14th.*    About 11.30am I had such a lovely surprise when my friend Joy came and brought a lovely little basket of spring flowers for me, so beautifully arranged. How dear she is! I know she came to cheer me because I told her in my letter that I was finding it very hard these days. Perhaps it is because I've had a cold that I've been so down-hearted.

*April 15th.*    Went to Montpelier for dinner. Sat near the fire with Alfred's Mother and did my knitting. I told her how I felt and how difficult it was to believe I did well in staying here. We all did what seemed best.

*April 20th. SUNDAY.*    I left for Bethesda at 10am. A fine sunny morning, though still cold. As I cycled down Jubilee Hill, how lovely the sea looked, and the gorse in full bloom all over both hillsides. My congregation was small, but including the children on the platform there were about 50 persons. The front was prettily decorated with Primroses and Daffodils and looked so cheerful and spring-like. I did not feel nervous and I hope the service was helpful to those present.

*April 22nd.* Lovely sunny day. We spring-cleaned the girls' bedroom. I put the beds outside and beat them. Washed paintwork etc.

*April 25th.* Tonight I spoke to Mother as we sat by the fire. It helped me for she thinks I was guided by God to stay here, and I must not worry over the matter now. It is for my dear Alfred that I worry, to think that he came back from Africa and I was not there to meet him.

*April 26th.* Today, we each received a ration of French chocolate (two ounces) It was exciting! We had almost forgotten the taste of chocolate! It is supposed to be for cooking purposes, but we are eating it in the ordinary way.

*April 27th. SUNDAY.* Today came news that the Germans have entered Athens. How I have thought of those poor Greek people – how they must be feeling as we felt on the day the Germans landed here. One cannot describe the feeling, it was too awful!

*April 30th.* We are now allowed to send Red Cross messages so, as Dad was going to town, I prepared three for him to take to the Red Cross office.

*May 1st.* Alice here. Elsie came afternoon and we all scraped potatoes. Miss Winnie Arthur also called, on her way to fetch her weekly rations at Stan Le Brocq. Mr Oliver Mourant came for tea, so that the table was crowded out! Food is such a problem too! We had potatoes with their skins. We live on potatoes now!

*May 4th. SUNDAY.* Went to Bethlehem this morning. Sat with the children during service near a pair of dear little twins, just started! We have many new children now; the tiny ones are sweet! After dinner I cycled to town. Went to see Auntie Lulu and I could see that her face has got much worse yet. She has taken to her bed. Had tea at Montpelier. We all went to Wesley tonight. It was the Sunday School Anniversary and I enjoyed it very much indeed. The children took part in a Demonstration called 'The Shining Way.' It was all done so reverently and the whole atmosphere of the service was like that. There were bowls of Tulips and Irises in front of the stage which looked so lovely with the sun shining on them. Slept at Montpelier.

*May 11th. SUNDAY.* Bad news today of London being heavily bombed. Many casualties. Westminster Abbey and the Houses of Parliament damaged by fire and high explosives. I feel awful when I think of these things. I remember how lovely the Abbey and the Houses of Parliament looked that lovely evening in London when Alfred and I went for a short trip on the Thames (July 25th 1938). Dear old England – why should these dreadful things happen to it?

*May 13th.*   Today has come the astonishing news that Rudolf Hess is in England. He had flown 900 miles in an unarmed plane, landed by parachute in Scotland and given himself up to a ploughman! Why, no one yet knows. Somehow we feel so excited, for it must mean that things are not going smoothly with the Nazi officials. We must be careful not to speak about it when Germans are anywhere near.

*May 15th.*   We spent most of day trying out different potato-scraping machines which we had borrowed but, to my mind, our old vegetable-scraper is still the best!

*May 19th.*   After tea Joy came and I showed her all the farm animals and flowers and gave her some plants.

*May 20th.*   We had new potatoes for dinner for the first time this year. Mr Arthur Querée, a Local preacher, had given them to us.

*May 23rd.*   About 1.45am Elsie and I were awakened by a terrific crash! It terrified me as I thought it was a bomb. Then we saw lightning, so knew it was thunder. It was not, after all, the British come to rescue us!

*May 24th.*   Cycled to town after breakfast and went to Maine to buy a silver watch for John's birthday. They only had five watches left, as the Germans have had them all. Bought one for £5 and a leather chain for 2s.6d. A woman tried to steal my bike outside Le Marquand's at Charing Cross. I rushed out of the shop just in time to catch her going off with it! I was lucky! So many bikes are being stolen as one cannot buy any, except at £30 or more!

*May 25th.*   John's 21st birthday. His godparents, Mr and Mrs Le Rossignol, came to tea; also Leslie and Margaret.

*May 28th.*   I washed one lot of potatoes and we began scraping another lot. Tonight, we heard a Guernseyman speaking from Boston, America, about the Channel Islands. It was cheering to know that we are spoken of and not forgotten!

*May 29th.*   Scraped potatoes. Mother did washing. Kath's bees swarmed, and Miss Arthur came to put them in another hive tonight. What a wonderful sight to see bees swarming for the first time! I received another message from my dear Alfred today. I am so happy to know that he was alright.

*June 1st. SUNDAY.* I received a letter from Rev. W J Ward, Superintendent, giving me full authority to preach. I preached the sermon at a Girls' League service at Tabor tonight. Uncle Edward had come to hear me! Somehow I was not satisfied with myself though I had spent much thought on this Whitsun address. Tonight, came back from Bethlehem too late to hear Rev. E Douglas Gibson (who used to be in Jersey) broadcast in the Forces' hymn-singing. Sorry to have missed it, as one longs to hear any familiar voice from England.
Cycled a little way down St. Peter's Valley tonight to meet Elsie, to give her some milk and rhubarb to make something for their Brigade meeting to-morrow. I also gave her some Spider crabs to give Joy, in case they have not had any.

*June 4th.* Mother and Dad went to Mr Binet's (Cousin Wally) funeral at St. Clement's Church. The undertaker sent a taxi for them. Then, from town, they went in the horse-drawn coach.

*June 6th.* Granny had a bad turn this morning. We had Dr. Shone, and he said she had just escaped a stroke. Tonight she was bad again. Poor Granny, she has got very weak, quite suddenly. I went to town, afternoon. Bought handbag (12s.6d.) light blue leather, at De Gruchy. None elsewhere except second-hand ones, or summer ones. I was lucky to find this one, though it was expensive. Went to see Rev. Ward about Local Preaching and he is to put me on trial. I hope I have done well, but it seems wrong if I were to lose this opportunity which is given me, and I know Alfred would wish it. Rev. Ward did not think I would have thought twice about it, but I am afraid not to have time to do it properly.

*June 13th.* Went to town, called to see Lilian at the Office to tell her about Rev. Ward's letter. She agreed that I ought not to miss this opportunity of taking up Local preaching. Went to First Tower to see Joy. She gave me a ride in the 'chair' in which she carries her Mother at the back of her bicycle! It is indeed a wonderful affair!

*June 14th.* Kath's bees swarmed again! I found them just in time and syringed them with water, stopping them from going over the wall, and they settled on a small apple tree. Miss Arthur came and put them in a skep. What fun bees are!

*June 16th.* Sad news today of the sinking of *HMS Jersey.*

*June 17th.* News of the sinking by a Nazi bomber of another Jersey boat, the *St. Patrick.* I have travelled to and from England on it, and now it is gone. Mother went to see Auntie Lulu. She is getting worse rapidly. It is dreadful.

*June 19th.* I scraped potatoes afternoon. Reg. Jeune (from O Mourant's office) came to fetch a rabbit. He sat awhile with me as I was scraping potatoes outside, and we discussed Local Preaching. He is 'on trial.'

*June 21st.* Very hot. Did housework etc. Had more excitement with Kath's bees! Tried to capture the swarm in Mr. Bisson's chimney – they settled again in a tree and we tied a skep over them. But, after all our trouble, the whole swarm flew away this afternoon!

*June 22nd. SUNDAY.* News this morning that Germany has invaded Russia. Mr Churchill spoke very solemnly tonight and said that this is only a preliminary to invading England. How one longs for it all to end! Tonight we got quite a scare, for we heard that German soldiers were being billeted in private houses. 60 wanted accommodation at St. Peter and had to be treated as 'one of the family!' They went to Stan Le Brocq and he had to call the Constable and the Centenier to persuade them that he really had no room. They have not come as far as here; we are thankful, very!

*June 30th.* Washed potato flour. It is lovely and clean, not like that horrid stuff we were making with those old potatoes.

*New means of transport during the Occupation.*

*July 1st.* Mother went to see Auntie Lulu. She found her much worse, for now she can hardly speak. Poor Auntie. What an awful case. Uncle Edward called tonight. A year ago, at 7pm, German planes landed at our Airport, and we were occupied.

*July 2nd.* Tonight we heard a talk by a 'Col. Britain' who explained the V-sign which appears in all occupied countries and which the Germans fear. Really, it is an uncanny thing, and it makes us feel queer! I wonder if there is anything in the fact that this talk was broadcast just at the time when this V-sign appeared here in Jersey. I wonder if British secret agents have anything to do with it?

*July 3rd.* We scraped new potatoes for flour; sat in the garden to do it. Before the news tonight, we heard of a mysterious happening in France early in the war. Again, it was about this mysterious V-sign. We heard Beethoven's Fifth Symphony sound and three dots and dashes. It is so strange!

*July 5th.* Washed potato pulp. This morning, we heard a recording of a broadcast made by Col. Britain last night to occupied countries, again about the V-sound and sign. He told people in occupied countries to keep quiet until July 14th, then, on that day to let Germans see V-signs everywhere.

*July 7th.* Very hot. Scrubbed scullery floor and washed potato pulp. Finished afternoon, and put flour in the sun to dry.

*July 12th.* Feel very tired tonight after the week's work! Did cooking, as usual, washed dairy cans etc. Also washed my hair. Went to Mrs Willie Priaulx to get some bay leaves to put in the potato-flour pudding. Found it very good; otherwise it is rather tasteless! There are many Germans in the Island of late. They have occupied many evacuated houses.

*July 14th.* This evening I began drawing a border of Phlox on a large sheet of paper. Joy asked me to do it for her, but I've told her I don't know how to paint. She thinks I can!

*July 16th.* Weighed potato flour – have just under three pounds from 33 pounds of potatoes. Not bad!

*July 17th.* Went to Montpelier in time for dinner. Afternoon, we walked round La Collette, sat on the sea-front and read. Had tea at a small tea-place called 'Rest-a-while'. Of course, we had brought our own bread, etc. as one can only get tea! It was pleasant and I had a nice rest and change. Stayed to sleep at Montpelier. On my way I had called at Einnim and given Joy the red

At 2am:
*German:* "Oh yes, you can give me a bed."
*Le Ruez:* "No, not one, not one!"

Hydrangea which I have grown and kept so preciously for her for two years! I grew it from a cutting and this year it has one lovely bloom. it has been a pleasure for me to grow it for my friend!

*July 18th.*    Met Evie and Lucille in town and we chose books for Sunday School children. What a job! I went to every bookshop I could think of but no books to be found for my class! Even bookshops are practically empty now.

*July 19th.*    Very dull day. Have a bad cold and pretty miserable! Did house-work as usual. Not a bad day after all for we heard a talk about the Channel Islands by the Bishop of Winchester. How it cheers our hearts to feel that we are not forgotten!

*July 20th. SUNDAY.*    Did not go out on account of my bad cold. Uncle Edward here for dinner. Bethlehem Sunday Schoolroom has been taken over by the Germans. I am very upset, as it is such a lovely room and I fear it will be spoilt. We have been hearing a lot about the 'V' lately. Today was to be the mobilisation of the V-army all over Europe! We don't quite understand what it all means. Here in Jersey, this week, the Germans have been painting huge V's on the houses where they are and on cars, etc. They want it to mean Victory for them!

*July 21st.*    My Birthday. I am 26-years-old today. I had some lovely cards. How good it is to have such dear friends. I am very blessed! Joy sent me a beautiful Bible. I am so glad to have one from her, as the one I use is worn out! She and Emily came to see me tonight, Mother gave me a pretty crumb brush and tray. Spent day as usual, housework, etc. Very busy, as Christine was helping in the field.

*July 22nd.*    Mother went to see Auntie Lulu – poor Auntie can no longer speak and is in a terrible state. I feel for dear Mother.

*July 23rd.*    Uncle Gordon phoned to say that Auntie had died during the night. We know we must thank God for having taken her. She was so ill and it was so horrible that she longed to die. Postman brought me two Red Cross messages from my dear Alfred. I am so relieved to know that he is settled in England. I thank God for this news.

*July 24th.*    Went to town and ordered wreaths at De la Taste. One from Mother and Auntie Janet and one 'In loving memory of our dear Aunt Lulu from her nieces at Homestead and Olton'. I felt that the cousins in England would have wished it. Went to see Dr. Lewis as my cold is such a nuisance and I've lost my appetite. Sent my Red Cross replies, and also sent message to

Auntie Janet and to Uncle Fred in America.

*July 25th.* Mother and Dad went to Auntie Lulu's funeral this morning. Service was at the Town Church (her wish) and burial at St. Peter's church-yard. Mother is sorry that the service was not at chapel, for the Church service, led by the Dean, was so 'cold.'

*July 26th.* A strange thing happened today. Someone phoned to say that a Mrs Morley from town had received a Red Cross Message for us from 'Cox'. Joyce went to the house and Mrs Morley told her how in this message from her husband, who is at Olton, Birmingham, it said: *Le Ruez, Homestead Farm ... write Cox, Olton.* Evidently, Uncle Bert has met this Mr Morley and, evidently also, they had received no news from us.

*July 27th. SUNDAY.* Went to Bethlehem. The Germans are not yet in the schoolroom but we cannot use it, so we had Sunday School in chapel. It is rather awkward as the pews are not suitable! It would be lovely if the Germans never arrived in our schoolroom after all! Today marks the end of a very strange and eventful week – the death of Auntie Lulu, good news of Alfred. It all leaves us rather bewildered ... and in the midst of it all we are very busy digging our potatoes.

*July 28th.* Busy day, housework. Christine helping in potato field. Late after-noon, I went collecting subs. for the District Nurse. Found everyone at home, for a change!

*July 29th.* Sent Red Cross Message to my friend, Lily Briggs, in N. Ireland. I have heard nothing from her and I thought that she would appreciate a message from me seeing that we can send messages now.

*July 30th.* Terribly busy day again. However, we have finished digging the potatoes. We borrowed a potato-scraping machine from Mr Le Breton at St. Mary and I used it afternoon and evening. Machine does very well. We pulped 100 pounds of potatoes. I washed 60 pounds straightaway. Miss Du Val and Jurat Le Feuvre called to see Mother tonight.

*August 1st.* Uncle Ernest has had a calf killed; this morning, I distributed some of the pieces in the neighbourhood (to trusted friends who will be able to keep it dark!) I was glad to be able to have a piece for Mrs Walker. Joy came to fetch it.

'Military Zone Infraction'
*German:* "Identity Card?"
The swimmer was fined 10 shillings.

*Aug. 3rd. SUNDAY.* This evening I preached at St. Ouen's chapel for the first time and I enjoyed being there. John came with me and he is full of praise for a lovely service. I feel very happy about it tonight. Yet, before going, I felt very unfit. We have had so much work to do this past week (the potato flour has taken so much time) that I had not had time to prepare as I would have wished. But God has tonight helped me far more than I deserve, and I do thank Him. The chapel is large, but all said they heard me plainly. I enjoyed the music. Mr G Baudains is a very good organist. The singing too was hearty. There were about ninety persons present. Afterwards, John and I chatted to Auntie Florrie and others, then went to supper at Mr and Mrs John Malzard and Betty.

*Aug. 4th.* Had some excitement about 2am when we heard footsteps on the gravel outside, and the door of the porch was flung open! I called Dad and he looked out of the window. It was a German soldier asking for a bed! He had walked from town and was trying to find St. Ouen's Manor.
Did a bit of clearing up in the garden. My week to do the cooking. It *is* a job, on the wood fire, when one has to boil potatoes for the pigs as well! Joy phoned to thank me for the painting I had done for her. I did my best, but it seemed poor to me. However, if she is pleased with it, I am glad!

*Aug. 5th.* Dad and Grandpa went to Mr J S Arthur's funeral. He died at La Pompe on Friday. Another splendid old Jerseyman gone. He was a fine man, such a gentleman, and father of Miss Ethel and Miss Winnie, of whom we are all so fond.

*Aug. 7th.* Alfred's parents, Elsie and Enid de Gruchy, Joyce's friend, came to dinner. Afternoon, we had a round of clock golf on the lawn and sat talking. After tea, they took the last bus (6 pm) back to town. At Croix-au-lion bus-stop, we found many Germans and lots of crates and boxes etc. Evidently they are moving into the Manse again.

*Aug. 13th.* Rainy and cold all day. Alice Amy and I scrubbed 550 pounds of potatoes in the shed in the little yard. Francis took them to Mr E de Gruchy at St. Mary where, in ten minutes, they were crushed to pulp! (Quicker than all our scraping by hand!) They charged 11 shillings (two shillings per 100 pounds). We put all the pulp in a big tub, and covered it with water for the night.

*Aug 14th.* Pouring rain all day. Herbert and I squeezed potato pulp in the pantry all morning. Dad helped afternoon. Tonight, I washed all the flour a few times, and some, which was already clean, I put on dishes. Left off at 9pm to wash my hair, as it had got so wet fetching water at the tank. What a day –

water outside and water inside! An important announcement was made by Mr Attlee, deputy Prime Minister, at 4 o'clock by our time (3 o'clock in England). What a surprise to hear that Mr Churchill has met Mr Roosevelt at sea during the past few days. Thank God no harm happened to him.

*Aug. 16th.* Sun was shining this morning so I put out all the flour to dry on top of the porch outside my bedroom window. Spent most of day re-washing pulp of yesterday (the third time). Weighed last week's flour. We had nine pounds out of 120 pounds of potatoes – not enough!

*Aug. 17th.* Tonight we were thrilled to hear Lord Justice du Parcq broadcast an appeal to help those who evacuated from the Channel Islands – about 30,000 need help, he said, including 3,000 children. They are being very kind to Channel Islanders in England, but how wonderful it will be when we can all be re-united. May it be soon!

*Aug. 20th.* Tonight I meant to prepare a sermon, but Herbert needed help to pluck ducks, so I must leave my sermon for another time.

*Aug. 22nd.* Lovely day, for I received another Red Cross message from my dear Alfred. How happy I am that he is well, and longing to see me.

*Aug. 23rd.* Weather very difficult for the corn. We cannot get on with it.

*Aug. 29th.* Francis and Laurence took potatoes to be crushed, this time to Mr Querée at La Commune, St. Peter. Took 500 pounds and it cost ten shillings to crush. Uncle Gordon came to dinner. Mother was able to have a good talk with him.

*Aug. 30th.* Laurence and I spent most of day washing potato pulp, yet we have not done half. My back is aching with bending and carrying buckets of water.

*Aug. 31st. SUNDAY.* There have been rumours during the past weeks about Germans having deserted. Evie told me that a 'deserter' had gone into Mrs Dallain's yard, sat on a cattle trough and cried bitterly. He asked for bread, but Mr D. said he had none to give, as it was rationed, but he gave him a glass of milk. Finally, he ran away, when he imagined they had phoned the Commandant, saying he would be shot. Poor man!

*September 4th.* Fine. Put flour out to dry. Cousin Sylvia Le Brocq came. I walked with her to the bus at St. Mary's. Miss Ethel came to get the honey out of the beehives but could not finish the job as the bees got angry! Poor long time.

*Sept. 5th.*    Flour still drying outside. Sifted some of it. This morning, I helped Dad and Herbert to stack two loads of corn in the shed and barn. Hot work! Miss Clara Arthur had tea with us. What a lot of visitors we've had this week! I finished my Harvest sermon tonight.

*Sept. 7th. SUNDAY.*    Preached at Bethesda this morning for their Harvest. About 36 persons there, including the children. My text was, 'For we are labourers together with God.' I was very taken up with all the trouble that had been taken to decorate the chapel. There is interest there. Did not feel too cheerful about the service itself – I did my best but it seemed so poor.  At Bethlehem tonight, we had a lovely service. It was our Harvest also and congregation numbered about 150. Pastor Hanks preached a splendid sermon on 'some thirty, some sixty, some a hundred. We must, in our Christian life grow from thirty to sixty, from sixty to a hundred'.

*Sept. 8th.*    Finished drying all the flour and weighed it. Have 52 pounds out of 520 pounds potatoes – very good! Nice to have another lot finished.

*Sept. 9th.*    Lovely to get news from my dear Alfred today, dated July 2nd.

*Sept. 10th.*    At Montpelier. Elsie and I went into town, got rations, and one pint skimmed milk (queue of a hundred waiting for it in Don Street.) Went to Red Cross Office to take our replies. I went to see Rev. Ward. He was making the (preaching) plan. After tea, we sat on the sea-front reading. Then Elsie played in a tennis tournament whilst I went to see Uncle Gordon.

*Sept. 14th. SUNDAY.*    Went to Sunday School till 10.15 then cycled to Philadelphie where I was preaching at 10.45. My first time to preach there alone. Dad and Mother heard me for the first time. Congregation about 55; not many children. Had dinner at Jurat Le Feuvre's, as it was their turn to have the preacher. Mr Le Feuvre made one criticism about my preaching, which is true. I go too fast. I know, and I'm trying hard to speak more slowly.

*Sept. 15th.*    Alice here. We scrubbed 400 pounds of potatoes. Francis took them to be crushed and after tea I began washing pulp. Very happy to receive another message from Alfred, especially as it tells me where he is at last! I know he is now at Matlock in Derbyshire and I feel quite happy and satisfied about him being stationed there. But how I long to join him!

*Sept. 17th.*    Spent most of this lovely sunny day washing the flour and putting it out to dry. Miss Ethel Arthur here for dinner and tea. All day, she and Kath were about the honey. Laurence helped Miss Ethel to extract it from the hive – there is some, at last! Tonight, I went to Anniversary Practice at Bethlehem.

*Sept. 18th.* Afternoon, Joyce and I went blackberrying at La Moye with Léa Le Rossignol, who had asked us. Very few blackberries – they seem to have been picked already. We saw more Germans than blackberries! Place full of them, turning fields upside down, don't know what for. We saw huge cannons camouflaged and so on. Felt glad to get back home as it was not really very pleasant.

*Sept. 19th.* Dad's Birthday. Evie and Aunt Elize here for dinner and tea. Girls went blackberrying with Evie in our fields.

*Sept. 21st. SUNDAY.* Now that I am having news quite often, I feel so much nearer to Alfred. I have found it easier these past weeks, but how much better it would be if Alfred and I were together. How I long to talk with him. It is so long to wait. How I wish the war would end, but one does not see light yet.

*Sept. 22nd.* Alice here all day and we scrubbed 600 pounds of potatoes. Evie came to help. Evening Mr P Queree came with his crushing machine and crushed 100 pounds for Mr Bauche and 200 pounds for Uncle Ernest. By that time it was too dark to do ours. Feel very tired after all that scrubbing.

*Washing potato flour in the back yard: I am pouring water on pulp in a sieve while pulp is contained in barrel on right and flour dries on plates on table behind.*

*Sept. 24th.*    All day again washing pulp. L and C helped me afternoon and we emptied the tub before tea. I already have a large lot drying. Weather sunny, fortunately. Tonight, I went to the practice at Bethlehem – it is very discouraging work. The older girls cause Lucille and I much trouble. But my dear little ones make up for it. I carry little Dorothy Toy back on my carrier, and I enjoy doing it. She is such a sweet child!

*Sept. 26th.*    My dear Alfred's Birthday. He is 30-years-old today. How I have thought of him and prayed for him today and hoped we will be together next Birthday. How I wish we were married and that there was no more war. Went to Murchiston Lodge and had lunch with Mrs Walker and Joy, and then had tea at Montpelier with Alfred's folk. Then came back home. Raymond here tonight, slaughtering a calf, which is against regulations!

*Sept. 27th.*    Dad cut up the veal this morning and I weighed and packed for different friends. Took some to Evie and to Joy. One is so glad to be able to help friends when one can.

*Sept. 28th.*    Went to Bethlehem this morning. Philip Le Ruez preached a very good sermon on 'Let the lower lights be burning' (Chorus of Hymn 582). Went to practice afternoon. Tonight stayed with 'Mother'. Wanted to begin preparing a new sermon, but felt terribly tired after all that potato-flour making. However, I managed to  make out an outline.

*Sept. 29th.*    Planted Hyacinths and Tulips in bowls of fibre and put them in a dark airy place. Mother went to town in Mr Bauche's buggy for the first time. She is always nervous of horses, but she enjoyed the ride and returned safely, thank God.

*October 3rd.*        Afternoon, I went blackberrying in Mr. Bauche's field. Found plenty lovely, huge ones. Mother will make 'Occupation jam' – there is nothing else to make jam with! Today we have been threshing our corn, and the men were here for a meal at 6.30 pm.

*Oct. 4th.*    Today we threshed rest of our corn (at Mr Farrell, St.Ouen), and the men who helped were here again tonight for a meal. it is difficult, in these times, to find anything to give them. It is lovely to be having such fine weather, and still so warm.

*Oct. 5th. SUNDAY.*        Our Sunday School Anniversary at Bethlehem. Rev. Scott preached this morning. Poor congregation. However, tonight the chapel was quite full. Pastor Hanks was the preacher. Everything went off better than I had dared to hope! There was such a lovely moon tonight, just rising, as we were walking home from chapel and I longed very much for Alfred! I found it hard not to cry, when we were having supper tonight – there was such a lump in my throat! It seems so hard that we are engaged and yet never together.

*Oct. 6th.*    What a strange day! Meant to go to town – had got ready when, about 10.30am, our neighbour Mr Bisson called us as there had been an accident at the corner. I went, and found Joyce Egré, aged 23, suffering from shock and bruises and cuts on her face. She was put on Mr Bisson's sofa and I did what I could, but felt very anxious for her head. She was unconscious and moaning the whole time. Had great trouble to get help. At last, Dr. Nichols from St. Aubin's came and advised her to get to hospital which happened about 12.40, for we had sent for the ambulance already.

*Oct. 9th.*    Got up 11.30am. My cold worse. Felt very miserable all day! Was to have gone to La Pulente, to collect a kind of seaweed (Carrageen moss) with which we make milk-jelly. Evie called on her way. Quite a party were going, including Léa. However, Mother was rather nervous of my going for fear the Germans might start shooting practice around there. So my having a cold settled the question!

*Oct. 11th.*    Lovely to get news of my dear Alfred again, dated July 21st, my Birthday. Mother also got two messages from Auntie Janet.

*Oct. 12th SUNDAY.*    Had some excitement about 4.45pm when RAF planes came over Airport and there was plenty noise. Don't know if it was bombs or anti-aircraft. The boys saw the planes dive and leave a smoke trail! Glad they have remembered us. We don't feel quite so cut off from England when they come, even if it is high overhead!

*Oct. 15th.*    The Germans have taken over Victoria College – what indignities we have to suffer! News bad: Germans very near Moscow. How tired one is of it all. There are hundreds and hundreds of Germans in our Island now.

*Oct. 16th.*    News very bad about Russia. it is so difficult to keep up our faith and hope. I tried to re-arrange sermon for Tabor next Sunday but could do nothing. I don't know what is the matter, inspiration will not come these days. I pray God to help me so that tomorrow I may know what I must preach on Sunday.

*Oct. 21st.*    Tidied portico and put fresh pots of flowers etc. About 4.40pm our big open chimney caught fire. We 'phoned for the Fire Brigade but put out fire before they arrived with a pump, which I ran and  borrowed from Madeleine Luce. Two Fire Brigade men were here about 1½ hours, making sure all was safe in the hay-loft and boys' bedroom. We gave them tea. Uncle Edward also here for tea.

*Oct. 24rd.*    There was a lot of noise during the night. I was awakened by what I thought were bombs falling and sound of planes. Later, I heard planes again and the shooting sounded from all directions – *pom pom* and very heavy anti-aircraft fire. Felt very nervous and did not move from my bed. The others looked out and saw everything lit by two flares over the Airport and flashing of guns. Today, we have heard that bombs were dropped at St. Saviour's. Afternoon, Laurence went and saw huge craters in Mr Perrée's field at Oaklands. Houses in the district have all had their windows smashed. Thank God no one was hurt.

*Oct. 27th.*    Last night we heard planes passing very low, and shooting in the distance. At dinner-time John came back from working at Westfield, looking very excited! He had found a leaflet dropped by the RAF! So Joyce went out to look and found one in our field, the Neuf Jardin – she was pleased. The leaflets are intended for French people this time and are all written in French, but still, we are always glad when the RAF visits us with leaflets!

*Oct. 28th.*    About 9.20pm we heard a great deal of gunfire, very close, and saw the flashes. We heard the plane the Germans were shooting at. It makes us so nervous and it is awful having those huge German guns so near.

*Oct. 29th.*    Alice here. She turned up hem of my winter coat, as it is too long for 'fashion!' Sent replies to Alfred's three messages. Mr Le Rossignol came tonight. He told us that a German doctor just back from Germany had said that he had been unable to get supplies – things were bad in Berlin, and he expected a 'crack-up' there within six weeks! We hope it is true!

*November 3rd.*    BBC announced that a Spitfire had machine-gunned a German E-boat heading for Jersey. We were quite excited to hear Jersey mentioned! News about Russia very serious.

*Nov. 4th.*    Mother and Christine went to town by 9am bus. Kath and I had plenty to do with cooking, etc. I enjoyed making the rabbit stew. It is hard work to get all the cooking done in time.

*Nov. 7th.*    Uncle Gordon here for dinner and tea. I received another message from Alfred. How lucky I am to receive his messages so often. We were all thrilled also to receive one from Cousin Henry Le Brocq (in Bengal) dated May. It has taken nearly six months to come! Alfred's had taken nearly three months. Tonight, at 10.30, we heard a banging at the door. Two German soldiers, rather drunk, wanted to know the road to Dr. Evans' house!

*Nov. 10th.*   Mother had message from Auntie Janet, asking why we didn't write. Poor Auntie, they have waited so long for news, but it is not our fault. Saw on the *Evening Post* tonight that information is wanted about Denis Vibert, whom we all know has escaped. One is afraid of what the Germans might do to us, now that it is found out.

*Nov. 11th.*   Joy came about 11.30 and we cycled to First Tower together – Joy was very upset because she must give up Einnim to the Germans and she and her Mother are not safe at Murchiston Lodge either. The Germans have asked for the place a few times already. Had dinner at Montpelier. Met Miss Linda Le Seelleur in town and she asked me to have a cup of tea at Gaudin's. We waited in vain for it, as they could not get their water to boil! A cup of tea is all one can have, in any case! As we left, cup of tea arrived, but someone had already taken our seat! Today is the 500th day of Occupation!

*Nov. 13th.*   I went to Ennim. I took one egg, and Joy made an omelette for us both. Also took milk and potato-flour and she made a pudding. Brought a big parsnip too and, what with the soup she had made, we had a big lunch! We both enjoyed it. It may be the last time we have a meal there together.

*Nov. 14th.*   I meant to finish my sermon for Sunday tonight, but Mr. Frank Luce came and he and the boys made too much noise playing dominoes so I had to give up!

*Nov. 15th.*   Housework, as usual, but managed to finish my sermon for to-morrow. There's a notice on the *Evening Post* re billeting of German soldiers in our houses – it appears that thousands more are coming over. We already have little enough to eat, and they will draw on our milk and butter, which is scarce enough already, and our wheat, which we had grown for ourselves. I pray God to help us this Winter.

*Nov. 16th. SUNDAY.*   Preached at St. Ouen's afternoon. About sixty present – very good, considering this awful weather. Wish my sermon had been better. After service, everyone was talking about the billeting of German soldiers in our houses, and all looked very worried about it. This seems just the last straw! However, we must endure patiently, and trust in God.

*Nov. 17th.*   Mother and Joyce went to Les Potirons afternoon to see Aunt Elize and Evie. I spent most of day near the hearth cooking. Tonight mended two pairs of Grandpa's socks.

*Nov. 18th.* Most of day cooking; such a difficult job these days – wet wood, worn-out bellows, etc! Joyce took a message for Cousin Doris Adams to Red Cross office. They did not refuse it, as sometimes!

*Nov. 19th.* Had a lot of trouble with cooking – couldn't make the wood burn, as usual, so felt very grumpy all morning, and tonight I am ashamed of myself.

*Nov. 23rd. SUNDAY.* Afternoon, when Mr Querée preached at Bethlehem we had a French service, which we don't often have now. I enjoyed singing the French hymns. The French language seems much more poetical and musical somehow than the English! Girls Vibert and Raymond came for tea; we gave them a cup of coffee about 9.15 then they left for home to be back before 10pm which is curfew hour.

**December 2nd.** Alice came and we cut up sugar beet.

*Dec. 3rd.* I lit copper after breakfast, and put in our 60 pounds of sugar-beet. It boiled (with the same weight of water) from 11.30am to 8pm. I left it in copper. Mother went to Home Missions meeting at Philadelphie this afternoon; Rev. Scott was the speaker and Commander Brooks the Chairman.

*Dec. 4th.* I worked hard all day squeezing juice out of sugar-beet. How my back and hands ache tonight! Christine helped me morning, but afternoon Mrs Stan Le Brocq came with Beryl and Joan, so Mother and the girls 'entertained' them, whilst I carried on with my squeezing! How I wish I were very strong and could work without feeling so tired!

*Dec. 7th. SUNDAY.* Went to Bethlehem. Sunday School now at 10am. Preacher did not turn up for service. After waiting past 11 o'clock, I walked to Les Potirons, borrowed Lucille's bike and cycled home to get some notes. Arrived back at Bethlehem about 11.30, in time to preach the sermon! By then, Uncle John had gone through the first part of the service. I preached on 'Hope', the sermon I had given at Six Roads chapel. News today that the Japanese have attacked American islands in the Pacific. At one place there were 3,000 casualties. It is terrible. How long will this awful slaughter go on?

*Dec. 8th.* Did cooking all day except for an hour when I worked on my water-colour picture of Cosmos to give Joy.

*Dec. 9th.* Joy phoned to say that they must leave Murchiston Lodge as the Germans are taking it. Oh, how hard this is for people. One feels mad with the Germans – why should they have all they want?

*Workman to his friend: "Gas mask boxes, that's a nice Christmas box for somebody."*

*Dec. 12th.* Joy's Birthday so I cycled to Murchiston Lodge, my last time to visit them there. Everything was upside down – most of the furniture gone and Mrs Walker and Joy were sorting out papers etc. I did feel sorry about it all. Emily arrived and we had a cup of tea, sandwiches and a tiny cake I had brought Joy. I gave her a bowl of *pot-pourri* with things saved from our garden.

*Dec. 17th.* Alice here. Evie also came afternoon to help us cut up sugar beet. This morning we peeled apples for black butter. Tonight I knitted at my 'mittens' for a Sunday School child.

*Dec. 18th.* We killed a pig this morning. Boys very anxious lest we be found out! Put sugar beet to boil in copper and had a lot of trouble to make it boil. Boys began squeezing it tonight.

*Dec. 21st. SUNDAY.* Very full day. Went to Bethlehem for start of Sunday School. Cycled back to Philadelphie for 10.45 and took Service there. Got back 12.15, made my bed, made pudding and arranged flowers in the hall. Mr and Mrs Willie Le Brun here for dinner and tea. I carved pork as Dad had a sick headache. Left at 2.30pm and cycled to Les Frères chapel at St. John's to take 3pm service. I enjoyed being there. Cycled back to Bethlehem where Rev. Scott's service was just finishing. I was in time for the Communion service and I was glad. Came home about 5.30pm. After tea, washed dishes and then sat down and read a little and listened to a broadcast service – very good. God has helped me today, I know.

*Dec. 22nd.* Lovely weather, not cold. Irene here doing the washing – she has started coming to help us. Afternoon I went with Miss Ethel Arthur, K Laurens, Doreen Le Maistre and Eda Vautier to visit the 47 old ladies at the Home at Sandybrook. I played the piano and everyone sang Carols, then we gave them a small parcel each. What sad cases there are. I hope we gave them a little pleasure.

*Dec. 25th. CHRISTMAS DAY.* Joyce and I went to Christmas service at Philadelphie. Arrived back just in time to hear a Channel Islands broadcast. I was so excited, because Daryl Querée was one of those taking part.

*Dec. 29th.* Took bus to town and spent very pleasant evening at Emily's in Belmont Road with Joy, Elsie and other friends from Wesley chapel. Emily's uncle, Mr Curwood, was there. I like him and I'm afraid I was naughty as I took a piece of mistletoe and tempted him to kiss me! He kindly walked back to Montpelier with Elsie and me before curfew.

*Dec. 30th.* Took one o'clock bus back home. It was packed and very slow, running on charcoal.

*Dec. 31st.* I thank God tonight that another year of war is over – another year of occupation and of separation from my dear Alfred. God has kept us safe through this year with enough food and clothing to live, and He has helped us to bear it all patiently. I feel more hopeful now than a year ago. The future is hidden from us, thank God, but may 1942 bring Alfred and I together again, if God so wills.

**1 9
4 2**

*January 1st.* The year Alfred and I had been looking forward to so much, for July 1942 was the month in which we had hoped to be married. Well, Alfred is in England, and cannot come to me. I am a prisoner in Jersey and cannot go to him. Yet I will not give up hope – may 1942 see us with one another. We have been separated since September 12th 1938. It is a long time, but God has been with us and we have much to be thankful for. Mother brought me my breakfast in bed as I had slept very badly, with severe pain in my finger.

Mr and Mrs Watson-Allan here for dinner and tea. We enjoyed chatting over old times. Mrs Allan loves talking about all her music pupils and Mr A. is so interesting to listen to, as he has read so much. They had to walk coming and going from Bel Royal, as there are no buses today. Uncle Gordon also here for dinner and tea, having invited himself! Dad and the boys were ploughing for wheat all day with our mare and Uncle Ernest's (no petrol for much tractor ploughing this year).

*Jan. 2nd.*     Housework morning. Afternoon took bus to town. We were packed like sardines! Went to Dr. Lewis and he lanced my finger tip. Now it will soon be better. Called at 34, Belmont Road. Was told that Mr Curwood had, this very morning, orders from the German Commandant that he had to be ready to go by 6 o'clock tonight to be interned in France, because he is an American citizen. What a shock it has been for Emily. Her Uncle means everything to her. I feel so terribly sorry. She was weeping and so was Joy, who was there and trying to make a cake for Mr C. to take with him. Then he came. He had tears in his eyes, but he is so brave about it. He does not mind for himself but for Emily's sake. He came to the door, and we spoke for a few minutes and then kissed Goodbye. How I hope he will be kept safe – we will all pray for him.

*Jan. 3rd.*    Joyce brought back news from town that Mr Curwood had not left the Island yet, but he is in prison here. Mr O Mourant went to see the German Commandant to see if anything could be done, but to no avail. Poor Emily – if only her Uncle was allowed to remain here, even if in prison, he would at least be near. Rumours that two Spaniards are to be court-marshalled for shooting two German soldiers on Gorey Common; that 20 German soldiers were shot on the pier for refusing to go, presumably, to fight in Russia; that two large planes are waiting at the Airport to take away German officers, and that they have handed over some of their stocks to our authorities!

*Jan. 4th. SUNDAY.* Mr C. still in prison. His friends have been able to see him today.

*Jan. 5th.*    I received a letter from Mrs Robin in Guernsey today. It is quite exciting to receive letters nowadays. They are 'fairly well' like us all, and longing to see their dear ones again. Did housework, but haven't done much this week on account of my bad finger. Laurence and John went to Mrs Allan tonight – they want to learn to sing!

*Jan. 6th.*    RAF dropped leaflets early this morning. Laurence found one and Joyce found one in our garden near the bee-hive! They were all written in French. They were not addressed specially to Channel Islanders. German officers were searching the countryside for them, but our eyes are sharper than theirs! It is nice to think that our British friends were close to us today. We are not forgotten after all!

*Jan. 8th.*    Alfred's folk here for dinner, and Mr and Mrs C Alexandre and Norman for tea, and Blanche Perrée and Isabel and Miss Winnie called to see Granny. Norman showed us a piece of shrapnel which he had found embedded in the ground outside their stable door. It weighed one pound! It teaches us how unsafe it is even to look out when firing is going on. It was very heavy last night.

*Jan. 10th.*    Very cold day – bleak north wind. Morning, did dishes, peeled potatoes, swept floors, etc. At 2pm walked to Bethlehem for K de la Haye's Wedding. About eighty people were present. Kathleen was in white with three bridesmaids (in spite of Occupation and cold weather). One of the little brides-maids fainted (presumably with the cold) in middle of the ceremony. Party went off to town in horse-drawn coaches to have their photo taken. The poor horses were all skin and bone and looked as cold as the rest of us! I feel that I do not want to have my Wedding-day in Winter. I hope my Alfred will come for me in summer-time, when the sun is shining and the birds are singing!

*Jan. 11th.*     Raymond showed us another leaflet found by a farmer: *Francais .. quand nos avions viennent, mettez-vous a l'abri.*

*Jan. 12th.*     Went to St. Ouen to see Mrs Hacquoil and Valerie. They were surprised and pleased to see me! Mrs H. told me she wishes I still kept a school as Valerie learnt more than she does now where she goes! I did love my little school, and wish I had had time to keep it up. All the parents seem sorry I gave up. Well, I am thankful they were satisfied. I was not satisfied with myself and know I could have done better.

*Jan. 13th.*     Everything covered with snow when we woke this morning. Blizzard continued all day and the snow lies very thick tonight. Snowdrifts many feet deep in places. Very few people about.

*Jan. 14th.*     During the night it froze, so all the snow has remained. How beautiful everything looks – the trees loaded down with it. John walked to Westfield instead of cycling. This morning, I made a lovely big snow-man outside the back door! Uncle Edward, who came, told me it was the finest snow-man he had ever seen, and that it looked like George Washington or John Wesley! It is babyish of me to make a snow-man, but it seems a pity to 'waste' the snow! And I got lovely and warm! It is nice to be young and healthy and to be able to enjoy the snow, but it is hard for sick and old people who cannot get about and are cold. Fuel is so scarce everywhere too, and people suffer, especially in town. A young German airman came tonight: *Moi, chercher du savon pour la figure,* he told me, offering tobacco in exchange. Of course, we always refuse to 'trade' with them. But one feels sorry, for they are so like ourselves!

*Jan. 16th.*     As weather had improved, Joyce decided to go back to work this afternoon. So she and I set off to take the bus at Croix-au-Lion. We waited half-an-hour, and when it turned up it was too full to take us! So we came back home, very disconsolate! However, I was looking forward to going to town, so decided to cycle. Plenty snow to top of Beaumont; walked in bad patches. After that the roads were clear. Went to Belmont Road and stayed with Joy and Emily till 6pm. Enjoyed it so much. We sat by the fire – they knitted and I mended socks for Uncle Edward. Mrs Walker came and we had a cup of tea. I had brought one 'Jersey wonder' [type of local doughnut] each, and they were thrilled to have such a treat! What a luxury for days such as these.

*Jan. 18th. SUNDAY.*     We've been excited to hear that yesterday the RAF had visited Guernsey and bombed the harbour. I hope no Guernsey people were hurt. Tonight I feel cross and irritable for no reason whatever. Sometimes it is difficult to understand one's feelings. I have just read, as a prayer, Hymn 550; Verse 2 helped me:

> *My heart to Thee I bring,*
> *The heart I cannot read;*
> *An evil heart indeed.*
> *I bring it, Saviour, now to thee,*
> *That fixed and faithful it may be.*

How I long for Alfred; if only I could share all my thoughts with him, it would help so much. It is hard that we cannot write as we used to. I expect that he misses that very much too, and he needs me. May the time of reunion come speedily.

*Jan. 20th.*    Miss Gertie Le Rossignol and her brother are in Hospital as they cannot get insulin. It is very serious for them, as for all diabetic people. Some have already died. Doctors cannot even get insulin from Germany.

*Jan. 22nd.*    Germans are moving their big guns from Les Jardins as they think the RAF has seen them. Those guns were pretty obvious, I thought! We are glad if they move them, as they seem unpleasantly near us!

*Jan. 23rd.*    My second finger of left hand bad again; it tortured me last night – did not sleep one wink! All day I've kept putting it in very hot water.

*Jan. 24th.*    Slept all night without pain, what a relief. Cycled into town afternoon. Called for Joy at Einnim, First Tower. It began to rain heavily. Joy came with me to Dr. Lewis to hold my other hand whilst he cut open my finger-tip again. He did not hurt me but I was glad when it was done! Afterwards, we went to Emily's where I took off my wet things and we sat by the fire, had a nice talk and cup of tea. Mother had given me a bottle of milk, a small 'loaf' and a scrap of butter, which Joy and Emily appreciated very much. Town people have so little, never good Jersey and very little milk. It is dreadful! Cycled back home in pouring rain, getting back at 7pm just getting dark. Things are depressing all this time. Almost every night, the *Evening Post* reports sudden deaths. It is very strange – lack of proper nourishment must be the cause. Then there are lots of 'foreign' workmen in the Island, brought by the Germans. These are half-starved and half-clothed, and reported to have strange and dangerous diseases.

However, we have all had a ration of a quarter pound of chocolate each this week. It was wonderful – chocolate!

*Jan. 28th.*    Alice here as usual. She and Herbert chopped up sugar-beet whilst I did ironing. An amusing incident happened this afternoon. We had a slight thunderstorm and the first flash of lightning and clap of thunder was at once followed by a long blast from the air-raid siren at the Airport. Evidently the Germans thought the RAF had come. It shows how scared they are!

*Jan. 29th.*    Emily had news from Mr Curwood. She is very anxious as he hasn't enough food and a very bad cold. How tried she is, poor Emily, from every direction. Her only brother in the Forces, and no news from him; her Uncle interned somewhere in France, with not enough food, and herself not well.

*Jan. 31st.*    Finished reading the life of Priscilla Johnston tonight. She was the niece of Elizabeth Fry. This book has been not only interesting, but profitable. What wonderful women these were and how near they lived to God. Tonight, planes are passing and German anti-aircraft guns are making a terrific noise. It is awful that they are trying to shoot down our own British planes. My first Hyacinth bloomed today indoors. How one loves the first Spring flower that blooms! It seems to bring hope somehow!

*February 3rd.*    Mrs Le Brun and Mrs Reis came afternoon. It is always so pleasant to see them. How lovely it is to have good friends, and Mother has such lovely friends. We heard today that there are two lots of British airmen here. There are plenty rumours concerning them. I suppose they baled out into the sea near here after their raid on Brest last Saturday night when there was so much gunfire here. They say the prisoners are wounded. How one would like to have a talk with these men, fresh from England. And how sorry we are that they have been shot down. Herbert caught quite a large eel from Mr Bauche's stream when they were clearing it today.

*Feb. 5th.*    Cycled to town – snowing all the way. Went on to Montpelier. Brigade girls came and we all had a nice afternoon together, working and chatting. Elsie asked me to close with a short prayer, before they left, at 7pm.

*Feb. 6th.*    After breakfast helped with dishes, then went to First Tower where Joy introduced me to their new residence, 'Tingghi'. It is a cosy little house, and I was quite charmed with it. There is a view of St. Aubin's Bay. I am so glad they are settled at last. Mrs Walker was busy tidying and getting her books in order.

*Feb. 7th.*    Mother received Red Cross message from Auntie Janet; they had not yet heard about poor Auntie Lulu. The message was dated October 7th. I am sure messages are purposely delayed by the Germans. I heard that messages being delivered now had arrived before Christmas, but the Commandant said that only a few must be delivered. No wonder we have to wait so long. I am still hoping to hear from Alfred in this batch.

Freezing hard tonight. We heard that German bodies have been washed ashore at Grève-de-Lecq. It must be true for Miss Bauche's maid told us that no coffin could be got for Miss Marcus' relative who died two days ago. The undertaker said the Germans had taken all the coffins, also that there is hardly enough wood to make them. What a state of affairs!

*Feb. 8th.*    Wrote to Mrs F Ahier (Springside) as it was her Silver Wedding Anniversary last Friday. Heard that over thirty German bodies have been washed ashore here. The boys saw Germans carrying a large wreath towards St. Ouen's. What a horrible thing is war.

*Feb. 9th.*    Went to see Dr. Lewis, as I have a queer lump in the neck. Thank God, he does not find it anything serious. For some moments, however, I was terribly anxious, because of the look on his face as he was examining me. At first, he also was anxious. I am so thankful it is nothing to worry about. I do want to keep perfectly well, for my dear Alfred's sake.

*Feb. 10th.*    Margaret Le Ruez, our cousin from Westfield, came today for lessons. I am giving her two hours every afternoon until the weather is warmer, when she will start school. She was six-years-old on February 3rd. She is a little Miss. She asked permission to 'leave the room' and, finding she was a long time gone, I went upstairs to investigate! I found her in Granny's bedroom by the fire, talking to Grandpa! Evidently, she was already tired of lessons! Things are depressing. Yesterday, the BBC announced the landing of Japanese troops on Singapore Island – it looks as though we cannot hold it much longer.

*Feb. 11th.*    Received message from Auntie Janet – they had heard in October about Auntie Lulu and were very distressed. I had one from Alfred dated September 21st. He was evidently in his new Circuit and living near Willersley. We wrote our answers tonight, but it is so difficult when one cannot say what one would like.

*Feb. 12th.*    What a hectic day! Men were ploughing. We had dinner late, at about 1.30. There were the twelve of us, as usual (including Granny upstairs), plus Mr Oliver Mourant and Elsie who arrived about 1.50pm. In the midst of this, Cousin Frank Le Gros turned up and sat there whilst we finished dinner.

At 2.30, Margaret came for lessons with me. Then tonight Raymond came, but it was so late by the time all our work was finished that we only sat down by the fire for a very short time, as supper had to be got in time for Raymond to get home before curfew at 10 o'clock. We were delighted this morning to get our first Red Cross message from Queensland – from Cousin Henri Picot. We had sent him an 'Enquiry' last April!

*Feb. 13th.*    A trying day, somehow! Perhaps because, to begin with, the news were bad. British yesterday lost 40 aircraft in an action with German warships and planes in the Straits of Dover. And, at Singapore, things can only get worse. Dad, as usual, sees the black side, and what with Uncle Gordon (who is always finding fault with the English, though he is English himself) sitting in the breakfast-room all the afternoon, whilst I was trying to teach Margaret! Then Miss Elsie Lucas called, also Evie. Finally, we finished the day by us girls arguing with the boys about the war and women. And I got mad and hit John. However, I feel quite happy again now, after having been to his bedroom to kiss him goodnight. These days are so horribly trying and we must pray for patience.

*Feb. 14th.*    Today we had a wild rabbit for dinner. Laurence saw it and stunned it, poor creature! Yet how glad we were to have it, as we have been short of food of late. We are always so hungry when we get up from the table. Yet we must be thankful that we have enough to live. Some have yet less than we.

*Feb. 20th.*    I typed out some of my sermon for Sunday after Margaret had gone. I pray that it may be acceptable to God. It is so difficult to judge one's own work. After I've taken much trouble in preparing an address, it seems to me to be worth so little. How I wish Alfred were here to help me!

*Feb. 20th.*    Mother received by post a pair of gloves and a scarf to match, which Joy had made for her. Dear Joy, she had worn the scarf twice herself, which makes Mother appreciate it all the more!

*Feb. 22nd. SUNDAY.*    Granny's 85th Birthday. Did not go to Sunday School as I was preaching at Philadelphie. I have been very encouraged today. I feel that God has helped me and felt happy as I preached (Text 1 Kings XIX v.11 and 12). Service in schoolroom; weather very cold). Dad praised me afterwards. It means so much, as Dad never praises unless one really deserves it. But I don't deserve praise, because whatever is good in me is a gift of God. I had dinner at Mrs E Querée and went with her and the two girls, Doreen and Ruth, to afternoon service at Philadelphie, when Mr Sarre was the preacher. Tonight, I read a few of Alfred's old letters from Africa to find material for a missionary talk.

*Feb. 23rd.* Dad spoke to me again about yesterday's service. He had liked my prayer and said it fitted in with his own sentiments. I do feel happy about this, as I always find the prayer the most difficult part, and I had asked God to help me and to teach me how to pray. It is wonderful how God answers prayer.

*Feb. 26th.* Went to see Dr. Lewis. Felt rather upset when he told me that he wanted Dr. Halliwell to see my neck. Went to Montpelier and told them why I had been to the doctor, though I hate to worry them. They are so afraid anything would happen to me, for our dear Alfred's sake. They said they would pray for me, and Elsie cycled all the way to Bailiff's corner with me. I was so thankful for her company. The Valley is so lonely, and lots of strange men about nowadays; also I was feeling a little upset.

*Feb. 27th.* Afternoon, Mother said it would do me good to go out, so I obediently went out! I had tea at La Caroline with Constable and Mrs du Val, and Miss du Val. On my return, Mother said she had phoned Dr. Lewis in my absence. Naughty Mother!

*Feb. 28th.* Uncle Gordon turned up for dinner. He has not yet ever brought his bread ration, though we told him last time that we were very short! Today, we heard that six of those 'foreign' workmen brought here by the Germans had died beside a brook from which they had eaten poisonous weeds, after they had eaten all the water-cress. 30 more are said to have been taken to hospital. Those poor men are starving and yet forced to work. Grandpa (through no fault of his own) has given Mother lots of trouble again today, and tonight Granny was upset and nearly fainted. Mother and I just kept her from falling. How I wish my dear Mother did not have all this trouble.

*March 2nd.* Herbert's Birthday: aged 18 today. Cycled to town. Joy came with me to Dr. Lewis. The waiting-room was full and we waited over an hour for my turn. I am trying not to worry. I feel very well in myself, so can't think there is anything wrong. Doctor took a sample of blood from a vein in my arm.

*March 3rd.* Laurence's Birthday: aged 24.

*March 4th.* My first blue Primrose bloomed. I sowed the seed about two years ago but it is worth waiting all that time to see the flowers bloom. I am very fond of these, so is Mrs Walker. I received a Red Cross Message from Alfred, dated November 6th. What joy it is to receive these messages, short and late as they are! I have not yet heard from the doctor. I hope he will phone tomorrow, to rid me of suspense.

*March 5th.* Grandpa received an Enquiry from Mrs Dorey, Montreal. After dinner, cycled to Wesley Chapel, as Elsie had asked me to go to a Concert given by Mrs Baudains and the First Tower choir. It was very good indeed and I enjoyed it, for one does not go out much to things like that these days and I love good singing and music. Stayed to sleep at Montpelier. Alfred's parents looking a little better though poor Mrs Du Feu's chilblains on hands and feet are still very bad.

*March 6th.* Breakfasted with Alfred's people, did a few things for Mother in town, called at Emily's, then at Uncle Philip in Pierson Road. Saw Auntie Julia in bed. She spoke quite sensibly, but what trouble she gives Miss D. – same as Grandpa gives Mother. Mother phoned Dr. Shone to send him some medicine today, to see if it will help. We kept him in bed.
Tonight, a dog attacked one of our lovely geese, one which had been laying well. It was so bad that it died after a few minutes. Laurence was very upset. Today I was delighted to receive a Red Cross message from Lily Briggs, my friend from Newry, N. Ireland, which was a reply in her own hand to my enquiry sent July 29th last year. So I can keep the form.

*March 9th.* Phoned Joy to tell her what Dr. Lewis had said about my blood test. He has found 'nothing conclusive' but I must go and see him and Dr Halliwell on Thursday. I try not to worry, it is in the evening that sometimes I feel a little worried, as now.

*March 10th.* We are all feeling down-hearted about things tonight. Heard on BBC of the awful atrocities that the Japanese have committed to British officers, civilians and women at Hong Kong. One can hardly believe that men can be so evil. Why must there be so much suffering in the world? Our questions can never be answered in this life, I know, and so we can only have faith in God, though we cannot see or understand. But I am only human, and long, above everything, to be with Alfred!

*March 12th.* We all have a great weight lifted from our minds tonight. I have seen Dr. Halliwell and he said that the lump in my neck is nothing serious at all – something to do with a vein. Dr. Lewis had told Mother he feared diseased blood, something very serious.We all thank God tonight that I am perfectly healthy; I felt so and could not believe there was anything seriously wrong. I went to the doctor's with a smile on my face and a flower in my buttonhole (a blue primrose). Joy came with me. I went straight into Dr. Lewis' consulting-room and after a few minutes he and Dr. Halliwell came in. The latter examined me, and pronounced the verdict. Dr. Lewis said "Thank God" very fervently! Later I asked him if the lump would disappear, and when he said, "No," I said, "What a pity." To which he replied, rather sternly, "Don't say that, but thank God it is nothing serious, for I had all sorts of horrible ideas in my head about it." When I got home and told Mother I was all right, to my surprise she wept for joy and relief on my shoulder. I fear I had not realised how dreadfully worried my dear Mother had been. The doctor had frightened her, and she had been imagining me in hospital for months, or even years! Well, I do thank God again and again, especially for Alfred's sake.

*March 17th.* Herbert went to town, to fetch our ration of dates (seven ounces each). What a treat!

*March 19th.* Worked in greenhouse, took Chrysanth. cuttings, etc. Joy phoned to thank for eggs we sent. Hens have laid well this week and mother has been able to spare eggs to many friends. People in town don't see eggs!

*March 22nd. SUNDAY.* Went to Bethlehem. Returned as usual, part of the way with a number of dear little girls hanging on to my arms and hands. How happy one feels when children seem to enjoy one's company. It gives me great pleasure on Sunday mornings to have all these dear little ones around me – Eunice, Iris, Daphne, Ivy and Margaret Le Hegarat; this litle one, aged nearly five, came to Sunday School for the first time today and Dorothy, Margaret and Joan (aged three) – these eight lovely little girls. Then there is Audrey Anquetil, whose home is this way too. She is about 13-years-old. Tonight, Herbert cycled down to Bethesda Chapel with me and I preached. Mr Arthur Querée had asked me as Mr F Du Feu, who was planned, was ill. I was glad to be able to help, but I wish my preaching were better than it is!

*March 23rd.* Cycled to town. Had tea at Emily's with her and Joy. Stayed chatting by the fire (and, incidently, blowing on the fire; this is the usual 'Occupation' occupation in winter, as fires will not burn!) Went on to Montpelier and stayed to sleep. I was very happy indeed to find that Alfred's folk had received a message from him, and such a lovely message too: *I arrived home on Aug. 13th 1940. Keep smiling. We shall not for ever be separated. All will be well. Love to you all. Alfred. 5th Dec.1941.* So at last we know when Alfred arrived in England, and it was in the middle of the heavy bombing, when hundreds of German planes came over at a time. I feel I just cannot be thankful enough that Alfred was kept safe through it all, and through that long dangerous sea journey from Africa.

*March 24th* Found on my return from town that Judy had had five puppies during the morning – first time we've ever had puppies on this farm. And, to my joy, there were two messages from my dear Alfred awaiting me, such loving messages too.

*March 25th.* Miss Elsie Lucas, Mrs Lucas and her little girl (aged four) came, afternoon. The child is so pretty, but very shy at first. But she enjoyed seeing the puppies, and stayed with me on the lawn whilst I pruned the Rose bushes.

*March 28th.* Last night we did not sleep till about 4am as British planes were overhead seven or eight times and the German gunfire was terrific. We had not heard it so strong before. I really thought the windows would break. Mother and us girls kept on getting up each time we heard a plane in the distance and stood together under a doorway on the landing. We were tired out by the time all was silent. This morning, we found many pieces of shrapnel around the house. BBC has announced a combined raid on St. Nazaire.

*March 29th. PALM SUNDAY.* Mother's Birthday. I gave her a posy bowl which I had filled with Spring flowers – Polyanthus, Crocus, Lenten Lilies, Violets, Periwinkle etc. Went to both services at Bethlehem as usual.

*March 31st.* Had a message from Alfred dated October in which he says, *Adèle gets married in Nov.* It was a surprise. So Adele Cox has now been married for four months; not one of Auntie's messages mentioned it, no doubt many have failed to reach us. I've been feeling quite unsettled all day after hearing about cousin Adèle being married. Alfred and I have waited for so long! Yet I envy no one. Poor Adèle, though married, is probably separated from her husband now. I pray God to keep him safe. It is so hard on young people who love one another to marry, only to have to separate soon after. May this wicked war soon end.

*April 2nd.* Cycled to town afternoon. Took beans to Cousin Sylvia and eggs to Mrs Gulliford and to Enid de Gruchy for her Granny. What a charming girl Enid is, and so grateful for the little we do. Went on to Montpelier for tea. Mr Howells, who is a baker, made some lovely Hot Cross buns (without fruit, of course) and gave some to Mrs Du Feu. They had gathered the ingredients between them. We had some for supper. What a treat, and how lovely they looked. To think that we did not appreciate them more when there were plenty!

*April 3rd. GOOD FRIDAY.* Went to United Service at Great Union Road Chapel. Rev. Fell preached. Dinner at Montpelier then went to Grove Place to hear 'The Messiah' sung by Free Church Choir members, about 30 voices. The whole performance was inspiring, especially at the end, when we all stood up for the Hallelujah Chorus. There were three German officers present in the gallery. They had a copy of 'The Messiah' and they followed it all. It gave me a strange feeling to see them there – a sort of sadness. I've thought a great deal about Alfred today, and that first Good Friday we spent together four years ago, at the time we became engaged. What a long time ago it seems and how much has happened since.

After service this morning Mrs Fell spoke to me. She told me that the same thing had happened to her as happened to me. Rev. Fell was going abroad but she did not pass the medical test, so he could not go. She said: "There is a providence in these things, I am sure, and it all turns out all right in the end." This conversation has helped and cheered me very much, somehow. Mrs Fell told me that she often thought about me – and I did not even think she knew me!

*April 4th.*     Jobs in the house, as usual, and in odd moments I finished preparing my sermon for tomorrow. Wish I had time to settle to it properly, but with all there is to do my preparation is always done in spare moments. I feel it is a great responsibility to be preaching on Easter Sunday and I am not fit to do it.

*April 5th.*     Joyce cycled out to Les Frères chapel tonight with me. I don't know what was the matter – though I did my best my congregation seemed unresponsive. It may have been my fault, or my imagination! But I was glad to see two rows of lads, about 14 -17 years of age, who seemed attentive. All of them shook hands with me, and as I was getting my bicycle in the shed one ran in, whistling the tune of the last hymn: 'I know that my Redeemer liveth.' That made me glad! On our way home, we called to see Aunt Elize and Evie at Les Potirons. (Lucille was eating a piece of cabbage stalk near her poultry run – she thinks it is good for her health!)

*April 6th. EASTER MONDAY.*   Mr and Mrs Watson-Allan, music teachers, here for dinner and tea. We had killed a 'fatted calf' in great secret last Saturday, so we had something to give our visitors to eat today. Afternoon, Mrs Laffoley called (Laffoleys are back at Auvergne after being ten years at Grève d'Azette). So what with Mr Allan and Mrs L. we had plenty entertainment! I laughed so much that I soaked a hankie in drying my eyes. Then tonight I feel as depressed as anything. The news is so discouraging. Japanese have raided two places on the east coast of India, and we are anxious about dear Cousin Henry in Bengal.

*April 8th.*     A lovely day for we have received six Red Cross Messages! I had three from Alfred, mother two from Auntie Janet and one from Cousin Doris. Alfred's messages rejoice my heart. They are so lovely, and so hopeful, this time. *I have great hopes for 1942,* he says, *the best is in store, and is worth waiting for, darling.* How dear he is: worth waiting for, I should think so!

*April 9th.*   Wrote out the answers to our Red Cross messages. It takes quite a time to concoct these messages of only 25 words. Spent part of the day running to see to the fire under the copper in the wash-house, as we were boiling sugar-beet. What a lot of wood one burns to do it!

*April 11th.*   Received a reply from my dear Alfred to an enquiry I had sent last  October. It is especially lovely, because it is all written in his own hand, and I can keep it. It is the first one I have had of these, and I am so happy about it. So, three months ago, Alfred was writing those 25 words to me and he was hopeful, and wrote, *All will be well.* Mother has received a reply to her enquiry sent to Auntie Lucy a year ago! This is our first news from America. How lovely to see Auntie's handwriting. So today we have had two very unexpected pleasant things. Thanks be to God for His goodness and blessings.

*April 12th. SUNDAY.*   Uncle Edward came tonight and told us that the Germans have taken over his house.

*April 14th.*   We all went, at intervals, to Philadelphie Chapel schoolroom, where all the St. Peter's Parish folk were having their photographs taken, on German orders. Everyone on the Island has to have a photo to put with their Identity card.

*April 17th.*   Went to the German Post Office in Beresford Street and posted a letter to Mr Curwood who is interned in France. In town also, I had my teeth examined at Mr Mallet. He began to tell me about having visited the prison and there being lots of Jersey people in it amongst a list of names, he mentioned Uncle Edward Le Brocq. I was surprised. The Germans are supposed to have found cartridges in his house. Later I saw John Le Brocq (baker) who told me that Uncle Edward had been arrested and was going to France for trial. I fear it is very serious.
Had tea with Alfred's parents, then met Elsie at her office and we went to see 'The Pirates of Penzance' performed by the Green Room Club at the Opera House. Enjoyed it very much; had not been to any entertainment since the beginning of the Occupation. Thinking about Uncle Edward, and hoping the worst rumours are not true, especially for Mother's sake.

*April 19th. SUNDAY.*   Went to Bethlehem. After Sunday School I took the service. Had a congregation of about 80 as there were so many children. Was a bit bothered as I had made a mistake in my figures and announced the wrong Hymn to begin with! A few minutes later, I upset the glass of water over my

Notes etc. under the pulpit. However, no one knew about this little accident! My brothers and sisters liked the service, they told me!

*April 21st.*   Lovely weather. Alice came, as usual. Margaret and Leslie here for tea, also Miss Ethel came to spring-clean Kath's bees. Mrs E Querée and her two daughters came tonight. Laurence and John went for their singing lesson. Mr Allan told them that he had heard on BBC news that in the House of Commons Lord Portsea had asked if food and supplies could be sent to the Islands, to which someone replied that it was impossible to send a ship or a plane, but that the Channel Islands were not being forgotten. How lovely to hear that!

*April 24th.*   Margaret came and I went to see Auntie Edith, who paid me £4 for M's 32 lessons, up-to-date. We were all very 'thrilled' to hear a talk on the wireless by a Guernseyman about the Channel Islanders who are in England. He said they had settled well, but often feel an indescribable longing to see their lovely isles again. But they feel apprehensive when they hear of raids over the Channel Islands. He assured them all that the greatest care was being taken not to harm their own people.

*April 25th.*   All the usual Saturday housework. Tonight I prepared for Sunday School tomorrow and for preaching at Philadelphie. This week we have again heard the rumour that the Germans are taking away all the young men but heard also that the Bailiff refused to sign a certain paper, and said he was prepared to be shot rather than do it. I hope nothing like that will happen. One lives in dread of what the Germans will do next.

*April 28th.*   Christine's Birthday. Uncle Edward 'phoned to say he had come out of prison this morning, after 12 days there. We had not been able to find out anything certain about him. We are glad he has not been taken to France.

*April 29th.*   Uncle Edward came to tell us all about it. He appears to have been rather 'tried' there in prison, especially through the suspense of not even knowing he was to be released until yesterday about noon, when he was told to pack up as the Governor of the prison had the order to release him. He just escaped a minimum of two years imprisonment in France and he was told that if a gun had been found he would have been shot. It was a box of cartridges the Germans found in his house. Uncle did not know they were there! He has not enjoyed his 12 days in prison, especially, as he said, being treated like a convict when he wasn't one!

*May 1st.*   Constable Du Val came to tell us that we must give up one boy's bicycle to the Germans – the newest one of course! No use protesting, they would only take it on the road. He thinks the Germans are getting more nervous and irritable every day.

*May 3rd.*     Poor Miss Bauche is very ill indeed. Mrs Collas was sent for and the Matron from Bon Air Nursing Home came out with her in a Police van, there being no other means of conveyance, and saw Miss B. for a few minutes. Dad and Mother went but she only recognised mother for a moment.

*May 4th.*     Went to Royal Crescent Chapel, where I gave a Missionary talk about Alfred's work. Had felt nervous but enjoyed it after all, easy to talk because the ladies were so sympathetic and the Chairman, Mrs West, was very charming also. It was a pleasure to meet these people. What a lot of nice people there are in the world – every day one realises it more. I meet plenty anyway!

*May 5th.*     Irene brought us four lovely spider crabs! What a pleasant sur-prise! The first this year. Her husband is now allowed to fish at Grève-de-Lecq again, but has to give ninety per cent of his catch to the Germans. Fortunately, however, they are not fond of shell-fish!
Last night, about 11.30, we heard a sound as of bombs on the sea, and every-thing shook. We thought the RAF was attacking shipping, and it was so, as Irene said her husband had been all day bringing in wood to the shore – broken parts of a ship. The Germans asked him to help them. He found a suitcase full of women's clothing, and inside was the name and address of a Jersey-woman from town. So the RAF sank a ship quite close last night. What can that woman have been doing on board with the Germans? There has been an account on the *Evening Post* of a 'boating tragedy' in which a young Audrain has been drowned. But no one goes 'boating' nowadays. Rumour has it that he and two friends were trying to escape – the two others jumped overboard and swam ashore. It is far too risky for anyone to try to escape. I hope we shall not be punished for it – one always fears for the men of this Island.

*May 6th.*     I went to see Miss Bauche – she was sitting up taking a little beaten egg. She knew me and spoke just like her old self, with her humorous smile, though she is very weak. It is wonderful how she has rallied.

*May 9th.*     We have had an awful shock tonight. We can hardly realise it, but our darling cousin Florence has died. About 9 o'clock, as I was finishing my sermon in my bedroom, I heard a knock at the front door, I went down and found Madeleine Norman there and, with tears in her eyes, she said: "I am so sorry to have to bring you bad news," and she brought out a Red Cross enve-lope. She was sympathetic, and full of feeling for our sakes. I waited till after supper to tell the others. We all loved dear 'Fof' so much, and to think that we shall not see her again. She was such a lovely character, deep and serious-minded, gentle and so sweet. Why did she have to go so young? Poor Auntie Janet, and Uncle, and Adèle and Marion – how they must be suffering. We don't know why she died. The message said: *Our darling Florence passed peacefully away on Feb. 13th. Tell the others.*

*May 10th. SUNDAY.* Cycled down to preach at Bethesda for their Sunday School Anniversary. John came with me, and Raymond Vibert. Mr and Mrs Willie Le Brun were here for dinner and tea. It has helped to have them with us – to take our mind off our sorrow a little. Tonight, we all listened to Mr Churchill's speech – it was one of the most encouraging he has made and we felt cheered and began to hope that the war and this Occupation might end this year. There were 16 of us in the breakfast-room listening-in, for there were the 11 of us (Granny was upstairs, as usual, so one can't count her, then there was Mr and Mrs Le Brun, Uncle Ernest and Leslie, and Raymond Vibert. I wonder what the Germans would have said if they had seen us, smiling at our Prime Minister's remarks!

*May 11th.* Went to give a missionary talk at Wesley Sisterhood. Joy and Emily sang a duet 'Jesus shall reign' to a tune composed by Joy herself! Mrs Clarke, the Congregational minister's wife, was in the chair. She told me that her husband had meant to go out as a missionary to New Guinea, but she did not pass her medical test so he never went. So I am not the only one who does not pass medical tests for going overseas!

*May 13th.* We had lobster for tea. How lucky we are! Irene brought it yesterday and we paid her 8 shillings. It was a huge one.

*May 16th* Had another Red Cross message from Auntie Janet and Uncle Bert saying that they were all well and had heard from Alfred and he was all right. They were all well and yet only 13 days after Florence died. And this message, dated January 27th, sounded so cheerful.

*May 20th.* We had thunder and lightning and heavy rain from mid-morning to late afternoon. I washed flower-pots in greenhouse and re-potted ferns and begonias, etc. Tonight we had quite a do when Dr. Lewis came to vaccinate us against small-pox (which is reported to be in France). We were all vaccinated except Francis and Herbert. They will be done later, but we had to leave someone out, in case there would be no one well enough to milk the cows. Miss Marcus and Helene the maid, Mrs Ellen Amy and a little boy called Turmel also came here to be vaccinated. The sitting-room was the surgery, and the breakfast-room was the waiting-room! When the doctor had finished the puppy ran in, so we asked him to give it a name! Dr. Lewis said 'Victoria' so we shall leave it at that! Last night we had slept little as British planes were over and there was so much shooting. BBC said they went to St. Nazaire. Bombs fell at Trinity.

Mr and Mrs Le Seelleur here for dinner and tea. It was at their place I met Alfred, and we were looking forward to seeing them. Then Joy and Emily came, and we all (15 of us) had tea together in the breakfast-room. Laurence went to Trinity and saw the 11 craters made by the bombs which had fallen in Mr Querée's field – the whole field being sort of ploughed up and no grass to be seen, as before. Thank God, no one was hurt.

*May 22nd.*    A party of 10 of us from Bethlehem YLU cycled out to La Rocque this afternoon to visit Mrs Evans' Home for Babies. Enjoyed our visit. Sat on a patch of grass close to the sea and had our tea there, Mrs Evans and Morwen kindly making and serving us with cups of tea. (I don't know where they got the tea but it was lovely to have some, as one gets it so seldom nowadays.) The countryside everywhere was a joy to see today – everything so beautiful, fresh and green after the rain... all lovely, except where the Germans have spoilt it with their huts, their guns, their barbed wire, etc.

*May 23rd.*    Much firing during early hours. British planes overhead – St. Nazaire again. I wish they did not pass over here and put themselves in danger of being shot at. We all feel tired – don't know if it is the effects of vaccination, or lack of sleep. Today, our vaccinated areas have been itching and both spots are raised like blisters. We are watching developments with interest! Mrs Du Feu had a message from Alfred on which he says: *Look after my Nan.* How lovely it is that he should speak of me as 'my Nan'!

*May 24th. WHITSUNDAY.*        Empire Day; Mrs Walker's Birthday. Mr Zugg preached at Bethlehem – first time we heard him. He is a Salvation Army man who has lost his right arm. His wife and children are in England – he found himself cut off here, like so many others, before he could get away. The Germans have stopped the Salvation Army so he helps us now. Phyllis and Beryl Vibert here for tea. Kath and I have developed a lump under the arm which is painful. The vaccine has taken.

*May 25th.*    John's Birthday; he is 22-years-old today. Margaret came, as usual, for her lesson. I am beginning to feel sick – the gland under my arm is very painful.

*May 26th.*    I received a post-card from Mr Curwood from an internment camp in France. Felt very miserable all day with bad pain along arm and left shoulder-blade. Worse tonight. Didn't do much today but lie on the sofa.

Laurence stayed in all day too, and the others didn't feel too well. Joyce, however, felt able to go town to work. Joy phoned to see how we were getting on! She hasn't been vaccinated yet – there is no more vaccine in the Island for the time being, so many people are waiting.

*May 27th.*    Today I received two messages from my dear Alfred. He says he has permission for us to get married as soon as we are together. It is just like him to ask for permission now, so as to make sure to be able to marry me as soon as we meet again. But I fear we have to wait a long time yet. Laurence and I stayed in bed until tea-time – I had slept little, the pain being so bad. It is nasty altogether. A good thing we didn't know what we were in for! Dr. Lewis came and said our 'spots' were 'beauties!' Only one of Mother's has taken so she is only guaranteed for four years instead of seven.

*May 28th.*    Had an awful night. Feel absolutely rotten this morning – bad head, sickness and pain. The others are feeling worse too but are not in bed, except Laurence and Christine. And that naughty doctor told us yesterday that the worst was over! I hope dear Mother will not be as bad as us. This afternoon I was to have gone in for my Preliminary Local Preacher's exam; I am very disappointed that I could not go, for I want to get on with it soon.

*May 29th.*    Got up for dinner but have felt awfully ill all day and my arm is beginning to swell. Rev. Scott called and said I'd be able to do my exam. soon. Kath, Christine and Laurence not at all well. What a family! I pity Francis and Herbert who still have their turn to come!

*May 30th.*    Very disappointed to be feeling bad still. Managed to get up in time for dinner and to help Joyce scrape potatoes for tomorrow. My arm swollen from shoulder to elbow tonight. Kath has suffered dreadfully in her arm today. She was even jumping right up in bed tonight with the pain. And Laurence had a temperature of 104° today. Mother phoned the doctor who said there was no need to worry.

*May 31st. SUNDAY.*    Evie came to see how we all were. Christine felt well enough to go to Bethlehem this morning. Kath and I only got up at 4pm. Still had bad head and swollen arm. Mr Luce, Lady Vernon's butler, came to see us tonight. Over a thousand British bombers were over Berlin last night. It is terrible that such things must be done – wish Germany would collapse before we have to destroy all her cities. Well, Germany began, and how many lovely and historic buildings in England's cities have been destroyed!

*June 3rd.*    We are all on the mend, though not too bright yet. I feel as giddy as anything and Laurence has bad pain in his legs. There are all sorts of

71

rumours about the vaccine – some say it was old stuff that the Germans didn't want. It certainly has made people very ill!

*June 8th.*     Margaret did not come as she was going to be inoculated against diphtheria. There are several cases of it at St. Ouen's and the school has been closed. Notice on *Evening Post* that we must give in all our wireless sets. Everyone is upset about it, but hoping the Bailiff will be able to do something to prevent it. Now that things are going better for 'us' the Germans don't want us to hear, I suppose!

*June 14th. SUNDAY.*     Preached at Philadelphie this morning. Walked back with Mrs Le Feuvre, as I was having dinner there, it being their turn to have the preacher. They had kept a cockerel for a special occasion, so we had it for dinner. I felt quite honoured! The love affairs of my brothers and sisters seem to have gone all awry today! L. is very upset; J. does not know what is best to do and C. has been weeping! The boys have hardly eaten all day and Mother says she has a headache with it all! Well, I think it will all come right in the end!

*June 15th.*     I went to see Mrs Roland (Olive, who went to school with us at Miss Rowe's) whose husband has died. It is so very sad. I could not speak at first, when I saw her sitting there with her little boy on her knees. At 28 years of age she is a widow with a boy of seven, and a girl of nearly six. Poor Olive, how terribly hard it must be. Her husband was taken with TB about four years ago. It is a dreadful illness, and since the Occupation there are many cases of it. Then I visited Mrs Anquetil who has just had a little girl and lost her at three days old, the third baby she loses in this way, through jaundice. I spoke to Mr Anquetil; what a nice man he is. I did not know him much before. I do feel so sorry for them. Audrey, who is 14, would so have loved a baby brother or sister. It is very sad.

*June 16th.*     Went to Montpelier. Elsie had asked me as she is having a few days' holiday. After dinner, we sat on 'the front' at the bottom of Beach Road, Elsie sewing and myself reading *Christian Foundations*, part of my Local Preacher studies. After tea, we walked to First Tower chapel for their week-day Sunday School Anniversary service. The chapel was packed.

*June 17th.*     Elsie and I went to town to see if we could get any fish. There were about 100 - 150 people in the fish-market, and not one fish to be seen! All the counters were empty. However, there were a few mackerel hidden underneath, and Elsie got three for themselves and three for Mrs Howells. She was lucky; many people were disappointed. Fancy no fish to be had in Jersey; to think that the Germans deprive us even of that! Went on beach and paddled with little Rosemary Howells – sea-air does one good and is a pleasant change.

*June 18th.*    Very glad to hear, on my return home, that the love affairs of my brothers are now progressing happily – misunderstandings settled etc. Saw a meadow in St. Peter's Valley full of cows which the Germans have brought over – black and white, red and white, and all with white faces, so unlike our dainty Jerseys.

*June 20th.*    This is a black day, for we have had to give up our wireless. Herbert packed it, and took it to the Parish Hall. Everyone feels it very much as it is our only link with England. One feels so mad against the Germans (wrong as it is to feel so) for we have done nothing to deserve this. However, let us be thankful that it is only our wireless sets that have been taken and not our young men. We shall never be at rest until the Germans have gone – may they depart soon! Then, another disturbing thing: today on the *Evening Post* there is an Order from the German Commandant: He has arrested ten persons in Jersey, as hostages, because of  leaflets with 'inciting contents,which have been printed and distributed; also for sabotage in connection with the tele-phone. If the perpetrators don't give themselves up, these ten persons are to be interned on the continent. One has heard of this sort of thing in European countries under occupation and now it has come to this little Island. Some girls had shown me one of these leaflets, trying to persuade people not to give up their wireless. I wish people would keep quiet, and not put us all into trouble. It is no use going against the Germans unless it is a matter of conscience. Well, we do feel depressed about everything tonight.

*June 21st. SUNDAY.*    Fewer children at Sunday School this morning, owing to vaccination. Lovely warm weather, so we sat outside this afternoon. Tonight, Laurence came in with the news that he and Phyllis Vibert are engaged. We are all very happy about it. She is a lovely girl. She is 19 and Laurence is 24. I find it terribly hard when I hear of engagements and marriages. Tonight, Laurence went to fetch Phyllis to introduce her to us as his fiancée. We were all very shy, somehow! Phyllis looked so sweet and Dad made her such a nice little speech!

*June 24th.*    Alice here and we picked gooseberries. All this week I've missed Alfred terribly and have had a lot of wicked thoughts, such as anger, disap-pointment – don't know really how to express it all, because Alfred and I are having to wait so long for marriage. We are getting old, and it is over four years since we got engaged. It seems to spoil things to wait so long.

*June 25th.*    I gave the greenhouse a good clean this morning. Dad has finished thinning the grapes. Reggie Jeune called to see about buying some hens. I had a chat with him about 'Sermons' and 'Local Preaching ' as I usually do when I see him. He has just passed his last exam. so is on 'Full Plan' now. He is only 21. Afternoon, I went to Montpelier. Muriel Le Seelleur came, and we went on the beach. But soon there was heavy firing and red smoke on the sea, quite close, and shells seemed to be exploding on the other side of the rocks. We did not know if it was practice or not but felt it safer to go back to the house. When the firing stopped we went back. Apparently, the Germans were shooting from big guns on the hillsides towards the harbour. After tea, Bunty Le Seelleur arrived – she had been doing a Nursing exam. at Hospital.

*June 26th.*    Laurence went to town to see if he could find an engagement ring, but there are none anywhere. Never mind, he will buy Phyllis a lovely one when the British are here again! Margaret has not come at all this week; she is not yet well. And now Auntie Edith has been taken ill. She has *Erysipelas* and her face is unrecognisable. I think it is dangerous too. People's vitality is lowered through lack of proper food. They are getting all sorts of illnesses. There have been a number of cases of lock-jaw, two of them fatal. It is time the Occupation finished. Have heard that Herbert Gallichan and his brother have been arrested by the Germans for being concerned with printing those leaflets. In spite of this the ten hostages are still in prison.

*June 27th.*    My Sweet Peas are now coming on beautifully; picked several lovely bunches today. We are missing our wireless very much. One hears news which others are supposed to have heard, but one does not know if it is true or not. There is an Order tonight to all fishermen in Jersey to paint their boats blue, white and red (French colours). I wonder what that means?

*June 28th. SUNDAY.*    At Bethlehem I had to play the piano for the hymns as Uncle wasn't there to play the organ, Auntie being ill. And Lucille went home after Sunday School to look after Evie and Eunice who were bad after their vaccination. Rev. Skyrme here for dinner and tea. I would have liked a chat with him, but Grandpa spoke the whole afternoon! Mother and Dad went to tea at La Pompe and Raymond came to supper. I have lent my diamond ring (which Cousin Frank le Gros gave me on my 21st Birthday) to Laurence, for Phyllis, until he can buy her one when the Germans have gone and we can get rings from England. She is delighted with it. I am so glad.

*July 1st.*    A very nice day. Phyllis came to tea, also Rev. and Mrs Scott. We all sat on the lawn this afternoon. Phyllis is already less shy. She is very sweet indeed. The ring looks lovely on her finger and is just the right size. I am very glad to have had it to lend her. Alice was here today and she was ever so nice to Phyllis.

74

*July 2nd.*     We all went to fetch our registration photos at Philadelphie. Most of them are awful. Mine is, but even then it is too good for the Germans! Tonight I cycled to Galaad for my Local preacher's exam. The examiners were Rev. Ward, Rev. Scott, and Ph. Noel (Mr A de B Breton did not arrive in time!) Rev. Scott asked me the questions – not quite what I expected! They seemed satisfied, though I wasn't with myself!

*July 3rd.*     Mother and Dad's Wedding Anniversary. They have been married for 29 years. We had a busy morning. Dad was cutting up veal (we killed a calf yesterday). Then Granny and Grandpa give us a lot of work these days. They both have the 'Occupation Malady', as we call it, and it is so much work for Mother always to be having to change their clothes and bed and wash the floor. How I wish mother did not have all this trouble. I went to the Walker's for dinner. Joy was very pleased to have some veal for her Mother who is still not yet well, unfortunately. Took veal also to Mrs Le B., Elsie and Uncle Philip Le Brocq. Found Auntie Julia bad – she has got worse these days.

*Shopping in town.*

*July 5th. SUNDAY.*     A very nice day. Went to Sunday School and gave a talk to the children (story about Naboth's vineyard). Then cycled on to St. Ouen's chapel to take the service there. Spoke to the children on 'Vaccination' and drew a lesson from it. They were very attentive. They have all been vaccinated by now. The older people told me they also had found my talk interesting! Miss Florrie Du Feu was looking and feeling quite bad after her vaccination and was not fit to be there. I was thankful she did not faint during the service. Quite a lot of people fear to be vaccinated, when they see how ill others have been. For the older people my text was, 'What went ye out for to see ... a reed shaken with the wind?' (Matt. 11, v. 7). I found it easier than sometimes. The atmosphere was very helpful. Phyllis here for dinner and tea, also Fred and Cis Le Brocq. They went back after supper. They had enjoyed their day with us (and the veal at dinner!) I thank God, at the end of the day, especially for the encouraging time at St. Ouen's this morning.

*July 6th.*    Alice came and we picked blackcurrants nearly all day. They are lovely and very plentiful this year but, alas, we have no sugar to make jam. It is hard! Alice told me that Auntie Florrie had much appreciated my prayers yesterday morning. Yesterday, for the first time, I had no notes at all for the prayers, so I certainly was helped. How I wish I could preach the sermon without notes also; I must persevere. We've been disappointed not to have had any Red Cross Messages – many people had some last week. Some must get lost. Alfred sends me one every week and they don't even come once a month!

*July 7th.*    Kath and I washed potato-pulp all day. Edward Laffoley had crushed about one hundred-weight for us. The new potatoes are better than the old for flour-making. Feel very tired tonight after pumping all that water etc. Margaret came afternoon and I made her bring her little table and books on the bricks in the yard and taught her as I washed the pulp! Mr Bauche is ill (he must miss his sister); he had heart attacks yesterday, so Dad and the boys went to do some of his work and put him back to bed when he fainted.

*July 9th.*    Breakfasted at Montpelier; later saw Emily, who told me the glad news that her Uncle, Mr Curwood, has been released from internment and is now in Paris, on his way to America. It is far away but he will be free and safe when he gets there. It appears that there has been some sort of exchange of prisoners and Mr C. and another American citizen from Guernsey have been allowed to return to America on payment of money. The other internees in their camp in France are not to go free, as they are of military age. Well, how I hope Mr C. will arrive safely in America, but what a long time Emily may be without news of him. Called to see Cousin Frank le Gros to tell him about my having lent the ring he gave me to Laurence and Phyllis. He doesn't seem to mind. Edward Laffoley crushed some more potatoes for us tonight and Willie came and helped me for about three-quarters of an hour to wash the pulp. He pumped the water for me.

*July 10th.*    Pouring rain, so had to work indoors. All day, I was in the pantry washing potato-pulp. Christine pumped the water for me this morning and Kath this afternoon. What a job! But we finished by tea-time and tonight I washed the flour and emptied the tins. A tiring day!

*July 11th.* Cycled to town and got my hat at Petit Louvre, which they had made for me out of a piece of material I took. Very satisfied, I think! Paid 13 shillings. Called at Uncle Philip. Auntie Julia much worse, has had a slight stroke and her throat is paralysed. Miss Deslandes is very patient and kind to her, I am sure. I discovered tonight that John has been secretly listening to the wireless (the one we kept) from the place where it is hidden. It is risky of course.

*July 12th. SUNDAY.* Mr and Mrs Stuart Pepin here for dinner, tea and supper. We were very lucky, as regards dinner. We would have had to put them off, except that Irene turned up on Friday night with a lovely dog-fish which we had fried today. We are so fortunate in knowing a fisherman's wife. Lost my vaccination scab today, almost two months since we were done.

*July 13th.* What a lovely lot of potato-flour; I began sifting the dry one today.

*July 14th.* Cycled to town. Took four pounds blackcurrants to Mrs Du Feu and six pounds to Mrs Bunting.

*July 16th.* Had an unexpected pleasure in receiving a lovely long letter from Mr Curwood, in Paris. It is very dear of him as he hasn't known me long. I wrote in return. But no Red Cross messages to cheer us all this time.

*July 17th.* Mother and I went to see Mrs Du Val for her sister, Cecil (Mrs Hamon) died suddenly early this morning. I felt so sorry poor Mrs Du Val. She is so upset. I often met Mrs H. in town. She was always so bright, even though she was almost crippled with arthritis and, lately, her heart was bad. She was always doing something for others, sewing especially, like 'Auntie Marie', another sister – they never lost a moment! What a fine example for us to follow! Doing something for others. This morning, Mrs Hamon's table was found full of sewing she had been doing for poor children – working until the very last, a beautiful death.

*July 20th.* Mrs Du Val managed to get a taxi tonight to go to St. Martin's to see another sister, Mrs Dorey. Kath took this opportunity to go to see her friend, Kathleen Picot, who has TB. Kath had not seen her for months and found her changed and very ill. How sad it is.

*July 21st.* My 27th Birthday. And this was the day when Alfred and I had hoped to get married. Well, I never dreamt that I would still be separated from him when this day came. My darling 'little Minister'; it is so hard for him to have to wait so long for me. Perhaps before another birthday comes we shall be together. Went with Herbert to Mr Laffoley's to take two hundred-weight of potatoes to be crushed. How quickly done by machine! Then went to town. Found Joy and Emily crushing potatoes in a hand-machine – we have more advantage in the country for doing that sort of thing. Don't know why potatoes people get in town are so poor, for they are fine everywhere this year and people should be getting better stuff. Tonight, Elsie and I went with Joy and Emily to see a play at the Opera House called 'George and Margaret'. The acting was very good, but the play not much! Jokes too much on the vulgar and suggestive side – not worth acting! I wonder what Alfred has been doing today. I suppose Methodist Conference is on and perhaps even this week he is being ordained, and I cannot even be there.

*July 28th.*    Better weather, so I put out all the potato-flour to dry, and began weighing it and sifting it this afternoon. Spent the whole afternoon up there on top of the porch, outside my bedroom window, seeing to the flour. Tonight went to see Aunt Elize, who is now very frail. Then went on to Bethlehem for Rev. Scott's weekday service.

*July 29th.*    Mother went by bus to town. Mrs Le Brun had invited her to a pupils' Concert, given by Mr Herivel. It was a change for Mother. It does her good to go out because Granny and Grandpa, through no fault of their own, give her much trouble these days.

*July 31st.*    Went to see Auntie Edith. She paid me £4.17s.6d. for 39 lessons given to Margaret. Tonight I finished sifting all my potato flour; it has dried so well in today's hot sun. Have more than I expected – 36 pounds out of 300 pounds potatoes. So, with both lots from last week, we have altogether 65 pounds of flour, and so pure and white!

*August 3rd.*  Dad and the boys scrubbed two hundred-weight of potatoes and cut off the diseased parts, and Mr Laffoley crushed them for us this afternoon. Potatoes are full of disease this year, such a pity as they are lovely big ones. Making potato-flour with them at once is the only way to save them.
Mr O Mourant arrived at noon and asked if we had any dinner for him! We made him earn it by helping to wash the potatoes! Received another nice letter from Mr Curwood from Paris. I do feel terribly sorry because, after all, his hopes about being repatriated are all off. All those Americans who were released must now return to internment camp. Mr C. wrote the day before he had to go back.

*Aug. 4th.*    Have spent all day washing potato pulp. Irene had come wash the clothes, and she helped me when she had finished.. we washed over two hundred-weight. What tiring work. Tonight Evie called and entertained us for three-quarters of an hour telling us about the 'sick ladies' she had visited. Evie should be on the stage really! Hearing her tell of her adventures is far better than going to the Pictures! And it costs nothing! Poor Mr Bauche is very ill. Dr. Avarne has been today and said it is a hopeless case. How sad it is that so many people must suffer before they die. Why can't they go peacefully? And no doubt Mr Bauche has felt his sister's death, and maybe this has hastened it.

*Aug. 5th.* Lovely sunny day but almost too busy to enjoy it, as usual! I finished washing flour, and put it all out to dry. Christine was helping in the field picking potatoes, so we had more to do indoors. Mrs Le Brun and Mrs Reis came afternoon, so Mother sat outside with them till 5.30pm and we took them tea there. I am so glad that Mother had this opportunity of a little rest, as she is very tired by Granny and Grandpa, and also not too well, from the food. Very often the bread makes us unwell – I found some mouldy bits again this week. There has been an order today for farmers to take their horses to the Parish Halls for the Germans to choose some for themselves. It appears that they are taking away all the lovely horses they had brought over, and are going to use ours instead. And farm horses are all thin and overworked already. But maybe it is a good sign that they are taking theirs away, we hope so anyway. How we wish they themselves would all go! We are feeling very sad tonight because Judy, our little brown and white bitch, mother of Vicky, has gone. Laurence has given her away, and two men came and took her away as she was in the field with the others. I suppose we can't keep so many dogs, but we've had Judy for three years and one does get attached to one's animals. I never thought Laurence would part with her, she was such an affectionate little creature.

*Aug. 6th.* We scrubbed more potatoes and I finished drying and sifting the other lot. I had 28 pounds flour out of two hundred-weight of potatoes – very good indeed. Those big potatoes, though diseased, are full of flour. We finished digging today and we had a man to begin cutting the oats. The fields of corn and oats look so beautiful just now. There had never been so much grown before as during these Occupation years, but we grow less potatoes.

*Aug. 8th.* Kath helped me to wash potatoes. I was at it all day and evening. Feel very tired tonight but I have prepared a Sunday School talk. It helps me tremendously to have to prepare and look things up for Sunday School – it teaches me to know my Bible better. I've been disappointed to get no news from Alfred this week, nor last week, when others had messages. I long for a word from him, and how much more to see him and be with him.

*Aug. 11th.* Joy came and I took her to Laffoleys as I wanted her to see Edward's potato-crushing machine at work. She thinks it is a wonderful invention! Edward is undoubtedly clever at that sort of thing. His machine crushes better than any other that I've seen. Irene brought us another lovely lobster last night which we had for tea today.

*Aug. 13th.*    No sun, so could not dry the potato flour. Laurence went to town and saw about 500 Russian men and boys which the Germans have brought here – some say that about 1,500 to 2,000 have arrived and are being put in those big camps which we have seen the Germans putting up lately. I feel very sad when I think of it all – those poor men and young lads taken so far from home and having little food. They were dressed in rags and barefooted.
Had a pleasant surprise – received a Red Cross message from Alfred today and he says he longs for me more than ever. As I do for him! I had not heard from him since June 14th. Phyllis came about 7.30 tonight, but did not see Laurence till 9.55 as he was busy about the oats in the field, and did not come in till 9.35, and then he wanted to change his clothes. So, when he was ready, it was time for supper, then time to take her home. He has not much time to spend with Phyllis when she comes on a week-day. I wish the boys could take work a little easier. It is always rush, rush here! It seems to me they ought to have a little time to rest and think of other things and to read to improve their minds.

*Aug. 14th.*    Rain all morning. Christine and I went to town by bus. We were packed like sardines, as usual, and many were left behind. A long time since I had taken the bus. Went to see Dr. Lewis as the food has been upsetting me too.

*Aug. 15th. SUNDAY.*    Stayed in tonight, washed the dishes and dairy cans etc. had about a half hour to spare before the others came back from chapel, so played hymns and wrote out part of a sermon. Phyllis came for tea.

*Aug. 16th.*    This morning poor Mr Bauche was taken away in the ambulance to Bon Air for an operation, but we fear there is no hope at all for him. The Germans have now got to our field (Laffoleys) making their railway, and today they have Russians working on it. Hundreds have arrived, even women. It is said that people in town wept to see them pass. One Russian, at work today, asked John if he were English: "I Soviet, you English," and he clapped his hands joyfully! It is a strange thing that we should be allied with Russia. One does not know what to think about these things. Yet we feel so sorry for these Russians – far from home, half-starved and half-naked. Then, the fact of us all being under the Germans is a link. One feels friendly towards all who are suffering in the same way as oneself. Francis slept at Mr Bauche's house tonight, so as not to leave Miss Marcus and the maid alone.

*Aug. 18th.*   Cycled to town. Tried to get shoes for Mother and myself but there is nothing but clogs with canvas tops. At last, I bought a pair of sandals with wooden soles and fancy leather top, for myself. But I had to pay 27s.1d., a price I have never even paid for a good pair of leather shoes. It is awful! And it is impossible to get shoes to wear in cold or wet weather. (May the British come soon, with shoes, sugar, flour, etc.) Very hot day. All the flour dried so I sifted it afternoon. Have 30 pounds from last Tuesday's lot. Mr Laffoley can hardly believe it. It is certainly a record all this time with our potato flour this year, and all made from the good part of diseased or green potatoes. Mr L. crushed us another two hundred-weight tonight, so I washed the pulp. I seem to have time for nothing else these weeks, and I would like to do some reading and preparation for sermons, Sunday School Anniversary and so on. However, I must not be impatient and we must have food.

*Aug. 19th.*   Mr Bauche was having his operation about noon. All afternoon we have awaited news. Mother tried to 'phone the Nursing Home but could not get through. Went to Frank Luce's same thing. Tonight 'phone was working again so we heard that Mr Bauche had had his operation. Then we find that because the British landed and made a big raid on Dieppe the Germans have got 'the frit' as we say. So they took command of the Telephone Exchange in town, they stopped all their 'works' and shut up their Russian workers. In fact, people say the Germans seem to have disappeared today! No singing to be heard in the streets! John had heard (in secret) about Dieppe. It is the biggest raid they have yet made. The Germans thought that the British had landed for good! It is said that the German officers have been practising to evacuate, and that if the British landed in France they would run away from here, leaving the common soldiers to man the guns! Well, I wish they would go without offering resistance. We don't want any fighting in this small place. There is nowhere civilians can go. We haven't any shelters, not that they would be safe either.

*Aug. 20th.*   Dad and the boys very busy reaping and binding wheat – reaping with a neighbour's machine today.

*Aug. 21st.*   New order today: curfew is to be at 10pm instead of 11pm. We all had supper earlier, so that the boys could get to Mr Bauche's place in time. Thank goodness that is the only new Order today. We feared more after the happenings in France. Everyone still talking about it (in whispers, of course, or we might find ourselves in prison, or worse). It doesn't take much to annoy the Germans, especially when they are feeling nervous! They have put a big account on the *Evening Post* about a 'frustrated British landing' but we are not taken in by that.

*Aug. 24th.*   The Russians have been uprooting and eating our potatoes in the field where the Germans are making a railway track, so Dad and the boys

have been digging them tonight, else there will be none left for us. One feels so sorry, though, for these men – they must be dreadfully hungry to eat all those things raw. Mother went to Mrs Laffoley's and was much amused at the 'latest' from her: "Did you see those planes, the other day? Well, a 'Big Bug' came over from Germany, visited everything and said the Island was of no military use at all to Germany, but Hitler says, 'you must build a railway for my prestige!"

*Aug. 26th.* Mrs Bunting and Margaret came for dinner and tea. They were forcibly removed from Sark, having been forcibly removed by the Germans. Mother and Mrs B. had not met for 25 years so they had plenty to talk about! And I was glad to see M. again and to discuss views on different subjects with her. I enjoy finding out what other people think. We have all been saddened at the tragic news of the death of the Duke of Kent in an air crash in Scotland. We are not supposed to know!

*Aug. 27th.* Left for town at 10.30am. Called at Joy's and Bunting's. At Alfred's folk we had a plate of vegetables and a cup of coffee substitute, then all left with Mrs Howells and Rosemary to take bus for Gorey. Being early, we just managed to squash in; about half a dozen were left behind. We went on the beach awhile. Mr Howells joined us. We picked a few blackberries in lanes then had tea at Long Beach Café. Sun was boiling hot! We had brought our bread and milk, etc. and they gave us stewed fruit or vegetables and coffee substitute. So it was a good tea for these days! When we got back tonight I sat on the beach at end of Beach Road and paddled. Very refreshing, and quite a change for me this day has been. Had been so busy with making potato-flour that I had not come to Alfred's folk for about five weeks.

*Aug. 28th.* Bought a six-week-old rabbit at Stanley's. Paid ten marks, more than ten times the price they were before the war. Shocking! But I understood they were five marks each and meant to take two. When I discovered my mistake, I did not like to go off without a rabbit, especially as both were already in my basket. I do hope this one will not die. Came home for dinner and fixed up my rabbit in a box in a pig-sty, as Herbert's are not doing well in the shed. No one seems to know the cause of all these rabbits dying off. It is just, well, Occupation, the cause of all our troubles! Went collecting subscriptions for the District Nurse tonight. Went to Mr Trachy's and he gave me two lovely rabbits, three-months-old. It is much too good of him to give them to me. I have been fortunate in being able to get rabbits at last and I hope they will do well for we need food so badly. It is about three years now since I kept any but my old interest in them is still there! It is a pity one has to kill them though, because one gets to love them.

*Aug. 29th.*    The thunderstorm which has threatened for some days has come at last, with sheets of rain. It got so dark after dinner that we could hardly see indoors. The ducks were actually swimming in the flooded yard – they had the time of their lives, poor things!

*Aug. 30th.*    At Bethlehem this morning. Rev. South preached on the Parable of the Talents: (a) nothing we have is our own, it is God's gift; (b) if we use our talents they increase, if we don't use them, we lose all; (c) our reward is the Praise of our Master, with opportunity for greater service. This afternoon, John arranged for me to listen to the Overseas news, from the bathroom, with the blinds down in case anyone came into the yard and saw me. Had not heard the News myself since our wirelesses were taken away. It is risky to have kept one. The Germans must know there are some somewhere.

*Aug. 31st.*    · Joy came to fetch apples and grapes. Then, Dad said she could glean in our cornfield so I helped her. Tonight I began preparing my Trial Sermon.

*September 2nd.*    Alice here, as usual, and Margaret to have her lessons. Reggie Jeune came to do some gleaning. I helped him awhile and he stayed for dinner. Everybody talking about the 'latest' in Occupation news, which is that all the farmers in the Coin Varin district must evacuate within ten days, taking all their cattle, etc., but leaving their furniture in their houses. The reason is supposed to be that the Germans expect the British to land in St. Ouen's Bay, proceed to the Airport and to town, whilst the Germans will shoot at them from Coin Varin, where they have lots of heavy guns. I don't know what the farmers are going to do, Where can they go and where find land to replace their fields? The Germans are mad! Jersey is too small a place to be so heavily fortified.

*Sept. 3rd.*    Today was a National Day of Prayer in England, for today we enter upon the fourth year of war (may it be the last). So, at 12 o'clock (11am in England) I thought of and prayed for King and Nation and for Peace.

*Sept. 4th.*    Today, Mr A. who comes to help Miss Marcus to pick Mrs Bauche's apples, has come rushing in twice, all red and excited! First, because a heifer was loose, next because Mr. B's cow was calving in the field. He is not used to the farm, and he does amuse us!

*Sept. 5th.*    The men ever so busy with the wheat. And I had to go to Beth-lehem to help decorate for Harvest service tomorrow. Then, tonight, there was an Order that work must be done tomorrow as the wheat must all be gathered in by tomorrow night. I wonder why the Germans are so interested in our wheat?

*Sept. 6th. SUNDAY.*    What a strange day, not at all like a Sunday. Farmers at work bringing in their wheat. I have worried all day as to whether it was the right thing to do or not, but I can't make up my mind. However, the boys were able to go chapel tonight. Mr Sid Querée from town had tea with us as he had kindly offered to help. The German Commandant, Knackfuss, has been out all day seeing that farmers were busy. He came round St. Peter's but, fortunately, not in our fields. Uncle Ernest and other Inspectors had to go to town this morning to see the three German Commandants. Uncle says they are all in a bad temper and say that if the Inspectors and farmers do not get on more quickly with the wheat and oats they will be severely punished. They got mad and thumped on the table several times. They are getting the wind up we all think, fearing a British invasion. In the midst of all this, I went to preach at Galaad this morning, and tonight we went to Bethlehem for our Harvest Thanksgiving service. So, this strange Sunday is over! Never before had Dad and the boys brought in their wheat on a Sunday. The weather has been hot, one of the loveliest days we've had for a long time.

*Sept. 7th.*    Dad and the boys very busy loading the oats into vans. Tonight it was my Trial sermon at Galaad chapel at 7 o'clock. I got there in good time. Rev. Scott prayed for me in the vestry and Mr P A Huelin came in to give me Rev. Ward's best wishes. I was disappointed that Rev. Ward could not be present, as his opinion would have been of more value to me than that of the others! However, Rev. Scott, Pastor Hanks and local preachers A de B Breton, E P Ahier, P A Huelin were all there to report on my preaching. Mr Howells and Lilian also came. I preached on Rev. ch. 3, v. 15, 16. Felt nervous as I began my sermon and did not say all I meant to say. I am never satisfied with my sermons. It being a weekday, there were only 20 persons present including one little boy sitting alone at the back. One farmer, Mr Coutanche, told me that he was very busy today, but the Lord told him: 'Surely you can spend one short hour with Me tonight.' So he came to the service.

*Sept. 8th.*    The men were threshing oats at Mr Farrell at St. Ouen's today. So we girls and Mother had a busy morning preparing dinner for them. Herbert had to kill three rabbits as we had nothing else and the rabbits were not yet really fit to kill. We gave them dinner in the breakfast-room – 12, including our own men. We girls had dinner in the kitchen and Granny and Grandpa up-stairs. Irene was here washing, so we were 19 altogether at dinner-time. Everything went well, fortunately, and weather is perfect for threshing. It was lovely to see the vans all loaded.

*Sept. 10th.* Did not feel at all well after dinner, so lay down for an hour. Later I gleaned with Roger de Faye who was here for tea. Tonight went to Bethlehem to finish giving out parts to the children for the Anniversary. Called at Somerleigh to fetch the two rabbits Jurat Le Feuvre had promised me. He very kindly gave them to me – two fine, six-week-old ones. Tonight, Dad gave us a fright by having very bad indigestion – all those wretched potatoes, I suppose. Then, after eating, Dad worked too hard, as usual! High time we all had a change of diet. Margaret Bunting phoned, whilst I was out, to congratulate me on the good report that had been given about my trial sermon at the Quarterly Meeting at Grove Place this afternoon. It was nice of her to phone and to know that the report was good.

*Sept. 12th.* Sent a Red Cross Message to my dear Alfred. It was four years ago today that he sailed away from Jersey. All this week I have thought so much about him. When he left me, we never dreamt we should be separated for so long. We said Goodbye for eighteen months, then he would return from Africa for his furlough. I could never have let him go had I known what was going to happen!

*Sept. 13th. SUNDAY.* Threshing machines were all working today – German orders. Preached at Les Frères chapel this morning. Went to Bethlehem afternoon for Anniversary practice. Stayed in tonight with Kath and Joyce. We washed dishes and dairy cans, fed rabbits, etc. – whole evening occupied. Just sat down to read a few minutes when we heard heavy footsteps in the yard. Saw two Russians making signs that they wanted food. We gave them a crust of bread each, apples and a cup of tea we had left over. I brought a map and one showed me where they came from – east of Moscow. He asked, "English?" Then said: "Russe, Russe", for himself. All the rest of the evening I have felt so sad in thinking of these poor men. They looked so dreadfully tired and sad, so far from home, and one is constantly hearing of the bestial way in which the Germans treat them, beating them even to death. It is unbelievable, yet it is true. This afternoon, another Russian had come – a young, bare-footed one – and he kissed Francis' hand. Yesterday one came, also bare-footed and in rags, and we gave him boiled potatoes and apples. He put the potatoes in his tin bowl and all the apples inside his shirt, then lifted his cap to us. How we wish we had more to give them. If only we had more bread, but we have only just enough for ourselves.

*Sept. 15th.* What a blow has fallen on the Island again tonight. On the *Evening Post* there is an Order from a higher authority (Hitler!) saying that all

Englishmen, aged 16-70 years, are to be evacuated with their families to Germany. Oh, it is shocking, one can hardly believe that such a dreadful thing is coming to pass. There is no word bad enough to describe the cruelty and beastliness of the Germans. Of course they give no reason whatever for this. Then, to spring this upon us so suddenly; tonight people had orders to leave tomorrow. We have so many friends amongst the English people – it is too dreadful, one can hardly think. Our poor ministers, I don't suppose they will be exempted. Laurence went to see a Mr Brown, St. Peter's Mill, and there he was, packing, a wife and three children, one a baby in arms. Laurence was very upset when he got back.

*Sept. 16th.*    Lovely and sunny, not in keeping with all the happenings. What a day! The evacuation to Germany begins. I went to Alfred's folk for dinner and tea. Went upstairs to see Mrs Howells: poor Mrs Howells, she is so afraid to get the Order to go, with little Rosemary too. As she says, if she could only leave Rosemary behind, it would be better. Mr Howells feels like all the Englishmen, that they don't mind going themselves, they can rough it, but it's their wives and kiddies they don't want to take with them. How awful it all is! Afternoon, I went to Grève d'Azette to see if Uncle Gordon had heard anything about himself. It was a shock, as I walked up to the door, to see his small suitcase packed and to hear women's voices saying, "Well, best of luck, Mr Amoore," and so on. Oh, I thought, he's going. And yes, there he was, just leaving. I couldn't believe it! He has been in Jersey for 40 years. Last night, at 9 o'clock, two Germans, with Constable Crill, arrived to tell him that he must be off by the 4 o'clock boat today. All his neighbours, ladies, were wishing him goodbye, with tears. I put his suitcase on my carrier and we walked to the place where a special bus was to pick up all those who were going. Found a good number waiting, so brave, with a smile on their faces as if they were going for a holiday, instead of what I fear, to their deaths perhaps. It is cruel and wicked. Fine boys and girls from our Colleges, waiting there, with blankets on their arms, and their parents with them. One, a typical Englishman, a Mr Fenton, I think, leaning against the wall, with a careless, nonchalant air, as if it did not matter at all! Not a sign of what he really felt. As some women were saying to me: "We must not on any account show the skunks what we feel. We will keep a cheerful face." How wonderful those English folk are. There was, too, an elderly gentleman with his wife who has often served me at Boots. I don't know his name, but I went up to shake hands and told him how sorry I was. At last, after an hour's wait, the bus came, and they were all herded in by German soldiers to be driven to the pier. I couldn't help crying a little as the bus went and Uncle waved goodbye. His neighbours took my arm and told me to be brave, such nice women.

Left Montpelier about 7 o'clock and called at Mr and Mrs Allan to see if anything had happened to them. Found them standing amongst several cases and packages. "Well, you see, we're back," said Mrs A. to me. "What," I said, "you don't mean to say you've been?" Poor things, at midnight, they were roused by German officers with the Order that they must be off today. Mrs A. was on the point of collapse. At noon, at the last moment, she got a certificate from her doctor saying that she had just recovered from a very serious operation, and that saved her. They had got to the Weighbridge amongst crowds of others and were finally sent back home on account of her health. Mr A. says she would never have lived through it. He said it was dreadful at the Weigh-bridge. Of course, no one was allowed to see what was going on. Germans with fixed bayonets were guarding the area, and soldiers were shouting and bullying the English people. "Dreadful," Mr A. said. Quite a number were exempted, some being farm-workers, others ill. Got home about 8pm. Francis said the Bonn family had just passed so Laurence went to see them. He found great rejoicing! They had been sent back because they had a very small baby. People (Uncle Gordon amongst them) told me they expected *all* would be evacuated, Jersey people too. People say this is only the beginning of what they will do to us, now that (we think) they see themselves lost.

At Georgetown, they were having a Prayer meeting at 9pm, the time the boat was due to leave. At home, I went to my room and prayed with them, in spirit. Mother is very upset about Uncle Gordon but she has nothing to reproach herself with. She has been more than good to him every time he came. How sad one feels tonight, how bruised, shaken and strange.

*Sept. 17th.*   Lilian phoned Mother to say she was on the pier last night (being a St. John's Ambulance nurse) and Uncle spoke to her and told her to tell Mother to see to his clothes. Poor Uncle, I am glad she spoke to him. He was alone amongst a crowd. In town today, I met Pastor Hanks and got off my bike to speak to him. He told me he had just been to the Town Hall and seen his name on a list of those to be evacuated. I had hoped he would be out of it, but, as he told me: "Why should ministers be exempted?" (How splendid he is.) If he gets the Order to go, he will go and be a minister to those with him. If there is no minister with them, who will pray for them, and cheer and comfort them? He will take it as an opportunity to minister to the needs of the suffering people, and to do something for his Lord. But when he thinks of his Mother and sisters in England, he doesn't want to go to Germany. He is torn between two, but whatever comes will take it in the right spirit. Well, the decision is not with him.

Heard that the Germans were to put out yet worse Orders soon, but did not tell anyone, for I hope it is not true. I know that we are at the mercy of Hitler, but God is more powerful than him. Tonight Mrs Crill phoned and said that her husband (Constable of St Clements) was out with the Germans warning people for tomorrow's boat. How our Jersey officials suffer, being forced to do these things. It is said that our Bailiff even went on his knees pleading with the

Germans not to carry out their Order, but in vain. Also that Knackfuss, the Commandant told someone: "I am very sorry about this, but we can't do anything about it. The Order comes from a man who has no regard for human life."

*Sept. 18th.*    Mrs Crill phoned early to say that her husband got back at 1.45am and the Germans called for him again before 7am. He said we could go to Uncle's house to see about his clothes, but later we decided not to touch anything for we know not what other Order is coming out, and we fear to do anything that might bring us into trouble. Anything may annoy the Germans in the state they are these days. We would rather lose all Uncle's stuff than get into trouble. What are clothes and possessions? It is our lives that matter. We are so afraid of seeing the *Evening Post* because of what may be on; we are in a state of suspense the whole time these days.
A young Russian came. He comes from the Ukraine – he showed me on a map. We gave him potatoes and beans which he ate in the pantry. One who came yesterday showed me photographs of his sisters, such good-looking girls.
*10.30pm.* The night has come and thank God there was no new Order on the *Evening Post.* How we think of those English families now on board ship on their way to France, open to all dangers. Everyone is in suspense, expecting their turn next, even Jersey folk, wondering if anything is going to happen to us also. We have had many dark days, but none so black as now. Will the dawn come soon?

*Sept. 19th.*    Dad's Birthday. We heard that one of the boats taking away English families had come back; all sorts of rumours afloat as to the reason. All feeling hopeful, thinking that perhaps the British had intervened. But, when I got to town my spirits sank low again, on hearing that the people who were sent back, must go again on Friday and that during the week others must go, as arranged. Lilian, who has been on duty on the pier both days says that the English that have left are all showing such a splendid spirit. They sang, 'There'll always be an England' and 'God save the King' as they sailed away. The Germans said nothing and were treating them well, so far. This has been such a strange week. One feels as if in a very bad dream. I was very cheered by a verse that appeared on the *Evening Post* today:

> *Tread gaily,*
> *Yet not unaware*
> *That He hath counted every step*
> *Thy feet must climb.*

Cheered, not only by the lovely words, but by the thought that someone had put this on the newspaper.

*Sept. 21st.*    Constable Du Val has had another list of people to 'warn' today, to be off next Friday, 48 from this Parish alone. They are taking women who have no menfolk here also. He had to warn one English woman whose husband is in England. The poor woman wept so when she heard she had to go. It is cruel. I feel anxious about my dear friend Joy, and her Mother, Mrs Walker – they stand in great danger.

*Sept. 22nd.*    Mother and I went to Uncle Gordon's house to see to his clothes, but we found other things of poor Auntie's that should have been removed. It is awful poking about in the house – lots of things of Auntie's were left in her drawers. Uncle does not seem to have touched anything since she died 14 months ago. Poor Uncle. I wonder if he is in Germany now, and how they are all being treated? On our way back, Alfred's mother gave us a cup of coffee which did us good. From the bus, which was terribly crowded, as usual, we could see the wrecked ship (which went on the rocks in the gale last Sunday night, with some of the German crew being drowned) quite clearly.
I went to Bethlehem about 4.40pm for the children to practise their hymns and recitations for the Anniversary. I do love those little Sunday School children. To be with them awhile cheers me up in these dark days. They are so inno-cent, happy and sweet. Sometimes I think that there is hardly anything more lovely than to be loved by children. I had tea with Evie and Aunt Elize then went to the week-night service. We were glad to have Rev. Scott with us. We had feared to lose him, but he went before the Commandant today, and has been let off, for this time. So he will not go on Friday after all.

*Sept. 23rd.*    Today's *Evening Post* brought good news: the evacuation (deporta-tion!) is postponed until further notice on account of this bad weather (we wonder if that is the true reason!) but all those warned, must keep themselves in readiness. I know we must not be unduly hopeful for the Germans love to spring evil surprises upon us.
More Russians came for food today. The young one who had refused shoes a few days ago made signs that he wanted them today. He showed me photos of his two lovely sisters. He must come from a good family. I wish we under-stood each other's language. However, talking by signs and actions is fun! Poor Russians, they are made to work in the pouring rain with no shoes or socks, and whatever clothes they do have get soaked. The Germans are putting rails in Mr Bauche's meadow and knocking down his apple trees. Our field comes next. I spent most of the day with Herbert in the large pig-sty cleaning and arranging our rabbit hutches. We are putting them in the sty as one does not keep many pigs nowadays, since one is not allowed to kill them for oneself, and food-stuff for them is so scarce. I rang up Joy. So glad to hear her voice and to know she is still here.

*Sept. 25th.*    Mother and I went in the lorry with Laurence to Grève d'Azette to Uncle Gordon's house. We brought back some furniture and other things to keep for him, so that the Germans don't get them. But the house is crammed with china, pictures, etc. Uncle had no time to give instructions. It is a worry for Mother and she has enough worries already. Distressed to hear that the Germans have been all day warning people for evacuation.

*Sept. 26th.*    My dear Alfred's Birthday. He is 31-years-old now. I wonder what he has been doing today? Had all gone as we expected we would have been married for two months by now. Order tonight that next batch of evacuees are to be on the Weighbridge at 2pm next Tuesday. Russians have been coming all day for food.

*Sept. 27th. SUNDAY.*    Spent all afternoon trying to finish preparing for tonight, but had a headache and couldn't get on somehow. Did my best. Cycled to Six Roads for 6.30. Preached on 'Call ye unto Me, etc.' (Jeremiah 33 v 3). Finished early as I wished to have a Prayer meeting to intercede for all those who have been taken away and who expect to go. These include several of our Local Preachers: Mr Bull, Mr Watson and others. Everyone stayed (there were about 35 present, with quite a number of children). Three ladies stood up to pray, such fervent, heartfelt prayers. I was so thankful, I felt that those women were more fit to preach than I. God bless them. I had never conducted a prayer meeting before and I did as I thought and I felt that God was with us. One of the ladies who had prayed told me that she was English with three children, and she was expecting her Order to go any day. May something happen to prevent it.

*Sept. 28th.*    Tonight Kath was extracting the honey from the honeycombs. Phyllis and Beryl Vibert came and we took turns to turn the machine. The Russians, under German orders, have started cutting into our field, having done Mr Bauche's meadow. It is terrible to see that lovely field being ruined. Dad is upset. And yet it is nothing compared to the deportation that is going on. We killed a small pig tonight, in great secret!

*Sept. 29th.*    More than a thousand English people were due to leave today. We heard that many Jersey people, too, had been warned last night to go today. These were  men or women who had served sentences in prison for so-called sabotage, curfew and black-market offences. Some of these had served a month in prison in France, come back home, and are now called to be taken to prison camp in Germany. All day we've been thinking of those hundreds being taken away, and all day Russians have been coming to the house for food – they escape for a few minutes when the Germans backs are turned. One stayed a long time munching new turnips and carrots.

*Sept. 30th.* Thank God! The deportation to Germany is stopped. Heard today that last evening, after two boat-loads of people had left, the Germans announced, through a microphone on the pier, that they had the number required, and all who were left could go home. I am so thankful that amongst those remaining were both of Audrey's uncles who were being taken away for having been discovered with a wireless. (An Englishman who boarded with them gave them away – despicable traitor! It makes one's blood boil to think of people who can be so wicked.)

*October 3rd.* We are very much bothered by so many Russians coming for food. The boys are annoyed because, though we give them food, they steal our tomatoes and apples. A lovely boy aged about fifteen years came. He told me he was Polish. I gave him some porridge we had left over and an apple. He thanked me by raising his cap and making me such a lovely bow! Poor little fellow, I wonder if he has any of his family left in Poland? One had heard many stories of how the Germans beat the Russians and I've seen it happen several times myself this week. The Todt guard, in charge of the prisoners working in our big field beats them with a thick stick, and today I think he killed one. From indoors, I could hear the sound of beating and through the trees I could see a stick being brandished. A few minutes later, John came in and said he had seen a Russian being carried by others out of the field and put on a lorry. His body was quite limp and John thinks he was dead. It is so cruel. I don't know how the Russians stand it. But, of course, they would be shot if they resisted. We think the RAF passed quite close today. It cheers one up, for we feel so lonely of England.

*Oct. 4th. SUNDAY.* Our Sunday School Anniversary. Very nice services. The chapel was quite full tonight. Rev. Fell preached on, 'There is a lad here.' We did enjoy having him with us and to think that he has nearly been taken off to Germany too! I hope the boys and girls and their parents were touched by his message. Little Dorothy sang so sweetly, and all my other little ones did their best and enjoyed it all.

*Oct. 5th.* Had a pleasant surprise this morning. Joy and Emily came to see me. When they arrived, I was just digging a grave for one of my rabbits which had died. Very sorry, as it was one of those Jurat Le Feuvre had given me, and a very fine one. The Russians have got on very quickly in our field, and today a train was already coming half-way up the field to carry away the ground which that huge machine shovels up. It makes me sick to see our poor field, and we have nothing to say. How much longer must we endure having the Germans here?

*Oct. 6th.* It was very foggy this morning, and we thought perhaps the

British had landed in France: (1) because the Russians were not at work; (2) because Raymond told us that the Germans were all on guard at Les Niemes; (3) the baker told us that the Germans had been at the Telephone Exchange all night. But our hopes were dashed when the Russians, in charge of the Todt man, arrived late in the morning, also the telephone rang, as usual, etc. One of the Poles amongst the squad spoke to Laurence in the field (when the Todt was not looking) and said he came from Warsaw. He came to the house later and we gave him porridge and pig potatoes. Poor fellow. Margaret here for her lessons this morning. I peeled potatoes for dinner as she worked. We needed a big lot of vegetables as we had men to dinner who had been helping us to thresh. We threshed our last lot of wheat at Mr Farrell's.

At dinner-time lots more Russians came. When too many come, we can't give them much, but they all had a big handful of boiled pig potatoes each. One of them appeared very ill (we had noticed him lying in the field all morning) and we gave him a cup of hot milk and water.

Another little lad sat on a box in the yard for about three-quarters of an hour eating potatoes and what he could find of bits of raw vegetables we had thrown there for the pigs. Mother asked him his age and he said 15 (on his fingers). Then he began to say "Kaput, Kaput", trying to show, I think, how many of his family were gone, then the poor little fellow burst into tears. We all wept to see him. Mother put her hand on his shoulder. He showed me an immense hole in his trousers, so we gave him a needle and thread and he mended it and was quite pleased with himself.

Finally, John felt so sorry for him that he gave him a cigarette and a match, and how pleased he was! He stroked John's coat and kissed his hand. How can the Germans be so evil as to take away lads like that from their homes, I don't know. As we were leaving, tonight, the same little fellow was working with the squad in Mr Bisson's field. He recognised us and gave us a broad smile. I winked at him, making sure the Todt was not looking. One has to be so careful. Another Pole from Warsaw came also.

Well, we had a busy time with all these interruptions, in the midst of giving dinner to all our own men; we did not finish dinner till 3pm. So we just had time to wash up, get ready and have tea (Phyllis and Beryl were here) and rush off to Bethlehem for the Sunday School Anniversary week-night service. I did not enjoy it much because everything seemed to go wrong. To begin with, I had made the programme in too much of a hurry this afternoon and had left out a part, so Rev. Scott got mixed up and I had to rectify my mistake. Then the big girls sang at the top of their voices, quite out of tune for their hymn. And my little ones all got up at the wrong time and remained seated when they should have stood! However, a few did well and they all did their best, I suppose! The chapel was full. We gave all the children their prizes – books that had been given as there are no new books to be had. We hope by next year to have lovely new books for the children! But I thank God that, in spite of everything, we've been able to have the Anniversary at all. We should all realise that God has been very good to us in many ways, especially that our Sunday services have not been interfered with, that we have enough food to live, that our houses are still standing, and countless other blessings. We must pray for those who are far worse off than ourselves, especially those who have been taken from their homes.

*Oct. 7th.*     Very foggy again. The Russians did not come to work till 11am so evidently the Germans are still on the look-out! We had heard rumours that the British had made a landing on Sark and tonight we know for sure that it was so, and that they know all about the deportation that has been going on. They obtained all information in this raid, made without loss. We feel so excited about it yet afraid of reprisals on us. Also sorry to feel that people in England who have relatives here will be anxious, not knowing who has been taken to Germany and who hasn't. I hope Alfred and Auntie Janet are not too worried. I have realised that it is a very dangerous thing for me to write all this in my diary, in case it should be found, and how my family would be in great danger. It is almost wrong of me to keep it, unless I can find a place perfectly safe in which to hide it.

*Oct. 8th.*     The little Russian lad came again at dinner-time and he kissed my hand when I had given him some food. He brought another young one with him. Others came and many others went to steal our apples and vegetables. Many times the boys had to go and chase them.

*Oct. 9th.*     Feeling tired and downhearted about everything tonight! Went to town and the wind was so strong coming back. Then Elsie told me that she had been told that the British had announced that there was an Order out in France (which included all the Channel Islands) that all single women over 21 could be conscripted by the Germans. She thinks it is true. I have only told John about this rumour, for the others would be so upset, and there is no need when a thing is not certain. I am anxious too, because Mother is not well. Dr. Lewis has come and says she has an overstrained heart and must take things very easily for a fortnight. This Occupation is so very trying, it goes on so long. There are times, like today, when it is so difficult to keep cheerful and hopeful.

*Oct. 10th.*     There is one thing to be thankful for this week – in spite of all our fears no more dreadful Orders have come out, just one about curfew, which is to be at 9pm instead of at 10 o'clock. One wonders if it means that the Germans fear something! The news about the Sark raid is very exciting – they even have copies of Jersey and Guernsey papers, as well as of Sark. How wonderful that they were able to do it. It is all so thrilling, and we are not supposed to know.

A disturbing incident took place in our little yard about dinner-time. I saw what I took to be two Russians coming up. A young one came, opened the door and shut it behind him. The other, a very tall older man dressed in mechanic's overalls, stayed, looking on. I gave the little one a handful of potatoes, and he asked for an apple which he saw on the window-sill. I gave it to him and he went out at once. When he reached the other, they seemed to argue. The big one looked very angry. I got scared, realising somehow that he was, perhaps, a German. I called Dad, and he went out. The big one was a German and he appeared very angry with Dad, but Dad couldn't understand what he said, except "Kaput, Bolshevists." We think he was angry because we gave food to the Russian. But why did they come together? It looks as though the German wanted to see what we would do. We feel rather disturbed and hope we won't get into trouble. After that, we dared not give anything to those who came this afternoon. We closed all the doors and felt awful doing it. It was raining hard, and the poor fellows waited so patiently but we never went out to give them anything. It is so difficult to know what to do.

*Oct. 11th.*     I preached at Six Roads chapel this morning. It was their Sunday School Anniversary. The children sang very nicely. Constable and Mrs Crill came afternoon, also Uncle Ernest and the children. Phyllis here for tea. Raymond was with Christine, as usual every Sunday now! He had to go home early at 8.45 because of curfew and Laurence and John had to come back early too. We lit a fire in the sitting-room and Mother rested there all day. We always wanted her to rest every afternoon, but she always said there was too much to do.

*Oct. 12th.*     Mother stayed on the sofa in the sitting-room all day. A poor little Russian came and we were afraid to open the door to him, for fear the German in the field might see us. I tried to explain to the boy, by saying 'Chef' and pointing to the field, whereupon he looked terrified and ran away as fast as his bandaged feet would allow him. All day I have felt sorry to have refused him, it looked so pitiful to see him running with his poor little bandaged feet. He had one shoe only.

*Oct. 13th.*     The same little Russian came today and I was glad. I risked giving him some cold porridge and apples.

*Oct. 14th.*    Had dinner at Montpelier, then went on to speak at the Overseas Missionary meeting at Aquila Road. Mrs Harrison, Senior presided and Mrs Harrison, the Solicitor General's wife, sang two lovely solos. I spoke about Alfred's work and ever so many came to thank me. I had a very happy time with them all and I need not have felt so nervous. It was my first time to speak there. I wonder what Alfred would think about my talk, made up of things he told me about his work in his letters from Nigeria.

*Oct. 15th.*    We girls all overslept this morning! I had had to get up twice to put Granny to bed again, as she wanted to go downstairs in the middle of the night. Had a very busy morning.. had to wash the floor in Granny and Grandpa's room and so on. Finally, left at 1.15 and cycled to Montpelier, had a rushed dinner, met Miss C Alexandre in town and others and we cycled to St. Martin's where I had to speak at their missionary meeting. They even had two stalls, one of fruit and the other of miscellaneous articles. After the meeting we had a cup of coffee, a plate of apple sauce and potato flour, and one oatmeal bun each. We paid a shilling for that, towards missionary funds! I cycled back via Trinity, St. John's and St. Mary's. Asked my way twice! Had never done this long cycle journey alone before. It took me just under an hour. I was sorry I had to go out today, having been out yesterday and so much to do. But I didn't know Mother was going be ill when I accepted Mrs Le Seelleur's invitation to speak at their meetimg.

*Oct. 17th.*    This week there has been another death from tuberculosis, Mr Ed. Perrée from St Mary, aged only 21. We had often seen him going about with his arm in a sling. Poor fellow, he didn't have much chance. It is dreadful, young people are dying of TB who would live if they had proper nourishment, especially fats and sugar.

*Oct. 18th. SUNDAY.*    We were not visited by Russians today. Yesterday they cleared all the rails and sleepers from our field and that horrid scooping machine went away, crawling like a huge monster along the road, having done its evil work in our field.

*Oct. 19th.*    Mr Salmon Le Rossignol, aged 45, has died at hospital of diabetes because there is no more insulin in Jersey and Germany won't let us have any. There is no hope for his sister either, unless we are released soon, nor for any diabetic people. We all hoped the British would invade France this year but there is not much time left.

*Oct. 23rd.*    Went to town and got some more medicine for Mother. I wish she would show improvement. The doctor is not anxious, so perhaps she just needs to rest for a while.

*Oct. 24th.*     Kath's Birthday. She is 26 today It has been lovely to receive a Red Cross message from my dear Alfred – a reply in his own hand to a message I sent last January. What a pity they take so long to come. It was a lovely message, telling me of his love. I am blessed indeed.

*Oct. 27th.*     Postman brought us a Red Cross message meant for Uncle Gordon, which he asked us to read, then he took it back. I had wondered what happened to Red Cross messages which came for people who have been deported. Evidently, the Germans allow relatives to read them, but not to keep them. Uncle's message came for a lady friend of his ... I wonder what he would say if he knew we had read it! A young Russian came; poor fellow, he had a leg all swollen and purple and seemed anxious. They know that their German masters have no pity on those who are sick and let them die. I hear that about 13 Russians died at a camp last week, some being taken away in wheelbarrows before they were quite dead. A man who lives close by says he will have to move because he does not want his children to see the Germans beating the poor Russians. To think that such awful things happen in our little Island. These are dark days indeed for Jersey.

*OT (Organisation Todt) Officer forcing Russians to work, beating them with sticks if disobedient.*

*November 1st. SUNDAY.* I'm now going to Sunday School only once a fortnight, so today I took my turn to stay at home, and what a busy morning, cooking etc. I did miss going to Sunday School but now that Mother has not been well I feel it my duty to take my turn home on Sunday mornings. Tonight we sat by the fire in the sitting-room and I began to write notes for a new sermon. Time for getting supper comes all too soon. By the time one has washed the tea-things the evening is really very short, for about 9 o'clock I must start making the grandparents' gruel and Christine makes the porridge. Supper is over about 10, then I wash the dishes and we all go to bed. By the time we've said good-night to one another, said our prayers and read our Bible portion, it can be 11pm or later by the time we finally get into bed. How thankful I feel every night for a nice comfortable bed, how lovely it is when one has worked hard all day and one is feeling very tired! There are so many who have no nice beds to be in these days, so many far from home and sleeping one knows not where. I do think of them and pray for them, every night, as I get into my own bed.

*Nov. 2nd.* Last night we put back clocks one hour (German orders). We are now same time as in England. We all got up earlier as it was lighter so got on more quickly with our work. So, apart from the usual housework and seeing to Granny, I was able to clean all my rabbit hutches and some of Herbert's and do some washing this morning.

*Nov. 4th.* Auntie Julia died last night, aged nearly eighty. She had been helpless for quite a long time. I did not realise she was that age, she never looked old until she was ill. I did some mending today, put a big patch on a pair of stockings. We are so short of them. Yesterday, there were some in town but only for those who had put their name down ages ago! Also people were queuing up in hundreds for permits for boots or shoes. Some waited all day and did not get in. People tried to push past each other and women were almost fighting, Emily told me it was awful. Some better arrangement should be made.

*Nov. 9th.* One hears plenty about the Russians stealing these days but the Germans are worse. Mr Hidrio of St. Mary's opened his door one morning only to find a German with fixed bayonet who forced him to remain inside whilst they stole several barrels of his apples and two fowls, then departed in a car.

*Nov. 11th.* John heard (from his secret place) that Mr Churchill has reviewed the situation and says that there may be great changes within the next few days. He also spoke of the Germans having planes which they have kept for when the British invade France. One fears the loss of life there will be when invasion comes and, according how things go in Africa, it may be very soon. What it will mean for us here no one knows; I suppose our friends and relatives in England are anxious. I sent Emily some beans and potato flour to send to her Uncle interned in France. I hope he will get the parcel, but as things are? We have had no news of Uncle Gordon yet.

*Nov. 13th.* There is an Order on the *Evening Post* forbidding us to feed foreign workers, especially Russians, so we'll have to be very careful in future.

*Nov. 15th. SUNDAY.* This afternoon I preached at Ebenezer, for the first time. Congregation about 50. Singing very good. Someone even struck up the chorus again of the hymn, 'I need thee every hour', so they were enjoying it. Mrs Picot had invited me to tea, also Laurence and Phyllis. It is so sad to see her daughter, Kathleen. We sat for a while in her room, where her bed is, and she coughed a lot. What a dreadful illness TB is and poor Kathleen has dragged on for so long and there cannot be any hope at all for her.

*Nov. 16th.* We were very much bothered by Russians all the morning and we're so afraid of being seen feeding them. One poor fellow was in a terrible state, his face bandaged and terribly disfigured. We put a bowl of porridge for him down in the vegetable garden. I planted some tulips, some that I had found in Uncle Gordon's house, no good leaving them there to perish.

*Nov. 17th.* Ellen A. called and told us that Mr and Mrs W Le Brun's house at Bel Royal had been broken into by thieves who stole all their jam and honey (some of Kath's) and even a watch was taken from a little table between the two beds in which Mr and Mrs Le Brun were asleep. They slept through it all. The thieves took their clothes and left dirty rags covered with lice in the clothes basket instead. It makes one very nervous. It is so strange that there are so many robberies when no one is allowed out after curfew, except the Germans, and the 'foreign workers' are supposed to be shut up in their camps.

*Nov. 18th.* Two exciting events have taken place today: (1) John has got engaged to Beryl Vibert. It was her 18th Birthday today and John was 22 last May. They are both very young but know their own mind. I think Beryl is very fortunate! John is such a fine boy, tall and fair. But he is fortunate too! I am glad my brothers have chosen such sensible girls and I pray that they may all be very happy. John has been telling us for the past week that Churchill had said that 'many things are going to happen within the next few days,' and we knew that he was thinking of getting engaged! (2) An RAF plane has made a forced landing in a Mr Perchard's turnip field. Apparently, he was waiting a quarter of an hour before Germans turned up to take him prisoner. When they came they were fully armed and the pilot was standing on his plane (unarmed) awaiting them. Several persons were able to speak to him before the Germans arrived. It was hard luck on that pilot but he was lucky not to be shot at – fancy the Germans not seeing the plane before!

*Nov. 19th.* About 5.30 John went to fetch his fiancée and so we had another 'engagement tea' – fried potatoes and one tin of fruit kept from before the Occupation! Well, we are all very pleased. How lovely Beryl looked tonight. She always does and so does Phyllis, both so fresh and sweet.

*Nov. 20th.* Mr Bauche had a sale today. His old broken-winded horse, for which he had paid £30 years ago, went for £160!

*Nov. 21st.* Poor Kath had to have teeth out so Laurence took us to town in the lorry (though we are not supposed to use it in this way) to Mallet's the dentist. Dr Lewis gave the anaesthetic. I waited in the next room and was very glad when it was over. Kath had quite a bad time, we have such strong teeth. I hope Kath won't have neuralgia any more. What a day – going to town and all the work to do besides.

*Nov. 22nd. SUNDAY.* Four people in bed for breakfast so it was rather a rush to get off to Sunday School. Arrived ten minutes late, just in time to give the introductory talk. My rabbit from Mr Trachy had little ones this morning and the grey one from Lucille had some on Thursday. I do hope they will do well and not be stolen. One can't afford to lose rabbits now.

*Nov. 23rd.* Mother told me tonight that Raymond had proposed to Christine last night! I think he has got excited over his two sisters' engagements and can't wait! Mother told Christine to tell him to wait until he is 21, which will be next January. I thought something must have happened because Christine was all smiles this morning and Raymond turned up whilst we were still having breakfast, supposedly to fetch some corn and again tonight. He and Christine will be well suited and I am glad.

*Nov. 26th.* Many more robberies during last night. Thieves went to Westfield and stole Uncle's overalls, sabots and farm coat but fortunately could not get further into the house. They went to Les Potirons and stole Uncle John's pants which were drying in an outhouse. Other farms were 'visited.' I expect our turn will come. I am sure the Germans could prevent these thefts but equally sure that they don't care. We even suspect that they put the Russians up to it.

*Nov. 27th.* A Russian Commission from the Red Cross has arrived in the Island to try and improve conditions for the prisoners. They went to Westfield and told Uncle that those that have escaped are dangerous and must be caught. We must not feed Russians any more or give them clothes for it puts us in too great danger. This Russian told Uncle that the Germans dress up as Russians so as to catch us. Already some farmers have been caught that way. One at St. Ouen's gave potatoes and a pair of trousers to a Russian who implored him. Later, Germans arrived in a car and the farmer found that it was a spy that he had helped and now the Germans are going to punish him.

*Nov. 29th. SUNDAY.* Did not go out at all today. Have a bad cold. We all have. Mr Churchill was making a speech tonight. In secret, John, Herbert and I heard it. I think the purpose of his speech was to keep the English from getting too elated over the victories lately. He spoke very seriously and again, did not promise anything. He said 1943 would be a stern, terrible year. Felt rather depressed as I listened, but thinking it over, not so much. Mr Churchill never raises false hopes. And he knows his people, how they must always be 'kept up to it.'

*Nov. 30th.* Mr Churchill's Birthday. He is 68 today.

*December 1st.* A shocking tragedy has occurred during the night. Our neighbour, Mr Ernest Le Gresley, aged 62, from the little shop at Carrefour-a-Cendre, has been killed by a Russian and Miss Le Gresley is at hospital seriously injured. All the neighbourhood is very upset. Mr Le Gresley was so liked by everyone, always so cheerful and interesting to talk with and such a good man. We cannot realise that he is dead and in such a dreadful manner. And we were all sleeping peacefully, unconscious of what he and his sister were going through. The Russians had been twice before to steal, once to steal the bread rations for people. This time, it was about 1am Mr Le G. heard a noise, dressed, and went downstairs. A window-pane had been removed and the Russian was hiding in the garden. There was a struggle. The Russian snatched a stick from Miss Le G. (who had come down and was trying to help her brother by beating the Russian) and beat them both, then ran away. Miss Le G. ran for help. Constable Du Val phoned the police. The German Gendarmerie arrived and some of our policemen from town. Poor Mr Le G. was dead and his sister badly hurt and the Doctor ordered her removal to hospital by ambulance. So, when the neighbours arrived to fetch their milk ration (the shop was a milk dépôt) they found the police there, and the tragic story was soon told. Mr Le G. had diabetes and I am sure was not strong enough to struggle for very long. He may have been stabbed, for people say he bled profusely, right through the sofa. How his sister must have suffered to see him killed before her eyes. And they were so happy there together. The thought comes, Why does God allow good people to suffer so? To which there is no answer. About 50 German police and soldiers have arrived to hunt the Russians. Quite a scene to see them running across fields, and they trapped two just in front of our windows in the back lane – we saw them jostled into a car and driven away. All morning the Germans have been at it, farmers helping to try and track the killer or killers down. After all that the farmers have done for the Russians, they feel mad at the way good has been returned with evil. We are in a strange position. We don't want to help or co-operate with the Germans in anything, yet these dangerous Russians must be caught. But, once caught, we cannot trust the Germans to keep them safe. They have no business to let them escape from their camps to settle in unoccupied houses or old tumbledown places and live by robbing us, and now, murdering. I suppose they want to point out to us what sort of Allies we have. There is no protection for us anywhere. When Mrs Godel, Mr Le G.'s sister, arrived on the scene this morning, she was so upset that she said to a German officer: "All the Russians ought to be shot." To which he replied, sarcastically: "You're very loyal, Madam!" I felt mad when I heard this. The Germans are so horrid! We are in a fine pickle here in Jersey. As we say, 'It is high time the English came!'

*Dec. 2nd.*    Everyone talking about poor Mr. Le G. People feeling nervous. Every time dogs bark at night, one imagines Russians are about. I hope my rabbits won't be stolen, I've put a defence of prickly Rose prunings at the entrance of the pig-sty, where I keep them!

*Dec. 4th.*    The post-mortem on Mr Le G.'s body has revealed nine stab wounds, one two inches deep in the groin, which severed a vein. The death was caused by heart failure through loss of blood. He bled to death as well as being beaten. How is it that the Germans allow the Russians to carry clasp-knives? They have stolen weapons too. Miss Le G. was very badly hurt, on face, head, and neck and had cuts in the side.

*Dec. 5th.*    We had three Red Cross messages today – Mother two from Auntie Janet and I had one from Alfred. Disappointed that there is no news of his ordination. This is dated August 26th. so I suppose the previous ones have got lost, just because I wanted them specially! Dad and Francis went to Mr Le Gresley's funeral at St. Mary's Church.

*Dec. 7th.*    About 1.45pm we heard planes close and gunfire. Later heard that German ships near Noirmont had been attacked by the RAF – one or two sunk and one crept into the harbour on fire. Ambulances seen going to and fro. Spent an hour in garden planting Tulips which should have been done before.

*Dec. 8th.*    Went to town to try to find a Birthday present for Joyce. Shops full of nothing or of second-hand stuff. Managed to find an amber brooch, paid 12s.6d, I suppose two or three times its real value. BBC (we know!) has announced that three ships were attacked and damaged off Jersey. One hates to think of the poor men on board. German bodies have been washed ashore.

*Dec. 9th.* Dr. Shone called. Finds Granny failing and says she will only give more trouble as time goes on. Oh dear, we have enough of a job already and so difficult to get washing dry. Weather damp and no heat in airing-cupboard, of course! This morning, Laurence had to go to the Police Station to identify certain Russians he had seen in the district. Germans took him and another man from St. Mary's to the Fort at South Hill, where they saw 40 Russian prisoners. Laurence recognised one whom we all know by sight, and thinks he is the dangerous one. He used to come here out of working hours, dressed in brown check suit, waistcoat and trousers, a good pair of Wellington boots and a slouch hat. No doubt he had stolen all this. He is pale, round-faced and has a grumpy expression. Last time he came to the back door he asked for salt, which we refused, for we are rationed. When we showed him the German order about not feeding Russians, he smiled (knowingly!) for the first time and went away. He may be the murderer's accomplice. Mr B. from St. Mary's thinks he knows the murderer, for he saw one full of blood, washing at a stream. One of the Germans afterwards asked Laurence to have a cup of tea at Gaudin's with him. Of course, Laurence refused!

*Dec. 10th.* Joyce's 21st Birthday. Had a nice little tea-party. Phyllis and Beryl, the Misses Ethel and Winnie Arthur and Evie. So nice to have them, but time was short, as they had to leave at 6pm, darkness coming on. Miss Ethel told us that one of the ships sunk on Monday was manned by Dutchmen who were bringing timber. Many were badly burned and are lying in hospital in cotton-wool. We feel very sad. Thefts continue in this district. The whole place at Lady Vernon's was ransacked, and all her whisky stolen. (What does she want all that whisky for!) Even the Grandfather clock was opened. Her butler thinks it must have been the Germans, as some had been billeted there several times.

*Dec. 12th.* My dear friend Joy's Birthday. Cycled out to First Tower to see her. Had made her a small cake, decorated with cream. So sad to think that her Mother would have liked to make her one but had nothing with which to make it. In the country, one can manage to have a little flour and other things.

*Dec. 13th.* Miss Barbour phoned to say she had had a letter from Uncle Gordon. First news since he was taken away. Glad to know he is all right, though he is in hospital with bronchitis. Says they were five days in the train on the way to Germany – very wearying. They get Red Cross parcels from England with food.

*Dec. 15th.* Joy phoned to say that they had just had an Order from the Germans to be out of their house within eight days! Well, it's too bad. Last year, about this time, they were forced to leave Murchiston Lodge in the same way, just before Christmas too! As Joy said, she felt quite stunned, it was so unexpected. She was already packing when she phoned. Only consolation is it might have been worse, for having to move out of one's house seems nothing compared to getting an Order to leave for Germany the next day.

*Dec. 16th.* We've been delighted to receive Red Cross messages today, especially one from Cousin Henry in India. And I had one from Joan Davis, with news that she was married last October. We are glad to know that the Ovaltine Dairy Farm is all right and carrying on. Alice was full of news today, for thieves went to John Pirouet's. One night 45 boxes of potatoes were stolen. Since then he kept watch every night at a window, and last night he saw a man climb over the yard door and then open it to two others. They tried kitchen door, Mr P. shouted at them and they ran away. They were dressed in white overalls, so were Germans. Thefts continue every night: rabbits, ducks – thieves pluck them and leave feathers and beaks lying about! German Order on the *Evening Post* about wireless sets again. They know some have been kept and if they are not handed in by December 31st there will be very severe penalties, even death penalty in very serious cases.

*Dec. 20th. SUNDAY.* Very busy morning. Went to Sunday School at 9.45am. Led a short Christmas Service there, then cycled on to St. Ouen's Chapel for 10.45 Service. Preached on St. Luke 2 v.10. About 50 present. Children were very attentive especially when I spoke to them. But two girls in the choir whispered through all my prayers, during the sermon and even during the Benediction! I fear they must be rather empty-headed and did not hear or care about a word I said! Went to service at Bethlehem tonight. The younger Sunday School Scholars recited about the Shepherds and others sang.

*Dec. 21st.*　　John had a dreadful scare today. Uncle and he found two Russians asleep in Uncle's cottage. Uncle went to phone the police, and they suddenly turned on John threatening him with knives. John was very frightened and we are so thankful that he managed to get away safely.

*Dec. 24th.*　　Alice gave me a lovely silver dish, which she had meant as a Wedding present. Dear Auntie Alice – may my Wedding take place soon. Went to town to deliver various parcels and to see Joy and her Mother at St. Mark's Road where they have now moved. It was formerly occupied by Rev. Stuart who has been deported to Germany from Guernsey. Tonight I made wreaths with holly and packed gifts.

*December 25th. CHRISTMAS DAY.*　　Dad, Christine, Herbert and Joyce went to Philadelphie for the service. The rest of us were too busy to go, sadly. Francis went to take various bags of foodstuffs to Mr and Mrs Allan, who had little for Christmas dinner, poor things. I am sure lots of people haven't had much, only their miserable ration of hard French meat. We had our own goose, and very good it was. Very thankful it had not been stolen. Mr Bauche had two ducks stolen this week. Mr O Mourant and Rev. and Mrs Scott here for dinner and tea. All the Vibert family here for tea also, so we were 20 altogether. Tonight John showed us the magic lantern that Dad used to show us when we were children. John also screened other pictures with a machine he had made but they were not very clear and not as successful as we had hoped. We screened pictures of ourselves and the Viberts! Then we played Travelling Post and had supper before the Scotts left. Curfew was at midnight tonight! We sang Carols and Laurence and Joyce sang a duet. The Viberts left at 11.30, and we washed the supper things before going to bed. The day passed well, very quiet considering we were so many. But we are never very noisy!
There was no notice on the *Evening Post* about curfew being extended to midnight today and many people did not know. It is said that the reason why it was not announced was because the Germans here had not had permission to do it and did it on their own, so did not want the Higher Command to know. A notice on the paper would have given them away. I wonder how Alfred has spent this Christmas Day? We have never yet spent a Christmas Day together. May we be together before another comes round.

*Dec. 27th.*　　My turn to cook this morning. Weather so fine that I decided to go to Alfred's folk's for dinner. They were delighted to see me! We all went to the 4 o'clock service at Wesley. Mr Howells preached. I enjoyed the service.

back home at 6.15. It was getting dark. I passed a large company of Russians at the bottom of Les Routeurs waiting to be driven back to camp. They were chattering away for all they were worth and didn't seem to have a guard, so no wonder they escape. Glad I've been to town and given pleasure to Alfred's people. Tonight I thought over my sermon for next Sunday.

*Dec. 28th.*　　Received a letter from Uncle Gordon, our first since he was deported on September 16th. He is at a place called Laufen. We are not sure where that is. People think it is in Bavaria and not far from Switzerland. We are glad to have news.

*Dec. 31st.*　　Mr A de B Breton phoned to say that he had had a letter from Guernsey, and someone there had received a Red Cross message with this news: *Young Du Feu from Jersey ordained at Methodist Conference in July.* This is the first news I get of Alfred's ordination. So he has been a real minister for some monthe now and I'm not there to share his work. I do feel so sorry to have missed his ordination. We had so looked forward to this and to our Wedding afterwards. But I must not complain. I have much to be thankful for – that Alfred is alive, for one thing. And yet, when I hear news of him, a lump comes into my throat.....for I long so much for him. Copy of letter from Uncle Gordon in Internment camp in Germany, received on December 29th 1942.

*Allowed three letters per month. five days in train, very wearying. Was going to do dentistry,but am in hospital. Bronchitis. German doctor very nice. We understand each other in French. Is my home safe? Anxious. We do all our own washing, house-keeping, cooking etc. 500 in camp. 50 in my room. Fire all night. 15° below freezing. Sleep in 2-decker bunks on straw mattresses. Much coughing and snoring. Soup twice a day. Breakfast at 8am bread and marg. Red Cross supply tea, cocoa, sugar, tins of meat and veg., chocolate, jam. Books very scarce. Many from Guernsey here and children in prams. Have not the energy to learn German ... do not feel strong enough. The eternal conversation is food and cigarettes and exchange. I gave 30 cigarettes for tin of Nestle's milk. Just washed my pyjamas. Growing a beard. How long will it take? Have I time? No news since leaving. Spent 1st week in kitchen preparing vegetables for 500. Christine not in it. Hope all are well and shall be glad to know my house safe. Happy Christmas.*

*Dec. 5th 1942.*
*Gordon Amoore.*

**1 9**
**4 3**

*January 1st.* The year has opened with a wet mild day, with hopeful thoughts and feelings and hopeful news (it is said that the Announcer of the News in England greeted this year as the year of Victory and Liberation; may this indeed be so!) I really believe it possible, more than I have believed it since the Occupation began, that this year will bring us Liberation, and the joy of seeing my dear Alfred. The thought of it makes me feel beside myself with joy! Mr and Mrs Watson-Allan here for dinner. How delighted they were to have goose! We were glad to share it with them – people have only vegetables for dinner these days. The Allans left at 6pm as they had to walk back to Bel Royal. All the family, except Dad, Mother, the grandparents and me, have been to the Viberts at Les Nièmes for tea. Curfew at midnight tonight.

*Jan. 2nd.* Busy day – housework. Tonight, finished typing out a sermon and thought out a Children's talk.

*Jan. 3rd. SUNDAY.* Mother had a bad bout of indigestion during the night so did not get up for breakfast but it's better, thank God. I arrived late at Sunday School, just in time to take my class. How dear my little girls are, and how I love teaching them. At 10.45, I took the service. Ed. Le F. had asked me to take his place as he has hurt his leg. About 50 present, majority children. I spoke to them about life being like a book, each year a page, quoting the lovely little poem, 'The New Leaf'. Preached on Hebrews XI v. 8, 'And Abraham went out, not knowing whither he went.' Finished in good time, as the chapel is cold without heating. Noticed a stranger present, and afterwards he shook my hand heartily and told me he had enjoyed the service very much and that he had come to see the Old Year out, and the New Year in, and was glad he had come. "I congratulate you, Madam," he said. He is a Mr Dunkley, staying at the Le H's for a few days. Well, I feel thankful if it did him good to

107

be with us, and if God used me to help him. Then, Miss Florrie Luce told me that it seemed I had preached just for her. How strange is the way in which God guides one in choosing one's subject. And Uncle Ernest rang to tell me it was one of my best sermons!

At 3pm I preached at Philadelphie. Had a good service in the schoolroom which looked well filled. There were two lovely fires burning! The singing was hearty and attention good. Dad and Mother enjoyed the service. Mrs L. and Willie had come specially and Mrs L. said the sermon was just what she wanted as she had always been 'bothered' about 'faith'. I wish the result of my sermon was that they would attend worship more often, regardless of who is preaching – people should go to worship God, not to 'hear So and So!'

Mr Hubert, organist, chose a fine tune, 'Evening Shadows', to fit the hymn, 'Spirit of Faith come down', and it went very well. How I enjoyed it! I wish this lovely tune had not been left out of our new Hymn Book. I have received the praise of men today for my preaching. Let me beware, for there is danger in this; let me give God the glory. May God keep me always humble,and may I never seek the praise of men, but remember, as the hymn says,

*If there is aught of good in me, it comes from Thee alone.*

*Jan. 5th.* Pruned the Hydrangeas in the Avenue, and did tidying in the greenhouse. John has come back from Westfield with quite a story about the Russians. Last night, four German soldiers, together with Constable Du Val's men and Uncle Ernest (ten men altogether), went down to Uncle's cottage in the meadow to look for Mr. Le Gresley's murderer. They left Westfield at 11pm. Had trouble to find their way, pitch dark. They stumbled on, got there and watched. Nothing happenend and Germans got fed up with watching. They went back to Westfield, where they visited the cows in the stable. One said he was a farmer in Germany, using bulls instead of horses for farmwork. They then stayed in the kitchen looking at a map of Europe which Uncle has on the wall. About 2.30am they all went down to the cottage again, some going to the back and others at the front. Opening the back door, which leads to the stable they saw a Russian standing flat against the wall, holding a crock full of chopped wood. Germans took him and searched the cottage. They found lots of wood, ready chopped, in a cupboard, a saucepan of cooked potatoes and meat, cooked beans, two bottles of benzine, and a plucked cockerel. The Russian was just about to prepare a fire to cook it. The Germans asked how he lit a fire without matches and tried to force him to reveal the hiding-place of his comrade, by holding two pistols at his head, but all he said was "Nix, comrade." Then they took him to the stable at Westfield, where they questioned him again and he would divulge nothing. So they took a cow rope, made a loop, put it round the Russian's neck and hung him to a nail, support-ing him, whilst they tried to force him again ... poor fellow, he still would only repeat "Nix, comrade." They almost strangled him, only just let him down in time. Next, the Germans all had a go at 'booting' him dreadfully. Finally, they tied a rope round his body, with the other end tied to the back of a bicycle, and forced him to run behind whilst a German cycled as fast as he could to the Alexandra Hotel at St. Peter.

So that is the *horrible* story. It is awful, and we are terribly upset that Uncle was a witness of all this. One feels bewildered – one hates to think of anyone being thus treated. On the other hand, one remembers poor Mr Le Gresley, our good neighbour, dead, killed by a Russian prisoner. It appears that this one, caught at Uncle's cottage, had escaped from the Five Mile Road camp and been out three days. We are told that after lashing him, they put him back in the camp. But the two 'wicked ones' are still at large. I suppose they make these others steal and cook for them. What a state of things!

Joyce came back from town with news that, during the night, a German ship was wrecked off La Moye – supposed to be about 300 soldiers on board, also some women who had come to entertain troops at Christmas, also eight large guns. 200 persons are said to have been drowned. One cannot know the true facts, but Joyce saw lots of small craft on the sea, searching for bodies, and all the undertakers have had orders to make coffins. Poor soldiers! Germans say the ship struck a rock in the dark, but just as likely it was a mine.

*Jan. 6th.*     Damp mild weather, had no winter yet. Alice here as usual on a Wednesday. Did some mending afternoon, patching my green frock which is threadbare. We shall be in a fix about clothes if Occupation goes on too long.

*Jan. 7th.*     Had dinner at Montpelier, then went to Sunday School Council meeting at Grove Place. Called to see Joy and saw Emily, who told me that her father had been forced to make coffins for shipwrecked Germans. Curwoods had orders for 20 coffins, and all the undertakers had to make some. Evidently there were many drowned, and there was no room for the bodies at hospital. They had to be piled up at the Yacht Hotel. Enemies or not, it is very sad. May this dreadful war soon end and we all live in peace and friendship.

*Jan. 11th.*     Mrs C Le Gresley came and begged me to give lessons to her little girl, Dorothy. She's been at St. Mary's Central School since last May and does not know her letters yet. Feel sorry for the poor child and will try to help her, though I really haven't the time. Joyce brought back news from town that all men who have been Colonels or Majors in the British Army are to be deported. We had hoped that deportation to Germany was over for good. However the date is not fixed, so we hope it will not take place.

*Jan. 12th.*     We have received two Red Cross messages, with not much news and very stale. Auntie Janet's was sent last June! I feel disappointed not to have had one from Alfred. There was some excitement in town about 11.15am when an RAF flying-boat came very low over town and harbour – low enough for the markings to be clearly seen and identified. Some say they saw the pilot wave. For some people, it is the first time they have seen an RAF plane since the Occupation began. How I wish I had seen it! Spent greater part of day washing Granny's things; weather turned windy and rainy, and my washing blew off the line. I had to do it again! What a job we have to get Granny's things dry these days!

*Jan. 13th.*     People think that the plane that came yesterday was laying mines. It is said that there were three other planes with it, and that today the Germans had two mine-sweepers at work. More people have been warned today to appear before the Commandant with a view to deportation.

*Jan. 14th.*     The harbour is closed. No ships can come or go, it is said, for mine-sweepers are at work. Anyway, this means that deportation cannot take place for the time being.

*Jan. 15th.*     People are quite excited because it is thought that the British have laid mines all round the Island. Tonight RAF passed low several times and there was heavy firing from German guns.

*Jan. 16th.*     Housework most of day. Three of my eight-week-old rabbits are sickening – very discouraging, as one takes so much trouble with them. No one can find any cure or prevention for this sickness, which has killed so many much-needed rabbits since the Occupation began. The harbour is open again and boats have come in from France. There has been an *Evening Post* today, so some paper must have arrived! Have had several disturbed nights this week – boys have got up, dressed, looked around house and farmyard, thinking Russians were about – but, fortunately, false alarm every time.

*Jan. 17th. SUNDAY.*     Went to Sunday school and chapel at Bethlehem, as usual. Stayed in tonight, have a cold. News good today, though we shouldn't know it! Everything seems ready for an offensive. RAF over Berlin again last night. One feels excited, yet nervous as to what will happen here. One tries to imagine how we shall be released, and pray that there will be no fighting. Our island is so heavily defended. Well, we must not worry. But to think that perhaps we shall be in touch with England again this year! It seems so impossible, yet it is possible.

*Jan. 19th*     Christine and Raymond Vibert got engaged today. We are so pleased. All of us are very fond of Raymond. This afternoon we had a party for our Sunday School children at Bethlehem, about 75 of us, including teachers. We gave them tea, provided by teachers and friends: baked apples, blancmange (made with potato-flour and carrageen moss) bread and butter, black-butter sandwiches, mixed cakes (all plain, of course) scones and sugar-beet tea. It was a real feast for these days, and how the children ate! Then we played games. Rev. and Mrs Scott were there. We had not given our children a treat of any kind since the Occupation began, and I enjoyed seeing them enjoy themselves.

Tonight comes a German order that all dances must be cancelled – supposed to be owing to the diphtheria epidemic .

*Jan. 21st.*    Margaret and Dorothy came for lessons. Raymond has brought Christine a lovely cut-glass vase; don't know where he managed to find it. Typed out part of a sermon today.

*Jan. 24th. SUNDAY.*    One more rabbit dead. Cycled to Montpelier for dinner, then preached at First Tower this afternoon. My first time there, felt nervous but got on all right. Alfred's parents and Elsie came, also Mrs Averty, who has just lost her daughter from TB of the throat – so very sad. Mother and Dad were invited at the Viberts to celebrate the engagement of Raymond and Christine.

*Jan. 25th.*    Mother and I went to Somerleigh to take something to send to internees in Germany. Mrs Ed. Le Feuvre arrived with her little boy – the little chap seems keen on farming already, though he is only four-years-old!

*Jan. 27th.*    RAF passed very low during last night. This morning early, Germans were apparently searching for British parachutists. They asked Mr C. if he had seen any British soldiers about, and they searched his house.

*Jan. 28th.*    I received a Red Cross reply message from Alfred. It was lovely to get 25 words in his own hand!

*Jan. 29th.*    Slept at Montpelier last night. Called at Rev. Ward and we arranged for my Dedication service. Mrs Ward called from the kitchen for me to go and see her. She was lying on a couch near the grate, and I had such a nice talk with her. She gave me this advice for when I am married – never to go into any Manse without first having seen it. She thinks she has harmed herself doing the housework in a too big awkward Manse, and now she must go for an operation. But I think that it is because people haven't got the necessary food and have got thin and weak, that they are not fit to do all the work that they used to do. Every time I see the Wards I like them better. I do pray that Mrs Ward may come safely through her operation.

*Jan. 30th.*    Tenth Anniversary of Hitlerism. Everything quiet here and, by what one hears, there have been no celebrations in Germany either – no flags flying and Hitler himself not even making a speech.

Dad received a letter from the Department of Public Health, as follows:

> *Dear Sir,*
> *I have to call your attention to the state of the milk sent by you to the Jersey Dairies Ltd. Samples of milk have been taken for the detection of dirt, which proved very unsatisfactory. I should be much obliged if, therefore, you would call at the office.*

Francis was very upset, but, as we told him, there is no need to be when we all know that our milk is perfectly clean, we who take so much trouble with it. They are so stupid in town, they take a sample of what they think is our milk and don't realise that the dairyman mixes the milk long before it arrives in town, so what is in our cans is quite likely not ours at all. In any case, other milk has been mixed with it. All farmers are not as careful as we are. Dad is going to write them a letter that will 'settle them'! He will tell them that he will be very pleased to call at the Office when they've taken a sample of milk at our farm, or just as we arrive at the dépôt with the dairy cans before the milk has been tampered with. He'll also tell them that it is a curious fact that our neighbours have specially asked for our milk, knowing the way in which it is handled! *Chenna les f'tha rentrer lus cornes!* – ['That'll make them retract their horns!'] Poor Francis, this is the reward he gets for taking so much trouble with his cows, and being so particular to send enough milk to the dairy.

*February 1st.*  Margaret and Dorothy here for lessons this morning. News has leaked out that a service was held at St. Martin's-in-the Fields for Channel Islanders yesterday. Preacher was the Archbishop of York (formerly Bishop of Winchester) and George Whitfield read the Lessons. How I wish we had heard it all. It is lovely, however, to know that it was held, and that they spoke of us and prayed for us.

*Feb. 2nd.*  Joyce has brought the news that Miss Vivienne Mylne (daughter of Rev. Mylne of Great Union Road has been arrested by the Gestapo on charge of spreading news, and has been imprisoned. I am very sad and pray she may be released soon. One never knows who will be arrested next.

*Feb. 2nd.*  Margaret's Birthday. She has burnt her foot so will not come for lessons for a few days, but Dorothy turned up. Laurence, Phyllis and Kath went to Westfield for tea, in honour of Margaret's Birthday – she is seven. One more rabbit dead today.

*Feb. 4th.*  This has been an important day in my life. At Grove Place this afternoon, I was publicly recognised and dedicated as a Methodist Local Preacher. The service was held in the vestry of the chapel which was crowded, there being about 45 present. Dad came, also Uncle Ernest, Uncle Philip Le Brocq, Alfred's parents, also Joy and Emily, Mrs Bunting and Margaret, Mrs Averty. Others were mostly from Grove Place, also several local Preachers and all our Circuit ministers except Rev. Skyrme. The Charge to the candidate was given by Rev. Ward, who told me that a preacher must never deal in subtleties, must have a warm regard for his congregation and remember that the most sinful of men can be saved; never to neglect the Old Testament, for it has a message as well as the New. There is much to be learned from stories of its splendid characters, and we cannot rightly understand one without the other. I must always remember that the preaching and expounding of the Word of God is the most important part of the service. Music has its uses, but it must never take the place of preaching. Try to preach without notes – never read your sermon. Rev. Ward was splendid.

The Charge to the Church was given by Philip Le Ruez, Local Preacher – very good also. Pastor Hanks gave the Opening prayer; Dedicatory prayer was by Ph. Huelin, preacher, and Benediction by E J Ahier, preacher. Rev. Scott presided. I had to give my 'testimony' before them all – my conversion and call to preach. It was more of an ordeal than if I'd had to preach a sermon. Felt nervous and did not finish properly, as I'd intended to. All the ministers were sitting behind me – so close, I was almost treading on their toes! And everybody else was only separated from me by the big desk! Rev. Ward, on behalf of the Grove Place Circuit, presented me with a copy of *The Rise of Gentile Christianity* by Foakes-Jackson. This was instead of a Bible because one cannot buy a Bible now, nor any new book. When the British come back I shall be given my Bible! The whole service was very solemn and inspiring and made me feel what a great responsibility it is to be a preacher, what a great calling it is. I do so wish Alfred had been here for this service. He will be glad when he hears of it, I know.

*Feb. 8th.*     Cousin Sylvia Le Brocq here for dinner – a long time she hadn't come. She did make me laugh, says she is afraid the bottom of the bus will burst one of these days! It is true, they have so few that they pack people in like sardines and lots are often left behind. The bus has to run on charcoal too, and makes slow progress. Deportation is to take place again – those who have been warned to go on Wednesday.

*Feb.11th.*     Joyce and I went to Mr and Mrs C Alexandre to tea. We did enjoy going. They are such nice people, and Norman is such a dear little boy. He is very interested in music. He played hymns for us on the piano and the harmonium. He even plays at Philadelphie if no organist turns up, and he is only eleven. I think Mrs Ward was having her operation today. I have thought of her a lot.

*Feb. 13th.*    A beautiful sunny day, the first really dry day for weeks, so we got all Tuesday's washing dry without any trouble! We have heard that the deportees were put on board last night, for an hour, and then told to go home. Don't know if this is correct. No one seems to know if they've gone or not. How the Germans love to torture people, keeping them in suspense as long as possible. Received a very unexpected letter from my old Headmistress, Miss Clough. She had seen the report on the *Evening Post* about my Local Preachers' Dedication Service.

*Feb. 14th. SUNDAY.*    Went to Bethlehem this morning. Afternoon went with Mother to Philadelphie as Herbert was being received into Church membership, also Raymond Vibert. Rev. Scott preached a very good sermon on 'Rejoicing in Hope.' Tonight we heard a quiet knock at the door. It was a young Russian but so smartly dressed that we had to ask him for his 'papers' to make sure he was one. He was wearing a white summer hat with black ribbon, a thin black coat and green trousers (such as Germans wear), and rubber clogs. He told us that the Germans had given him these 'togs'. He explained how he had been taken from Russia, through Germany, France, St. Malo, La Manche to St. Helier, Jersey. He comes from Moscow. I expect he is much better educated than those poor dirty ones. We gave him a glass of milk and something to eat.

*Feb. 15th.*    Stormy. Rain, hail, sunshine. M. and D. here for lessons this morning. Afternoon, I cleaned out all my rabbit hutches. Miss Trachy called. She wanted to congratulate me, having seen the report about my Local Preachers' service. I didn't know one was supposed to be congratulated!

*Feb. 17th.*    Christine and Mother went to town. C. was having a perm given by Raymond! Mother went (in a car which brought Mrs Collas to see Mr Bauche) to see Cousin Sophie at Bon Air Nursing Home, and Uncle Philip. So I had a busy day here – teaching, cooking, etc. Felt quite tired by end of afternoon. Alice here. Ellen Amy called, and we went to the end of the orchard to see the huge scooping machine which the Germans were forcing to pass in the lane. It was much too wide, so its caterpillar wheels brought down part of the hedge, together with stumps and roots of trees, as it slowly forced its way along. The OT men were laughing at the mess they have made of our hedge. They don't care!

*Feb. 18th.*    Tonight we went to a concert in Philadelphie schoolroom, given by the young people of Ebenezer chapel. Rev. Scott presided. We had a very enjoyable time. Howard C. has a lovely tenor voice. He sang 'You are my heart's delight', which I specially appreciated, as Alfred used to quote that to me! Alice Amy was there with 'Auntie Florrie.' What a surprise.: 'Auntie Alice' who never goes anywhere!

*Feb. 19th.*    M. and D. here for lessons. Beautiful day. The dogs barked furiously in the night. Russians went to Mr Conan, also to Mr Frank Luce, where they stole seven fine fat does. I'm sure Madeleine is in a temper about it! They found the seven rabbit skins in a field. One of the does had a litter a fortnight old. It is a shame as they will die now. Alice told us that Russians had been to Auntie Florrie's, stolen her flour, four sheets and three bottles of bottled pears. The Pirouets found the empty bottles, broken, under a hedge. This afternoon, Mother took Kath and I to see Mrs Amy, the mother of our baker, whose husband has just died. When the Amys were married they lived in the cottage here at Homestead. I was very glad to meet this dear old lady. She spoke of Heaven, how she was looking forward to it, and to meet again all the dear friends. She said that if Jersey is so beautiful, how much more lovely must Heaven be. She and her children, grandchildren, sons and daughters-in-law are all so united. It was a joy and inspiration to meet her. She told us how, when she lived in the cottage here, Mother, who was then a child, would sit at her feet, on a little stool, and help her to sew, or she would read a little book, or listen to her stories, and she was so good and quiet! Mother loved sewing when a child, and reading fairy tales. Mrs Amy took us to see the bake-house – very interesting. She showed us the window through which the Russians had entered and the sack they had left behind. Well, we have so enjoyed this visit and the walk with Mother in the sunshine was lovely. It isn't often we have the pleasure of going out with Mother.

*Feb. 21st. SUNDAY.*    Beautiful sunny day. My turn to stay in, so very busy morning cooking etc. Blowing and blowing on the fire with the bellows, as usual these days. Afternoon, I preached at Les Frères. It was lovely there – the chapel, with its coloured windows lit up by the sun. it must be one of the prettiest chapels in the Island. But I did not feel that I had done very well today. Perhaps I was tired after the hard morning's work.

*Feb. 23rd.*    Went to town and had lunch with Mrs Walker and Joy in St. Mark's Road. Did a few things for Mother in town. Got four shirts for the boys at Amyson. Paid sixty marks for the four (£6.8s.2d). They are of very thin cotton.

*Feb. 24th.*    Alice tells us that the stealing every night at St. Ouen's is dreadful. Lots more people have had fowls, rabbits, wheat etc. stolen. One working woman had just bought twelve pullets at £1 each, and have been taken. Does are taken and the young left to die. It is very hard for people. How tired we are of the Germans being here. It is said that there is typhus amongst the Russians here and that those infected have been taken away. It is said too, that

Advocate Ogier and his son are being taken to Berlin to be tried, and that Mrs Ogier is almost distracted. Is it any wonder? It is an awful affair, for Mr Ogier and his son are in danger of being shot for spying, and the Germans have their eye on their friends too. It is rumoured also that all 'undesirable' women are to be deported, i.e. women who have had babies by the Germans, women who've got any form of VD (and, supposedly, have passed it on to the Germans) and women who've done anything to annoy the Germans. Well, those women who've had illegitimate children, because they've carried on with German soldiers, only get what they deserve if they are taken to Germany. Better for them to be taken, rather than innocent people, like all those families that were taken just because they happened to be English.

*Feb. 26th.* Rev. and Mrs Mylne and their daughter have again been arrested by the Germans and court-marshalled. It is said that special officials from Germany came for the purpose (and I suppose to try Mr Ogier and son also). The Mylnes are both condemned to a year's prison and their daughter to ten months for keeping a wireless and for spreading news. Everyone feels upset about it. The Mylnes are very brave. Prayers were offered for them at the Girls' College, where Vivienne is a teacher. I fear that the Mylnes will be taken away from Jersey. Everyone is praying. We have heard that the Rev. and Mrs Foss from Guernsey have been deported to Germany, for no reason at all.

*Feb. 27th* Lots of rumours about. It is said that there is a smoke screen over England as they are getting ready to invade. Here, important officials are said to have come, to decide whether to give up Jersey or to defend it. More deportations are to take place next week. One man, who was deported with the last batch, asked what he was being taken for. He was told 'sabotage': He asked what he had done to be deported on such a charge. He was told that he had taken too much skin off the potatoes! (He was working for the Germans.)

*March 1st.* Dad was at the Assizes today. On his return, he told us that he had been made Foreman of the Jury. The Jury at the Assizes have never before been allowed to go home until a case was finished, but the Court passed a special regulation for this year to allow them to come back, as many of them did not want to leave their families alone at night, on account of the Russians. The case this year is concerning the tunny fish and liquor stolen from the Essential Commodities.

*March 2nd.* Herbert's Birthday. He is 19 today. Mr Bauche had a stroke this morning. Miss Marcus was in town and Mrs Hawkins and the maid were alone, and except that Mother went to see him, they would not have realised that he had had a stroke. So we phoned doctor at once. Mr B. recognised Mother but the doctor could not make himself understood.

*March 3rd.*   Laurence's Birthday. He is 25 today. Phyllis came to tea. Alice told us that someone had told 'Auntie Florrie' that Mr Churchill had double pneumonia and that his case was hopeless. She wept and wept! And it is not true – we know that he is better. Dad still at Assizes.

*March 4th.*   Mr Bauche died in the night. We will all miss him, especially the boys. They were fond of him and have seen quite a lot of him since he's been ill and they've done much of his work for him. So that lovely house will have to be sold as there are no children.
Dad has finished at the Assizes today. Both cases were very long. The second concerned theft of foodstuffs from the Mental Hospital. Mr D., a lazy loafer, was condemned to prison for two years.

*March 5th.*   Feel quite down about things tonight. The Mylnes are supposed to go on Monday. Advocate Ogier and his son have gone – they are in danger of being put to death. Poor Mrs Ogier. Joyce knows her husband, having worked in his office for a few weeks. Mr Fred Le Brocq works there. I suppose they will carry on the business for the present. One never knows what dreadful things to expect next. We started planting our potatoes today.

*March 7th. SUNDAY.*   A Russian came this afternoon. I think it was the same one who had a white hat a few Sundays ago. He is very superior to the majority of those who are here. He is clean, neat, polite, and good-looking. Quite the opposite of one who came during the week, filthy and ugly, and he wiped his nose with his cap, then put it back on his head – ugh! Tears were running down his cheeks – we cannot understand how they can make themselves weep like that; it is amazing. I gave the one this afternoon some cold potatoes and beans and he ate in the sun. I wish I had given him more.

*March 8th.*   M. and D. here for lessons. Dad and Francis went to Mr Bauche's funeral. Mother's trio of friends came this afternoon – Mrs Le Brun, Mrs Pepin and Mrs Reis. We love seeing them. Today they amused themselves discussing my wedding! I'm sure I'd be glad if they arranged it all for me! Anyway, it is no use making plans, but I pray that Alfred and I will be married this year. We have waited so long.

*March 9th.*   Went to town and saw Mrs Ward who is convalescing at Mrs Averty, Casa Marina. I do enjoy talking to Mrs Ward. The Mylnes are supposed to be taken away on Thursday. Mrs Ward says it is dreadful the way the Germans are harassing them, treating them like felons. Rev. Mylne had appealed to have his wife left here as her heart is weak and she has to have treatment. A judge is supposed to come over to consider this appeal. In the meantime, the Germans keep the Mylnes in suspense, torturing them mentally as much as they can. There is much talk in town also about the fact that the Germans are asking for Jerseymen to go to work for them in Alderney. They are bringing eight hundred Russians here from Alderney. The Bailiff has refused to do anything to help them to find men. I don't know what will happen – no one can stop the Germans getting their own way.

*March 11th.* I planted out my Sweet Peas today, which I had sown indoors in pots is the autumn. Tonight, we four girls, with Phyllis and Beryl, went to a concert at Bethlehem, given by the 10 girls of the Sion Chapel Girls' League. I enjoyed the singing, especially.
Mr Bauche has left the eight of us £25 each in his will. We had never expected such a thing. None of us are related to him in any way. The boys have done a lot for Mr Bauche, of course, but why he should think of us girls, I don't know. I suppose he liked us all for Mother's sake. We are very sorry that he has died, poor Mr Bauche. One would rather have people than their money. I wish he had been a Christian and not so worldly. I wonder what happens to such people when they die? Mr B. was such a clean, honest, kind gentleman, but not interested in the things of God. Poor Miss Bauche was always praying for her brother.

*March 15th.* I read some of the letters Alfred wrote to me from Handsworth College before we got engaged. It is interesting to trace the growth of our regard and love for one another. We made quick progress, I think. It is a good thing to be able to write one's thoughts to one another, and it didn't do us any harm to be separated at that time, but, rather, good, I am sure. Well, we have known plenty separation, before engagement and before marriage. It is time we were together. There have been more arrests of people found to have wireless sets, or to have spread news. One man, having been found with a set, saved his own skin by turning it over to the Germans, and is now paid by them, so it is said, to betray his own countrymen. It is shocking and one feels ashamed. But what would one have done – it is all so frightening.

*March 16th.* I've been absolutely delighted to receive a Red Cross Message (a reply to one of mine) from my darling Alfred, in his own hand, in which he says that he will have a house next year and asks where I would like it! I am thrilled to think that we shall have a Manse when we get married. I feel quite excited. May the Germans soon depart from here and may God keep us both safe through all. Poor Alfred, what a long time he has had to wait for me. May I be the very best of wives to him!

*March 20th.* Went to town this morning to Dr. Lewis and got a tonic for myself and medicine for Dad's headaches. I admired a photo of Dr. Lewis' wife, and he said: "Isn't she beautiful?" It is so sad that he got separated from his wife and has a little boy in England whom he has never seen.

*March 21st. SUNDAY.*    Preached at Bethlehem this morning on Ezekiel ch. 2. v. 7. It was Overseas Missionary Sunday. Miss Trachy came, the very first time she has attended a Methodist service! She was surprised at the Children's talk, as she had never heard of a Children's talk during a service before. I'm sure she found the whole service very different from the Church services she is used to! I went on to town and heard Elsie preach at Samarès. We had a good service and I was quite taken up with this little building. Stayed to sleep at Alfred's folk. Before I had left home we had had quite a discussion as to whether I'd stay to sleep in town or not. I imagined something might happen in the night and I might not be able get home in the morning. As one says: 'It' (the Invasion by the British) must happen one day.

*March 22nd.* After breakfast played a little with Rosemary Howells. She enjoyed my pretending to be a bee! Lovely ride back. Everything looked so beautiful in the early morning sun and mist. Elizabeth Castle, with the sea all hazy, looked like a dream Chateau. Then St. Peter's Valley – the only ugliness was the places which the Germans have so spoilt with their fortifications. When I got back, I found Margaret and Dorothy waiting for 'teacher.' Cleaned out my rabbits afternoon. Delighted to receive another message from my dear Alfred.

*March 24th.*    Another message from Alfred today – a reply to one I sent last September. A Russian has been killed in a night raid on a farm at St. Ouen's. It appears that four Russians went to steal. The farmer's son heard them, went down and was attacked. His father and brothers came to the rescue with heavy sticks. (The Russians were armed with iron bars, specially prepared for forcing windows and removing nails) In the fight, one Russian was killed by a blow on the temple and another knocked unconscious. One of the farmer's sons had a severe blow on the jaw, knocking out his teeth, which, fortunately, were false! It is all so dreadful.

These last three days, we have been feeding a young Russian who has come to the door. He would give us two boxes of soap-powder one day, and two tablets of soap. We didn't like taking these things, not knowing where he got them. Poor little chap, and he will kiss my hand! I fear that I wash my hands well afterwards. One sees no sign of the Germans 'cracking up' here.

*March 26th.* As we were having breakfast the Germans were practising in Mr Bisson's field opposite our windows – horses and gun-carriages etc. It is interesting to see the horses. It was the sale of outdoor effects at Oaklands this afternoon – lots of people passed. The little mare, not yet broken in, has been sold for £130. It is sad to see all Mr Bauche's things going.

*March 27th* The thousandth day of the Occupation. Oh dear, what a long time they've been here, and how tired we are of it all. Received a letter from Uncle Gordon, from Laufen. He does not appear to be enjoying prison-camp life. It must be very trying to be herded together like that, and shut in for months, even years. There is an appeal from the Todt Organisation for baby-clothes for pregnant Russian women. I do feel sorry for those poor women, separated from their families, brought here and treated in this bestial way by those horrid Germans, for I feel sure that those babies have German fathers. What evils war brings in its train. It is awful to think of the things that are happening here.

*March 29th.* Mother's 59th Birthday, We gave her a low tea-table for when her friends come in the afternoon. We moved the clocks one hour ahead today. Victoria (Vicky) had seven puppies this morning.

*March 30th.* Had dinner at Montpelier, then went to Georgetown chapel for the Women's Work Quarterly meeting, where I was the speaker. Very good company of women present, between 70 and 80. Mrs Fell presided, to my joy. They all seemed to enjoy my 20-minute talk. I felt nervous at first but it passed off as my thoughts were on my subject and I hardly used my notes. Afterwards people from three different chapels asked me if I would go and speak at their meetings. I had to refuse as I have plenty speaking to do already, and preaching, and I must not overdo it, nor neglect my work at home. Curfew changed from 9 o'clock to 10 o'clock. Young couples here pleased.

*March 31st.* Dad went to the sale of Mr Bauche's house. It went for over five thousand pounds.

*April 1st.* Mr Michel from Val de la Mare has been taken by the Germans; whether to be imprisoned here or away, no one knows. About a year ago he had annoyed them when they took his lorry. He has already paid a big fine and, I think, considered himself safe. Then suddenly, he gets a telephone summons from the Commandant. Once a person is on the German Black List, even for the slightest offence (and they are easily offended), it is impossible to escape. They may pretend to be lenient with you, and then! It is terrible for Mrs Michel not knowing what will happen to her husband, and she has several children and a farm.

*April 4th. SUNDAY.*      Lovely day. Went to Bethlehem morning. This after-noon, we sat outside reading. Tonight I preached at Tabor. The cycle ride was lovely. The countryside so beautiful, and from Tabor, lovely glimpses of the sea. Léa came back as far as here with me. Was very amused to hear about the preacher at Bethlehem tonight, a Mr P. from the Salvation Army. Wishing to illustrate the point that people do not always practise what they preach, told how, some time ago, he had heard a splendid sermon. He was very impressed – the preacher did not lack words, and his sermon was about not being of 'unclean lips'. Then, to his sorrow, Mr P. discovered that that splendid preacher was himself a man of 'unclean lips.' For, the following day, he passed Mr P.'s shop with a pipe in his mouth! (I think it must be Rev. South that Mr P. was referring to.)

*April 5th.*      Beautiful weather, like a summer's day. Mrs Barbour, Uncle Gordon's friend, spent the afternoon here. She enjoyed coming, very much. I took her for a walk and showed her the damage in our fields (for the German railway tracks) and I fetched rabbit food at the same time.

*April 6th.*      The Germans have found out that several farmers have been harbouring escaped Russian prisoners, feeding and sleeping them in exchange for work. We very anxious for them and their families. Some have been 'hiding' for a long time, and one has even been to the Pictures in town with a Jersey girl on several occasions. One dreads to think what will happen if they are found out.

*April 9th.*      Today is Adèle Le R's Birthday. Her Mother brought us a piece of her Wedding cake, made in 1939! They had kept it, hoping that Adèle and Philip would have been able to come home from Africa; they decided it was time to eat it. It was in perfect condition. But I felt sad to be eating Adèle's cake when she is not here. Perhaps her Mother could have kept it a little longer, hoping things will change soon.

*April 15th.*      It was the sale of furniture at Oaklands today. Lots of people passed and many left their cycles and horses here. When the sale was going on, there were so many people in the rooms downstairs that the floors began to sag (there are cellars below) and Mr Maillard, the auctioneer, had to order everyone outside. Everything is sold at a shockingly high price.

*April 18th. SUNDAY.*      In his sermon tonight, Rev. Scott mentioned an illus-tration given by Dr. Leslie Weatherhead about a cowboy who, hearing for the first time about Jesus entering Jerusalem riding an untrained (unbroken) colt, remarked, "What wonderful Hands He must have had." Yes, this gives one something to think about.

*April 20th.* Irene here and we turned out Mother's and Granny's bedrooms. Yesterday when we were having dinner a seagull alighted on the wall, picked up a mole that lay dead beneath the window and swallowed it whole and her neck didn't even look fat as she flew away! Today the same thing happened. It is wonderful how seagulls can see so clearly from a great height. And what a throat and inside they must have!

*April 21st.* As the Hymn says, 'O happy day that fixed my choice!' Five years ago today, Alfred bought me my engagement ring. What a long time ago it seems. Thank God that we could be happy then, not dreaming of all that we would have to go through before our Wedding Day would come. And it is not yet in sight. What is there yet for us to go through? God Himself only knows. May He give us strength for the future, as He has wonderfully supplied it so far. I was able to send Alfred a Red Cross Message; I am sure he will be thinking specially about me today.

*April 23rd. GOOD FRIDAY.* Stayed in with Christine this morning. Others went to chapel. Afternoon, I took bunches of tulips to Miss Trachy and Aunt Elize. Had tea with her and Evie. Then Evie, Lucille and I cycled to Six Roads chapel where the Choir had a programme of Sacred Songs and Recitations, arranged by the Misses Skelton. I presided. The chapel was beautifully decorated – Arum lilies in the front and vases of Tulips in every window. When we came out about 8.45pm it was pouring and I got soaked coming home. But, thankfully, rain has come – we have been wanting it for a long time.

*April 25th SUNDAY.* Cycled to Sunday School – got very wet. Came home, changed and cycled into town. Rain all the way. Dinner at Montpelier. Went to Grove Place where they had a Children's service and I had been asked to speak. (It was the 97th Anniversary of the Dedication of Grove Place chapel). Children were very attentive, except two of the older girls who giggled the whole way through. I felt very annoyed with them! First time I had ever gone into, or spoken from the Grove Place pulpit. Had tea at the Misses Alexandre and went with them to Grove Place in the evening. Rev. Ward preached a very good sermon on 'The Power of the Resurrection'. Stayed to Communion. Slept at Montpelier.

*April 26th.* Had breakfast, dinner and tea with Alfred's people and the Slades, who are there for the weekend. Morning I called to see Mrs Walker, Joy and Mrs Ward, who is not yet well enough to leave the house. Afternoon, we went for a walk. Found it cold and bleak. Went to Uncle Gordon's garden. It is full of grass and weeds and in a dreadful state. Felt sad as I looked at the empty house and neglected garden. Poor Auntie Lulu, who was always so proud of her house and garden. I wish she were alive now, though she would have been taken to Germany with Uncle, I suppose.

*April 27th.* We heard the fog-horn blow this afternoon, so knew there were RAF planes about. Uncle, coming back from town, saw crowds of people on the Esplanade, all looking out to sea, where ships were plainly visible, smoking. One man saw them being bombed through his binoculars from his office in town. The attack was short and sharp. Uncle could see small craft looking for survivors.

*April 28th.* Christine's 24th Birthday. We went to Bethlehem tonight for the Young Leaguers Union tea and entertainment. We took our own food, of course!

*April 29th.* Joyce's friend, Enid, here for dinner and tea. Her father came tonight. What a nice family they are. Thank God that there are still some good people left in this wicked Island. So many seem to be given up to pleasure and sin in its many forms – illegitimate babies are being born and people cannot be trusted as they used to be; some spies and traitors here and there. That is what War and Occupation bring, I'm afraid. Herbert helped me to change the ground on the Rose-beds today.

*May 1st.* We received a Red Cross message from Cousin Laurence Picot in Queensland and one from Alfred. Great excitement about 3 o'clock this afternoon. I was just washing the saucepans, heard a plane but took no notice, thinking it was a German. Then, suddenly, there was terrific machine-gunning. Ah, I thought, RAF! Rushed upstairs, but in the wrong direction and missed it. Saw puffs of smoke from German anti-aircraft guns. Plane sounded very low. Laurence was able to recognise the markings. He was excited! It was a two-engined American bomber (Flying Fortress, people think). John also recognised the markings and saw two fighters with it. In town there was heavy cannon fire. Planes roared over town and dropped two bombs in the harbour. How I wish I had gone to the right window and seen the markings, even Mother did! Several times this week Frenchmen have come begging for food. Some said they came from Paris, others Vichy. All tell the same tale: taken away suddenly by the Germans. The Tulips have been very lovely. Had several hundreds that I'd got from Uncle Gordon's – have given away many. Everything has bloomed early this year. Have already picked two Roses!

*May 2nd. SUNDAY.* Went to Bethlehem this morning. Tonight cycled to Wesley chapel. It was their Sunday School Anniversary. The Demonstration was rather long! A teacher and child fell down the stage steps and gave us all a shock, but they were not hurt, fortunately. Laurence and Phyllis, John and

123

Beryl had been invited to tea at Montpelier, and after service we all went back there for a cup of coffee (substitute!). At 9.30 the five of us left. Cycled through rain all the way home, getting dark and no lights. Got back here at 10.15, and very thankful to be safely back home too! How nice it is always to come back home, never mind where we've been... this is the best place in the world! And I thank God once again for this lovely Home, and a good Father and Mother and brothers and sisters.

*May 3rd.*     Very strong wind all day. Irene here doing the washing. Did gardening, housework etc. Fetched rabbit food in the fields. Very busy day. Feel quite tired tonight.

*May 5th.*     Mrs Resch and her little daughter came to choose a puppy – we gave them afternoon tea. Mother and Dad went to Philadelphie to a concert given by Girls' League from Sion Chapel. We heard very heavy bombing during the evening.

*May 6th.*     Laurence, Phyllis and I went to pay a Silver Wedding visit to Mr and Mrs D C Le Seelleur (where Alfred and I met). It was really on April 30th but there were still people visiting them today. I counted over 60 vases of flowers! We were glad to get back. Felt tired, such a long cycle ride, it took about an hour each way. Uncle Edward came. He had had a very cheerful message from Auntie Hazel. Red Cross messages sound cheerful lately. Heard that a German soldier had said "If only England knew how close she is to victory. We're done!"

*May 7th.*     Irene here spring-cleaning the drawing-room. I polished the brasses. Notice on *Evening Post* that bread is to be rationed more from next week. We had heard that this would happen in July and no one expected it so soon. People are very upset as we already don't have enough bread. Don't know how people will live if this goes on much longer. Fortunately, we feel hopeful about things – the news that gets through (in spite of no wirelesses) is good.

*May 9th. SUNDAY.*     Gale continues; unexpected at this time of year. Quite cold too. Felt worried lest I would not be able to get to Georgetown this afternoon. Cycled down to Bethesda to take their morning service (Sunday School Anniversary) in place of Mr W Querée, whose Mother died on Friday. Had very short service – only five people in congregation and 25 on the stage! Got back at noon, fed the rabbits, rested a few minutes, had dinner (Peter Crill here) and left at 2 o'clock to cycle to town to preside over the Sunday School Anniversary at Georgetown. They had a long programme of recitations and songs by Primary and Junior children. Very good congregation. I gave a

124

10-minute talk to the children. Enjoyed being with them. Had tea at Montpelier, called to see friends, then cycled back with the wind against me. Had to walk in some places. Got home at 7.30pm. Fed rabbits. Read for a short time, too short. Not much rest these days, but thankful I've managed to get to both my services, in spite of boisterous weather. Everyone knows that the war news is good, and we expect the British to strike soon. There are still some people who are very pessimistic, however. Of course, if we judged by the look of things here we would have reason to be gloomy. Germans so busy always with their fortifications and their propaganda on the newspaper.

*May 12th.*    A German officer told Uncle Ernest today: "Tunis is finished. Hats off to the British Army and General Montgomery, we salute them!" And it is said in town that there has been a riot amongst the Germans at the Ritz hotel. About 16 soldiers got drunk, stuck their bayonets in a large portrait of Hitler, then threw it out of the window, also set fire to furniture. Francis had to take a cow to be slaughtered for rations.

*May 13th.*    Amazing how news spreads. Everyone knew this morning that fighting in Tunisia is over. The postman asked specially for Mother, to tell her the news. She is one out of only four people whom he trusts enough to tell the news. Well, we will not betray him! (He does not know our secret!)

*May 14th.*    Margaret and Dorothy continue to come every morning for lessons. Lovely day, but I did not have time for gardening, unfortunately. We had new potatoes for tea, our third time – they are very good. I went with Herbert tonight to the secret place to hear Mr Churchill broadcast from America. First time I had been to the hiding place.

*May 16th. SUNDAY.*    We are back in our Sunday School again. Though the Germans commandeered it, they never used it, so it has not been spoilt.

*May 17th.*    Grandpa is 85 today. Alfred's Mother, Mrs Howells and Rosemary spent the afternoon here. I went round the farm with them and showed them the railway track in our field. Rosemary enjoyed seeing all the animals and poultry. It is said that the Germans intend to use the Airport to go and bomb England; they are supposed to have brought lots more ammunition to the Island lately, and that our dockers refused to unload the bombs, so the Germans had to do it themselves. There have been rumours before about lots of planes coming to the Airport to bomb England. So far, it has not happened since they had fighters here during the Blitz over England. We hope and pray that our Airport won't be used in that way again. But it may well be the intention as more hangars have been built.

*May 18th.*    Irene here spring-cleaning the hall and breakfast-room. I sold her eight week-old rabbits, all for 10s.8d; cheap, as one can't buy them under five shillings each in town.

*May 20th.*    Had tea at Montpelier, then went to Sunday School Convention at Grove Place. Dad and Uncle Ernest came. Very interesting meeting, which lasted two hours. Various questions were debated with speakers For and Against. My part was to speak For in answer to the question whether the Catechism should be re-introduced when the Occupation is over.

*May 24th.*    Mrs Walker's Birthday. Joy had invited me, but I found it too stormy to cycle out – disappointing. But I had taken a bunch of Geraniums for Mrs W. yesterday and a little flour, butter and eggs, which Joy had asked if we could spare, otherwise she could not have made a cake for her Mother.  I had also sold her a rabbit for their dinner, and sent some new potatoes and a bottle of milk.
We have been told that the German who started the riot at the Ritz Hotel was caught (he had run away), made to dig his own grave, then shot. Horrible.

*May 29th.*    Afternoon, we heard great noise of 'planes and Laurence counted about 50 coming back from France and going towards England. There were many others and they passed so close, yet the Germans did not shoot. We were glad – perhaps they were afraid!

*June 1st.*    The Colorado beetle has been found in Jersey. The German Commandant, Knackfuss, on his return from France, at once found it on some wheat. Some people think he might have put it there himself to cause trouble to the farmers. So everyone must spray now. Mother received a message from Uncle Bert, saying that Auntie Janet has been ill since Christmas. We feel upset about this, and Uncle does not say what is the matter.

*June 6th. SUNDAY.*        Tonight at Bethlehem we had a most inspiring sermon on Rev. ch. 3. v.15. "I would thou wert cold or hot." Pastor Hanks is a splendid preacher, the words flow easily from his mouth, and he puts his whole soul into it. I had taken that text myself for my Trial Sermon, so I was very interested tonight.
Bodies of British airmen have been washed up here this week, and the funeral was held today. Crowds of people gathered for the funeral at 7am but only a few State Officials were allowed into the cemetery.
It was Francis' Birthday today. Mr Trachy and his sister Blanche came and had supper with us. They were talking to us about their adventures with 'Togo' on Evacuation days, three years ago. How they meant to go to England and went to town to get Togo put to sleep at the Animal's Shelter. But there were so

many waiting with their pets (women crying) that they had to return home and they never went at all.

*June 7th.*    Grandpa received Red Cross message from Mrs Dorey in Canada. On the *Evening Post* there were photographs of the funeral of the two RAF men whose bodies were washed up here. One of them was a Methodist – his New Testament was found on him so Rev. Ward was allowed to take part in the short service held in the Hospital chapel. Hundreds of people followed up to the gates of the cemetery at Mont-a-l'Abbé and nearly 200 wreaths were put on the grave afterwards. The Germans themselves put wreaths, one from the Lufwaffe! Our Bailiff put one 'on behalf of His Majesty the King.' Many were marked 'for the sake of freedom.' We wonder why the Germans have made all this fuss for bodies of British airmen have been buried here before, but very quietly. It seems as if the Germans want to be friendly, if anything happens, I suppose. And they make propaganda out of this. They themselves carried the coffin, draped with the Union Jack. This afternoon I did gardening, and tonight carried on with the preparation of a sermon.

*June 10th.*    Went to town afternoon. Called to see Joy and her Mother. They have both had tonsillitis and don't look very well yet. There is no good food and sick people cannot pick up as they ought. Went to Methodist Quarterly Meeting (my first time) at Grove Place – about 38 present. Amongst other things, it was decided to celebrate Rev. Ward's jubilee as a minister. Evie cycled back with me, and I had tea with her and Aunt Elize. Got back at 9.20pm. Washed dairy cans and made porridge for supper etc. I wish there wasn't so much work to do, and we could go to bed earlier and have a little time to read. I've not yet prepared my Children's address for Sunday, but my sermon is ready, however. Some boats had left the harbour, all loaded with our potatoes for the Germans, when they were ordered to return and everything was unloaded. I wonder what happened? We don't want the Germans to have our potatoes, and they want to take all they can – will they be able to, I wonder?

*June 11th.* A farmer, Mr Coutanche, has been killed by the German train at St. John's. He was deaf, and was walking through his field after putting out his cows when the train, loaded with stone from Ronez quarries, came along. He was struck and killed outright, his right arm wrenched right off. It is so shocking, especially as it could have been avoided – the train does not go fast. It is rumoured that there has been a Commando raid on Alderney and that some of the Englishmen and Jerseymen from here who had been forced to go to work in Alderney, have been captured and taken to England. What a fine thing for them – if the rumour is true! There is to be a double ration of potatoes next week, as those that were unloaded must be eaten. No one knows why they did not go.

*June 13th. WHIT SUNDAY.* Felt very bad in the night with my cold, but much better this morning, and was able to preach at Philadelphie. Asked Beryl to read the Scripture lesson for me, to save my voice. Had dinner at Somerleigh as it was their turn to have the preacher. Jurat Le Feuvre was in bed with a bad cold. I was glad and encouraged to hear, later, that Dad thought my sermon was good. I had specially prepared it for Whit Sunday.
An interesting thing has happened at Grève de Lecq this afternoon. A British pilot has been rescued from the sea by the Germans, after being seven days adrift in his rubber dinghy. They got a sea-plane to pick him up, but the seaplane was never able to rise again and had to be towed back to the harbour. Many people who were on the beach saw the excitement. Lucky people to see an RAF man. Poor man, to think he had been so long adrift, it is a wonder he is alive.

*June 14th.* M. and D. here for lessons, as usual. Irene here washing. She told us that her husband, Mr Renouf, saw everything, as he was fishing and the Germans had to use his boat to bring the pilot in. He managed to tell Mr R that his plane had been machine-gunned and he had been at sea for seven days. I cleaned out rabbits this afternoon, and tonight we went to Young People's Rally of the six Western chapels, held at Philadelphie.

*June 18th.* Mother not very well – she stayed in bed all day. Miss Marcus here all day. Glad she came as there was so much to do, and she helped with the dishes and potatoes.

*June 20th. SUNDAY.* Mother still in bed. Wish the doctor would come. She looks a little better, but it is so difficult to know what to give her to eat. I stayed in this morning. Preached at Bethel tonight. Had tea at Mr and Mrs Luce.

*June 21st.* Dr. Lewis came tonight. Says Mother is the same as last year. Her heart beats too fast and she must stay in bed another few days. I'm glad he has come, feel reassured.

*June 22nd.* Went to town morning. Called to see Joy and her Mother. Mrs Walker not at all strong yet. Joy looks fed-up with the Occupation. She does not want to hear any news because she no longer believes anyone when they say that the British are coming soon. It's been said so often and it hasn't happened. Well, I wish people would not lose heart. It is hard to wait so long and we are all getting fed-up! One must keep hopeful for one's own sake, as well as for other people's.

*June 23rd.* Picked blackcurrants with Kath. Mother still in bed.

*June 24th.* Mother got up for dinner and stayed on the sofa in the sitting-room. Afternoon, I cycled with Phyllis and Beryl to Grove Place for a Women's Work meeting. It took the form of a Concert with items from each Circuit, including two Missionary plays. Weather was lovely. Schoolroom was full. I enjoyed it, but felt very tired when I got back. Find the long cycle ride tiring. So much so that often I prefer to stay at home. There is so much work to do here, that one cannot go out without having more to do afterwards, and going out wastes one's energy.

*June 26th.* Working hard all day and did not manage to get to bed before midnight. Only had a few minutes to read through my talk for tomorrow. When will this awful Occupation end. Feel quite tired and depressed tonight. It seems that I shall have to wait an awful long time yet before seeing Alfred again.

*June 27th. SUNDAY.* Lovely weather. Terribly busy morning cooking. Misses Alexandre here to dinner. (Miss C. was preaching at Philadelphie this afternoon.) After dinner, I rushed off on my bicycle to town where I was giving the address at a Children's service at the Congregational Church. Rev. Clarke, the minister, had asked me to speak. Got back at 5 o'clock. Stayed in tonight. The Misses A. left about 8 o'clock, then I washed dairy cans, fed rabbits, prepared supper etc. A busy day, very rushed, and not one moment for reading or rest. However, we have given pleasure to the Misses A – they seemed glad to have come. It is good to be able to give pleasure to others.

*June 28th.* Dorothy here for lessons, but not Margaret, who was sick, having eaten too much fruit, as usual! Cousin Sylvia Le Brocq here for dinner and tea. Tonight I went with Madeleine Luce to see the people who had belonged to the 'work-party' before the Occupation, to see if we could recover some of the shirts and socks that had been given out three years ago. Got several things; other people who had used wool etc. for themselves paid us for it. Quite enjoyed going round, as I went to houses in St. Peter's that I had never visited before. Saw poor Mrs Touzel who has TB in the hip and has been in plaster for five months. She looks so well, is as bright as anything and always laughing. I do hope she will recover – they were just married. There is so much TB in Jersey now; I suppose it is due to lack of fats and sugar. Got back after 10 o'clock. Fetched cabbage leaves for the rabbits, supper, washed dishes, bed, nearly midnight again! It was three years ago today that the Germans came to bomb us – what an awful day that was!

*June 29th.* Spent afternoon in the pig-sty cleaning out all my rabbit boxes, what a job! But I enjoy doing it, except that I haven't enough time, because it was time to get tea ready, so I had to leave two hutches. I like looking after animals, it is so interesting.

*June 30th.* Alice says that a Mr Le Boutillier from St. Ouen's had a 60-pound pig stolen after being killed in the sty. Dr Lewis came and found Mother much better.

*July 1st.* Herbert, in secret, heard a wonderful speech by Churchill last night. Three years ago today, the Germans landed here by plane and took over our Island. What an awful day it was! We now look forward to being released soon. Everyone hopes it will be this year, we feel hopeful after C's speech yesterday – everyone knows about it! How I wish the Italians and Germans would give up before more dreadful things happen. Not only for our sakes, but for their own peoples who are being so dreadfully bombed.
Margaret and Dorothy did not come today, as we wanted to finish picking the blackcurrants. Elsie came to fetch some.

*July 2nd.* We finished bringing in the last remnants of the hay today. Weather has been fine and all the hay has been cut, dried and brought in without any trouble. Mrs Festou has had the very sad news that her son, Ernest, aged 23 (twin brother of Leonie) has been killed in action in Africa. He used to work at Westfield. In the last batch of Red Cross Messages, there has been sad news of several Jersey boys killed.
Today has also brought the news of the death of Donald Price, aged 31. He had been ill since the beginning of the Occupation with TB and, lately, one saw his mother wheeling him in a bath-chair. Alfred will be very sorry to hear of it,

for they worked together at the Income Tax office before Alfred went to College. When we were schoolgirls and he got on the same bus, we nicknamed him 'Tall One' but he did not know. Alfred meant to introduce me to him when he got back. But a few weeks ago, I saw him in the bath-chair, so I introduced myself. Unfortunately, I was, as usual, in a hurry and did not speak for long. But I thought that next time I saw him, I would tell him how we schoolgirls used to admire him and call him 'Tall One' I thought it would amuse him. He always seemed to us to be a jolly sort of fellow. Now there will be no next time. I'm so sorry. I never thought he was dying, but his hands were so thin.

*July 3rd.* So much work and bed so late, very tired! Mother not able to do anything yet, but I am glad she is resting. She always works too hard.

*July 6th.* Alice came today, as I went to town. Bought a pair of shoes (sandals with wooden soles, all that one can buy) for 12s.9d. Dined at Montpelier, then went to Bethel chapel to speak at their Sisterhood. Spoke on 'Hope'. Mrs H Luce presided. They are all so nice there. We had a cup of (substitute!) tea afterwards – one does not expect it these days. And one lady, who like myself is called Annie Margaret, gave me an oatmeal bun she had in her bag, as she did not like to think of me going back, so far, without anything to eat. How very sweet of her. Met Joyce and cycled back with her. Wind against us, felt dreadfully tired, that hill takes it out of one. I suppose the lack of sugar takes away our strength. I feel sure that is Mother's trouble.

*July 8th.* Elsie came for dinner and tea. She helped me to pick raspberries and to fetch rabbit-food in the fields. Russians went to Westfield last night. They broke the window of Uncle's shaving-room and took the mirror. They went into the greenhouses and tasted the tomatoes, and took a key and entered Mrs Lucas' scullery and turned everything upside down. Fortunately, they got no further.

*July 11th. SUNDAY.* A dreadful tragedy has occurred. This afternoon, Gordon Le Herissier, aged 16, has been drowned at Grève de Lecq. He had been a Sunday School scholar at Bethlehem, and of late Uncle had asked him to be in the choir. He was a promising boy and I liked him. I always had admired him, because once, when having failed his Scripture exam, I asked him to try again next time. He did so, cheerfully, and it pleased me so much. Others might not have had the pluck to try again. Poor Gordon, one feels stunned, it seems too terrible to be true. The weather was not really good for bathing today. Three other boys were with him and they were hardly in the sea when he got into difficulties. One boy caught his hand, but a huge wave separated them, and Gordon disappeared. There was no one near to help. The

Germans were called and went out with a boat. One wanted to dive, but his Officer did not let him, as it was too dangerous. Tonight, his body was washed up at about the same spot as where he disappeared. We feel so upset, and keep thinking of his parents and brother and sister. I preached at Bethlehem this morning. Went to Philadelphie tonight, where Rev. Fell preached. He is so good always. He is not very strong lately and is sad and down-hearted at everything that is going on here, and he longs for more news of his relatives and friends away.

*July 12th.*    Slept badly. Kept on thinking about poor Gordon and his stricken family. Then, had to get up to put Granny to bed. She was wandering about, naked. She thought it was time to go and milk the cows, at 3am! I couldn't get to sleep again, and when I did it was to dream about Gordon's family. Picked a big bunch of Sweet Peas and arranged them in separate colours, for Mother – pink, mauve and white. I wish I had more colours, and long for the time when one can get seeds from England again.

*July 13th.*    Had to tell Margaret and D. not to come today, as poor Grandpa is giving us so much washing and Irene could not come to help. So I spent all morning washing his shirts and long pants – scrub, scrub, scrub! Tonight, I went to see the Le Herissiers at St. Mary's. Poor Clifford was sweeping the yard, and I felt so upset that I could not speak. His father came and took me to see Gordon, and I laid a small bunch of my white Sweet Peas beside his body. God gave me the strength to pray beside the coffin and I hope it helped his father, who is very afflicted. Then I went upstairs where the poor Mother was in bed. She is very brave. She said to me, "I must not cry any more. I have asked God to help me." Then she spoke cheerfully about Gordon. She told me how wonderful old Mrs Bower has been. She is so full of faith. She knows what sorrow is, having lost several grown-up children many years ago. I did not see Doreen. It is so sad for her and Clifford. And all such promising young people – there are not enough like them in the world, so well brought up, and in the Christian Way.
John went with Beryl to her cousins at Trinity, the Vautier family with 11 children. The Germans have ordered them to quit, as they mean to knock their house down. The poor man does not know where to go with his large family and farm animals, such lovely people too. The Germans evidently don't intend to go. They keep on, harder than ever, making their defences.

*July 14th.*    How dreadfully sad this day has been. At dinner-time I heard a knock at the door and saw a letter pushed underneath. It was from Uncle Gordon, for me, written in French, from the German Internment Camp. All unsuspecting of its contents, I began reading it aloud to the others, as we ate our potatoes. Then, suddenly, in the midst of Uncle's usual grumbles about the camp, I saw this sentence: *Kate, mon ami de B'ham m'a dit que votre tante Janet est morte, il y a un mois.* I felt stunned but managed to leave that sentence out, and to go on reading, so that no one would know just then. I put the letter in my pocket and went into the kitchen, wondering how I was ever going to tell Mother this news. Then she came into the kitchen and asked me why I had put the letter in my pocket (I usually pass it round) and was there something I had not read? I said, "I'll tell you after dinner." Mother said: "Auntie Janet is dead." I put my arms around her. I could not answer. Poor Mother. This is terrible. She was just living to see her dear sister, Janet, again. How many things she longed to talk to her about. The end of the Occupation, for Mother, meant seeing her dear Janet again, just as for me, it means seeing my dear Alfred again. And poor Uncle Bert and Adèle and Marion. How can they bear it, when they lost Florence also, just over a year ago. Mother was expecting her friends, Mrs Le B., Mrs R. and Mrs P. and it was too late to put them off, so I went to meet them at the gate and told them. However, I was glad they came. It helped Mother. What a sad day altogether.

Dad, Francis, John and I went to Bethlehem for the funeral of Gordon. The Chapel was full except for a few pews in the gallery. There was a lorry-load (two layers) of wreaths. Rev. Scott conducted the service in chapel and in the Church cemetery. It was so difficult to keep from weeping. It is wrong of me, I know, but I feel sort of angry today, to think of people like dear Auntie Janet and young Gordon being taken away when they are so needed in the world, whilst Granny and Grandpa live on, unable to enjoy life any more and, worse still, being a great trial to us, the very last thing they would have wished. So many things one cannot understand, and life can be very hard and tragic.

I rang up Dr. Lewis, without telling Mother, and asked him to call, as I was afraid this shock would make her ill again. It was 9.45pm when he called. He was so nice and sympathetic, and I am glad he came. He showed us a picture of his son, aged three, whom he has never seen, which he received today from his wife in England, through Germany. He was so thrilled. Uncle Gordon also said in his letter that he has received the photo which I sent him, and that he will forward it to Alfred. How delighted he will be if he receives it!

*July 15th.*     Alice here, and M. and D. for lessons this morning as usual. Afternoon I went to St. Brelade's Bay with Alfred's folk and Howells. Had tea at Miramar where Elsie has been having a few days' holiday. It was very warm as we sat on the beach. I felt sad. Everything looks so lovely, and dear Auntie Janet and Florence will never see Jersey again. They had so loved coming to Jersey and to Homestead. There are some places on earth that are so lovely that one cannot feel that Heaven can be lovelier. One does have strange thoughts! Uncle Edward came. He is very upset about Auntie Janet. He tossed Uncle Gordon's letter aside, angry that he should write so callously – and in French, as if to air his French!

*July 17th.*     Went to town and had my hair washed and set. Mrs W. who did it told me that a German had been drowned in front of her very eyes at St. Brelade's Bay whilst bathing with a party. Though they recovered his body within 20 minutes, he could not be brought round again. How quickly those things happen.

*July 18th. SUNDAY.*     At Sunday School we had the Easter Service – it was suitable to have this as we thought of Gordon: 'All who trust in Jesus shall not die, but live'; we sang, also, 'Love is stronger than the grave.' I spoke to the children about this. In chapel old Mr A. preached. He had brought two bottles with him, to try and 'scrounge' some milk from someone!

*July 20th.*     After washing breakfast things, I rushed out to get food for the rabbits as weather looked like rain. Suddenly, thunder and very heavy rain came on and continued all day. So I've had a great disappointment because I could not go to the 'At Home' in connection with Rev. Ward's ministerial Jubilee. (50 years on July 18th since he went in for the Methodist ministry). I got quite ready, but in vain – weather too bad to cycle all that way. I'm sure Alfred would have liked me to go.

*July 21st.*     My 29th Birthday. How old I'm getting and still separated from my dear Alfred. I had hoped to be in touch with him this Birthday, at least by letter, if not to be seeing him. I must be patient still and may next Birthday see us together. I keep wondering where Conference will have stationed Alfred, for that will be our future home, surely. Well, it has been quite a happy and quiet day. Audrey Anquetil came to the door early with a lovely bouquet of Carnations. I did appreciate them! Then I rang up Rev. Ward to say how sorry I was about yesterday. He was so nice and so pleased and thrilled – he and Mrs Ward were nearly bowled over when he was presented with a cheque for £150! The schoolroom at Grove was packed and there were splendid musical items. It will have done Rev. Ward good and put fresh courage into him, after all the worry and problems he has had to deal with. Then M. and D. came for lessons. How lovely it was to see little Margaret so happy because she had a present for Teacher – a hot-water-bottle cover, and gloves from her Mummy. Did Granny's room when they had gone, fed rabbits, changed, and rushed over my dinner. Not quite finished when the bell rang and Joy and her Mother had arrived by bus. This is the first time Mrs Walker has had tea here and I was so glad she came. Mother and I and the two of them had tea in the sitting-room. We sat out and walked round the farmyard. Alice came. She gave me two lovely salt-cellars, and a lustre-ware tea-pot, well over one hundred years old. Dear Auntie Alice, how she loves us all and gives us her precious things. Mother gave me a sugar-basin to go with it and a pound note (not German money!) Kath had made a hankie with lace for me, Joyce had found a picture-frame in town, Alfred's Mother gave me a tray-cloth and Elsie a clothes-peg bag. So in spite of Occupation and empty shops, I've had all these lovely things, and the thoughts of the givers makes one so thankful.

*July 24th.*     My heifer, the one I had named 'My Lady Louise,' calved this morning. She is a perfect beauty! I now have 39 rabbits, and what work they give: fetching food in the fields, feeding and cleaning the hutches. But we must have something to eat.

*July 26th.*     Good news today – Mussolini has resigned. Don't know what this will mean, but one dictator has gone – pity it wasn't Hitler though. Laurence took potatoes to town early and all the men on the pier were talking about it and calling out something about 'macaroni' in front of the Germans! People are excited about it. Dad, Kath and I washed potatoes this afternoon, took them to Edward L. to be crushed. Tonight I worked till 10pm washing the pulp.

*July 27th.*     I washed potato pulp all day (Herbert pumped the water for me this morning) till 10.15pm. Finished my four hundred pounds. What a tiring job. I rested for half-hour after the dinner dishes were done and half-hour after tea, otherwise I'd have had trouble to manage – my back aches so! Put a few dishfuls of flour out to dry, weather being warm and sunny.

*July 28th.*     Spent most of day washing potato-flour and putting it out to dry. Alice helped me. Laurence took more potatoes to the boat. It is hard to have to let the Germans have them. Our people starve whilst the Germans have the best part of our milk, butter, potatoes etc.

*July 29th.*     At last we've received another Red Cross message, one from Cousin Doris, such a lovely message – she says we're not forgotten! She says nothing about Auntie Janet, and poor Mother hopes to the last that it is a mistake. Spent all afternoon sifting the potato-flour and finishing to spread it out. Have 21 pounds so far. Roger de Faye and Miss Winnie here for tea.

*July 30th.*     Margaret and Dorothy here this morning for last day of this term. I shall be glad to have more time for potato-flour, gardening etc. I like to see the children, but haven't really the time to teach them! Finished drying and weighing flour. Have just over 40 pounds from my 400 pounds of potatoes.

*July 31st.*     Received message from my dear Alfred at last – a reply to my enquiry sent last October. Well, it has taken long enough to come! But I feel very sad for he says "Auntie Janet none too good." The men have been reaping wheat and oats all day. A very busy day and late going to bed. I've not had enough time to prepare for Sunday School and for preaching, and I don't really feel fit for all that awaits me tomorrow morning. Plenty lightning tonight. Herbert and I watched it from the attic window.

*August 1st. SUNDAY.* We have been very upset tonight because the sad news of Auntie Janet's death has been confirmed, and we can no longer hope. Monica Le M. came to the door about 10.30pm on behalf of the Red Cross. She had two Messages. One which I read first said that Auntie Janet was improving slowly, and the other said that she had died after a relapse and urgent operation. I hope she did not suffer too much. She died on March 16th. I took the messages to mother in the sitting-room and she gazed at them for a long time. Oh, how sad I was for Mother. I never imagined that we would never see Auntie again. She was so kind when Joyce and I stayed there and always so bright and humorous. Oh this cruel separation caused by the Occupation! How one yearns for things to change.

This morning I went to take my Sunday School class, also gave talk to the whole School, then cycled to Galaad (strong wind, felt very hot when I arrived!) to take the 11am Service. Sat outside short time afternoon. Went to Bethlehem tonight. Got back and washed dairy cans, fed rabbits, and we had just finished washing the supper dishes, when the bad news came.

*August 2nd.* Wrote out the replies to the Red Cross messages from Uncle Bert and the Death Notices for the *Evening Post*. I had trouble to do it, the tears would keep on falling. Poor Mother is looking so pale. How hard it is for her, and how bravely she bears it.

*August 5th.* Very strong wind blowing. Many stooks blown down in the fields. The boys went to put them up again tonight but, as fast as they put up those sheaves, down the wind blew them again! One does not expect this weather in August. Old friends of Auntie Janet's have phoned Mother and others sent cards of sympathy. I have written out a message to send to Uncle Fred in America. How sad he will be.

*August 7th.* Went to town, took apples etc. to various people. They are all so grateful. The trouble is that I cannot carry as much as I would like on my bicycle. As I walked through the crowded town (where all those people come from, I don't know – it is always like that on Saturdays). I noticed many foreigners especially men, dark-skinned, with black hair – maybe Italians – until I longed to see a friendly face. Suddenly, I saw Mrs Pepin and Mrs Reis. I caught Mrs P's hand – she was just thinking the same as I was! Got back, tired, had a bath, tea, washed dishes, fed rabbits, fetched rabbit-food for tomorrow. Then at 9pm came to my bedroom, to look up my sermon and Children's talk and to choose the Bible readings and Hymns for tomorrow. After that, had supper, washed dishes, Bible Reading, prayers and bed at last, about midnight.

What a busy day; Saturday always is.

*August 8th. SUNDAY.*     Strong wind still blowing. Got up about 7.50am, prepared and took up Mother's breakfast and Granny and Grandpa's, as usual.
Fed rabbits, breakfasted, washed dishes, got ready and cycled off to preach at
Six Roads chapel. 25 children present and 18 adults. I felt that somehow God
had enabled me to help someone there. There was a Mr D who lost his wife
some time ago, and Mr P. whose wife is very seriously ill at Millbrook Nursing
Home. And I did feel that my own sorrow over Auntie and what we had all
gone through in the past week helped me to understand these people better
and to pray more feelingly. I begin to think that one cannot help or fully
sympathize with people in trouble unless one knows what it is oneself. So I
think often that God is allowing me to be separated from Alfred, to be tempted
and to know sorrow, all so that in the future I may be more fitted to help
others and to understand them.
The rumour has been about everywhere that Hitler is seriously ill. Everyone
hopes it is true! I suppose it cannot be wrong to wish the death of such an evil
man. I'm glad it is not last Sunday all over again, with its bad news. Dear,
dear Auntie Janet, to think that we never again see her on this Earth.

*August 12th.* A lovely day of sunshine. Dad and the boys have been bringing in
the wheat so I asked Joy and Emily to come gleaning. They had tea here and
we've gleaned for nearly three hours tonight. I raked the whole field for them
and Joyce (sister) did some raking too. Then Joy and Emily cut off the ears of
corn. They had a good lot. Time goes on and no special news to cheer us. And
the end of the Occupation does not seem to mean the same now that dear
Auntie is dead. It seems so cruel that Mother won't be able to tell her all the
things she wanted so much to tell her.

*August 14th.* Dull depressing weather, drizzle all day. Did cleaning in the
house, also cleaned my bicycle, looked over sermon for tomorrow and fetched
rabbit-food, but everything was soaking wet. Vicky and Watch have caught
their fifth hare this week, so we've had plenty rabbit to eat!

*August 15th. SUNDAY.*   Went to Bethlehem this morning. Afternoon cycled to
town. Had tea with Joy and Emily, then went to Augres chapel. First time I've
preached there. Congregation 38 including a few children. People very nice.
I could have laughed when I happened to turn towards the choir where
Mrs M. was playing the harmonium. She struck me as being the image of 'Mrs
Benger' in the *Lax of Poplar* book. She was sitting straight and stiff, and had a
hat with huge pink roses piled in front. It is naughty of me to be so amused!

*August 16th.* Granny and Grandpa's Diamond Wedding Anniversary. Grandpa had a letter of congratulation from the Bailiff (Mr Coutanche) and from the Attorney-General (Advocate Duret-Aubin) and from Rev. Ward. Oliver Mourant came afternoon and Evie and Aunt Elize. It is such a pity that Grandpa is no longer fully able to appreciate things (he would have been so happy and thrilled). By tonight he had already forgotten he had received those letters. And poor Granny is past it too, she has been kind of dozing all day. However, we appreciate those letters. Both the Bailiff and the Attorney-General mention, not only Grandpa's service to this Island, as Constable of St. Mary's but also to Methodism as Local Preacher etc. I'm afraid Alfred and I will never celebrate a Diamond Wedding, not even married yet!

*August 17th.* Washed potato pulp all day, apart from having a cup of afternoon tea with Enid Le Feuvre who called to bring a letter for Grandpa from Jurat Le Feuvre. Then tonight, had to leave my work to go to a Sunday School meeting at Bethlehem to arrange for the 'Treat' and Anniversary. Got back 9.30, closed rabbits for the night and saw to potato-flour. Herbert had finished washing the pulp whilst I had gone – good Herbert.

*August 18th.* Felt very tired after yesterday's hard work. Alice came, as usual, and helped me very much to wash flour and put it out to dry. Don't know how I would have managed without her. About 5 o'clock, Joy and Emily came. I gave them tea in the sitting-room, then we went off to glean. Elsie came later, had tea with the others, then joined us. We gleaned till 9pm. Lilian called for some apples, and by the time I had fetched this and that for them all and they had gone, I was quite 'done-up!' Got into my comfortable bed very thankfully indeed! Yet it was so nice to see my friends, and to have the pleasure of doing something for them. One feels so thankful, in these days, that, living on farms, we have the wherewithal to help our town friends a little. Heard heavy bombing going on practically all day in France. At dinner-time, we were rather upset. A man from the German farm at the Airport came with one of their cows (an ugly French white and red one!) to mate her with one of our bulls. We didn't know what to do. We did not want to, because we could not have used that bull again with Jersey cows. We phoned the Department in town and they said we must refuse, and tell the Germans to buy a bull and keep it on their farm. The man with the cow looked in a horrid temper – said the German Commandant at the Airport had sent him. We managed to send him away, and hope we won't get into trouble.

*August 19th.* Alfred's father's Birthday, so Joyce and I went to St. Brelade's Bay where the three of them were spending the day. We were not there long but I paddled for a few minutes and it refreshed my weary feet. We took our sandwiches and ate them at Brown's Café. I wish we had had time to be there longer – such a change these days to get near the sea.

*August 20th.* Cloudy all day, but no rain fell till tonight, thank God, for we were threshing today. Everything is done and the straw inside (oats). We dined early, as the men had to be at the machine at St. Ouen's at 1 o'clock. So we had a nice long afternoon, part of which I spent about my potato-flour. At 5.15 we gave a meal to our men and to all those who had come to help. Christine made a fish-pie with our last tin of salmon (kept for three years!) and with it they had salad and tomatoes and bread-and-butter (we managed enough from our ration) – then apple-pie and potato-flour pudding, sugar-beet cake and coffee substitute – a very good meal indeed for Occupation time. If we didn't have a little flour of our own, but only the oatmeal ration like people in town, we could never manage a meal like that. The German inspector at the machine was decent today, and not too strict, and allowed Dad to have several sacks of oats for ourselves. After all, it is our own, why shouldn't we keep a little. We had our own tea about 6.15 and afterwards Joyce and I washed the piles of dishes. I think the invasion of France will take place soon – we hear such a lot of heavy bombing going on. One dreads it, but it must come, if we are to be released. May God bring us safely through to see our loved ones again. The Red Cross messages don't seem to be coming through these days and one longs for news.

*August 22nd. SUNDAY.* Quite a long time since I'd had a Sunday without preaching – glad of a rest, really. Stayed in to cook. Roger de Faye and his little brother here for dinner and tea. We had killed a cock as we know they have so little to eat in town.

*August 23rd.* Joyce and I went to tea at Montpelier. I arrived in time to go and paddle in the sea for ten minutes! Tonight, we went to Great Union Road Chapel where there was a Children's Festival. Five Junior Methodist choirs from town (75 children) gave some splendid items together, and there were also some solos and part-songs. Chapel was almost full. Joyce and I got back at 9.50pm, high time, as it was getting dark and we had no light.

*August 26th.* Mother and Kath went to Evie's for tea. So glad Mother was well enough to go. I wish she had opportunity to go out to tea more often and that we had the means of carrying her to see her friends. If only we had a nice little horse and trap!

*August 27th.* Had an upset this morning. About 7.15am Francis came rushing upstairs shouting: "A heifer, a heifer, swollen in the meadow. The piercer, quick, where is it?" As he was milking, a neighbour came rushing in to tell him that one of our heifers (which sleeps outside in Mr Bauche's meadow) was down, swollen. Poor Francis arrived and pierced her to let the gas out, but he was just too late. She died. We rang up the vet. He told us to bleed and skin

139

her so as to save the meat. So we phoned Ernest Le Feuvre who came at once and did it. Vet. came later, said the meat was good, and he would send some-one to fetch the carcase, as we are not allowed to keep any of our animals for meat. However, Dad got round him, somehow, and he said we could keep it, as long as we did not sell it at Black Market price. (Dad would never do that!) And, of course, the Vet wanted some for himself! It happens that there is no meat ration this week, so probably the Vet knew that if our heifer went to town, the meat would all go to the Germans. We have been fortunate, for we can have all the fat, which is so useful, and quite unobtainable these days. We have also kept the liver, and four people have been sent a small share ready-cooked. We have only kept one piece of meat for ourselves, for roasting tomorrow. Dad has been cutting up the carcase until long past midnight and Mother packing up the pieces for distributing amongst our neighbours. And yet there wasn't enough to send to friends in town that Mother would have liked to help. However, many of our neighbours will have an unexpected good dinner tomorrow. At the same time, we would much rather our heifer had not died. Francis is very sad about it and we can't make out how she came to die. She was loose, as if someone had untied her rope (one never knows, these days). There was nothing to hurt her in the meadow, but she was choked up with grass.

Someone has heard that the Germans intend to deport four thousand more people from here. I wish Mother had not heard that said. I knew it upset her, so I did not let her go to town, as she had intended. She might have heard it again, also she is tired after going out yesterday and I was anxious to think of her going in that crowded bus. It is also reported that eight German officers have committed suicide on hearing they had to go to Russia.

*August 28th.* Mother received a Red Cross message from Uncle Bert today. Poor Uncle, we are anxious about him. He does not say if Adèle and Marion are with him and his signature looks shaky. Two of my rabbits not well this morn-ing. I hope the others won't start being ill. I had taken two litters away from their mothers and put them loose in the bottom of the pig-sty and they all looked so well. This week has come the terribly sad news of Advocate Ogier's death in a German camp. People say he was broken-hearted to have to go a second time. The Gestapo arrived at his house without warning, and took him away immediately. That is how they torture people – they set them free and then pounce upon them again. And it has killed poor Mr Ogier. Mr F Le Brocq, who had worked in his Office since he was 15, is terribly upset. During all that time, he had never heard Mr Ogier say an unkind word to anyone. Many loved him. So that is another murder laid at Hitler's door.

*August 29th. SUNDAY.*   Constable and Mrs Crill here for dinner and tea. He told Mother that he admired her 'bevy' of girls! We feel quite flattered because it is usually the boys who are admired! Tonight, I preached at St. Ouen's Chapel. Congregation 81. Reggie was there with the young lady to whom he has got engaged, so I was introduced.

*August 30th.* Have three rabbits sick now, so gave them some olive oil last night. Disappointed not to have had news from Alfred. I long for message, but more for the day when I can get a letter!

*August 31st.* We had the treat for our Sunday children today – tea in the Bethlehem schoolroom. They brought their own bread-and-butter, and we teachers provided cakes, stewed pears and apples, with carrageen and potato-flour blancmange, and sugar-beet tea to drink. Then we had sports and games in Mr Le Herissier's field. I think the childen had a good tea and enjoyed themselves. I actually won the Teacher's race! My prize was one German mark! Clifford and Bertram Le Maistre looked after the sports. They are such nice boys. Poor Clifford, I'm sure he misses his brother dreadfully.

*September 1st.*     Mother, Kath and Christine went to spend the afternoon at Mrs Grace Pepin. Mother enjoyed it, except for the horribly crowded bus. I was glad to see them return safely. Mrs P. always has stories to tell about the Germans, because her husband, being manager of the Gas Works, is so much in contact with them. She told about two interpreters who had been working with him lately. One has been sent elsewhere and he was very sad to leave Jersey. He told Mr P.: "My heart is full of sorrow to have to go, for I have been very happy here with the British people." He has been here for three years, and never took a holiday. Mr P. asked him why he did not go to Germany, to which he replied: "I want them forget about me, for I don't want to go away from Jersey." He is going to Russia and he said: "I go to fight, but I don't know what we are fighting for."
The other German interpreter was from Hamburg. Some time ago, he visited Hamburg, and found that his entire family had disappeared and the place in an awful state through British raids. He came back very depressed, then he was told that he had to leave Jersey and go to work in Hamburg. He said: "Any place but there, I cannot, and I will not go there." Knackfuss, the Commandant, said: "Then, I will have to report you," and the Interpreter went straightaway and shot himself. There have been other suicides amongst the Germans because they don't want to go to Russia. Poor things, what Hitler has brought upon them!
Tried to continue preparing my sermon for St. Martin's tonight, but have had an almost constant headache these past weeks and don't feel myself at all. A proper bother!

*Sept. 2nd.*    Another rabbit dead. Jurat Le Feuvre rang up Dad (who is

Inspector of Crops) to say that someone had dug up a huge patch of his potatoes during the night. He reckons that about ten barrels have been removed. He thinks it must have been the Russians who pass by with the train, for the potatoes had been pulled up out of the ground, without the use of a fork. There has been a dreadful accident to a German on part of their railway line that runs, just past the Huberts at Oakdale. The German was on a motor-cycle and evidently he thought he could cross the line in time, but he was too late. He was thrown on the line and all the trucks and engine passed over both of his legs. John saw him. Mr Hubert came with an improvised stretcher and he was carried on to their lawn. Other Germans came on the scene, and later the unfortunate man was carried away in an ambulance. German or British, one feels very sorry for anyone who is so hurt. Those railway lines which the Germans have put across our fields and roads are without gates or anything, and very dangerous. It is a miracle that more people are not hurt.

*Sept. 3rd.*     Today we enter the fifth year of war, and news got all over the Island quite early that British and Canadian forces have landed on Italian soil. Everyone is feeling excited – the Germans have not reported it on the paper tonight.

*Sept. 4th.*     Went to decorate at Bethlehem for the Harvest services. Miss Ethel was unable to come and I felt quite incapable of having the responsibility. One relies on Miss Ethel. However, I did my best and Kathleen Le Maistre, Isabel and Lucille came to help, also a few little girls. I did the vases and baskets for the tables in the rostrum and pulpit. We were just finishing, when Miss E. dropped in on her way back from town. How thankful I was to see her. She just moved this vase and that, just a little, and so on, and all was well! She has the knack and is so splendid at arranging flowers.

*Sept. 5th. SUNDAY.*     Rev. Fell preached for our Harvest, on Psalm 92 v. 5. 'O Lord,how great are Thy works, and Thy thoughts are very deep.' Herbert and I were invited to tea at Mrs Capt. Syvret and Joan so that we could go to their Harvest service at Bethesda tonight. There were other guests for tea whom we knew. Then I was introduced to a Miss Le Brun whom I found quite charming. We had heard about each other but not met. Though she is a good deal younger than I am, I don't feel it in conversing with her. Phyllis and I hope to meet again.
Bethesda Chapel was very tastefully decorated. I have thought a lot about Alfred today because, it being the first Sunday in September, he will have arrived in his new Circuit and be preaching there for the first time. How I long to know where he is stationed now, especially as it may be my future home. I have no idea what part of England he is in today. Maybe I shall not know

until the Occupation is over. It is hard to feel that he has had to go alone into his first Manse. I had so hoped we would be together when he was given a Manse. This time of waiting to be together is so long!

*Sept. 6th.*    I received a card from Uncle Gordon in the German camp. He says my photo has been received by a friend of his in England who will send it to Uncle Bert, who will pass it on to Alfred. I do hope he has received it by now. What a lovely surprise for him!

An unusual thing happened amongst my rabbits yesterday.The doe I had from Mrs Berry had a litter of 11 rabbits (she had actually had thirteen) already five-weeks-old. I found that she had made another nest and had another litter of twelve rabbits! So she had in her hutch 11 five-week-old rabbits and twelve-day-old ones! Thus in less than six weeks, she had given birth to 25 rabbits. The explanation is that a young buck had escaped from his box and entered the doe's box through a hole in the wire. I found him there one morning, but I did not expect the doe to have another litter! So I've had to remove from her the five-week-old ones and hope to save them – have given them coccidocis powders to try and prevent illness. What interesting things happen on a farm, be sure!

*Sept. 7th.*    All day washing potato-pulp. Herbert helped me and we got on well, because Mother and K. washed the dishes for me so that I could get on with the job. But the flour is not settling as well as last time and I fear we will have some bother.

*Sept. 8th.*    Wonderful news has come through tonight: Italy has surrendered unconditionally. Though no one is supposed to have a wireless, the good news has spread like wildfire. We all feel excited. The question is: What happens next? What about us?

*Sept. 9th.*    Left at 2.30pm to cycle to town for Quarterly meeting at Grove Place. Soon it began to pelt with rain. I plodded on, had to call at Mrs Reis to borrow stockings which I changed on arrival at Grove Place, but my shoes were wet through. Nothing very interesting at meeting, though everyone feeling hopeful after yesterday's news, so we spoke of having a big united Thanksgiving Service when the Germans leave us! Still pelting with rain. Called at Cousin Frank Le Gros, got home at 5.50 almost wet through. Put my feet in hot water and felt none the worse.

*Sept. 12th. SUNDAY.*    Thunder, lightning, heavy rain, storm started about 9.30am and I was unable to leave for St. Martin's (an hour's cycle ride in that weather would have been folly) so 'phoned Mrs Le Seelleur who said she would take the service if I did not turn up. I was so sorry as it was their

Harvest and they had asked me specially. Cleared up afternoon so I cycled out, did the journey in three-quarters of an hour. Don't know how I managed it and with a head wind! They had a Children's Service, and they brought such lovely baskets of fruit and vegetables, all 70 of them. There was a congregation of at least 210 persons. I gave an address on Ruth 2 v. 19. 'Where hast thou gleaned today?' Chapel was beautifully decorated in the front and masses of fruit and vegetables. Really a sight! Had tea at Springside. Mrs Ahier gave me a plate which contained heaps of raw grated turnip, grated apple, tomato, something which looked like cold mashed potato, lettuce, Calendula petals, and a dab of custard to crown all! It  certainly looked colourful. Mrs Ahier is so interesting a personality. I love people! Weather looked ominous again, so did not stay to their evening service. Got back at 7 o'clock. Fed rabbits, then chatted to Mother. I like telling Mother about my 'little adventures' when I've been out. The boys went to St Ouen's Harvest service tonight.

*Sept. 13th.*    It is exactly five years ago that my dear Alfred and I parted – he to go to Africa as a missionary. How long ago it seems. I thank God for Alfred, and I thank Him also that the future was hidden from us when we parted, for we could not have borne it. It seemed awful to separate for eighteen months, but, thankfully, we did not know that the separation would stretch to five years, and over. Still, God has helped us to bear it.

*Sept. 14th.*    Margaret and Dorothy started coming for lessons again this morning. I always find that children's brains are much more alert and fresh after the holiday! We got a scare about 6pm. Thought the Germans had shot Vicky! She was barking furiously at them passing in the road and suddenly we heard the loud report of a gunshot. We all jumped up and John opened the door. There was Vicky, trembling. Maybe they only meant to frighten her or us, but, thinking she had been shot dead, we felt awful. One should perhaps not get so atttached dogs, but Vicky is so faithful and loving and a jolly good guard also!

*Sept. 15th.*    A year ago today (the 16th) the first deportees were taken away, when I found Uncle Gordon saying Goodbye to his neighbours. Thinking about it made me suddenly feel frightened again. One always fears more deportations, especially of the young men. One is almost afraid to open the *Evening Post.* Mr Mourant had a Red Cross message yesterday, so my hopes were raised, but there was nothing for me.

*Sept. 16th.*    Threshing wheat at Mr Farrell today and our helpers were here for tea. I was not there as I had to go to Bethlehem to speak at a Cradle Roll meeting. Miss Ethel had asked me to speak to the Mothers! I really did not feel experienced enough to speak to Mothers. However, I spoke about the power of suggestion and Imitation in training children. Not many present, as people are all busy threshing.

*Sept. 19th. SUNDAY.*    Dad's Birthday; he is 59 today. Went to Bethlehem this morning. Stayed in tonight as I have a bad cold. There is a long time that a Frenchman comes every Sunday about 7pm. He came and I gave him two pieces of bread, and milk to drink. He would like clothes, but we haven't any to give him. Like hundreds of others, the Germans took him away from his home and forced him to work for them.

*Sept. 20th.*    Freddie, the barber, came to cut Grandpa's hair. He is just back from three weeks in France. I'm sure I would not like to travel in these days, but he does not care and only goes for pleasure. The German Commandant gives him permission, only because he says he is going to help his folk there with their harvesting! And they do not charge him for the (dangerous) boat journey.

*Sept. 23rd.*    Another rabbit died, three months old, the sixth. It is very discouraging to lose them at that age.

*Sept. 26th.*    Alfred is 32 today – my hopes of a year ago have not been fulfilled. Had tea with his parents and Elsie. They were glad to have me to spend part of this 'special day' with them, and we spoke about A. and wished we knew exactly where he is now. Mr and Mrs Du Feu came with me to the Sunday School Anniversary service at Grove Place tonight and I stayed to sleep. I preached at Philadelphie this morning. Mr Le R. attacked me afterwards but it was only to tell me that I spoke too fast! I told him I knew it was my failing – I must try to get over that.

*Sept. 27th.*    Great excitement about 4pm when an American bomber came low over the Island. Joyce saw it plainly over town. Hearing a terrific noise, I rushed to the attic and was lucky enough to see the plane. I counted over 50 puffs of smoke from shells bursting around it. Was terrified lest it should be hit, but it passed safely through. But don't those wretched Germans shoot! A strange thing happened at Westfield whilst the shooting was going on. A lump of earth and flesh fell through Mrs Lucas' conservatory, breaking a pane of glass. Luckily she was not hurt. The top of the conservatory was also covered with earth – maybe a bomb exploded somewhere and scattered the earth far and wide.

*Sept. 31st.*    Another rabbit dead. So I'm killing the others in that litter to eat now, rather than risk losing them.

*October 2nd.*      Someone has had news through Germany that Helier Mourant has a son, so Oliver has been congratulated on being a grandfather, and he knew nothing about it! It is hard that he was not the first to hear the news. There have been a few Red Cross messages out this week, but none for us. Some people still believe that the Germans will be out of here by Christmas. Could anything so wonderful happen?!

*October 3rd. SUNDAY.*      The Frenchman came to the door again tonight. Told me he had not yet found a wife – so hard to find!

*Oct. 4th.*      Went to Mrs Allan's for a singing lesson. Hope to continue. Put clocks back one hour last night, so it was dark very early. Tonight, noticed a fearful glow in the sky. The boys went to see and found there was a very big fire at La Moye, at a German work-yard. There was plenty wood and barrels of oil burning fiercely. I wonder if it was an accident?

*Oct. 5th.*      About 9am two young Russians came including the one who used to come to the back door often, months ago – he had a bad eye then, was in a miserable condition, and dressed in rags. Today, what a change! His eye is better, he is decently dressed, with thick boot-clogs. His hair was not so close-cropped but fine, soft and wavy. He came, poor little fellow, to say Goodbye. He managed to make us understand that the Germans were taking them to work in France. He gave us a photo of himself and his name and address at Kiev. His name is Nikolai. He wanted very much to have a photo of us sisters, but we dared not give him one. We gave him our address, which, now I think of it, was worse. I hope we won't get into trouble. Other Jersey people, at St. Ouen's, had given him their address also. Poor chap, he intends to write to us when war is over, but will he still be alive? There is a terrible battle going on now at Kiev, the Russians trying to regain the city.

I so hope Nikolai will not be killed. He seems such a nice boy, and evidently quite educated, for he knows all the places on the map. He had with him another young one called Roman. We gave them some apples and a photo of a Jersey cow.

Germans are making young Jerseymen work for them now, driving their lorries and horses etc.. We have expected the boys to get a note to go before the Commandant. So far they haven't heard anything. Raymond had to go, but he was all right as he is a farmer. Of course, farmers are, in a sense, working for the Germans, without being able to help it, for they get most of our milk, butter, wheat, potatoes etc. It is hard that some are forced to work for them, but whilst it is in Jersey, it is not so bad as if they were taken away. May that not happen.

Mother and I called at Mrs Le Marquand (Joyce Maillard) to see her new baby boy. She already has a girl, three-years-old. What a sturdy child, and amusing too!

*Oct. 6th.*    Postman brought a letter from the Public Health Department saying that samples taken from our milk proved that there was a very poor fat content, and asking Dad to go and explain the reason! Second time this year that we have had a complaint, last time it was supposed to be dirty. And we who take so much trouble. Dad has written again, telling them that it is scandalous the way the milk is handled after it has left our hands. It gets mixed with other people's and who knows but that someone does not remove the cream! Really, one feels indignant with these 'departments'. Why can't they do their job properly – they worry those who do their best and leave the rogues alone. Hope Dad's letter makes them sit up!

*Oct. 8th.*    A message came to me today from some friends, asking me to pray because they are in very great danger. A Russian prisoner, who has escaped from a camp, has been hiding on their farm. I suppose it is because I am a preacher that I have been asked to pray, but it makes me feel very humble – to think that these friends, a lot older than myself, should feel the need of my prayers.

*Oct. 10th. SUNDAY.*    Our Sunday School Anniversary at Bethlehem. Not many people this morning but afternoon chapel was quite full. Children did quite well. Rev. Struthers, such a nice man, preached on Luke 2 v. 15, 'and when they found Him not, they turned back again to Jerusalem, seeking Him. Mary and Joseph lost Jesus, and people have been losing Him ever since,' so began his sermon.

*Oct. 14th.*    How delighted I've been to receive a Red Cross message from my dear Alfred at last, dated June. How long they take to come! The person who had asked me to pray phoned and asked me to go so that she might tell me more about it, but it has to be in great secret. One dares not think what would happen if the Germans found out – feeding them is bad enough, but harbouring escaped ones... .And this particular one is an added danger, because this person thinks that what he has gone through may be affecting his mind, as he is threatening them at times. He comes from Moscow, from a wealthy, well-educated family. The Germans took away everything they had. He knows English, and has improved it whilst he has been hiding on this farm and at other places where Jersey folk have risked their lives helping him. He has a quick brain. The only way to get rid of him would be to report him to the Germans, but neither the farmer himself, nor his family would want to do that – they are too loyal to England. So I keep praying ever so often that these friends may come safely through these dangerous days.

*Oct. 16th.*    What a hard thing God has given me to bear today. But I cannot and will not believe that my own dear Alfred is losing his affection for me. At dinner-time I received two messages from him. He says, *I find these days of separation increasingly difficult. My friends are good, but cannot appreciate how I feel.* (sent on May 11th) and on May 22nd he wrote: *I am weary of long and needless separation.* So cold, no love, and he does not reply to my loving message on the other side of the paper. I can see that he cannot understand why I did not leave in time.

Alfred, cannot you trust me to explain all? God knows that I prayed over it, with tears, and did what I thought was best at the time. Had I only known that he was coming home from Africa I would not have hesitated and waited that extra day or two, hoping to hear what he was doing. No one knew for sure that the Germans were coming. It is cruel, for I simply cannot explain on a short Red Cross message. What am I to do? Worse still, I phoned Elsie, and they have received similar messages from him, one which says: *Affection burns low, but honour survives.*

Oh, is it possible that he has ceased to love me after all we've meant to one another? I pray with my heart that he will yet be patient and wait till he sees me and misunderstandings can be done away with. And, horrible thought, has some other girl come into his life? I feel like saying ,"My God, why hast thou forsaken me?" Yet I will believe in God and I will trust Him to help me. I dread to hear worse news, I want to cry and cry, but I must not, for tomorrow, I am planned to preach at Tabor, and I must not wear myself out before. My poor Alfred, I know how he must have felt when he did not find me waiting for him in England, and he has perhaps brooded over it and imagined that it was because I did not care enough for him. And yet all his messages, so far, were so loving and true. In February his message said: *I am longing for reunion as much as ever, dear.*

*Oct. 17th. SUNDAY.*    Rather stormy, wind and rain. Could hardly sleep all night. Felt awful on waking. Food nearly chokes me. Could not go to chapel this morning – was afraid to break down. But I prepared for this afternoon, when I went to preach at Tabor. Managed to get through all right. Almost broke down as I prayed for 'loved ones far away' as we always do. Elsie met me at Tabor and came home to tea. She is so good, has great faith in her dear brother, and believes it will all come right. Yet to see her upset me and I wept bitterly and again tonight, when Dad came to say Goodnight. I could not help it. Poor Dad, he hates to see me suffer and he held me tight. I think he feels angry with Alfred, but I cannot think hard things. I love him too much. Spent the evening trying to write to Mr Curwood to try to get something through to Alfred that way, but it is so difficult to know what to put, and I am afraid to make things worse.

*Oct. 18th.*    Tore up letter to Mr C. and wrote another this morning. Tore that one up again and have written another tonight. I pray God that it is all right, post tomorrow. Could not possibly go to my singing lesson today. Instead, cycled to town in very strong wind to see Rev. and Mrs Ward and told them all. Felt they would help me. They were upset but Mrs Ward prayed for Alfred and me and it did me good. Rev. Ward wrote out a Red Cross message to send to Alfred telling him that all will be explained at reunion and that Nan's affection is beyond doubt, and there can be no blame attached to her, and not to worry himself. Oh dear, if only Alfred could get that message tomorrow, but it will be months before he gets it and so much can happen in between.
I wrote a message to Alfred myself, and one to his best friend, Bernard Titmus, asking him to try to help Alfred. But we are only allowed to send one message this week. The man at the Red Cross Office was sympathetic and said he would send Bernard's next week. It is comforting to know that Alfred is praying – he says so in his June message.

*Oct. 19th.*    M. and D. come for lessons this morning as usual. When I got up I wrote yet another letter to Mr Curwood. After thinking it over during the night, I felt must alter something. This is the fourth letter I write to him – Joyce has posted this one at the German Post Office. I phoned Elsie. She feels sure things will come right. I felt quite cheered after speaking to her, and for the first time since Saturday felt I could eat a little. I have read all Alfred's messages, so loving and full of longing for me, that I cannot but believe that it was a bitter mood that came over him. Satan entered his heart. So I pray that it will have passed and that God has filled his heart again and renewed his love for me. But oh, this awful suspense of waiting for more news – this is the severest trial of all.

*Oct. 20th.*    Could hardly eat my breakfast. I must not give way like this. I must be brave. I phoned Elsie and felt more cheerful. Alfred's parents have thought that perhaps he was not well when he wrote those messages. Elsie gave me the address of Mr Rodd who is in a German camp, so tonight I have written to him asking him to write to Alfred, telling him I am anxious fearing he is not well and assuring him of my faithfulness and love. I feel much happier after writing this letter. My poor Alfred, this cruel separation must be a terrible strain for him – how he must have suffered. I pray so earnestly for him.

*Oct. 24th. SUNDAY.*　　　Kathleen's Birthday. She is 27 today. I managed to find a book to give her but it had to be a second-hand one, of course! Tonight I feel quite happy and cheerful about Alfred and myself, after two services that have helped me very much. I seemed to feel very near to him and feel and believe that God will 'make all things well' in His own good time. This morning I went with Evie to Sion Chapel. The weather was lovely, quite a change after the rain and wind of the past week, so we enjoyed the cycle ride. Rev. Skyrme had asked my friend, Joy, to take a service or two on our plan and she was preaching there. We had a very good service. Joy is very original. She took no text, but spoke on 'Hands' ending with the thought that we are 'in His Hands'. The Children's talk and Hymns were all so well adapted to her subject. The whole service was very helpful, especially so to me this morning. Mrs Ward preached at Bethlehem this afternoon. She is a splendid preacher. What a lot she has to teach a young woman like myself. She preached on 'God is no respecter of persons.'

*Oct. 25th.*　　　Went to Mrs Allan, but only did piano, as I have a cold and could not sing (and I have not practised my singing since the upsetting messages). Poor Mrs Allan, she got wet through several times last week, there being no bus, and she had to walk home. Then no good food, no nice hot drink, no lovely fire to warm her when she gets back. On a farm, we are better, we have some wood, and we have started lighting a fire in the evening. The boys are standing the seed potatoes now of an evening and we girls sew, mend and read and I find it difficult not to be downhearted!

*Oct. 26th.*　　　Pruned a few Hydrangeas. Irene brought us a few sand-eels – what a treat! John cheered me up by telling me that the English expect a collapse of Germany any day.

*Oct. 27th.*　　　Mother and Dad went to Mrs Le Sueur's funeral. Miss Ethel Arthur came, bringing her Mother in a bath-chair. Lovely sunny weather and I had intended doing a good afternoon's gardening, but, never mind, I was so pleased to see dear Miss Ethel.

*Oct. 28th.*　　　Had dinner at Montpelier. Mrs du Feu, Elsie and I went to an 'At Home' at Mrs Walker's in St. Mark's Road. It was very enjoyable. My favourite item was a song by Miss Louisa Price, a very good soprano. We had a cup of 'coffee' and a biscuit during the interval. Joy had asked me to provide the milk as it is impossible to get any extra in town. Elsie cycled back with me as far as Bas des Routeurs. She is extremely good to me, especially at this time, doing her best to keep me hopeful about Alfred. It was so kind of her to come all through the valley with me.

*Oct. 29th.* Did not feel at all well today, with this wretched cold. So disappointed because there are some 'messages' out today, and I've not had any. Began to imagine that perhaps Alfred has not sent me any more. But, thank God, I have found comfort as I came to read my portion from *Daily Strength* – a verse just suited to my need:

> *Be patient, suffering soul! I hear thy cry:*
> *The trial fire may glow, but I am nigh.*
> *Greater than all thy pain,*
> *My love for thee.*

So I have thought on this, greater than all my pain, God's love for me and God's love for Alfred.

*Oct. 30th.* I thank God that I've had a message from Alfred. The fact that he sent one gives me relief. When I read the first part: *I still believe the best is yet to be,* I felt so thankful, but then he goes on to say, *it could not be worse than these days of separation.* I hope this message is not meant to be as bad as it sounds, but Alfred put the word *Love* at the end, which cheered me. I was planting Wallflowers and Tulips in the garden when Mother told me there was a message for me. I found myself trembling, and I went to my bedroom and knelt down to pray for strength before opening it.

*Oct. 31st. SUNDAY.* Preached at Bethesda this morning. Herbert cycled down with me. My voice still hoarse, so asked Enid Querée to read the Lesson for me. On way back, stopped to pick some heather for Mother on the *côtils* [Jersey-French word for to steep, sloping fields] at the side of Jubilee Hill. Mother was telling me a short time ago that she had a special corner in her heart for Alfred, and I know she is praying for him. I must try to rest peaceful in the knowledge that God will help him through this terrible time.

*November 2nd.* Another message has come from Alfred, dated April, a reply to one I sent in January, but oh dear, it is very cool, not at all like my own loving Alfred. However, I must not think about it, because I have received later ones. A letter has come form Uncle Gordon at last, but what a letter! So unlike him that I feel quite bewildered! He mentions 'le bon Dieu' several times, and that he thanks God for the days in which He specially manifests His goodness! Well, can it be that he is a changed man and that he has been converted? I can't imagine what has happened to him! He has heard from Uncle Bert that Adele has a baby boy. What good news and yet how sad we feel that dear Auntie Janet is not there to rejoice in her grandchild. Uncle Gordon seems cheerful and hopeful, as though he had heard some wonderfully good news. He seems to think that the end is in sight, and signs his letter with a big

Lady speaking in Jersey-French to Stan Le Brocq, owner of St. Peter's Stores:
"Tu n'as peux té. Hó! J'n'en ai pas d'peux."
[You are afraid of them, but I'm not.]

flourish as we had arranged he would do if things went very well.

*Nov. 5th.*     Two Germans, passing on bicycles, tried to shoot Watch because he flew at their Alsatian and pinned him against the hedge. Watch just escaped, but they were furious and even waited at the other gate to see if he would come out again. We'll have to keep him tied. I did some forking in the Avenue this afternoon. All day kept thinking of my dear Alfred and trying to puzzle out what can have happened to make him change, and apparently so suddenly. I feel so sad. How he must have suffered when he returned from Africa.

*Nov. 6th.*     Cycled to town with Joyce before 9 o'clock so as to get 'permit shoes' (10 marks). Mrs Stagg had done everything for us, got permits etc. She waited for us outside Dale's and took us in by the side door so we had our shoes without bother. There were only a few people queueing outside. This is the first pair of leather-top shoes we've had since the Occupation, the soles are wooden, of course.

*Nov. 7th. SUNDAY.*     Went to Bethlehem this morning. Preached at St. Ouen's afternoon, about 65 present. After service my St. Ouen's relations, 'Aunties' Florrie and Alice, Hilda and Lizzie stayed chatting. It was nearly half an hour after the service had finished that I left! For a change they are all hopeful about the situation. Many believe we shall be free before Christmas! If only that were possible!

*Nov. 8th.*     Went for singing lesson this morning. and M. and D. came for lessons afternoon. A young German nurse rang the front doorbell this afternoon and asked me if we had any vegetables to sell for the Sick Soldier's Home, not far from here. I told her we only had enough for ourselves. She said we had a fine house! She was extremely nice and polite and spoke English very well. Joyce has not been to the office today. She has not been at all well lately, terribly depressed, so Dr. Lewis called to see her tonight. He said there are many girls like that, the cause being the strain of Occupation, I suppose. Joyce is inclined to be introspective, which does not help. Dr. Lewis was telling us that people say that when the Occupation is over we shall not be allowed to leave the Island for six months. I do not believe this. I could not bear it. I shall want to go immediately.

*Nov. 10th.*     As we can use our schoolroom at Bethlehem now, we reopened our Wesley Guild tonight and intend meeting once a month, on moonlit nights. Young people from Bethesda visited us tonight and gave several items. Rev. Scott gave an address but spoilt it by going on for too long! Uncle Ernest presided.

*Nov. 11th.* Afternoon I did some gardening. Tonight I wrote a long letter to Alfred's Mother telling her some of my thoughts and feelings about this trying time. It is easier to write as one is stupidly shy of talking about one's innermost feelings.

*Nov. 12th.* Went to town to Mr Mallet the dentist to make sure that my teeth are all right. Glad I went as he found a tiny hole in my eye-tooth. I always have the feeling that I must take care of myself, for Alfred's sake. Last night, the Russians went to Westfield, entering the kitchen by forcing the window. They stole milk, butter, salt etc. and took away the dog. Uncle and family were terribly upset. The dog is one of Vicky's pups. Then, to their joy, they found it unharmed in Mr Beresford's garden – the Russians had thrown it over the high wire-netting. There are plenty thefts going on, but it could be often by the Germans, as there don't seem be many Russians left now.

*Nov. 14th. SUNDAY.* Very stormy – wind, rain, hail, cold. At Bethlehem this morning Reg Jeune preached on Prayer and Rev. Ward (afternoon) on 'Fret not thyself' (Psalm 37). His sermon was particularly helpful to me (he told me he had not preached specially for me!)

*Nov. 17th.* Alice arrived with a huge bunch of flowers, as usual, dear Auntie Alice. Today there has been a funeral in town for 29 British naval men whose bodies have been washed ashore. Those poor men, what a horrible death. I finished pruning the Hydrangeas, sowed more Sweet Peas in pots in the greenhouse, and brought my Hyacinths out of the dark. I spent most of the evening thinking out and writing notes for a sermon. I thank God for my preaching because having to prepare for my services keeps me busy in spare moments and I have little time to brood.

*Nov. 18th.* Elsie came for dinner, very nice to see her. She brought me a letter from Alfred's Mother which helped me greatly, she is so full of trust in her son. I thank God for Alfred's people – they help me so much to be hopeful. Mrs Capt. Syvret called and Roger de Faye here for tea, so a proper visitors' afternoon! Kath, Joyce and Christine went to the Viberts with Laurence and John, as it was Beryl's Birthday. She and John got engaged a year ago today. Beryl is only 19, so young!

*Nov. 19th.* Went to town. Called to see Joy, then went to The Limes Nursing Home to see Cousin Sylvia. She is quite down-hearted and weak. She told me that she only wants to live so as to spite the Germans! Everywhere people are now feeling absolutely depressed and fed-up. Morale is getting very low and some people hardly seem to care what happens! People hoped and believed that this coming Christmas would see us freed.

*Nov. 21st. SUNDAY.* Bethlehem, as usual. Stayed in afternoon and carried on preparing a sermon, fed rabbits, washed dairy cans etc. The Frenchman came begging at the door, as he has done for months.

*Nov. 24th.* Mother had a Message from Uncle Bert today, dated April 4th, telling us that dear Auntie Janet was laid to rest on March 22nd. and that Alfred was present. It made poor Mother weep and I wept with her. But Mother is so brave and will not let herself get too upset, but at once sets to work again. I am glad to know that Alfred was at the funeral. The Red Cross office has returned a message which I sent to Alfred a week ago telling me that I cannot send more than one per month to the same person, so I cannot send another before December 11th. It is hard – just another thing to try me on top of everything else.

*Nov. 27th.* Why must I suffer so? Mrs W. from the Red Cross Office phoned to tell me that there was a message from Alfred. She thought I would like to have it as it is not ready to be delivered for a few days. Oh, so hoped it was good news, but it is terrible. She read me the message, dated August 8th, which said: *These five years have been long and lonely for me. I do not know how much longer I can bear it.* Oh, my poor Alfred! I feel fearfully upset, don't know what to think or what to do. This is hell on earth. If only I could get to him. When will this terrible Occupation end? May God help me, and still more help my poor Alfred. How can I do my work in the house, prepare my sermon for Sion and another for Christmas Sunday; how can I find strength and courage to do all this?
I phoned Elsie. Alfred's Mother is also terribly anxious about him. Dear Elsie helps me, for she is so confident still that all will be well. She reminds me how we have always done what we felt best and prayed about everything, so we must not look back but trust in God that all things will work together for good. It is when I think of Alfred, alone, with these despairing thoughts and no one to comfort him – then I feel in hopeless despair. I cried on Mother's shoulder when she came to kiss me goodnight. She is so good and I hate that she should suffer also, for my sake. She comforted me, and told me not to worry, for she fears I will be ill. She said God may be giving me this trial so that I may be better fitted to serve Him. May God give us both faith in His power to help and keep us.

*Nov. 28th SUNDAY.* I thank God for granting me sleep last night in spite of my heartache and pain. I repeated again and again to myself, the words of Psalm 31 v. 7: 'I will be glad and rejoice in Thy mercy, for Thou hast considered my trouble.' Rev. Scott phoned about 9am and asked me to take the service at Six Roads chapel this afternoon, as the planned preacher was unable to go. Stayed in this morning. Weather very mucky, thick drizzle. Only 17 persons present at Six Roads. I hardly know how I managed, but God gave me strength to go through the service. Tonight I busied myself trying to begin a Christmas sermon, but how difficult it is to be brave! I must not let people know that I suffer, but I fear that I look dreadfully pale. It is so difficult to look cheerful when people ask if I've had news of Alfred.

*Nov. 29th.* Did not go to Mrs Allan as I felt too upset to be able to sing or play. M. and D. came for lessons. Tonight, I tried to compose myself by doing embroidery. I must be brave, because I can see Mother is afraid that I shall be ill. She says if I go on, I'll not be able to go out for people will see by 'my poor little face' that something is wrong. I keep on repeating to myself that God loves Alfred and He loves me.

*Nov. 30th.* I prayed earnestly yesterday for even one spark of light to lighten my darkness and despair. I have been much relieved by two messages. First, Mrs W. from the Red Cross rang up, saying there was an enquiry for me from Alfred, in which he said he had heard from Uncle Gordon and was delighted to get my photo. He has received it and he is 'delighted.' I know he would never say that if he did not mean it. Then, the postman brought a Message, dated July 17th, in which Alfred said: *Thanks ever so much for this message. I am staying here for a third year, and hope most of it will be spent with you.* How thankful I feel for these messages. I am still anxious and can't bear to think of my dear Alfred so lonely. I ache to comfort him. How cruel is this separation! When I had washed the dinner dishes, I lay on my bed and slept for half an hour. I felt more at peace than I've felt for over six weeks. But I feel tired, as though I had been ill. Mother would not let me go to our Guild meeting tonight. Joyce and Herbert went. I certainly felt too 'done-up' to go.

**December 1st.** Had dinner at Montpelier. They had had another message from Alfred, and he seemed more like himself. Tells them to keep smiling, and that he longs to see them and is very well. I spoke at the Samares Mission this afternoon, 24 women present. They had chosen the hymn about 'loved ones far away' and I found it so difficult to 'compose' myself, and being on the platform made it worse! However, God gave me strength as I rose to give my talk. Called to see Mrs Ward, and she knelt and prayed for Alfred and me.

*Dec. 2nd.* Joyce and I slept at Montpelier last night. This morning we went to the upstairs flat to see baby Howells after his bath. I held him in my arms and wished! Went to post a parcel of apples, beans and biscuits for Mr Curwood. One does not have to pay, but they are not pleasant men at the German Post Office. Called to see Joy and Mrs Walker. Joy and I discussed the Red Cross office here – we are not happy with some of the people there. Apart from being off-hand and unsympathetic, we fear that they discuss people's messages too much. I hope that Mrs W. won't phone me any more. I wonder why she meddled at all. Was she trying to be helpful or was she inquisitive about my affairs. Anyway, I feel very sorry that Alfred is being discussed by these people, as I am sure he is. It is awful to feel that none of our messages are private. Joyce and I went to a Classical concert at the Opera House. I thought it would do us both good. The Orchestra was conducted by P G Larbalestier. It was all lovely and I specially enjoyed listening to that marvellous pianist, Beryl Anderson. We cycled home with Phyllis Vibert. It was getting dusk in St. Peter's Valley, and we felt really frightened. The Germans were shooting with their big guns from the hills above us. The guns cracked terrifically, and we saw the red flashes, and the shells made such a noise passing over our heads. Oh, when will those Germans go?

*Dec. 3rd.*     Received a letter from Mr Rodd in the camp at Laufen, saying he had got my letter on November 3rd and had written immediately to Alfred, conveying my message. He writes me such a kind and sympathetic letter. I'm glad I asked him to do me this favour. It is a pity Alfred does not know him. He may imagine that Mr Rodd is a young man but I hope Alfred will realise that I was so anxious and desperate that I had to get in touch by some means or other even though I do not like so many people to know that Alfred's messages have distressed me so much.

*Dec. 4th.*     Have been in bed all day with a bad cold in the head. I expect I am rather 'below par' with all this anxiety. However, I've not been too down-hearted today and thought very lovingly of Alfred and held his photo close.

*Dec. 5th. SUNDAY.*     Stayed in bed all morning. Granny and Grandpa have been noisy all night, and this morning have given Mother so much trouble that I even prayed to God to take them. They are no longer themselves. Poor Granny and Grandpa, it is so sad that they should have got like this, especially Grandpa, after all he had done as a local preacher and Constable and always helped other people. I sat with Dad by the fire in the sitting-room this after-noon. Dad has also been in bed with a bad cold. About 5 o'clock, Elsie, who had been preachIng at St. Aubin's called to see me. How good of her to come all the way up that hill, in this cold weather, to cheer me!

*Dec. 7th.*     God is trying me to the very uttermost! I had been feeling so much more hopeful and confident, then Elsie has written to tell me that they've had a message from Alfred, dated August 30th, which shows how difficult he is finding this long separation from me, and he does not seem sure of his feelings any more. I'm afraid I cried in mother's arms again when she came to say goodnight.

*Dec. 8th.*    Didn't sleep much, was feeling so upset. But I prayed for Alfred as I lay sleepless. Alice here today. She would be very upset if she knew because she is fond of Alfred, everyone in the family is.

*Dec. 9th.*    My head bad all day with this wretched cold. I packed a parcel of apples, beans and biscuits to send Uncle Gordon. I painted a card for Joy's Birthday, also prepared part of my Christmas sermon. Thank God for plenty to do.

*Dec. 11th.*    When I woke it was snowing – huge flakes, the biggest I'd ever seen. Tonight there is quite a thickness everywhere. How lovely snow looks on the trees and house-tops and in the fields. It is not often we have snow so early! I posted Joy's card. I'd like to paint lots of cards if I had time. This morning, before getting up, I read a chapter from a book about Elijah, the Prophet, and I felt that it contained God's message for me. It was about the time when Elijah sent a lad to look for a sign of rain. Elijah prayed and six times the answer was: "There is nothing." but Elijah went on praying and the answer came. This is His message for me today. Let me, like Elijah, continue praying with perfect faith, that when God feels I am ready for it, He will answer, granting me my heart's desire, for my beloved Alfred, that this darkness may be lifted from his soul.
Dear Elsie phoned. Her Mother was glad of my letter, and that I was feeling happier and more confident. Alfred's folk help me so much. God bless and reward them for their faith. May they have the joy of seeing Alfred soon – our Alfred, as we all know and love him.

*Dec. 16th.*    Slept at Montpelier last night. Alfred's mother brought me break-fast in bed. How kind she is to me. Took a message for Alfred to the Red Cross Office. Mr D. read it with great interest, as I saw on looking through the window afterwards!

*Dec. 21st.*    How miserable everything is. This is by far the worst Christmas since the Occupation (except for the hope and belief that it will be the last like this). Not one shop 'Christmassy' – all dirty and second-hand things or totally empty. Cycled home from town with Joyce. It was fine again, after the pouring rain earlier, and I thought again how very *beautiful* Jersey is – the sea and sky and cliffs in St. Aubin's Bay were really a wonderful sight. The sea was very rough this morning and there were eight or nine German warships sheltering in the bay.

*Dec. 22nd.*    Dear Miss Clara Arthur sent Kath and I a box of three tablets of pre-war toilet soap! What a treasure – had not seen anything like it for years! Soap is not to be had except the ration of 'dirt' and 'grit'. A few weeks ago

Irene did the whole of our week's washing with a stick of shaving soap!

*Dec. 23rd.* What a busy day, preparing parcels of food for friends who have less than ourselves, making Christmas cards, and sending them. Many people called, especially this afternoon, wanting a drop of milk, a pat of this etc. Poor Mother is much too good and wears herself out sending parcels to friends in town who have so little to eat, we would like to have more eggs to give to those who needed them. Tonight Laurence has plucked several cockerels for friends, some he bought at 20 marks each (£2.2s.9d).

*Dec. 24th.* Rang up Rev. Ward to see what they were doing tomorrow. No one had invited them and they had nothing for Christmas dinner, so Laurence killed and prepared a bantam cock and Francis took it to the Wards this afternoon, with potatoes, beans, etc. so that they will have a Christmas dinner. The Wards are old now and separated from their children, and I wish we could have had them to spend Christmas Day with us but no means of transport at all. This day has been very busy. Mother and Christine cooking, Kath and Alice cleaning and myself making last-minute cards, packing bags and parcels for different people, peeling potatoes for tomorrow, and so on. Thank God for work to keep me from fretting and worrying.
This morning we saw three planes in the sky. RAF we knew, and it cheered us. We could watch their movements, though they were very high, because they were trailing smoke. The Germans shot a little, but they were wide of the mark, thank God. But after they had gone, the Germans started a terrific shooting. I was in the big shed and was quite scared to hear the shrapnel falling on the roof, so did not dare move till all was over. Alice arrived, loaded with presents for us – how she manages, in these days, to find all those nice things for us, I don't know. She has given me a lovely small copper kettle, which Aunt Jane had had given but never used. I look forward to making tea for Alfred and me. Dear Alfred, how I love him, I cannot believe that anything could really go wrong between us.

*Dec. 25th. CHRISTMAS DAY.* Weather extremely mild. Another Christmas Day is over, the sixth since Alfred went away. How I have borne these long years of separation, I don't know. I hardly dare think about it. It is no wonder poor Alfred has faltered under the strain of it. If only I could be with him, all these years he has wanted and needed me. I dreaded this day, but God has given me strength and I have not felt too sad or anxious, but confident that all will be well. I'm disappointed not to have had news through Germany or France, but letters are bound to be delayed at Christmas time. In spite of Occupation I've had some very nice presents. Kath gave me a lovely breakfast set – tea-cosy, etc. which she had embroidered herself. It was such a surprise and so beautifully done, that I could hardly find voice to thank her. Kath is so

159

good to do so much for me. Mother had made me an overall; dear Mother, who has so much other work to do. And Elsie has given me enough rationed wool to make a jumper and a pretty clip. Joy sent me a lovely pillow-case, embroidered by herself. Miss Marcus had sent a present for every one of us, how very kind.

One thing which has given me special pleasure, and helped me a lot, was a letter which Elsie had written for me to open this morning. At breakfast, I found it amongst my parcels. She had written to cheer me and it helped tremendously. But my heart-aches for Alfred in his loneliness. Mr Oliver Mourant here for dinner and tea. Raymond was here, whilst Laurence and Joyce spent the evening with Phyllis and Beryl at Les Nièmes. How fortunate they are to be together so much. I am glad Mr Mourant was here today, because he made me laugh so much with his jokes! It did me so much good to laugh, after all the tears I've shed (in secret). We played games with him too. Have prayed for Alfred again and again and wondered where he has spent this Christmas Day and how he is feeling about me.

*Dec. 26th. SUNDAY.*       Went to Bethlehem this morning. Afternoon preached at Six Roads, about 34 present. Felt very sad seeing the two Misses Skelton who have just lost their Mother. Chose Hymn 657, hoping it would help them, and had a special prayer. How I wish I could have comforted them. Death's so final. I have had them in mind all the evening.

*Dec. 27th.*       All the Vibert family here for tea and supper. Curfew was at midnight, as yesterday, but for Joan, it was at nine as she lives in the Military Zone. Just before tea, I felt awful when I saw the 'couples' arriving and I longed for Alfred to be with me too. A lump came in my throat and I felt I'd never be able to get through tea. So I went up to my bedroom and asked God to give me strength. I felt tempted to ask Him why I had to suffer this separation whilst the others see each other almost every day! As we played games in the evening, I forgot my trouble a little and it did me good. We had such a good game of Dumb Charades. Our side did Sunday and the other side did Cabbage. They acted so well, especially the cab scene, with Dad driving the horses and Mother being Mrs Ward going to preach! Also in the cab were Florrie Boulevard, acted by Joyce and Rev. Skyrme acted by Raymond. It was a cabful of preachers going to their appointments! Well, it did me so much good to laugh! How Alfred would have enjoyed that game.

*Dec. 28th.*       Had dinner at Montpelier – feel I must see Alfred's people every time I go to town, as they help me so. Spent an hour with Joy, then cycled back with Joyce. As usual, some young Germans in the valley rushed at our cycles to try and frighten us. They shouted and ran after us. Really, it is hardly safe to cycle that way alone. And I don't like all those foreigners about, some such strange-looking men. Where they come from, nobody knows. The Germans pick up men from the countries they occupy, and force them to work for them.

*Dec. 29th.* From six o'clock till ten we had young friends – the seven Le Brocqs from the Stores, the three Viberts, Doreen and Ruth Querée. So, with ourselves, we were 20 young people. They are all so nice and well-behaved. Laurence Le Brocq did some of his conjuring tricks!

*Dec. 30th.* Exactly six years ago that Alfred and I met at that Christmas Party at the Le Seelleurs. I feel helpless and frustrated, as I would specially have liked to send Alfred a message today but it is no use, the Red Cross would only return it.

*Dec. 31st.* Six years ago today Alfred du Feu phoned and asked for me. Said he was glad to have met me and wanted to meet me again. I had trouble to believe it was me he wanted, as I didn't think any young man would be attracted to a pale-faced creature like me! He has such a lovely voice over the 'phone, what novelists would describe as 'thrilling', and it was always the same! And it will still be the same. No letters from France or Germany yet, and I had so hoped for news, good news, before the New Year. About 1.45pm, we counted at least 40 RAF planes, high up. The Germans did not shoot. To see them makes us feel near to England, somehow! We are so lonely of the outside world, all shut up in this tiny Island! We have been the eight of us to Les Nièmes. The girls are sweet, especially in their own home. I can understand Laurence and John falling in love with them! We had such a pleasant time playing games. I am glad 1943 is over. We've had such bad news and shocks, and it ends, still leaving me in sadness, worry and suspense. But, thank God, still loving Alfred with all my heart, and still keeping my faith in God.

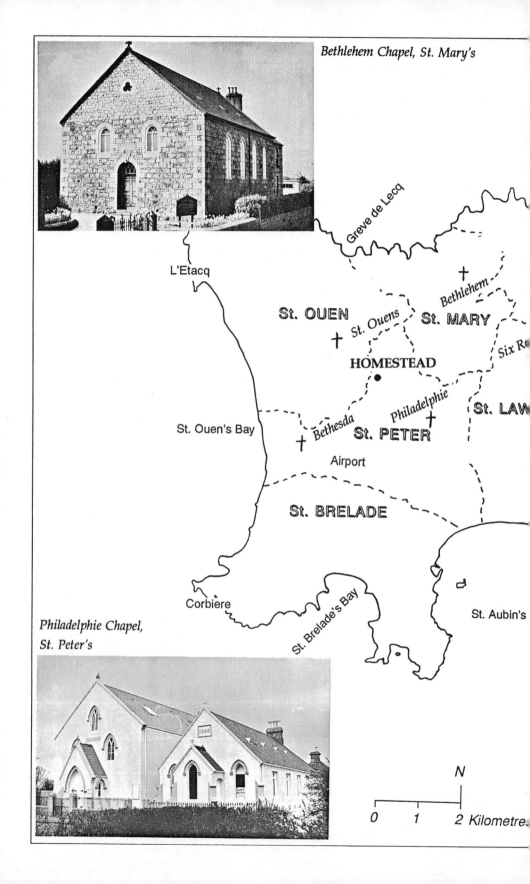

Bethlehem Chapel, St. Mary's

L'Etacq

Greve de Lecq

St. OUEN ✝ St. Ouens

✝ Bethlehem
St. MARY

Six R

HOMESTEAD ●

St. Ouen's Bay

✝ Bethesda

Philadelphie ✝
St. PETER

St. LAW

Airport

St. BRELADE

Corbiere

St. Brelade's Bay

St. Aubin's

Philadelphie Chapel,
St. Peter's

N

0    1    2 Kilometre

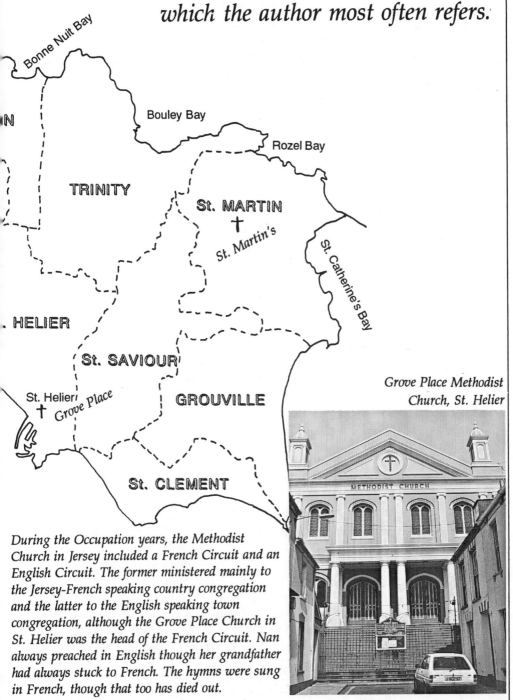

Outline map of Jersey indicating the twelve parishes, the location of Homestead in St. Peter's and the Methodist chapels to which the author most often refers.

Bonne Nuit Bay

Bouley Bay

Rozel Bay

TRINITY

St. MARTIN
✝
St. Martin's

St. Catherine's Bay

.N

. HELIER

St. SAVIOUR

St. Helier
✝ Grove Place

GROUVILLE

St. CLEMENT

Grove Place Methodist Church, St. Helier

During the Occupation years, the Methodist Church in Jersey included a French Circuit and an English Circuit. The former ministered mainly to the Jersey-French speaking country congregation and the latter to the English speaking town congregation, although the Grove Place Church in St. Helier was the head of the French Circuit. Nan always preached in English though her grandfather had always stuck to French. The hymns were sung in French, though that too has died out.

**1 9 4 4**

*January 1st.* We enter this year fully believing that we shall be liberated before its close, hoping even, that during its first half, we shall be freed, not only our island, but Europe. But, what bloodshed, what terrible things must happen before the enemy gives in. One feels afraid, one tries not to imagine how it will come to pass. Even here in Jersey, how will the Germans go? Will they harm us before leaving? Will the British land here? Will there be fighting? So we ask ourselves questions we cannot answer and feel thankful that the future is hidden! We pray that we shall be brought safely through to reunion with our loved ones. Feeling that perhaps the end of Occupation is very near, I would have felt so wonderfully happy at the thought of seeing Alfred, beside myself with joyous anticipation, but, instead, I wake with a feeling of sadness and anxiety. I am discouraged, bewildered and unhappy because I cannot understand what really is the matter with Alfred. Perhaps there is not so much cause for me to worry and upset myself as I imagine. Went to Montpelier for dinner. Afternoon, sat around the fire with 'Father', 'Mother' and Elsie and did some knitting, then we called next door, where, with other friends, we had a cup of *real* tea. How I enjoyed it! In the evening, Alfred's folk and I played Halma and Lexicon, after having had tea in the drawing-room.

*Jan. 2nd. SUNDAY.*      All went to worship at Wesley, Rosemary Howells accompanying us. She is a dear little girl, but with a will of her own! Mr Whiston preached. His service centered around Joshua 1, very helpful to me: 'Fear not, be not dismayed, I am with thee whithersoever thou goest, only be thou strong and very courageous.' Cycled home after dinner. Rained several times and wind very strong. Stopped several times to rest in Old Beaumont Hill, and to look at the lovely view of St. Aubin's Bay and its surroundings. God is full of beauty to create such wonders of earth, sea and sky. Then I felt sad and oppressed at the thought of Man's sinfulness, spoiling things. Felt terribly tired on my return, and was too late to go to chapel. Mother was home too. She is tired. I fed the rabbits, talked to Mother a few minutes, then lit the wood fire on the big hearth to get hot water, washed the dairy cans. Mr and Mrs le Rossignol were here till 9.50pm so I did not have time to do much reading. Glad to get to bed and rest!

*Jan. 3rd.*     Had letter from Uncle Gordon, dated November 29th, saying he had passed on my message to Alfred. He seems full of high spirits. I think he is hinting that the war will soon be over. It is rather difficult to make out his meaning at times. He tells us that Auntie Janet had a growth, and died of a haemorrhage after the operation. I still feel upset in thinking of her, she was so bright and full of fun, and I'll never be able to thank her for looking after Alfred on his return from Africa. I have replied to Uncle Gordon's letter. I felt he deserved it, for he says he had given two ounces of tea in exchange for a lettercard on which to write to me!
I was sad to hear that Cousin Frank Le Gros had died on New Year's morning. He was taken ill four days before and the young woman who looked after him did not tell his relatives until it was too late. I wish I had called to see him more often. There is a story going round that a German soldier shot his officer a few days ago, because the officer ordered him to shoot on British planes and he didn't want to. It is said also that 'White Russians' refused to shoot. These Russians are supposed to be with the Germans but I notice that they are never alone and there is always a German walking behind them with a gun.

*Jan. 7th.*     Dr. Shone told Uncle Ernest that he expects a collapse of Germany this month! Well, he is hopeful! How I wish he were right! The Germans look the same as ever here. I've seen plenty about town today, some singing as they marched up Hill Street. Called at Mrs Reis. She came with me to a milliner at Cheapside, to try and get a little hat made to wear with my coat. As I cycled home with Joyce I realised again the loveliness of Nature. The sun was like a flaming ball just dipping into the sea – a wonderful sight. The sunsets and sunrises all this time are very beautiful, and the weather is exceptionally fine.

*Jan. 8th.*     Very busy day. Christine` was out afternoon, so I was kept busy making the fire for boiling up sugar-beet syrup and heating water for the baths etc. What a job, with wood that is not very dry, and not too much of it either. Whenever my mind is not occupied the thought of Alfred comes and the desire to ask God to help him.

*Jan. 9th. SUNDAY.* My turn to stay in morning. Afternoon went to Bethlehem. Mr W Querée preached on Phil. 4 v. 5: 'The Lord is at hand. Be anxious for nothing, but in everything, by prayer and supplication, make your requests be made known unto God.' Everything was so helpful to me, his prayers and hymns; the last one was, 'Show me the way, O Lord, and make it plain, I will be patient Lord, Trustful and still.'

Rang up to see how Joy was. She is in bed with a very bad cold. I hope she won't have 'flu. Have heard that there is an epidemic of it in England. I wanted to write to cheer her, but have not found time, though I tried to find it.

*Jan. 10th.*　　Heard that hundreds of people In England died of 'flu in November and December, so now that has filled me with a terrible fear. We've not had a scrap of news from or about Alfred since his message sent to Montpelier on September 4th – four whole months. So much can have happened since then. Grant me faith, O lord.

*Jan. 12th.*　　I gave Alice a picture of Geraniums which I've painted for her Birthday on Friday. Went to town. Called to see Joy, who has been in bed for a week. Doctor has been. Had tea at Montpelier then went to Grove Place where I was speaking at a Young People's Fellowship Meeting. About 35 persons present, aged 14 years and upwards. The subject had been given to me : 'To love Him more dearly.' I had found it difficult to prepare, but God guided me, and the young people tonight were very attentive. I was glad when Mrs Ward told me she was glad to have been there. A word of praise from her means much to me in the way of encouragement. In another way she helped me – she whispered to me that Rev. Ward and herself keep on thinking about me and Alfred, and they were sure it will be all right between us. Mr and Mrs Howells and the two children left Montpelier this morning to live elsewhere, where they will have more room, but how empty the house seems without them, and how one misses Rosemary running up and down the stairs!

*Jan. 15th.*　　It is exactly three months today since the first of Alfred's disturbing messages came, months of suspense, anxiety and dread. I have strengthened myself through prayer and promises from the Word of God. Mother told me that I must wear my new coat tomorrow, but I will not. I cannot, whilst my heart is so heavy. When I've had good news from Alfred, I will wear it. Even then, I hardly like to wear anything so nice and new when, on the whole, others are shabby, having nothing new, because there is nothing new to buy! But poor Auntie Lulu had given Mother this mauve material years ago, and she had not used it. So she gave it to me because I needed a coat. Then I had no hat to wear with it, so Mrs Stagg gave me a navy blue one of hers. In exchange, I gave her a rabbit for her New Year's dinner. I've had the hat altered for myself. Now I have the hat and coat and I don't feel like wearing it. I have no pleasure in these things unless Alfred can share them! Physical separation from Alfred was bad enough, but it is nothing compared to this separation of the spirit. It makes me feel lonely and desolate.

*Jan. 17th.*     Last night I noticed a glow in the sky. We went up to the attic and could see that there was a big fire towards town. Today we've heard that it was at De Gruchy & Co. Again, caused by the Germans, who had taken over the bakery there. They have caused so many fires in this way, that one wonders if it is really by accident. The lovely Arcade is almost completely destroyed. Fire had taken a firm hold when discovered and it was some time before water was available, as permission had to be got from the Germans who hold the Waterworks!

*Jan. 18th.*     Mrs Syvret and Joan here for tea. They came with us to Bethlehem tonight when Philadelphie Guild gave us a repetition of their Christmas Sacred Concert. Very good. The play 'Outcasts' brought tears to my eyes.

*Jan. 19th.*     No news yet, how long this time of waiting and suspense is. The longer it goes on the harder it is to bear, and the more my anxiety grows. I cannot bear to think of the past five and a quarter years, of Alfred's loneliness and his disappointment at not being able to marry me in 1942, as we had hoped.

*Jan. 21st.*     Cycled to town. It did me good, going down Beaumont Hill fast – nice fresh air cheers me. Had dinner with Alfred's. We try to cheer each other up, but I can see Alfred's Mother is worried. She told me, as did Eunice and Gwen, whom I met in town, that Brian Le Boutillier from St. Martin's has just been imprisoned by the Germans and nobody knows why. After tea, on Sunday, he went to meet a girl and did not come home again. It was next day that they knew what had happened, when the Gestapo came to search the house, especially the boy's room. They must have arrested him on Sunday night. His family don't know what his offence is and what is going to happen to him. The Germans like to keep people in fear and suspense.

*Jan. 22nd.*     I'm thankful for two bits of news about Alfred which show that he is in good health, at any rate. Elsie had message from Ruby Dupré, who says, 'Cheerful news from Alfred, who is well and busy. And Mr Ph. Syvret phoned to tell me he had had a message from Lurline Dupré, who said that Alfred had received news of me through Amoore. This message was sent on October 6th. So Alfred must have been in touch with the Duprés and told them. It is quite cheering, because Alfred would not have written to them about me if there was anything seriously wrong.

*Jan. 23rd.*     My turn at home this morning. Went to Bethlehem afternoon. After service, Mrs Toy asked me if I'd heard from Alfred lately, saying she often thought about me, and how hard I must be finding this separation. She also said that she had told her little girls that 'Miss Nan' wasn't as usual of late, and she thought there was something wrong. I was startled to think that Mrs T. had noticed anything. I have tried so hard to be brave and to hide my pain and anxiety, but I suppose my face is bound to tell a tale. I sometimes wonder if this has made me look very old! I told Mrs T. that at Christmas-time I had felt the separation more keenly but that I'd had news yesterday indirectly, which had cheered me. John Pirouet and his fiancée, Betty Du Feu, who have just got engaged, came to tea.

*Jan. 26th.*　　Ruth R. came and brought the frock she has made for me out of rationed French material. John and Francis found leaflets dropped by the RAF during the night, just a little something to cheer us, even though they were printed for France, and not for us really. Tonight F H Joyce and I went to Mr and Mrs Alexandre and had a pleasant time (the Le B's from the Stores were there) their clock was slow and I knew it not – to my horror, 10 o'clock struck before we passed St. Peter's Church! Curfew is at 10 o'clock! I was afraid to be stopped by the Germans, but fortunately we got home without incident, though we met four soldiers. It is not easy or pleasant cycling in the dark and on a damp evening.

*Jan. 27th.*　　Cycled to town. Elsie and I went to the Syvrets. Frances had a party and the Brigade girls from Wesley were there, including Joy. We had a very enjoyable time. We had music and recitations, supper, then games till 9 o'clock. Back to Montpelier to stay the night and Elsie helped me with my knitting.

*Jan. 28th.*　　Left Montpelier early, visited several people before going home. Felt so tired pushing my cycle up Les Routeurs that I thought I'd never get to the top. Later, felt very sick as I was washing dishes and was sick, and had to go to bed. The cycle journey from town tires me – I always feel good for nothing when I get back.

*Jan. 29th.*　　Slept fairly well, but feel weak and worn out today. Stayed in bed.

*Jan. 31st.*　　I am not feeling too strong all this time, but I think good news from Alfred would bring back my normal health and strength. Today I feel much better than yesterday, and have kept busy. Taught Margaret, prepared vegetables, fed rabbits etc. and did some knitting tonight.

*February 1st.*　　Another month begun and still no good news of Alfred. Mrs S. has heard from Capt. Syvret through Germany. I am so glad as she gets so little news, and she is imagining that perhaps her husband was angry that she had stayed here. We can't explain anything till the Occupation is over. There seems to be quite a lot of news through Germany these days. I long for news, yet I tremble with apprehension. To think that in this time of crisis between us I can only send Alfred 25 words per month, open for all and sundry to read, which take months to reach him, or not at all. I am sad for all who are separated from one another in this way, knowing what it can mean.

*Feb. 4th.*     I've felt for the past few days that Elsie was keeping something from me. It must be hard for her as she had promised to tell me everything. I phoned her and forced her to tell me. She was afraid to upset me. She'd had a message from Alfred through a friend in Germany and he said, 'Tell Elsie that it is my desire to go abroad when the war is over.' It did give me an awful shock, because Alfred knows that I did not pass the medical for going to Africa. I don't know what he means and it was a reply to a message Elsie sent her friend last September.

*February 6th. SUNDAY.*     Lovely sunny day. I have thanked God for many things tonight. My prayers were answered in that I was given strength to preach, and I felt less worried about Alfred. Walked to Philadelphie with Dad and Herbert for 3.30pm service in schoolroom with about 45 present. Felt inspired and helped from the beginning as I preached my sermon from Rev. 3 v. 15 and 16. People thanked and praised me afterwards. I am afraid of praise, because it does not always mean that the sermon has done good. Elsie has been very good, she has come all the way from town to see me and had tea with us. She showed me the message from her friend in Germany. I did not feel like reading it. I think it is only because of the strange mood Alfred is in that he talks of going abroad. I think I shall send him a message telling him that I love him and will follow him to the ends of the earth, even if it kills me!

*Feb. 7th.*     Drizzly and dull but never mind, because I am so happy that I don't know what I am doing, for all is well between Alfred and me! My dear Alfred's love for me is as deep as ever. How did I get this news? I had been teaching Margaret and Dorothy, and had just gone upstairs when the phone rang and Mother and Kath called me: "Come quickly, Joyce Walker on the phone. Good news. Emily had just phoned Joy to say that she had received a post-card from Mr Curwood who had heard from Alfred who wanted me to know that nothing has changed between us, his love for me was as deep as ever, and I need not worry about anything. Also, he was anxious about my health." How wonderful it has been to hear this. It must be Alfred's reply to the message I sent him through Mr Curwood, when I felt so despairing. I phoned Rev. Ward and he is very thankful. "Thank God," he said, "An answer to prayer."

*Feb. 8th.*     We had great excitement at dinner-time. We saw a fighter plane which we took for a German as it was so low. Suddenly, terrific gunfire began from all quarters, so we realised it was British or American. Mother said: "Oh, I hope they don't shoot it down, and we looked anxiously out of the window, Suddenly someone shouted, "He's coming down by parachute!" We all rushed to the back field. Mother and I were just too late but Laurence saw the plane nose-dive to the earth and the pilot bale out and glide down by parachute. Mother and I were disappointed not to see it. Mother lost her slipper in the mud as she ran! It seemed as if the pilot had been trying to land at the Airport, for he circled it twice and seemed to make no attempt to escape. The postman told me the pilot had landed at Greenlands, not far from the Airport. He said his wireless was out of order and he did not know he was in occupied territory, poor fellow. He was wounded in the shoulder, by shrapnel, and is in hospital. Postman also, with a disgusted look, said that about 500 Germans rushed to the spot and all pointed their guns at that one solitary and wounded pilot. We feel so sorry he was brought down, but thankful he was not seriously hurt.

We have had our Sacred Concert tonight at Bethlehem. The schoolroom was quite filled. More news about the pilot, for the Viberts actually saw him when he was down. Beryl told me he was proper American, broad-faced and tall. He had black hair, and was very pale. The Viberts rushed towards him but could not speak to him alone as the Germans were arriving like flies! The American was smiling, and had just lit a cigarette. Someone said, "Hard luck," and he replied, "Oh, it's all in the game." The Germans who came from another area broke down Mr Jouany's door because they imagined they had hidden the pilot there and all the while he was in the custody of those at Les Nièmes. The Germans are so suspicious – they make one mad! The Commandant arrived later to fetch the pilot. It is amazing that poor man was not killed in the midst of that hail of fire. It was in parachuting that he hurt his shoulder a little. John was not well, the usual Occupation malady, and Dr. Lewis came to see him. He was so excited about the parachutist. He is supposed to have said to the civilians who first arrived, "Don't put yourselves in danger. It isn't worth it. It will soon be over."

*Feb. 11th.* I went to German Post Office and posted a letter to Mr Curwood, a parcel of onions and beans for Uncle Gordon and one for Mr Rodd in the same camp. I feel so grateful they have written to Alfred for me, especially as they are only allowed a certain amount of writing material. Went to the Wards. Mrs Ward knelt and prayed with me. More about the American pilot – Dr. Shone told Uncle Ernest that he had taken him a parcel on behalf of the Red Cross and was lucky enough to speak to him alone for a few moments. He said that his plane had been hit over France (he was not hit once here, in spite of all that firing!) and he was in difficulties. He had to land somewhere, but had lost his bearings and thought he was in British territory. That is why he made for the Airport and circled, preparatory to landing. Then, suddenly, he was shot at, so, realising he was over enemy territory, he managed to get his plane to rise, then he deliberately set fire to it, to prevent the Germans getting it, and came down by parachute. He did tell Dr. Shone that 'it won't be for long now'. I wish it wasn't for long! But it does show that they are hopeful in England.

*Feb. 13th. SUNDAY.*     Went to Bethlehem twice. Very good services with Rev. Fell and then Mr Arthur Querée preaching. Felt happier today and have worn my new coat at last! Mother was vexed with me because I would not wear it, but I wanted good news before.

*Feb. 16th.*     Emily phoned to say that she has received, through Paris, an actual letter written by Alfred on January 21st. to Mr Curwood. She read it to me. Alfred says that we know him well enough to know that we can trust him and that he would never let anyone come between him and me. And he hopes that when he sees me all his old affection will be restored, and he is doing what he can to make this possible. He is glad to know that it wasn't my fault about staying here. He says he did not know before receiving Mr Curwood's letter. So that is no doubt the cause of trouble – his inability to understand why I did not get away in time, which will have preyed on his mind, with our separation dragging on and on and us not being able to communicate properly. He has been disappointed in me and I in him; both of us, through not understanding. But I know God will help us, because we are both praying and doing our best. And I believed, from the first, that we were meant for each other. Mother tells me I need not worry now, but it is not easy.

*Feb. 18th.*     Mother said it was too cold for me to go to town but I felt restless and wanted to see Alfred's folk, so I cycled to town. Called first at Rev. and Mrs Fell to take a rabbit I had promised them. Had dinner at Montpelier. They cheered me. They have written a lovely message for Mr Rodd to pass on to Alfred and I am sure it must help him. Went to German Post Office and posted parcel of beans and shallots for Mr Curwood, and letters for him and Uncle Gordon containing my messages for Alfred. I do hope they will reach him soon. Went to see Mrs Ward and told her about the news through Germany. She was very satisfied. She helped me wonderfully and how I thank God for all that she is to me at this time. She knelt with me in the kitchen and prayed for my dear Alfred and me. Then, when we rose, she told me I must not worry and make myself ill like this, for she is sure God will answer all our prayers, and restore Alfred's love for me, and make all things come well between us. Saw Joy and her Mother, and Emily, and they all cheered me and said they feel pleased with the letters. So, as I cycled back with Joyce, I felt cheerful and hopeful and my heart full of love towards Alfred.

*Feb. 19th.* Granny was sick twice last night and gave Mother much trouble – washing floor, changing all her things etc. Granny was none the worse, her heart must be strong. I wish Mother did not have all that trouble. Busy day, cleaning, looking after wood fire, cleaning rabbit hutches etc.

*Feb. 20th. SUNDAY.* Cold and inclined to snow. Preached at Six Roads this morning. Congregation 30 but only nine adults. It is wonderful how God gives me strength to preach, in spite of all that I am going through. It is prayer that gives me strength.

*Feb. 21st.* I feel sad and anxious when I think of Alfred's parents, for the weather is very cold these days, and it is awful to think of 'Mother' being all day without a fire. She can only light it at six o'clock, when 'Father' comes back from the Office. The ration of wood is so small and often does not come every month, as it should. I felt like crying one very cold day last week when Elsie told me that 'Mother' was about town because it was warmer than staying at home.

*Feb. 22nd.* Granny's 87th Birthday. It would be a fine thing if only she were all right in her mind, but it is sad to see her as she is. Yet, physically, she is quite strong. Being in bed does not seem to weaken her. Mother has been anxious all morning because Francis and Laurence were walking our old bull to the abattoirs in town. They refused to fetch him even though they have a special cart. They were afraid of the risk and wanted to be bribed into doing it. So the boys walked the bull, and arrived safely. Our bulls are such dangerous creatures. And after all that trouble we are not allowed to have a scrap of the meat!

*Feb. 24th.* Margaret came for lessons afternoon and she and Leslie had tea with us. Leslie is 13 today. Grandpa frightened us during the night. He fell in his room and he made such a noise that we thought a bomb had fallen nearby. Dad and John put him back to bed but twice more Dad had to go and put him back. Today he has no strength in his legs. Dad washed him and we kept him in bed. It is very sad and such worry for Mother.

*Feb. 25th.* Elsie's 30th Birthday. I wonder if Alfred had remembered. I had dinner at Montpelier. 'Father' is in bed with a cold. 'Mother's' hands are in a shocking state through chilblains, and it hurts me terribly that she is all day without a fire. How people in town suffer!

*February 27th. SUNDAY.* Miss C. Alexandre here for dinner and tea. She was preaching at Philadelphie this morning and Elsie preaching there afternoon, so she came to tea also. Tonight I read another of Spurgeon's lectures, one on

'The Choice of a Text.' I find these lectures very interesting as well as helpful. I have prayed for Alfred many times today. Whilst I make the fire under the kettle for supper I pray and think of him.

*Feb. 28th.*    Last night about 11.30 there was a knock at the back door. Herbert bravely went down (one knows that only Germans and thieves are about after curfew) and found a drunken German soldier who had lost his way! Yesterday, one came begging for potatoes (they are very short of potatoes) and offered us sugar in exchange. Of course we refused, much as we need sugar! The German told John that he had a farm in Bavaria and was longing to get back, because he was wasting his life here. He had been several times on leave and said that everywhere in Germany there was decay.

*Feb. 29th.*    Bitterly cold wind. Girls here for lessons. Went to town, had dinner at Montpelier, then went on to take the Sisterhood meeting at Bethel where I gave a talk on 'The Shunamite woman'. Only 11 women present but such a nice homely meeting. Evening went with Elsie to Wesley Chapel where Rev. Quarrie (C of E) was speaking at the Guild. I was extremely glad of this opportunity of hearing him. He spoke on 'Temptation.' Two kinds of temptation: the one to wrong-doing, and the temptation (trial) of pain and suffering, which we often try to escape but is meant for our good. The tempatations of Jesus, he said, are the same as those which come to us – the world, the flesh, and the devil! If we take them in the right spirit, then angels will also come and minister to us, as they did to Jesus. Elsie presided and Joy and Emily sang a duet. Slept at Montpelier.

*March 2nd.*    Herbert's 20th Birthday. At dinner-time I heard the postman and went to the door. There was a Red Cross envelope for me. I hid it in my overall pocket until I had time to go upstairs. When I took up the grand-parents' dinner I went to my room. I found myself trembling as I opened the envelope. There were two messages from Alfred, replies to some I had sent months ago, and they were not too worrying after all, and Alfred put 'Love' at the end. I thanked God.

*March 3rd.*    Laurence's 26th Birthday. Dad in bed with a touch of 'flu and bronchitis and I have a cold coming on. Phoned Mr A Querée to ask if he could take my service at St. Ouen's on Sunday, and I'll take his the following Sunday when my cold should be better, I hope.

*March 7th.*    Dorothy came for lessons. Dad still in bed, and Mother in bed also. I am afraid she has a touch of 'flu. There is a lot about, though in a mild form, fortunately.

*March 10th.* Dr. Lewis came to see Dad and Mother. Dad has bronchitis and Mother has 'flu. Doctor said I am in for it too! He remarked that I had got very thin, saying, "I suppose you are fretting over that fiancé of yours." He startled me, but I did not tell him that he had guessed correctly.

*March 11th.* What a busy day. Eleven o'clock struck before we had even begun washing the supper dishes tonight. Dad and Mother don't seem to improve much and my cold hangs on but it is a blessing I'm well enough to look after the sick ones. Granny had given us plenty washing of nightdresses this week.

*March 12th. SUNDAY.* E P Ahier took my service at St. Ouen's as I was not yet fit. I was very sorry as it was Missionary Sunday, also at Bethlehem. Have been busy today looking after the patients. I do wish they would improve. Ever so many people are down with 'flu and pneumonia, and it worries one. I suppose it is the tail-end of what they've had in England. I do hope Alfred has continued to keep well.

*March 13th.* Have had a Red Cross Enquiry from Alfred, dated November 6th. It reveals how terribly discouraged he was. Also had a postcard from Mr Curwood – such a kind helpful message. How thankful I am for his help at this time. He has written to Alfred and is doing his best to help him. He tells me I must not worry. He trusts me to have faith in my Heavenly Father. (Later) Joy has phoned with very unexpected news – Mr Curwood is on his way to America! He is being repatriated. It has come as a shock to Emily, and a disappointment, because now she won't get news of her brother, nor about Alfred from that source. My last letter won't have reached Mr C. and Alfred will not get my reply to what he wrote to him. I have been thinking and praying for Emily. Yet one must be thankful that Mr C. is free and will be safe Mother and Dad worried us by still looking so ill so I called in the Doctor. We are relieved that he does not find them too bad but they must remain in bed at least two days more. Dr. Lewis said that the epidemic of 'flu and pneumonia is turning serious. It makes one very anxious, for everyone is below par through lack of good nourishment. Mr Frank Luce is very bad with pneumonia. We only knew today and Francis has been to see him. If only this bleak dry weather would change. One longs for a drop of rain. The ground is dry and white. It has been a very busy day. We had lit the copper, then Irene did not come, so Kath did some washing this morning. My cold is not better yet. Mrs Syvret very kindly sent a tin of grapefruit (pre-war) for Mother to try and tempt her to eat. Miss C Alexandre phoned to thank us for the drop of milk etc. we had sent her sister, who has been very bad too.

*March 14th.* Mother seems a little better but improvement is slow. I phoned Emily and offered to try and get a message through Uncle Gordon and Alfred to Tom, her brother. She told me that the Germans gave her Uncle and the others no warning. They left at 6am from the camp in a blinding snow-storm and told they were going to the States.

*March 15th.* Dad and Mother a little better but still in bed. Alice here; how we look forward to seeing her each Wednesday. Evie called, her visits always cheer us! Mr Luce died this afternoon, his heart could not bear the strain of pneumonia. He was only 73. I am sad for Mrs Luce and Madeleine. Nearly all the men in the neighbourhood are in bed with 'flu. A good thing Dad went to bed as soon as he felt bad.

*March 16th.* Mother got up this afternoon. We lit a fire for her in the sitting room. Dad still in bed. People are taking so long to pick up. We have all felt anxious about our parents.

*March 17th.* A few deportees from the same camp as Uncle Gordon (Laufen) have returned to the Island today, presumably because they are old. I wish Uncle Gordon had thought of sending us some message through them.

*March 18th.* I had such a disappointment today. Postman brought a parcel and I thought it was the one we were expecting from Uncle Gordon. But it was the one I sent to Mr Curwood on February 18th. If only I'd sent it a week earlier Mr. C. might have had it. It is very surprising that the Germans have sent it back, and intact. I sent it to Emily for herself! She has received a card from her Uncle, dated March 1st, written in a train at a small station, where, he says, they have remained for days – very cold, and not allowed to move from the train. But it seems that, somehow, he managed to give this message to some woman or child on the station, and it had been addressed and posted for him. It wasn't even a proper post-card. I feel sad to think of Mr C. there, in danger through cold, bombs and, who knows, very little food. It is worrying for Emily. My stupid cold not yet better – have had an awful headache all day, but had so much to do that it prevented me from thinking too much about it! Joyce in bed all day. Mother and Dad improving and Dad down for dinner. I've missed going to Montpelier these past weeks.

*March 19th.* Reggie Jeune had dinner with us. I had asked him to take my preaching appointment at Bethlehem as I was not fit to do it. This is the third Sunday that I've not been well enough to go to chapel. I expect that I'm pretty well run down! Hardly any time to do any reading today as there was so much work to do. We took Dad and Mother their dinner in the sitting-room and Joyce was still in bed. Every Sunday I pray for the services that Alfred is taking somewhere, and for God to lift him out of this depression and bitter-ness.

*March 21st.* Today, we have been delighted to receive Uncle Gordon's parcel – what a lovely parcel! The tears rushed to my eyes when Mother opened it. It is the first time Uncle Gordon gives us anything! And then, to think that all those lovely things have come from England. Uncle has saved all that for us from his Red Cross parcels, and all things that we need so badly. The contents were: five tablets toilet soap (real good soap), three tablets 'camp' soap (like the Russians used to bring us), two half-pound packets chocolate, three quarter-pound packets chocolate, two half-pound tins margarine, one quarter-pound tin Nescafé (had not seen this before), five quarter-ounce packets of tea, six packets of ten cigarettes, eleven packets sugar, amounting to three pounds and three tins (quarter-pound) of Rowntree's cocoa (Mother was just longing for cocoa) altogether weighing ten pounds. It is wonderful to get all this. Some of the things come from Canada, some from Buenos Aires, some from the 'Homeland'. It makes one long for England.

*March 22nd.* I've been to Les Potirons and had tea with Aunt Elize and Evie, my first outing for three weeks! I'm glad to be feeling better at last. I wish Mother looked stronger. Both she and Dad are still weak. When we were talking about Granny and Grandpa and Mother not being very strong, Evie said what a good thing I was in Jersey for she doesn't know what Mother would have done. Yes, for Mother's sake, I feel very thankful to be here as she has had so much anxiety and sorrow since the Occupation that it has sapped her strength, I know, though she never says anything. But oh, for Alfred's sake, I ought to be in England. For his sake, I am terribly sorry. For me, at present, everything seems awful and bewildering.

*March 25th.* Kath had her turn to be poorly in the night and I got up to help her. After that I couldn't sleep, thinking of Granny and Grandpa, the sorrow and worry Mother's had these past years, her not being too strong, Kath not being too strong, myself feeling tired and upset about Alfred, the war, the Occupation – everything was weighing on my mind, so it was nearly 6am when I got to sleep. How black things look in the night because when I got up after so little sleep and was getting breakfast, I felt much better!

*March 26th. SUNDAY.* Warm sunshine. Went to Sunday school again and to both services at Bethlehem. Rev. Struthers dined with us today.

*March 29th.* Mother's 60th Birthday. I wish she were ten years younger. Dear Mother, was there ever any Mother as good as she. I think not. I pray that none of us may ever disappoint her, and that she may live to see us all settled and happy, and that we may give her much joy. I pray that my Alfred may be to her as a son, that all her confidence in him may be restored when he comes home again, for she loved him from the first. Had dinner at Montpelier. Heard that Mr D, from the Red Cross Office, has been sacked. So I'm very thankful he won't be seeing any more of Alfred's messages or mine! I wonder why he's been sacked?!

*March 31st.* One is thankful March is over. It's been a bad month: not one drop of rain all through, much illness, pneumonia, 'flu, jaundice, tonsillitis and more cases of TB. Everyone feels tired, physically and mentally, and many people complain of loss of memory. And I've had a cold dragging on, which got me down. Tonight I came across a lovely message which Alfred had sent me in November 1942 and I realised again how much he loved me and how much he has suffered because he could not see me, or touch me, or talk with me. (I had been looking for Red Cross envelopes, as the Bureau are asking for them to be returned, as they can't get any more from Geneva, so must use the old ones again and again!)

*April 1st.* Good rain began about 7.30am. How lovely to hear it falling against the windows at last. But terribly cold, sleet and hail also. Elsie phoned, like she does now every Saturday afternoon to cheer me up!

*April 2nd. PALM SUNDAY.* Went to Sunday School and service this morning. Cold and foggy, then a lovely afternoon, sunny with a warm wind – how quickly the weather changes here! So thankful it was fine for our special service this afternoon. It was a new venture for us – a Flower and Egg service! I'm so pleased that it has been very successful. Our Sunday School children so enjoyed bringing their gifts and walking round the chapel with them. Some of their eggs and flowers were very tastefully arranged in baskets and boxes. Mrs F. Le Feuvre stood in the rostrum and received them, and Miss Ethel and I arranged them on the table. The choir sang: 'The Morning Breezes Softly Blow', that lovely Palm Sunday hymn from our S S Hymnal, as the children walked round. Then they lined up and sang: 'Here Lord, we offer all that is fairest', Rev. Scott gave the address and we had a few items by the children. We were agreably surprised at the number of eggs. I did not expect many, as they are so scarce these days. But we had eight dozen! So we've added the rest to make one hundred. How many sick and aged will have a pleasant surprise this Easter! There are some who can never get an egg at all, especially in town. We've made the children write their names on the eggs they brought, with Greetings. I feel very happy tonight about this service, and I so love seeing, and being with our boys and girls. On the whole, we have very sweet children at Bethlehem.

*April 3rd.* Pouring rain all day, will do much good. But it was too wet for anyone to cycle to town to take eggs. Had a letter from Mr Rodd thanking me for my parcel.

*April 4th.* I am trying to think out a sermon for Easter Sunday but I'm full of hay-fever. I've been very disappointed not to be well enough to go to town today to help Evie and the others to take the eggs. They went to Bella Le Breton's home and to Mrs Ward who will have 30 to distribute amongst the needy. And 40 were taken to Sandybrook Home for the Aged and Infirm. Mrs Walker phoned and said that Joy was not at all well again, so Mother has sent her milk, eggs and flour etc, hoping it will help, and I wrote her a little note.

*April. 5th.* 'The crisis is approaching with giant steps' so the Germans say in large print on the Paper tonight. This was supposed to have been said by Goebbels. They realise things are going badly for them; they can't stop the Russians now. But they would like us to believe that they are the defenders of all Europe from Bolshevism.

*April 7th. GOOD FRIDAY.* This morning I preached at St. Ouen's Chapel, congregation 23. Spoke on 'The Seven Words on the Cross.' Auntie Florrie and others told me they had been much helped. This sermon was inspired by a book I had read last Easter which was very helpful to me called *The Testament of Love.* This afternoon Kathleen and I walked to Val de la Mare and had tea with Mrs Syvret, who had also invited Miss F Hacquoil. What a character she is! Tonight we all walked to St. Ouen's chapel where an augmented choir gave solos and choruses from 'The Messiah.' The Girls Vibert and John were helping. We've heard that a German plane crashed in an orchard near Eden chapel last night and that many people saw it pass on fire. A blessing it did not fall on a house.

*April 9th. EASTER SUNDAY.* Preached at Galaad tonight on St. Luke 24 v. 26. Only 40 present, including 13 children. Congregation very attentive. I felt very much helped by my own sermon! Francis came with me as it would not be wise to come back alone through that lonely valley. We came back by Sandybrook. What a lovely view from the top of the hill! How beautiful Jersey is – the sea looks so lovely and yet it is so cruel, dividing my beloved from me.

*April 10th.* Went for dinner at Montpelier. Elsie and I cycled to see Doris Perchard. She seems very depressed. She says it is so hard to see that those who do wrong prosper and have everything they want and those who do their best to live rightly have the hardest time. She sees her neighbour entertaining the Germans and getting food from them and so on! Poor Doris. She is discouraged and feels at times that it is useless to try. I asked her if she would feel happy if she gave up doing right, and she said "No!" She is terribly, abnormally, nervous of Germans and of planes. I think the shock of the Evacuation and Occupation in 1940 told on her. She has a good husband and two dear little boys and I wish she were not so downhearted. Elsie and I stayed by the fire tonight, for I felt in need of a rest. We read each other's sermons, knitted, spoke about Alfred and I read a little from *The Vicar of Wakefield*.

*April 11th.* Called to see Joy, who doesn't look very well yet. Then on to Mrs Ward where I had a very helpful talk with her. She told me it isn't often she feels depressed about things, but the other day she did about the war. Then came to her the words: 'Without faith, it is impossible to please God', and that brought her to herself! She prays and believes that God will bring us through to victory. The trials of the British, especially now in Italy, she says, are a punishment, a just retribution, for failure to act aright about the League of Nations – something which she explained but which I don't understand, not knowing much about politics. I wish I knew my history better. I must read it up! Rev. Ward came in and said the news was better. In town this morning, I popped into St. Mark's Church. It was beautifully decorated for Easter and alone there in the solemn quietness I knelt at the altar and prayed. This afternoon I went into St. James' Church in passing and did the same. I wish our chapels were a little more like a Church. I don't like ceremonial but I like a building that creates the atmosphere of reverence. Came home at 5pm. The sun was so hot it made me tired coming up the hill. Fetched food for the rabbits on the side of the German track in our field. Tonight Joyce and I went to the Guild at Bethlehem. We had been asked to give a short item, so I had learnt a short recitation as I cycled home.

*April 12th.* Mother has a cold and has stayed in bed all day. I fear she has tired herself. I am so afraid she will be ill again. Dad has told me something cheering. He has been told that the Germans are dismantling all the hangars etc. at the Airport. An official came last week (when we saw a bomber accompanied by fighters – a rare sight of late) and is supposed to have said that the Airport was not suitable for the three hundred planes they intended to keep here, so to clear the Airport. There is some truth in the story, for the hangars are being dismantled and the material taken away; only a few days ago, some hangars were only just being finished.

*April 13th.* I have received a loving message from Alfred, a reply in his own hand and he has actually addressed me as 'Darling'. For six months I have pined for this loving word from him and it is so good to see it there on the Red Cross message. And I don't think Alfred would have written something he does not mean. He also says 'Look after yourself' and 'love.' This was written on November 22nd, before Alfred had received anything from Germany. Mother has had a message from Cousin Henry, dated June 1943, a reply to one we sent him in November 1942! Mother had a message from Uncle Bert. His signature looks ever so shaky. When we get his messages now

179

we feel the loss of Auntie Janet afresh. I am anxious for Mother today; she is in bed again. I see on the *Evening Post* tonight, in large print: CHITTAGONG THREATENED. It makes one feel very anxious about Cousin Henry who is there. I pray God to keep him safe it would be another terrible blow for Mother if anything happened to him. Finished my sermon after tea. Last night and tonight, we were ploughing and it was 10 o'clock when the men came in from the field, so it was midnight before I turned out my light. I've sent a message to Alfred to show him that his message of November 22nd. gave me new hope and life.

*April 16th. SUNDAY.* Mother in bed all day. Preached at Bethlehem this morning. Only 31 present, including children, owing to rain. It is Lord's Day Observance Sunday, so my text was from Exodus 20 v. 9. Lucille flattered me by saying that she was sure no better sermon had been preached in all our chapels today. But I don't believe her! I wanted to add another point to my sermon but it would have been too long. I wonder if I could condense my sermons more. I wish I had a better command of the English language. Took my turn to stay in tonight. Washed dishes, went upstairs to talk to Mother, read for about 20 minutes from the *Life of Henry Fawcett*. The evening passes so quickly. I lit the fire on the hearth for supper, and as I sat there blowing on the fire, waiting for the kettle to boil, I prayed for my dear Alfred. It is awful not knowing what he is doing and where he is going each day, and so not being able to share in his life in any way.

*April 17th.* Mother still in bed. I don't quite know what is the matter and am anxious. Saw Mrs Syvret today who told me that Capt. Ahier had sent a message to his wife which said: *Cheer up, the harvest will be a very good one this year.* That certainly sounds good; as Mrs S. told me: "They must know something we don't know!" And Mr Le Feuvre from Perry Farm told her that he expects the Invasion within the next fortnight. Of course, he does not know any more than we do but those remarks help to keep one hopeful! Have been so thankful to hear that Emily has had news from Mr Curwood from Spain! Says he arrived there after exciting journey through France and had just had a meal of roast beef, ham, oranges and bananas (makes one's mouth water!) and was on his way to Lisbon. I thank God he is safe, so far. I wonder if he is in America by now and perhaps in touch with Alfred.

*April 18th* Phoned Doctor for Mother. Whilst we were having dinner, Mrs B. came scrounging for rhubarb. To hear her talk puts one into fits of laughter. I feel like thanking God for people who are a little bit odd. It does one so much good to laugh!

*April 19th.* I've had unexpected good news of my darling Alfred. A letter from Mr Rodd of March 21st with a message he had just received from Alfred for myself and his parents. He writes like my Alfred of old, and especially I like this bit for me: *The nicest kittens in the world are not half as nice as the one at Homestead, and that is the one he will want in his Manse.* How lovely that he should use that playful term for me again! It is himself coming back to me. He also says that we must not be perplexed or distressed about the previous messages. Also, that he is leaving Matlock in September and has had four invitations, but nothing is decided yet. Will we be together in September? I can't bear to think of him going into that Manse alone.

We've had a day full of visitors. Alice here all day, as usual. Afternoon, Mrs S Le Brocq and three daughters came, and just as I had made tea for them (real tea, from Uncle Gordon) Mr Malzard and two other men came, then Rev. Scott. They drank up my tea and I could not offer Mrs Le Brocq a second cup! So, at that hour, we were 20 people in the house. And Ruth Reed called tonight. Mrs Le Rossignol told us that there has been a mutiny amongst German soldiers here and that 200 have been imprisoned. There was a Military Tattoo in the Parade at 10 o'clock tonight and the Germans put the curfew at midnight so that civilians could go, I hope nobody went! Anyway, it rained tonight. Joyce came back from town with a fine joke. She asked me: "Have you heard that the Gestapo is going?" I said, "No, why?" She said, "Because there is no crime 'ere!" (The Germans have lost most of Crimea lately).

*April 20th.* Have written a long letter to Mr Rodd enclosing message for my dear Alfred. I can hardly realise that good news has come at last. John had to go before the Commandant at College House today. They keep on calling young Jerseymen to work for them. Thank God, John was all right being employed in farm work, but it is hard for others. They say some are being put to demolish hangars. From six to seven o'clock tonight, there was very heavy bombing from the direction of Cherbourg. Our house and windows shook dreadfully. We also heard planes and we could see them, high up, shining like stars in the sunshine. The Germans only shot a little. We always feel excited when British or American planes pass. It brings England nearer. Have felt angry with E. who came to visit Mother (who is still in bed) and upset her by telling her that she was sure the Germans were going to take away the Jersey boys. Is that the sort of thing to tell a sick Mother? And she does not know more than anyone else.

*April 21st.* Went to town. Called at the Wards to tell them my good news. They were so thankful. Rev. Ward was in bed with one of his malaria attacks (relic of his time in Africa). He feels very tired and told me it was time he retired. Poor man, he's had too much worry for a man of his age. I pray they may soon be reunited with their children in England. Mrs Ward and I knelt beside a chair by the bedside, and she prayed and thanked God and asked him to bless Alfred and me. Came home with Joyce. Uncle Edward here, as usual on Fridays. Had tea, washed the dairy cans, fed rabbits, fetched grass, etc. for them on the 'track', and cabbage leaves. Evie here seeing Mother. Made fire for our supper, had supper, washed dishes, prayers, bed, and very thankful to have a nice comfortable bed to sleep in. Feel so tired now after cycling to and from town. I wonder what Alfred has been doing today? And how he has been feeling? For it is six years ago today that he gave me my engagement ring. I can't bear to think that it is so long ago. I must look forward and not back!

*April 22nd.* The doctor said Mother should stay in bed till Wednesday. I feel reassured because he says Mother will be all right when the Occupation is over and she can get more sugar. Doctor noticed a large handful of silvery stuff which we had found yesterday and we did not know what it was. Doctor told us that the RAF drop it to prevent the radio location from operating. Everyone was excited about this strange stuff – some said it was part of a Birthday wreath for Hitler! Mrs Moses Du Val called to bring Mother a pot of jam. How kind people are. She had heard that Mother was ill and longed for jam. Mother is always helping people, but she often tells us that it all comes back, that as you do to others, so they do to you. But it is lovely and cheering to be the recipients of little deeds of kindness, especially in these dark days when some people are showing a very ugly side to their characters.

*April 23rd SUNDAY.* Went to Bethlehem morning and evening. I am disappointed that Mother is not so well today, she hasn't eaten at all. It is worrying.

*April 24th.* Felt quite nervous during the night hearing planes passing all the time. I put on my engagement ring and went with Mother till they had finished passing. One has crashed at St. Ouen's, so we know there is always that danger. I asked Dr. Lewis to come – he says Mother's liver is temporarily enlarged. I hope it is not serious.

*April 25th.* Mother the same, ate no food and only drank a little skim milk. We kept Joyce at home as Irene is ill and could not come to do the washing. So Joyce and Kath spent all day in the wash-house! (No joke making the copper boil these days). We have decided that Irene should have more pay! Plane came over and made huge smoke trail again.

*April 26th.* Doctor found Mother improving and she has eaten a little. I think she has just escaped jaundice. Leaflets were dropped by RAF last night – boys picked up 45. Luckily they were not seen doing it!

*April 27th.* Sound of planes and heavy bombing all day. Planes dropped lots of that tin-foil again and a big piece of brown paper fell at John's feet at

Westfield. Rev. Struthers and his wife called and told me their children had found a whole boxful, complete, of that tin-foil. People are getting excited – they think invasion is on the way. And Rev. S. told me that he did not think I was too hopeful in thinking of being able to join Alfred in a Manse next September!

*Polish carts brought over by the Germans.*

*April 28th.* Christine's 25th Birthday. Uncle John Le Brocq, her godfather, here for tea, also Uncle Edward. Heavy bombing heard again and planes passing, morning. It is almost continuous now.

*April 30th. SUNDAY.* Very full day and no time at all to do any reading, which we like to do on Sundays. My turn to stay in morning. Washed dishes, did Mother's and Granny's bedrooms. Dinner, washed up, fed rabbits, cycled to Tabor to take the afternoon service. Enjoyed cycle ride, sunny and not too hot. Countryside lovely, fields covered with buttercups in the lane going to the chapel, beautiful sight! Noticed that several hangars at Airport were down – good sign! Got back in time for tea. Washed dairy cans then cycled to Bethlehem, arriving 15 minutes late, for service! Usual chores when I got back.

*May 1st.* Doctor found Mother improving though her heart is still beating too fast. We must take care of our dear Mother. Went to see Alfred's folk. Then went to Plumley's to have my hair permed (£2.2s.) for I hope to see Alfred soon and want to look nice. A year ago I did the same thing, for the same reason, and instead of seeing him, I've had anxiety and grief, and just as upsetting. The faith of both of us is being sorely tried.

*May 3rd.* Dorothy and Margaret started lessons again today. I really haven't got time to teach them, though I like doing it. They will start school as soon as the Occupation is over. We had a lot of callers this afternoon. Mrs Smurthwaite who came to fetch 'beestings' [milk from a freshly-calved cow]; Mrs Le Rossignol and Emmeline who came to see Mother; Mrs Du Val who wanted me to sell her some six-week-old rabbits, but I haven't any to spare; Mrs Berry who came to fetch a sitting of duck eggs; and Miss Winnie Arthur and Rev. Scott to see Mother

*May 4th.* Dorothy did not come because the Germans were practising sharp-shooting and she is nervous. (Well, so am I; I hate guns!) Had tea with E. and P. and heard the usual depressing remarks: "Your mother is failing, you aren't looking very well," and so on! It is no good expecting to be cheered up when one goes there. As for the war, it looks as though the Germans will always be here, I was told. I get fed-up with such remarks, because it is hard enough to keep cheerful. I've written to Uncle Gordon today; I wonder if he's heard from Alfred again.

*May 7th SUNDAY.* Fine, but bleak and cold. At Bethlehem Rev. Ward preached on the Story of the Emmaus Road. I do enjoy his sermons. Reggie here for tea. Francis, Herbert and I went to the Sunday School Anniversary at St. Ouen's chapel tonight. There were over 600 people there, counting those on the platform and in the choir.

*May 8th.* Margaret and Dorothy here for lessons this morning. Alice and Kath did the washing. Tonight Beryl and I (John joined us later) cycled down to Blanc Pignon as Mrs Resch wanted us to see the garden etc. She and her Mother took us to the top of the 'mountain' (as I always called it!) where, in the dear old days before the war, I had often walked with Joy – I don't like to see anyone else in possession of this lovely place! Then we saw the animals – the piebald ponies, a lamb with its mother, the cows, rabbits, dogs, etc. Everything so well-kept. Then we had a cup of tea and some food before leaving. We got back just before curfew! The moon looked lovely over the sea. Planes passed last night and dropped more silvery stuff – people say the birds are making their nests with it now! Doctor came, said Mother is getting on but her heart is still too fast. He is fed-up with French drugs which he says are not reliable. He longs for 'good British stuff.'

*May 9th.* Mrs M. Du Val came to see Mother, then I took her around the farm. She asked me about Alfred. I was glad to be able to say that I had had news through Germany. Thank God that Alfred has never stopped sending messages, even if he has felt bitter against me, because what would I have said when people ask me about him? The Germans seem to be expecting the Invasion, perhaps tonight! Constable du Val told Dad that they have posted a guard at all the telephone exchanges. And Irene told Herbert yesterday that they had put pillars all over Grève de Lecq beach, but this morning the sea had washed them away. So today they were putting more, digging them more deeply into the sand. Supposed to be to prevent the British landing. Irene's husband, who was fishing, laughed at them.

*May 11th.* Afternoon I cycled to town with Evie, Lucille, Audrey Anquetil, Eunice le Hegarat and Phyllis to a Girls' League Rally at Grove Place. We couldn't go by St. Peter's or St. Laurence as the Germans were shooting with their big guns (practice). So we had to go by Sion and then down Queen's Road. Countryside very beautiful and it was sunny and warm. I enjoyed the ride except when we got to the top of Queen's Road when we heard a plane overhead. And as the Germans had anti-aircraft guns on high stands near the road, I saw them looking through their field-glasses and training their guns in the direction of the plane And they shot at it, but missed, thank God!
36 of us at Rally and we had different speakers telling us about their jobs and answering questions. I presided for the afternoon meeting and Lilian for the short evening one. We had all brought our own tea. Got back before 9 o'clock. Mr and Mrs Allan had been here to tea as they had to leave their house at Bel Royal on account of the shooting. It seems that the shells often fall short. It makes one nervous.

*May 12th.* Worked very hard this morning as I expected Joy this afternoon, and wanted time to see her. Taught my pupils, peeled potatoes, cleaned rabbit hutches, Granny's room etc. Joy came but I did not have much time to speak to her. Showed her the ducklings, chicks etc. then gave her tea with Mother in the sitting-room. A Miss M. from this parish came with cow-book. She told me that she also had not seen her fiancé for six years. She is five months older than I am and her fiancé, in England, is 35, so she is worse off than I am. Her Mother refused to let her evacuate. Evidently her young man has not complained (at least, she did not say so). Perhaps he does not find it so hard to wait as Alfred does.
Mr H du Feu told us that, on a piece of silver paper dropped by the RAF which his children found, there was a message written: *Don't worry, Jersey, won't be for long.* They were so excited about it! Some airman, doing his best to cheer us, how it helps. I've looked on all the pieces I've picked up, but there's no message on mine!

*May 13th.* Very busy in the house all day. There is much to do and one has no time to oneself. But I'm glad Mother is improving though I wish she got stronger more quickly. We have been so used to see Mother running about, always so active, that it is strange to see her quiet. Alfred's Mother has sent her her ration of fish: one tiny plaice and one tiny whiting (four ounces altogether). Dear Mrs Du Feu, we know they needed that fish badly themselves. It would be such a treat for them, and yet they send it to Mother.

*May 14th. SUNDAY.* Went to Bethlehem this morning. Joyce's friend Enid here for dinner and tea. Mr Howells here for tea also. Mr and Miss Trachy came to keep Mother company whilst we all went to Philadelphie where the Bethesda folk were having their Sunday School Anniversary because the windows at Bethesda chapel have been blown in by the German blasting nearby.

*May 15th.* Alice and I spent all day in the wash-house. How my back is aching tonight! But we got all the clothes dry. It was very cold hanging out though. Mother got a postcard from Uncle Gordon today. He says he has sent my messages to Alfred but it is forbidden to copy the exact words. Another disappointment! I did want Alfred to get my exact words. However, I know Uncle will have done his best, as I've done mine, so we can leave the rest to God. Last night we heard much noise of planes going to England, and I went with Mother until they had passed. How those planes make my heart beat fast – it is frightening and not good for Mother either. On Saturday Uncle Ernest lost a cow through eating too much fresh grass. Uncle was in town and Auntie phoned Francis to go and pierce her, but she was already dead when he arrived. So Uncle has managed to have the meat. (The vet had to tell a lie though – he had to pretend the cow was unfit to eat.) As always happens now, crowds of people heard about it in no time and this morning about 60 people either phoned or went to Westfield to try and get some meat! Uncle let us have a piece big enough for us to let a few friends have some. I was so glad to be able to give some to Alfred's folk and a few other friends. We've had to take several bulls and cows to the abattoirs and never got an ounce out of them, yet one last week, lovely meat. Then when our ration came, it wasn't fit to eat, half we didn't dare even touch. Who gets all the good meat we send?!

*May 16th.* Our one and only goose has been stolen in the night, together with two laying hens, and about 550 pounds of small potatoes. Laurence was feeding the poultry with these, so now he must sell some pullets and laying hens as he hasn't enough to give them. We 'phoned Centenier Egré but when he came he said it was no use doing anything, for he is sure the thieves are Germans. Two of them were prowling around our back sheds on Saturday and pretended that they were coming to do exercises. They are stealing everywhere now. They seem very short of potatoes and are always begging. They also seem to have no food for their horses. They put them to eat on our hedges, and even turn them loose in people's fields where they are eating precious grass which farmers are keeping for hay. People who have had poultry and rabbits stolen say that if a dog barks they shoot it, and if people come out, they point their pistols at them.

*May 17th.*     Our application to be allowed to keep two heifer calves has been refused and the boys are not pleased. It is a shame to have to kill good pedigree cattle, and one was especially lovely.

*May 20th.*     Heard planes and bombs in the night. A German ship was sunk. Laurence saw lots of small craft in St. Aubin's Bay searching for bodies and Germans were gathering wreckage. He was told that 70 bodies had been washed up. Poor fellows. Germans though they are, one can't help feeling sorry. It all seems so dreadful and wrong.

*May 21st. SUNDAY.*     Cycled to town to take service for the first time at Grove Place. Found it difficult to know how to pitch my voice, the chapel being so much bigger than those I usually preach in. Felt nervous at first. (I suppose I looked like a midget high up in that big pulpit!) There were about 100 present, about half being children. They were very attentive, both adults and children! There were at least seven other local preachers present! God gave me the necessary strength, especially as I had been feeling disturbed again about message Elsie had had from a friend in Germany, with less encouraging news from Alfred. Had a chat with Mrs Ward after service, which did me much good, as usual. Got home just in time for dinner and afterwards I washed up. Fed rabbits, helped Granny to wash, made her bed etc. Rested on my bed for three-quarters of an hour then it was time to light the wood fire to boil kettle for tea, cut the bread, etc. Mr and Mrs W Le Brun here for tea, also two nice boys, Norman Alexandre and Arthur Querée. After tea, rushed off to service at Bethlehem with Joyce and had to stay till 9 o'clock to practise hymns for Whit Monday. Time to get supper ready when we got back. What a busy day for us all, but Mother has so enjoyed seeing Mr and Mrs Le Brun. He is very hopeful, expects the invasion within a week or so. He is sure the British Government has not forgotten us and made plans to help us. He is grieved that there are some traitors in the Island. It does make one sad, but some of them may have been driven to it out of fear.

*May 23rd.*     We got up in the night when we heard a lot of machine-gunning and other gunfire. Something was going on in St. Aubin's Bay; we saw dozens of flares and everything was lit up. We are having a cake ration for the first time this week but those who've had it have given it to the dogs and cats! Our baker says it was made in France for the Germans and they don't want it; they've forced our States to buy it and it is no good. The ration is one ounce at sixpence. We are not taking it – don't want to be poisoned! This afternoon I pulled up faded Wallflowers in the Avenue and planted Zinnias.

*May 24th.* Went to town. It was Mrs Walker's Birthday and she had invited me to lunch. Miss Lottie A. and Emily were there. Joy put on the gramophone to play 'God save the King' and the window was open so I hope some Germans heard it!. We played Lexicon and Pit. Mother had let Joy have a little flour to make a Birthday cake and there were little bits of sugar-beet in it instead of currants and it was very good. (Not iced, of course). Got back about 7 o'clock, tired after the cycle ride. Evie and Mr and Miss Trachy were here and we all went outside to watch a swarm of bees enter the hive. We went to have a look at the sweet baby ducks and other of our farmyard birds and animals. I shall miss all this when I am married! Mr T. found my litter of 12 little rabbits and their mother very fine.

*May 25th.* John's 24th Birthday. My pupils did not come as we were too busy. Laurence and Herbert spring-cleaned Mother and Dad's bedroom under Kath's supervision. How much more easily the boys do it with their strong arms! Yesterday they did the girls' room. We girls couldn't manage alone this year. Visitors (five of them) came to see Mother this afternoon, so I could not do much, as I had to give them 'afternoon tea.' Visitors have to do with sugar-beet tea nowadays! I've received two Red Cross messages from Alfred today and they were not upsetting and so I feel cheered and must try not to worry. But one is very stale – he sent it last November 12th! The other was sent on 24th. He says he is longing to see me again, and much love.

*May 26th.* Laurence and Herbert helped to spring-clean another bedroom. Again I did not have time for my pupils. Irene came to see us. Her leg is still in awful state and she won't be able to help us this Summer. Sometimes I am tired of all this work and having no time to sit with Mother a little while or to read but all day long washing dishes and clothes, peeling potatoes, sweeping floors, getting meals ready downstairs and taking them upstairs to the grandparents and so on! Still, after all, it is bliss compared to the anxiety which I suffer constantly about my dear Alfred. I am so anxious about him, suffering so much from loneliness, and my not being able to explain anything.

*May 28th. WHIT SUNDAY.* My turn to stay in to cook, etc. Managed to get about an hour and a half free this afternoon, so rested on my bed and then read for an hour, from *The Meaning of Prayer* by Fosdick – very helpful. Went to Bethlehem with Joyce tonight but it was awful because I felt so tired and sleepy during service and I couldn't help it at all.

*May 29th.* Laurence and Herbert cleaned my bedroom and I polished pictures etc. but only the glass as there is no furniture polish to be had nowadays. It is strange to do spring-cleaning without polish. Tonight we had a Rally of the Wesley Guilds of the six chapels in the West held at St. Ouen's Chapel. It went on for too long and we had to close suddenly because of curfew – and those who live in the Military Zone had had to leave. The names of 'absent friends' from each Guild were read out and we prayed for them and sang the 'special' hymn which I find very hard to sing and there are others like me, so we pray silently, as our voice refuses to sing!

*May 30th.*     Thunder rolled in the distance all day – the dark, black and menacing clouds looked so beautiful whenever the sun came out. Joyce and I spent all day in the wash-house. Margaret came for lessons so I made her do them in the wash-house! In spite of the unsettled look of the weather we got everything dry, but how my legs and feet ache tonight. It is awful having to do such a big wash without proper soap. One cannot get things really white. We washed with our last piece of rationed soap which melted away before we had finished and left, as usual, the bottom of the wash-tray full of sandy grit! Strange soap, that does not make one bubble or one scrap of foam. I expect people in England have no idea how 'tight' things are here, especially as people try to keep their Red Cross messages cheerful so as not to worry their relations and friends. Just for fun, I counted the things Joyce and I washed today, though 'scrubbed' might be a better word! 6 large sheets, 11 bath and hand towels, 5 kitchen towels, 3 tea-cloths, 3 traycloths, 2 large table-cloths, 2 table-centres, 2 dressing-table covers, 5 pillow-slips, 50 handkerchiefs, 8 men's collars, 4 women's overalls, 4 men's long pants, 6 men's shirts, 4 pairs men's working-trousers, 1 man's vest, 4 large pieces blanket, 4 night-dresses, 2 Granny's nightgowns, 3 pairs men's pyjamas, 2 girls' vests, 1 apron, 3 milking-aprons, 4 roller-towels and 1 mattress cover. We used tar and cinders for the fire under the copper, as one can't get coal and wood is scarce. It seems a long list of washing and yet yesterday Kath had spent all morning washing all the men's socks, vests and short pants etc. so there was that less to do today. Well, all good training, I suppose. I'll be able to understand and sympathise with women who have large families!

*May 31st.*     Laurence helped to turn out the Grandparents' room, and the sweep came and did four chimneys. I had a letter from Uncle Gordon. He had no news of Alfred and he says the post from England has now been stopped so he cannot expect to hear from him. It is another disappointment!

*June 1st.*     Alice helped us to spring-clean the drawing-room. Stealing by the Germans goes on. A farmer in our parish had all his fowls taken (24), their heads chopped off and left in the poultry-run, and one pig. And potatoes are constantly being dug up in the night; the crop, too, is poor, as there has been so little rain. People are getting anxious and even talking about famine.

*June 3rd.*     So busy and late going to bed. At 10pm. Laurence and Herbert were still gardening and they still had to pluck a cockerel for tomorrow's dinner. Dad, Francis, Laurence and Herbert had yet to have their baths and everyone to have supper. Then dishes to wash and I had to prepare my Sunday School lesson. When it is still daylight the men won't stop working!

*June 4th. SUNDAY.* Went to Bethlehem for both services. Had not had time to prepare my Sunday School lesson properly, and I felt it as I spoke to the children this morning. Work is good, but too much is not so good!

*June 5th.* Today has come the good news that Rome has fallen into British hands and, what seems a miracle to me – intact, without any buildings being spoilt. It is really wonderful, especially that the two million or so people there are all unhurt. It must be a big blow to the Germans. I wonder if they will have another big blow soon (Invasion) before they recover from this one. But I am sure the Germans will never collapse without an Invasion of France. Alice and I have been all day in the wash-house. It is very tiring carrying in so many buckets of water, filling copper, keeping the fire going, getting things out of copper, rinsing (more water needed), squeezing, and hanging out in the back field. I quite enjoy it all but wish I were bigger and stronger and didn't get tired, then it would be a lovely day doing the washing. Alice was depressing today, talking about a 'Communal kitchen' where everyone will have to go for food, when there's no more gas or electricity, and about next winter and how hard it will be. It was no good telling her that we expected the British will have relieved us before next Winter. We certainly hope so.

*June 6th.* Francis' 30th Birthday and what a day! At last, the invasion of France, so long talked about, has taken place! We can hardly take it in yet. So far, everything is quiet and as usual here, except that one has seen very few Germans about today – just a few Dispatch Riders rushing by on motor cycles. They are all at their guns and under the ground in their fortifications. Last night, I hardly slept a wink, nor did Mother, as from the time we went to bed till this morning there were planes passing continually and terrific anti-aircraft shooting by the Germans. And the house was shaken constantly by bombing which we presumed was taking place around Cherbourg. I put on my engagement ring and hid my face under the pillow! I wondered if it was the Invasion at last, but when I heard the wind, I thought it would be too rough at sea. Then, soon after eight, Herbert came rushing upstairs. I had at last slept, from seven to eight, and was only doing my hair. Herbert's face was white, and all he could say was 'Invasion!' I burst into tears, but checked them. It was because I realised what it meant for the soldiers, sailors and airmen. And for the people of France, on the coast, who have been told to leave everything and go twenty-five miles inland. How terrible it all is. Then I thought of myself and Alfred and how it may mean that I may hear from him and even see him sooner than I had imagined. Surely our reunion will be wonderfully happy! The British have landed in Normandy. Will the Germans go away from here or will they stay? We pray there may be no fighting. There is a Proclamation on the *Evening Post* tonight:

> *To the population of the Island of Jersey:*
> *Germany's enemy is on the point of attacking French soil. I expect the population of Jersey to keep its head and to remain calm, and to refrain from acts of sabotage and from hostile acts against the German forces, even should the fighting spread to Jersey. At the first signs of unrest or trouble I will close the streets to every traffic, and will secure hostages. Attacks against the German forces will be punished by death.*
>
> > *Der Kommandant der Festung, Jersey.*
> > *(signed) Heine, Oberst.*

Well I hope people won't get excited and cause trouble. We shall easily remember this date, it being Francis' Birthday! We have celebrated both events by having 'real' tea for breakfast and tea. We had been keeping this small packet for an occasion that would be worthy of it! We also killed a young cockerel for dinner, and had some of Laurence's strawberries for tea, so have had quite a Feast day! But all the time, we pray in our hearts for the men who are even now giving their lives so that we might be freed. Herbert went to the secret 'box' and heard the King's speech, and how he has called the nation to prayer, and has spoken of being conscious of our shortcomings. I thank God for such a King, for one can have hope for our nation whilst its King is a believer in God and in Prayer. Heard that the Royal Square was crowded with people this morning who imagined that the Bailiff was going to make a Proclamation! Of course, he never turned up! We are not free of the Germans yet! However, Heine did not come out to read his Proclamation!

*June 7th.*    We had a more quiet night because, though we heard planes passing and heavy bombardment, the Germans did not shoot. Tonight the BBC announced that more landings had taken place on the Cherbourg peninsula, and two small islands off the peninsula had been taken! No names were given, but I didn't think there were any other islands but the Channel Islands in that area, so would it be Guernsey and Alderney? Anyhow, at present, we are feeling rather excited and thinking that perhaps parachutists will land during the coming night. We've been to the attic to fetch our Union Jacks just in case! Yet we realise how awful it would be if the Germans offered resistance. They are strongly entrenched at Coin Varin and other strong points. A German soldier told a Jerseyman today: *Anglais en France, bon pour vous, mais encore meilleur pour nous.* [The English are in France; good for you but even better for us.] Because they are fed-up and glad the British have landed in France at last!

*June 8th.*  We are not allowed to use the telephone since the landing in France, so it is difficult to contact anyone. Alice was quite excited when she arrived. She told us that on the night of the Landing the Germans came with lorries and cars, and brought guns to put on the slopes, and they put up tents in Mr Pirouet's field. But the strange part of it is that they are rejoicing! Alice said that last night they had a concertina and they danced and sang in H. Vibert's meadow from 8 o'clock till midnight and people could not sleep with the row. It looks as though they were pleased to be expecting the 'enemy!' We've heard that there are about two dozen ships in the bay and others in the harbour. We wonder what it means – do the Germans intend to go away in the night perhaps? We saw one solitary soldier (airman) pass this afternoon, with his long heavy coat and all his kit and rifle on his shoulder. We wondered if he was going away. He looked very glum and didn't turn round to look at us as they usually do. I even felt sorry for him – I thought: 'He is somebody's son, somebody's husband or fiancé.'

*June 9th.*  Things are quiet. One feels very solemn at the thought of the great battle that is going on so very close to us – only a narrow strip of sea between us and Cherbourg peninsula. We have discovered that there are two small isles east of Cherbourg, so these are the ones the British have taken. Margaret Querée's brother, about Alfred's age, was killed in the Mediterranean last February and the news has only just come through. One feels so very sorry. How cruel war is. Dolly de Gruchy's mother died this week, so Dolly will never see her mother again. I planted Ageratum in the Avenue and Fibrous-rooted Begonias in the back border. Uncle Ed. here for tea.

*June 10th.*  Some excitement several times today, when British (or American) have come over. Much machine-gunning at 6.15am. Ships in St. Aubin's Bay damaged and some sunk. Later, planes attacked the gun at Les Landes. The boys saw the bombers plainly from the field. There was plenty shooting, and the Germans say they shot down a plane, but it is not true. All day planes have been passing. It is strange not to see Germans walking about the roads as usual – they are all hidden, watching and waiting, I expect. Tonight we hear that they want 450 tons of our potatoes to ship next week! I suppose it is to feed their troops in France, but I don't think the potatoes will get as far, as things are. I wonder if the Germans still hope to drive 'us' out of France, and are staying here in the hope of it.

I hope that we shall not be too long here without news of loved ones. We seem to be almost in a state of siege – can't telephone to anyone, can't expect any Red Cross Messages, nor letters from the German prison camps. Curfew is at 10 o'clock, all theatres closed, dances and entertainments. I've got a nasty cold and I feel tired, sad and anxious, and I just want to lie down and sleep until I wake up with Alfred's arms around me!

*June 11th.* A very noisy night again, many planes passing and very sharp anti-aircraft fire. And I was thinking again about my having stayed here, and now I simply cannot understand our blindness in not realising in time how bad things were, and again, not realising at all what it would mean if the Germans did come, and how long it would be. I must try to believe that it was for the best, though it is hard to see it at times. Jersey is in the News though we should not know it. John has just told us that the BBC has announced that RAF planes attacked a Radio location plant on the Channel Island of Jersey and also scored direct hits on three mine-sweepers and on E-boats off Jersey. So that is what they were doing yesterday. It is so strange – there was a time when we saw scores of German planes and never a British, and now things are reversed and we know the British have not forgotten us!

*June 12th.* It has been a bewildering day for me. Alice and I were doing the washing, and, coming in for dinner, I found a letter from Mrs Walker awaiting me, with news that Joy is at Bon Air, having been operated on yesterday at noon for appendicitis. What a shock it gave me, and I am in suspense, as I can't phone. When one's friends are in any danger one realises how much one loves them, and one wishes one had appreciated them more and been more grateful for their love and kindness.
Planes have come and attacked ships in St. Aubin's Bay again. Then tonight, we heard the most awful noise and shaking that we had yet heard. Don't know if it was a naval bombardment, or what. I felt more anxious about Joy – that awful noise and shaking can't be good for people who are weak and ill. Some Germans are getting 'ratty'. A man told me that some soldiers had slapped two little girls in the face, just 'because they were British.' The soldiers are given cognac and champagne, Raymond's father told me, and that is why they sing. At Les Nièmes they were rejoicing and told him: *Nous sommes gai.* It is to prevent them from being depressed about the Invasion, I suppose, but one does not feel too safe going about now, especially as they are all armed and ready to shoot at any moment.

*June 13th.* The friend who had asked me some weeks ago to pray for her family came today and told me how much it helped to feel that someone knew of the terrible danger they were in, and was praying all the time. I feel so humble that I am honoured with their confidence. I haven't even told Mother – she would worry too much. This particular Russian is a proper Bolshevik, and has a very uncertain temper, which makes it all the more dangerous to harbour him, but these people are much too loyal to Britain to betray him. I pray so earnestly that they may come through safely. The danger will always be there until the occupation is over. Last night, the noise of planes and explosions kept one awake. The Germans are holding on hard in Normandy, and we know how strongly entrenched they are here in their underground bunkers and tunnels. They are not in a good temper; sometimes they spoil all they can – the hay and the crops – taking what they want, and trampling purposely on the fields. Buses are being curtailed and travelling on them is only by permit. Bread ration lowered, and some say, no meat at all.

*June 14th.*    It has been a very upsetting and trying day. At 9 o'clock I was just writing a note for Joyce to take to Elsie when suddenly the air was filled with the noise of gunfire of all kinds and of planes. I went to the attic, which I shouldn't have done, and I was scared for a shell exploded quite close and I heard falling shrapnel and a plane very low. The Germans were shooting all the time and I found it strange that the plane was going so slowly, instead of trying to escape. It disappeared behind trees, and then I saw a huge column of black smoke. Even then, I hoped the plane had not crashed, but to my sorrow, it had. Raymond went to find out where. The plane had crashed straight unto Grantez Farm, where Maman Amy used to live, and the house and outbuild-ings have been completely burnt out. No attempt could be made to save a scrap of anything, and no Fire Brigade was sent for because the Germans refused to let anyone near. They were pleased to see it burn, no doubt. They said it was 'nothing'.

So, everything has gone, the room where old Aunt Jane used to sit, looking like a mere skeleton; the scullery where I used to cut Alice's hair, and the little rather dull kitchen, where Maman Amy used to sit by the grate – all gone! Yet what is a building compared to lives. Thank God no one was hurt. The people who live there escaped, just in time, by a miracle. The cattle were saved, except one poor little calf that had remained indoors, I'm sure Alice and 'Auntie' Florrie are terribly upset. They will have had such a fright too, so close. Some-how we've been upset all day, thinking of the occupants of the plane – it was too low for anyone to bale out. Bullets were flying everywhere, how no one was hurt is a miracle. In the very early hours we had heard a lot of noise, and apparently planes came and sank German E-boats off Plemont and they've been bringing in dead and wounded sailors all day. It is all terrible and fright-ening. Will there be fighting here – the Island is so small. I wish the Germans would just go, evacuate whilst they've still got a chance to do so. I've been trying to finish a sermon tonight, on 'Come unto Me,' etc. but I realise that I need to preach it to myself! I think I often preach to myself really – my ser-mons are what I experience and what experience teaches me that I need.

*June 15th.*    A quieter day. But in the night many planes passed high up, at times continuously. They pass every night now, I suppose on their way to the battle-front in Normandy. I can't bear to hear them in the night. They make me feel nervous and trembly. Alice came. She is so sad about Grantez. She had tears in her eyes – she and all her sisters were born there. People are mad with the Germans for not allowing them to save furniture and clothing. Much could have been saved. Not a bucket of water was thrown on the fire, and part of the house could have been saved as the plane fell at the back. The Germans refused to allow anyone to rescue the poor calf, and it was only because J. Rosquet defied them and entered by smashing a window that he saved the terrified horse. Sadly, the pilot was burnt to death and the undertaker went to fetch the body last night. Maybe the pilot could have been saved, had not the Germans shot at it when it was damaged and trying to make a forced landing. As one man from St. Ouen's said: "They would shoot a dead dog." They are trying to ship our potatoes, in spite of having had four ships sunk and two damaged off the Island only two nights ago. They were angry because not more were taken to town, and said it was sabotage. One farmer got into trouble some days ago because he accidentally moved some of their barbed wire. A guard came up and accused him of sabotage, of trying to make a gap for parachutists! Then his man-servant laughed and the guard threatened to shoot them both. One must always be careful not to be seen laughing, the Germans take offence at that. Roger de Faye here for tea. Laurence's strawberries are the finest I've ever seen – one weighed two ounces. I planted out Chrysanthemums this afternoon.

*June 16th.*     Went to town – dinner at Montpelier, then went to Bon Air to see Joy. And there she was, my dear friend, half-sitting up in bed, looking her usual self except for very thin cheeks and with such a welcome in her face and voice that I felt quite shy, and couldn't say much at first She has been so brave (though she wouldn't say anything about it). I am so thankful she is getting on all right.

*June 17th.*     I wrote a message for Alfred. The Red Cross Office is accepting them, though they hardly think they will go. A German soldier, fully armed, came to the door, and asked me for potatoes and milk. He was so nice, even when I refused. One feels awful refusing, and I wish I had given him a cupful to drink. Some of them make themselves very nice, then one feels that one cannot trust them. They might be polite one minute and shoot you the next. They do things which make one feel so bitter towards them, yet when they come to the door, and act like this one, one can't help feeling friendly towards them. Last night we heard many heavy explosions and much noise of bombing all day. The Allies are getting nearer.

*June 18th. SUNDAY.*     Planes came early and attacked ships in St. Ouen's Bay; they were going towards Cherbourg, people think, but they all turned back and most of them were sunk or damaged – more dead and wounded brought in. I saw Germans on the beach with horses and carts, salvaging, I suppose. One can't but feel sorry for all those poor sailors. From the attic, Dad saw the planes diving. Everyone knows the news of today, that the British have reached Carteret, the nearest point opposite Jersey. We have been mentioned on the wireless and that makes us feel quite excited. German prisoners have been captured, who had just arrived in barges from the Channel Islands, where they had been for two years and they spoke English fluently. I wonder what they've told the Americans about us! I was pleased, also, to hear about the capture of a German bunker in France, with the loss of only one British soldier – these are the sort of things they are hiding in at Coin Varin here, underground – a sort of house, complete with hot and cold water, electric light, furniture etc. So I feel that now that the Allies know how the bunkers are made, they will know what to expect here and how to deal with it. I was anxious that they wouldn't know.

Went to Bethlehem this morning and gave talk at Sunday School. Afternoon cycled down to St. Aubin's chapel to preside at their Sunday School Anniversary and to give a short talk after their Demonstration. Got home just in time for tea, then went off to Bethlehem to take the evening service. Congregation 65. Francis came to kiss me goodnight and said I had preached well. Praise from him means a lot to me. But, above all, I felt very thankful if anything in my sermon had helped him. I am thankful the day is over. I was rather dreading it, having so much to do. After service tonight, I called at Westfield to see Leslie who is in bed with bronchial pneumonia. On my return, I wrote to Joy who is still at the Nursing Home, then got supper ready.

*June 19th.*    Planes visited us again, dropped bombs at La Rocque, missed target and damaged houses instead, but no one hurt. Noise going on all day. Alice and I did the washing but no luck with the weather – strong wind then rain, so dried nothing. Gave Margaret and Dorothy their lessons as I did washing. They came by turn and did their reading at the end of the wash-tray. I really have no time to teach them now that Mother is ill. I am anxious about her. This morning she was quite flushed and her throat hurt her and she asked me to send for Dr. Lewis. We can't use the phone now, so Dad went to Mrs Priaulx, and asked her to give him the message if he went to see her sister. Fortunately, he did, so he came on here, and said Mother has a septic throat and must stay in bed otherwise she will be the whole Summer recuperating. He has several other cases. This will pull Mother down still more, especially as she has trouble to eat, in any case. How I wish we had good things to give her – sugar would help and cups of real tea; we have a little left, which Mother had exchanged for something else, but she won't let us open the packet. It has to be kept for a special occasion.

*June 20th.*    Very strong wind, too strong to put the sheets out, but got the rest of yesterday's washing dry. Cleaned rabbit hutches afternoon. Tonight we heard shooting and saw a barrage balloon that was drifting towards the house. Kathleen was terrified, and imagined it was one of the German 'secret weapons' which they are now sending over southern England. It was the shooting that was dangerous. The shells were exploding so close, and we got away from the windows. The balloon disappeared. I suppose they shot it down. Mother's throat still hurts and she has eaten so little.

*June 21st.*    Planes came low in the night and there was a lot of machine-gunning – apparently a German plane crashed on the Florence Boot Playing fields. I hate waking in the night now, because my thoughts are so depressing. I must be over-tired, I think. Yet, with each morning, God gives me new strength. Doctor found Mother much better today, but her pulse is still too fast and she is weak and nervous. Oh, if only there was no more war and no more noise of planes and bombs and gunfire, I'm sure Mother would improve. The same German soldier came to the door again asking for potatoes. I gave him a cup of milk, but he really wanted a bottleful, to make a pudding, he said! He said he would bring us some sweets, but I said we did not want any (we would have loved to have some, of course!)

*June 22nd.*    Same noisy night. Mother not yet up today. She eats so little that it is making me very anxious. All day long there has been terrific noise going on from the direction of Cherbourg, and the windows shook so much at times that I felt they might break. The sky to the north-east got covered with smoke for a time and, in the wind, we could smell it. There is no sign of the Germans intending to leave us of their own free will. They have just put up five guns in Mr Priaulx's orchard. Everyone thinks they will fight hard. I dare not think of it. I distempered the kitchen today; in the morning, I was teaching Margaret and Dorothy at the same time! Had letter from Joy – she's had her stitches out and is returning home.

*June 23rd.*    A lot of shooting last night and plenty star shells going up; heard that shipping off coast was being attacked again. This morning an American fighter plane made a forced landing at Val de la Mare – plane quite undamaged, it had run out of fuel. Pilot got out and put up his hands when a German officer approached. Pilot is reported to have said to the German, "Hello, buddy, can you tell me where I can get some more juice?" Herbert saw the plane tonight when he went down to Mrs Syvret.

*June 24th.*    A lot of noise of planes again in the night. They make me feel nervous and afraid. So I went to talk to Mother awhile and then to my sisters. One feels better moving about than lying still. There are several nights that a few planes, could be German, pass at intervals, terribly low, right over our house, and very fast. We can't sleep peacefully when we expect them any moment. Don't know what they can be doing. However I lay down again and felt much helped when I remembered, and repeated to myself, a verse which

Miss C Alexandre had quoted in a Children's talk:

> *Anywhere we journey here,*
> *We may find Him ever near*
> *Therefore we need never fear.*

Mrs Allan called at Mr O Mourant's office to tell Joyce that they had packed a suitcase and wanted the boys to fetch it. Someone has been frightening poor Mrs Allan and she expects to have to evacuate. She also said that should anything happen to them both, the 'silver' was to be for me. I've no idea what the 'silver' consists of, and I prefer that she should live than have her silver! And I don't know why I should have it more than anybody else. They want to come here for shelter if they have to move but our house is not safer than any other. Everyone will be in great danger if anything happens.

*June 25th. SUNDAY.*      Irene de la Perrelle here for dinner, after she had preached at Philadelphie. The Frenchman turned up again. We thought he had been taken away and probably drowned. He said they'd been imprisoned in St. Helier fort for a fortnight. They were taken there at 3am when the Invasion of France took place. Pastor Hanks preached at Bethlehem tonight. Congregation 94, better than usual.

*June 26th.*     A quieter night, planes did not sound so near. Woke to the sound of falling rain and it has continued all day. Hasn't rained like this for months. It will do immense good to the parched earth. Francis has been bemoaning the fact that all our hay has not yet been brought in but it will dry again! Alice and I did the washing though we could not get it dry! But it was so lovely to have all the water we needed. I must have handled dozens of buckets of water today. It is all heavy work and I am careful not to hurt myself, because I want to keep as well as possible for Alfred's sake.

*June 27th.*     Much shooting in the night. Saw star shells going up so knew there was an action at sea. The shore batteries went on shooting for a long time. I prayed for all the poor sailors, perhaps some losing their lives at any moment. Went to Mrs Capt. Syvret for tea, and Joan, who came in from school. Mrs Syvret walked all the way back with me. We went first to see the American plane. A German was guarding it. It is being dismantled, the wings were off – a heavy looking thing, and yet only a fighter. It makes one shudder to think of huge bombers and what happens when they crash. Mrs Syvret and I had a good talk as we walked up Jubilee Hill. We spoke about 'separation' and we mutually agreed that there was nothing worse to bear than that. She told me how she often cries herself to sleep and I was comforted to feel that, if an older woman does it, it wasn't so babyish after all. Poor Mrs Syvret, she has a constant anxiety at the back of her mind and the worry of what her husband really thinks about her having stayed here. I can see it worries her dreadfully, and I certainly can sympathise; I was so afraid that she would ask me if Alfred had ever mentioned it in his messages.

*June 28th.* The Jerseymen who had been taken to work for the Germans in Alderney have returned safely this morning, together with many foreigners, French, Algerian etc. Joyce saw crowds of them, men and women. There is a rumour that the Americans have sent an ultimatum to Alderney – even if this is so, it is not likely that the Germans will surrender. Things are not going as we had hoped. We used to hope, or make ourselves believe, that as soon as the British set foot on French soil, the Germans would be off. Now it seems as if they will never go, and people are thinking that there will be fighting here. I wrote a note to Mrs Allan to try and cheer her up, though I need cheering up badly myself! She's even gone and made her will and left me her silver, so she says.

*June 30th.* A quiet night and we all slept better, but I keep on thinking about people in southern England who have that dreadful pilotless plane of Hitler's to fear every night. It is awful. I am sure that people are very brave about it, braver than I would be. I am such a coward and frightened of everything, especially at night. How I admire those women who go out to the battle-front as nurses, etc. Girls did not come for lessons today so I took the opportunity of forking the flower border at the back, cleaning out rabbits, white-washing part of the pantry, as well as usual jobs. Uncle Ed. here for tea. Thousands of those foreign workers were seen last night getting into boats, absolutely packed, but they were still here this morning. Some had left and got nearly as far as St. Malo but then had to turn back. This afternoon again they tried to leave. I wonder if they will get across? I expect the British know everything. They did not bomb those boats last night, but neither did they allow them to reach France, apparently. Dad and the boys have finished bringing in all the hay today. Francis took a load of potatoes to town, and brought back Mrs Allan's trunks! We really don't know where to put them. I feel cross with everybody and everything tonight – it would relieve my feelings to smash something! I can't bear this state of things – I'm not able to hear from Alfred and imagine all sorts of things!

*July 1st.* It is four years ago today since we were occupied. I still hope we'll be free for my Birthday this month. Very busy day – one longs for a rest from physical labour, but it is work, work, work from morn till night, and no time for reading or other mental refreshment!

*July 2nd. SUNDAY.* Went to Bethlehem this morning. Rev. Scott preached

199

and we had the Sacrament after. I always pray especially for Alfred then, and remember that Sacrament service just before he left Jersey, when we knelt together and clasped hands. Miss C. Alexandre here for tea. Went down to preach at Bethesda tonight. It rained. Herbert came with me. Mrs Syvret was there to welcome us as there is no caretaker now. Half the windows are boarded up and patches of the ceiling have come down, owing to the nearby blasting and shooting by the Germans. The pulpit has had to be put halfway down the chapel.

*July 3rd.*      Alice did not come so Kath and I did the washing; we gave up at 5.30pm though we had not managed to do it all. I feel bruised all over tonight – this washing is such heavy work for my small body. Mr and Mrs Folin, who lived at Grantez, came tonight with their two little boys, and we gave them china and other things to help them build a home again. I felt so sad when she was telling us about their destroyed home. It must be very hard to lose every-thing, all one's treasured possessions in one blow.

*July 4th.*      Still feeling weak and tired, but cycled to town, as arranged. Called at Walkers and found Joy dressed, but looking very thin. Brought her a small rabbit, milk and potatoes. It is awful that people in town are so short of potatoes, and during the digging season too. Where do all the loads of lovely potatoes we take into town go? Had dinner at Montpelier. It does one good to talk together about Alfred and to share our worries.

*July 5th.*      The friend who had asked me to pray for her family had invited me to tea specially. She thought it only right that I should know more about the escaped Russian whom they are harbouring. When we were alone after tea, she told me a story which I must not breathe to anyone; they are all in enough danger as it is. This particular Russian is only 22-years-old, and he has been secretly harboured by this family and others for about two years. He comes of a good family in Russia. One of his sisters, if not two, married doctors. He wanted to be a doctor, and began studying, but finally became a mechanic. He was educated at a school in Leningrad, where he imbibed Communist ideas. He had to go into the army, was captured by the Germans and punished by them many times which caused him to be very ill. Once he was strapped to a chair for a whole fortnight, being dependent on his fellow-prisoners for every-thing. Finally, he was brought to Jersey with hundreds of prisoners and put to work in a quarry. Within 24 hours he made an escape, found a furnished evacuated house, where he lived for some weeks, sleeping in a proper bed and serving himself like a gentleman, using dishes he found in the house. He never stole, but begged for his food during the day. Then someone disturbed him, he was chased but escaped. After that, with a companion, he slept in a cupboard in a school building (locking it from inside) but one day the Germans came to

see the building and from the cupboard he heard and understood their speech, so he had to go away from there. At last, he found a loft on this farm, where he slept for many weeks without discovery. He begged his food from houses in the neighbourhood, doing it systemically, going to one house on a Sunday, because he got apple cake, which he liked. One day he was seen by one of the farm-hands but he did not 'split' on him. Later, he offered to do a little job, and he was given food. So gradually he just stayed, helping to work on this farm and getting his food and shelter in return. He was gradually learning English, asking many questions and writing down English words, and so on, until he got to speak quite well and to read magazines. He even learnt to speak our Jersey-French language. He is, however, a hot-tempered young man, and as he has grown more confident it has showed up, and the women of the household have got more nervous and frightened of having him around. The situation is fraught with danger. When the farmer sees that the Germans are suspicious, he passes the Russian on to someone else for a while.
I was told of other people who are harbouring Russians. One family that I know has been patiently teaching English to one of these escapees until he has read *The Pilgrim's Progress* and the Bible right through four times! It would be wonderful if some of these Russians were to learn the Christian way of life through the influence of those people who are risking their own lives for them here in Jersey. God works in mysterious ways.

*July 9th. SUNDAY.*        Stayed in morning with Christine. Plenty work to occupy us both. Afternoon washed up, fed rabbits, rested on my bed for half an hour and read 12 pages of theology. But the Frenchman called so I had to get up to give him something to eat, and by the time he had gone it was time to get tea. He says the Germans expect the British next week, and he is afraid of being bombed, poor fellow, whilst shut up in the camp. Went to Bethlehem tonight.

*July 10th.*    Spent the whole day till 6 o'clock, doing the washing with Alice. Poor Granny is giving us so much trouble these days. Tonight, I thought I would have a short time to do some reading, but no, I had to go and wash Granny instead. I feel that I have nothing to give, next time I preach, for my time has all been occupied with household tasks and with Granny these past weeks. I'd like to find a little time each day to improve my mind. Rev. Scott's book on Theology is so interesting, but I'll never find time to read it through. I miss Alfred more than ever. And when Mother happened to mention his hair, just after tea, the tears began to fall down my cheeks, and I just managed to hide them.

*July 11th.*    A friend came to see Mother and told her that a young Russian who reminds her of one of my brothers had been to their house and begged them to shelter him as it is no longer safe for him to remain where he is. They gave him some dinner, and they were all terribly upset because they could not take him. (I know they have very good reason). It is sad. May the Americans or British come soon and all these troubles be over. Two young Germans rang the front doorbell this morning, and when I opened it, one laughed and said: "Now don't be afraid when you see some Germans." They wanted potatoes. I sent them to Dad who was also told not to be afraid! They wanted a whole load. They did not get them! What's the matter with me? I've been crying again tonight. It was when Raymond came to see Christine, and there they were, together as they are almost every evening of the week. It suddenly made me so long for my 'young man' to be with me too. So I ran up to my bedroom and had a jolly good cry!

*July 12th.*    All sorts of rumours flying round. Some say Knackfuss has arrived on the island on important business. Others that the Germans are going because they've cancelled all their orders for vegetables and meat for the end of the week; others say that the Americans are landing here tomorrow! Meanwhile the Germans go on making booby-traps, moving guns and digging trenches in people's orchards and fields and showing no signs of retreat.

*July 13th.*    Thought it would do me good to go to town – it would take me out of myself. So I prepared my parcels of food for town friends and set off at 10 o'clock with Joyce who was going to her singing lesson. Saw Mrs Allan, then Elsie at the office, then Mrs Ward. And how it did me good to talk with her! I had not been since before the Invasion of Normandy. She said she felt downhearted on waking today, then the text: 'Have faith in God' came to her, and she felt comforted. I too must have more faith and not give way to tears and despair. She told me that I had not changed at all and looked as youthful as ever. I was comforted, for I feel so very much older. Called to see Mrs Walker and Joy, who is looking much better. I feel so thankful. Got home, had dinner, washed up, then gave Margaret and Dorothy their lessons. Mr O Mourant here for tea.

*July 14th.*    I had called in Dr. Lewis, as we were all anxious that Mother was not improving more. We feel reassured. He said Mother will be all right when 'all this' is over. We hope that she will soon be about again as usual. People no longer expect the Americans – they think we shall be like this till the end of the war. Many have already eaten their iron rations, especially the tin of sardines. I had a postcard from Uncle Gordon, dated June 13th. He was expecting to go to England; he says the sick and aged are being repatriated via Lisbon. He does not sound so cheeerful as in previous letters. Perhaps he dreaded the journey.

*July 15th.* Six allied planes passed low tonight, and there was terrific anti-aircraft fire. Don't know how those planes passed through such a barrage of gunfire.

*July 17th.* Lovely summer's day at last. Alice and I did the washing and got it all dry. Afterwards I had to go and lie down on my bed awhile to rest my back which felt nearly broken with scrubbing those heavy men's trousers. Saw on the *Evening Post* that someone had had news through the Red Cross, so think there may be some on the way.

*July 18th.* Mother's 'trio' of friends came for afternoon tea, and it did us good to see them, as always, because they make us laugh so much!

*July 19th.* I made blackcurrant jam with part of the extra ration of sugar we've had – first time we've had an extra sugar.

*July 20th.* Heard that Phyllis Le Brun was ill, and meant to go and see her. But the Germans were shooting so much that I didn't want to go out.

*July 21st.* My 29th Birthday and news that an attempt has been made on Hitler's life. People everywhere are discussing it (when there are no Germans within hearing) and feeling quite excited. Is this the beginning of the end at last? If all had been well, Alfred and I would now have been married for two years. Disappointed as I am, I know it is wrong to complain and I must be very thankful today that things are looking so much more hopeful. Audrey Anquetil came early with a nice bunch of Carnations for me and a card with a verse she had copied, which has helped me very much:

> *Rejoice this Birthday morning*
> *For Jesus is your Friend*
> *His Love which passeth knowledge*
> *Is yours unto the end.*

Mother has been so good and made me a few things, and I never saw her making them – an overall, a petticoat, a nightdress and an apron. Dear Mother, she is so good, and I long to see her strong again. Poured with rain all morning, too bad to go to Montpelier for dinner, but later, thinking it was improving, I set off, but by the time I got there, I was soaked! Alfred's Mother had given up expecting me; she lit a fire specially to dry my clothes and gave me a cup of 'real' tea, which she had kept for a special occasion. Made three other calls, then cycled back with Joyce. Tonight I worked on a sermon, and that helped me.

*July 23rd. SUNDAY.*     My turn to stay in morning. Had tea with Evie and Aunt Elize, then Evie came with me to Sion where I was preaching. Congregation 68 and a very helpful atmosphere. It was lovely cycling back, weather fine and fortunately no planes passed over when we went by the German guns.

*July 24th.*     Another washing-day over! We finished early, so I was able to rest on my bed before tea. I am trying to take care of myself, for I still feel weak inside, and so tired. Alice here today. She brought me two pillow-slips and a Flower jug. Dear Alice, she is giving us all her own things now that there is nothing to buy. We've heard that some internees have arrived at Lisbon; I wonder if Uncle Gordon is amongst them.

This morning, Uncle Ernest said something to the Germans because they had put five horses in his field and they pointed their guns at him and ordered him to 'get out!' One has to be so careful now – they are not in too good a mood. Yesterday came news that the Channel Islands are 'open to free bombing' (fishermen have been warned). We wonder if the Americans are thinking of landing here after all. Planes have been passing in great numbers all day and there was anti-aircraft fire and noise of bombing either close at sea or on the Island itself.

*July 25th.*     During the morning we saw hundreds of British planes pass, it was a lovely sight. They were heralded by one which passed right overhead, flying from east to west. The Germans shot at it all the way, and we watched it, fearing lest it should be hit. But it pursued its course quite undisturbed, and probably rose gradually higher, for the shells exploded beneath it. Soon afterwards all the others passed, and we tried to count the specks. The Germans only shot at one lot. The siren at the Airport has been going many times today. I suppose the planes were returning from a raid in France. One dares not think of the hell that is let loose then. We are all feeling tired and unwell these weeks – we think the bread is no good; it goes mouldy, and we have to cut off the whole of the crust of some loaves.

*July 26th.*     There was a big cloudburst this morning and the loveliest rainbow I'd seen for a long time. I thank God for it, for somehow it gave me courage and new hope – a sign, it seemed, of God's Presence and Love, which will never cease. I felt that God hears all my prayers for Alfred and will help us both. Poor Francis had his turn to be poorly in the night – if only we had good bread and more substantial food. The boys have been digging potatoes – hard work, without proper food to give then the necessary strength. I know it is one of the things that worries Mother.

*July 27th.*     Had dinner at Montpelier, then joined Mrs Capt. Syvret, Phyllis and Beryl at Victoria College Prep, where the Girls' College (Joan's form) were acting 'Much Ado About Nothing'. It was done out-of-doors and I felt slightly nervous when we heard planes, lest shooting would start. Had a very windy and tiring cycle journey back. John has brought back news that the Gestapo has been searching Perry Farm twice because five German soldiers have deserted, and one went there yesterday and asked Mr Le Feuvre for civilian clothes, which he didn't get. He also wanted to give up his belt and rifle. We must not be alarmed if the Gestapo were to arrive, for they will search every-where, probably. Unless, of course it was only a trick because they wanted a reason to search that farm – one never knows!

*July 28th.*    Margaret and Dorothy here and it is end of the term. I suppose I won't teach them any more, because M. is going to school, and D. must find another teacher because I hope to be able to get married soon, and in any case, I have so little time to teach, with Granny and Grandpa to look after, Mother not well, and everything else! But I shall miss seeing their bright little faces each morning, and Dorothy's funny little ways! Went to see Phyllis Le Brun tonight, having heard that her leg was bad, after an accident, when she was thrown off her cycle by a German car.

*July 30th. SUNDAY.*    Bethlehem this morning, then tonight preached at Tabor. I didn't think I had got on very well but perhaps it was my fault, because at dinner-time I complained of the unpleasant job I had to do in Granny's bedroom on my return from chapel which made me late for dinner. And I was angry because Granny and Grandpa give me so much trouble, especially on a Sunday! Afterwards I was ashamed of myself for having grumbled, when I remembered all my blessings, and I asked God to forgive me. I did not deserve that He should bless my preaching tonight! And it is so sad for our dear Grandparents to be like that – they cannot help it. We met three sheep on the way to Tabor (one does not usually see sheep in Jersey) and then saw a small flock which the Germans keep. We noticed quite a number of tanks camouflaged under trees, in fields and tracks, and their crews peered at us over the hedges. May those tanks never be used here.

*July 31st.*    We had such a fright during tea, such sudden sharp gunfire very close, then we saw a plane rush by at a terrific rate and very low. It gave Mother a shock again. Apparently, there were several fighters and they appeared suddenly and machine-gunned at the Airport and in the St. Peter's Post Office area where there are many Germans at their gun-emplacements etc. It can be dangerous to be about, but what can one do! The Gestapo are still searching for deserters. Alice said they had been to Jack V. and made a careful search in house and out-buildings, having their guns ready to shoot. The Americans have made a big advance and are now at Avranche, so that is good news.

*August 1st.* There was much shooting with very heavy guns during the night and we felt nervous as the shells passed overhead. Nobody knows what was up but we think the Germans were shooting at something at sea – the guns sounded very close and seemed heavier than any we had yet heard. I am sorry that happens, because it gives Mother no chance to get well.. one cannot but help being very startled. This morning I spent an hour trying to get in touch with a District nurse or Doctor for Mrs Bisson, whose little girl hurt her foot last night. Even the Constable did not have the use of his phone, and I could find no one to help. Suddenly, about noon, our phone rang! I couldn't believe my ears! After two months without being able to use it, now we can! One can never understand the Germans, but it is lovely to be able to use our phones again. One was always anxious lest someone would need a doctor quickly.

*Aug. 2nd.* This morning I collected the Subscriptions for the District Nurse. Alice here and we spring-cleaned the boulangerie [the bakehouse] this afternoon and I distempered the walls. The news is good – more advances in Normandy. Heard heavy bombing in the direction of St. Malo yesterday and today. The German guns last night sounded even nearer and heavier, and explosions made everything shake. Mrs Barbour had a card from Uncle Gordon dated July 4th and he was still in camp. I hope he is in England now, that he will write to Alfred and that it will help him. We are anxious and downhearted tonight, because John and Herbert have (secretly) heard Churchill's statement about the war, and Hitler's V1 weapon is causing much damage and many casualties. Worse still, an even more deadly weapon is expected.

*Aug. 3rd.* Someone has told the Germans that Edward Laffoley charges batteries for people and he has had to go to College House today. The Germans are trying to find out whose batteries he has charged. Already, the Gestapo have searched several houses, including Beach Farm. They found no wireless there, however. We couldn't help laughing when we heard about those German police going to a certain little cabinet in a bedroom, opened it hopefully and saw 'deux pots'! It is strange how, in so many of the tragic happenings, there is often a spark of humour.

*Aug. 4th.* Miss Marcus here. She helped me to weed back border this morning and did the rose-beds for me this afternoon. Went to Wesfield to fetch some tomatoes. Margaret was just going to give the mare a drink, so I got on her back for that short distance, because it is so many years since I had sat on a horse's back, and our Dolly is too frisky to be played with! Miss Marcus told me that Mrs Cohu had had a letter from her husband, Canon Cohu, who has been two years in solitary confinement in Germany. He says he hopes things will end soon, because he does not think he can bear it much longer. He was a man full of spirit and humour, and the Germans have done their best to break his spirit. They have even torn up some of his wife's letters before his eyes without letting him read them.

*Aug. 5th.*     Heavy explosions at intervals all through last night. Things quiet today. The usual housework, cleaning of rabbit hutches etc. More houses in St. Peter's have been searched. So, I am afraid for this diary, and don't know where to hide it for safety. We have made a new kind of tea lately with dried green pea-pods – quite good. This week we have been drinking a mixture composed of sugar-beet, bramble, raspberry leaves and pea-pods, all dried in the oven, then used as tea. Best mixture, so far, I think. News from France very good: the Americans have arrived at Brest. Thank God things are moving more quickly and the fighting not so fierce.

*Aug. 6th. SUNDAY.*     Lovely warm weather so we sat outside afternoon. My turn to stay in this morning – went to Bethlehem evening. The Frenchman came for food as usual. He is so disappointed still to be in Jersey. The Germans intended to ship them to St. Malo during the week but the quick American advance has prevented it. This poor Frenchie finds it dull here: no women to go out with on a Sunday; he can't find any, he told me!

*Aug. 7th.*     Alice and I spent all day in the wash-house. It is Bank Holiday, but no holiday for us! It would be nice to have a whole day without having to work or just having a change of work, like gardening! The Airport siren has been on the go all day; planes were passing. Alice and I ran into the shed, for the Germans were shooting whilst we were hanging out the clothes. All day long the house has been shaking with the bombardment still going on near St. Malo. It is strange how the Germans hold on there when they know they are being cut off. I feel sure they would do the same here if the British or Americans were to attempt to take us now.

*Aug. 8th.*     About midnight last night, we were startled by those heavy guns again. Dad thinks the Germans were shelling from Noirmont. All day long there has been heavy bombardment in the south. It gave me a headache whilst I was gardening. How it must be for those right on the spot, one dares not imagine. The sirens have been busy today – many planes have passed. Mrs Le Seelleur came to see Mother. She said Bunty had seen the wounded American prisoners that arrived at Hospital last week. The Germans evacuated them from a hospital at St. Malo. In spite of the risk the Germans still try to go by sea. Mr G Avery from Beaumont, with his own eyes, counted ten ships leaving our harbour during the night. Today we were reaping, neighbours helped Dad and the boys. I wish I felt strong enough to help, if I had time. However, I did some gardening afternoon.

*Aug. 9th.* Lovely warm day with thick haze, early morning. Heard much bombing again all night. Then much gunfire quite close at 6.30am until 8 o'clock. Allied planes came and attacked shipping around St. Aubin's Bay. Dr. Shone told Uncle that yesterday the Germans brought 320 of their own wounded men here from France and performed 95 operations during the night and they intend to fetch some more (they don't appear to be leaving us). Siren has been on many times. Tonight Herbert counted a hundred planes passing. How I long for news of my poor Alfred. I've been thinking of one sentence in the last letter he wrote to me from Nigeria in 1940, when he said: *I am very happy, my own lovely Nan.* God grant that he may feel like that again when all this is over, if not before. For, I know he truly was very happy with me.

*Aug. 10th.* Our neighbours have been having their rabbits stolen, and now it is my turn. When I went to feed them I saw at once that the boxes had been tampered with. All the fat ones ready to eat had been taken, and another, with a litter of nine. I am thankful that some were left, but now there will be nothing to make a dinner. I had been taking so much trouble, so that we could have one rabbit a week, for vegetables are not enough for the men who have so much hard work to do. I feel very sorry and angry too. We don't think the thieves were Germans this time. We phoned Centenier Egré but he has not found out anything. We think it might be someone who will sell them on the Black-market.

Went to town, called at the Wards, and it did me much good. Mrs Ward asked her husband to pray, just as he was coming in from the garden. His hands soiled with ground and his face covered with sweat (he had been digging his potatoes). He came in to his study, and standing there whilst I knelt, he prayed for Alfred and me. He talked to God so simply and so intimately, praying that our love for each other might be even stronger than before. I wish I could remember the exact words he said. And Mrs Ward again urged me to have faith.

Saw other friends and had dinner at Montpelier. There were lots of Germans about town, especially sailors, and the harbour was full of boats. Also, I saw large caterpillar-wheeled vehicles under trees in the Parade, and I was told that there are fresh guns too, brought from St. Malo. So, instead of evacuating from here, as one had hoped, the Germans are bringing more stuff and showing every sign of staying. The general belief now in the Island is that we shall be in this state till the end of the war. People don't think the Allies would try to take us by force, neither do they think that the Germans will surrender, nor evacuate, because they can hardly do so now.

*Aug. 11th.* Spent most of my spare time cleaning the rabbit hutches and moving them to the heifer stable where I hope the rabbits will be safer, with Vicky keeping guard. As we were having tea, about 6 o'clock, heavy bombardment began from the St. Malo direction, and went on until midnight. The windows and doors rattled, the house shook to its very foundations as though it was an earthquake. We thought it must be the Royal Navy shelling the French coast. Uncle Ed. here for tea, as usual on Fridays.

*Aug. 12th.*   The Germans were firing their heavy guns in the night. One could not sleep, and it gave one a headache. I felt nervous and miserable and longed for peace! The guns frighten me, and I long for morning! At dawn there was a naval engagement in the St. Ouen's Bay area. Yesterday the Germans announced on the *Evening Post*, that they had sunk two American E-boats off this island and we hoped it wasn't true but bodies of Americans have been washed up around our coast today. One feels very sad. Mr Le Brun came this afternoon and cheered me because he is very hopeful that the war will be over by October! I was just helping Herbert to milk the cows in the back field as the others were busy cutting the oats. What a long time since I had had a chance to do any milking, and I do enjoy doing it! The Germans have taken some American prisoners to have their hair cut in town today, and a crowd gathered outside the shop to see them. The Germans took away their Identity cards because they refused to move. Yesterday I heard what I took to be a sea-plane passing very low and was surprised that the Germans did not shoot at it. I have heard now that it was rescuing American survivors and that a message had been sent to the Germans not to shoot, and they didn't!

*August 13th. SUNDAY.*   The guns started firing again about midnight last night, and it sounded like a naval battle going on in the west, whilst in the east one saw flares and searchlights. The firing was sharp and continuous, our house was shaking and there was an explosion so heavy that I thought the stair window would be blown in. All day there has been the sound of bombardment. After breakfast and washing-up, went to Bethlehem, took my Sunday class and played the piano for hymns, then took the service in chapel. Congregation 65, mostly young people. Took as my text: 'Where hast thou gleaned today?'
Cycled back home, washed dishes again – they accumulate so when cooking is done during the morning. Then I did Granny's bedroom. What a job! She had got herself into a state again, so I was late having my dinner. After dinner, washed-up again, fed rabbits , rested for half an hour. Then Mrs Syvret and Joan came, also Léa. We chatted, had tea, then all went off to Bethlehem (Joyce stayed with Mother). We had a French service for a change with Mr A Querée as preacher. We all walked back together. About 9 o'clock, I lit the fire to boil kettle for supper etc., took trays up to grandparents, rest of us had supper, washed-up again, then prayers (especially for my Alfred), then bed!

*Aug. 14th.*   Irene came back at last. I helped her by taking the worst off

Granny and Grandpa's clothes and putting out all the clothes (and what a tiring time I had because of that wind). Noise of battle went on all last night, and has gone on all morning. The Germans are still digging themselves in everywhere – making rifle-holes, and even putting up more guns. It is not very cheering or reassuring. There are thousands of them here and they can't go away.

*Aug. 15th.*    At dinner-time Herbert came in with the news of a landing of the Anglo-Americans in southern France and also that Alderney had been bombarded by *HMS Rodney* this morning; and that the Channel Islands were now being directly attacked. As he was telling us this, there was terrific shaking of the windows by bombardment somewhere. We all got nervous thinking that either Jersey or Guernsey was being attacked. We opened all windows and began discussing where we could best hide, if there was fighting on the island. We could not think of a safe place. Dad suggested making a hole in the cement floor of the kitchen. We felt afraid, and yet there was in our hearts a longing to be released from the Germans, which is greater than our fear! We thought of phoning Joyce telling her to come home early, then realised that we were not supposed to know the news. Anyway, our appetite left us, and we expected anything to happen. In the midst of this, Priscilla du Heaume phoned to ask if she could come next week. This calmed us down a little though we thought she was mad to be phoning just then, but, of course, she wouldn't have heard the news. I told her to come Tuesday 'if all goes well.' So we calmed down and I washed the dishes. I wondered if Phyllis Le Brun would come, as expected. The noise of battle was going on all the time but suddenly we realised that the noise came from the south! So we were not being attacked after all. Phyllis arrived and she and Kath and I sat in the sun awhile and then had tea in the drawing-room. The first time Phyllis had come to tea. We looked at photo albums, fetched apples for her, then cycled down Jubilee Hill to Mrs Syvret's to fetch a rabbit for our dinner tomorrow. Then walked up as far as Phyllis' house and went in a few minutes. The German was on guard at that strong fortification in the rock on the hill, but he said nothing.

*Aug. 16th.*    Alice helped me to sweep bedrooms. I washed some night-shirts which Mother is giving to the Red Cross for the American wounded whom the Germans have as prisoners here. The Red Cross have nothing left.

*Aug. 17th.*    Christine at Evie's all day, so one missed her being there to do the cooking, so I did that as well as the usual jobs. Boys were busy stacking wheat and oats. The Germans are making farmers thresh early so that they can have the corn to feed their soldiers and sailors trapped here, and the straw for their horses. We would starve if we were left too long like this. It is awful to feel that a large part of France is now liberated, and all around us are the British and Americans, but we are here crowded in this small Island, with thousands of Germans! How shall we be delivered from them? That is the question that fills one's mind at present. Yet we have no cause to complain when we remember what people in the London area are suffering with Hitler's secret weapons. We've had no reliable news for some days, as the 'box' is out of order.

*Aug. 18th.* We were anxious about Mother so got Dr. Lewis to call and his visit cheered her up wonderfully, and us all! She was worrying about herself but he said her heart is much better and she is only suffering from too much acidity in the blood. Mother was so bucked by this news that she got up and went to see my rabbits and the oat stack which Dad and Mr Trachy were making in the back field. It is good to see Mother brighter! Then Doctor told us the news was very good – German débâcle in Normandy and the Allies 20 miles from Paris etc. Whilst the goings-on here are not cheering to behold – now the Germans are going to slaughter several hundred old Jersey horses to make sausages, and they will lend some of theirs to farmers. Everywhere they still put up defences, poles in the fields, more mines etc. Doctor told us that when those 300 German wounded were brought here they were lying in rows at the hospital waiting for treatment. The Germans did not have enough blankets for them, so tore them, and covered each man with half of one. Their suffering aroused the pity of our own doctors, who offered to help operate and offered our operating theatres but the Germans refused. So, one German doctor worked for hours, operating, and after 36 hours some wounded had not yet received attention. Doctor said their suffering was awful and the German doctor had no adequate supplies of anaesthetics or other medical necessities. Spent the day doing housework, gardening and cleaning rabbits... prepared tea and washed dairy cans. Tonight, I spent about half an hour in back field watching Dad and Mr Trachy finishing the stack. I was so afraid they would fall whilst making the point at the top. How I wish I could have taken a photo of them silhouetted against the sky, which was full of white clouds. Laurence was passing up the sheaves, Vicky was sitting watching her Master and the cows and calves were munching grass nearby. How peaceful it all seemed. Yet, so close, those dreadful battles are going on, and men killing each other. I was soon reminded of that, when the air-raid siren from the Airport gave a long wail. But, it did me good to be in the field then, as dusk fell everything looked so lovely and peaceful.

*Aug. 19th.* Had several peaceful nights – what a relief to sleep soundly! This afternoon there was heavy gunfire from the Germans here, towards the sea, from where we could hear what sounded like a warship shelling. It went on for about an hour and shook doors and windows. Now that St. Malo is down we shall hear no more noise of battle, unless it be on or around our Islands. At times one feels very anxious because there are so many Germans here and not too much food. We hear today that all our rations are going to be halved in two weeks' time, and already we are short of bread. We get up from the table hungry. Today it is Alfred's father's Birthday. There is nothing to buy, so I packed a tin of fruit for him, which Francis took to Elsie: one apple, two plums, two figs and a bunch of grapes.

*Aug. 20th. SUNDAY.*    My turn to stay in with Christine to do cooking etc. Cycled down to St. Aubin's chapel tonight to take evening service. Preached on Heb. 12 v. 7. Congregation 50. Thought the front of that chapel was lovely. Herbert came to meet me. We have felt quite lost these past days without having heard any news. John was quite upset about the 'box' being out of order and he could not manage to mend it. However, just before dinner, he started making a crystal set, and by 3pm he was already listening to a band from Normandy. He was so excited! Then he managed to get news from this British station in Normandy. It is wonderful and quite clear, but with head-phones, of course. The big problem is, where shall we hide it? Though the Germans can't take us to Germany now, they can still punish us, and we don't forget it.

*Aug. 21st.*    This afternoon I began looking over my 'bottom drawer', and packing the different gifts I've had for Birthdays (china, etc.) and I put them all together in a large box. It was time I tidied up my things, but it made me long for Alfred and sadder than ever at the dragging on of this awful separation.

*Aug. 22nd.*    Boys saw two Allied planes which were heavily fired on by German guns. Alfred's Mother has written me a short letter. She is so anxious about her son being so lonely. We know that by September 1st he will be in his Manse and the thought that he has to go into it alone is just about more than I can bear. If only we could get news, but one can see no hope of that, as things are here.

*Aug. 23rd.*    During the night thieves have come again and stolen Grandpa's clothes from the line – two shirts, two pairs pants and Granny's best nightgown! I cycled round the neighbourhood, and looked on people's lines to see if I'd find them, knowing that they must have been wet when stolen as it rained! But, no luck! One feels annoyed at people's meanness – we have so few clothes for Grandpa, and can't buy any. Alice helped me to sweep bedrooms this morning, and with the washing-up after dinner, then we picked a big bowlful of lovely blackberries in Mr Bisson's field. Afterwards we scrubbed two hundred-weight of potatoes to make flour. I had so hoped not to have to make any this year! Good news today: Paris has been liberated by French patriots. Church bells ringing in England, don't I wish I could hear them!

Tonight, I've been to see Aunt Elize at Les Potirons and was very sad to find her much changed and very weak. I fear she is dying – she knew me and spoke a little, but her eyes must already have been getting misty, because she thought it was getting dark and seemed anxious lest I would stay late and be afraid on the way home. Yet it was full daylight still. How sad I felt for Evie as I saw her supporting her dear Mother and resting her head on her shoulders. This has come so suddenly.

*Aug. 24th.*    Emmeline phoned to tell us that our dear Aunt Elize had passed away at 6 o'clock tonight. Dad had been at dinner-time and she was unconscious. One feels thankful she has died so peacefully, just as though she had fallen asleep. It would have been her wish to give no trouble, and especially she did not wish get like poor Granny here. It is so sad for Evie. She will be so alone, as, though her Mother was over 80, she was so well yet, in full possession of her faculties and able to read and converse, and one wishes for Evie's sake that she could have lived a little longer and to see the war ended. Aunt Elize leaves a lovely memory behind and her influence will live on. It won't be the same going to Potirons without seeing her. How glad I am to have seen her yesterday.

Mr and Mrs Allan here for dinner and tea. It is nice to feel that one gives them pleasure and a good meal. If I'd only had a rabbit, we could have given them more. However, we opened the last tin of salmon which we'd had given and had kept for a special occasion. It is wonderful how well tinned stuff lasts.

Rev. and Mrs Struthers came to fetch beastings again. He is always very hopeful. He says Jersey will be left till the end of the war, but that is only a matter of a month or so. I only wish he were right. Mrs Allan was telling us about two of her pupils who, in 1940, evacuated with their Mother, slept one night on the beach at Weymouth with other refugees, went as far at Southampton and found things so bad everywhere that they returned to Jersey, by the last boat that came before the Occupation. I hope one day that Alfred will be able to understand how difficult it was for anyone to know what was best to do at that time.

*Aug. 25th.*    Spent all day (apart from washing dishes and cleaning rabbit hutches) washing potato pulp, having had two hundred-weight crushed last night. Herbert helped me, yet I am so tired and aching tonight. It is all that lifting and carrying of buckets of water, for one thing. And I've felt sad all day thinking of Evie. And one thinks anxiously for one's friends in England with that dreadful V1 still going over. Alfred may be in the danger zone too – I don't even know where he is going to be living when he has a Manse.

*Aug. 26th. SUNDAY.*    Got up early and picked all my Zinnias and Ageratums to put in water to make a wreath for dear Aunt Elize. Put out all my flour to dry. Dad had a bit of a scare, just after 9 o'clock, when a car with German police, drove into our yard, but it was only to ask the way somewhere. (Herbert had just been listening to his radio!) Joyce and I went to Sunday School. Lucille spoke a few words about Aunt Elize, as did May Luce who, with Margaret Du Feu, was taking our morning service. Afterwards, I went to see Evie. I walked in and she met me, just between the little kitchen and her sitting-room. I just put my arms around her and we kissed one another. We wept together and she said, "I am so alone now. I used to tell Mother everything." I went in the room with Evie and laid a few flowers beside the body of dear Aunt Elize.

After dinner and washing-up I turned the potato flour over to help it get dry, chose hymns for tonight, rested for half an hour on my bed, sat outside and read book on Theology for 20 minutes, helped to get tea, and after tea cycled to Les Frères to take their evening service. Got back about 8 o'clock. Mrs Syvret and Joan were here. Spoke to them a few minutes, picked more Ageratum, fetched cabbage leaves for rabbits and fed them. Then Francis told me that Margaret had come to say that Leslie had hurt his head. So I got on my cycle and went off to see if I could do anything. Found Leslie in bed and 'diagnosed' slight concussion. He has a deep cut at the side of his head and does not remember anything. He was pushed outside Bethlehem and fell. Meanwhile Uncle had gone off to St. Peter's Telephone Exchange (as we can't use phone after 8pm) and managed to get permission from a German officer to phone the doctor, who will come tomorrow. Came home with Francis, who had gone to Westfield to bring in Uncle's cows. Back just in time for curfew! Supper, washing-up, bed, and so ends a busy and tiring day. But all my burdens I tell God and He comforts and strengthens me and I commend my beloved Alfred to his care.

*Aug. 28th.*　Irene here washing; had no time to help her today. Went early to take my flowers to Mr A Le Brocq, who has made a lovely wreath for us. This afternoon we four girls with Phyllis, Beryl and Raymond, Dad, Francis, Laurence and Joyce went to the funeral at Bethlehem. It was very trying. We sang, 'What a friend we have in Jesus', 'Blessed Assurance' and 'Peace, Perfect Peace'. Rev. Scott spoke very well. Aunt Elize had been Assistant Superintendent at Bethlehem Sunday School for over 40 years and always prayed for her scholars. We knew she prayed for us. I don't know what the world would be like without such splendid Christians. As Rev. Scott said: 'the salt of the earth.'

*Aug. 30th.*　Cycled into town about noon. Took a few potatoes to Mrs Ward (and dropped nearly half on the way!) though this is not allowed. Called to see Alfred's folk, then went on with Joyce to a bungalow near Green Island and had dinner and tea there with Mrs Walker, Joy and Emily. We were not allowed to go on the beach but the German guard let us go and wash our hands in the sea and I just put my feet in for a moment as it is so refreshing. How I would have liked to remain there for longer, but Jersey is not ours to do as we like with at present! All the afternoon we heard bombardment – don't know where it came from.

*Aug. 31st.*   Called to see how poor Evie was and found her cooking in her little kitchen, and looking very sorrowful. She so enjoyed cooking and doing things for her Mother, and she said: "Oh, it seems that I shall never cook for anyone again." Afternoon, I sifted potato flour and put more out to dry. People are saying that the Germans in Guernsey are going to surrender owing to lack of food. We have also heard that here in Jersey they are putting up flagpoles so as to be ready to fly the white flag! I wish these rumours were true! The noise we hear is apparently coming from a small island near St. Malo, which is still holding out and is kept supplied with water from here.

*September 1st.*   First thing I heard this this morning was Herbert calling: "Get up quick, there are lots of leaflets!" I jumped out of bed and was soon gathering what I could find. There were several in the back field and in the bushes on the hedge, some in the orchard, and plenty in the vegetable garden most were soaked with dew, but we've put them to dry and will spread them in the roads (making sure we are not seen) as they are written in German and are meant for them – the British want the German troops to know how far they've advanced in France. As I was picking some up I could hear the German soldiers coming from all directions, shouting as they searched for leaflets. I just escaped one soldier as I was going into their railway track in our field! I turned back quickly on seeing him on the other side of the hedge! I had heard a plane flying low in the night. We feel excited when leaflets are dropped, even though they may not be for us, but it cheers us to feel the British have been near.
Dr. Lewis came and found Mother much better. We are so thankful. He says there are very few medical supplies in the Island, especially anaesthetics, and they cannot possibly last longer than the end of October. He thinks the Germans might be forced to surrender or they could be tried afterwards and found guilty of cruelty to the civilian population and shot! How we would rejoice if they were to put up the white flag! There are many sailors here. Joyce says they came out of the Forum and all marched down Hill Street and Mr Mourant counted 1,150 of them

*Sept. 2nd.*   Afternoon went to Bethlehem to help decorate the chapel for Harvest, and I made a little cross with mauve Ageratum to hang on the pew where Aunt Elize sat, in memory of her. Joyce says people are actually putting up flag-poles, everyone looking forward to flying the Union Jack, whilst the Germans will put up the white flag. Mr Mourant is having a flag-pole made!

*Sept. 3rd.*    Went to Bethlehem. Rev. Scott preached a very good Harvest sermon. Poor Evie was there, it must have been very trying for her. I thought of her mother as we sang the Harvest hymns. I thought of her as 'a golden sheaf, to garners bright elected,' and the last verse which tells of the saints of God in that blessed land above, and the wonderful thought contained in the lines: 'the strains of all its holy throng with ours today are blending.' Do those above still share in some way in the lives of those on earth? Was Aunt Elize worshipping with us?

After tea I washed the dairy cans, then went to Tabor to take the evening service. Mr Ambler and his wife were there and when he saw how small the congregation was and knew that many had gone to other chapels because of Harvest services, he asked me if I was going to have the hymn about the 'straying sheep'! He is a humorous old chap really, and not at all as grumpy as he looks! Mrs J Le Boutillier was telling me how she longs for news of her boys who are in the Forces, and how she gets so anxious and down-hearted at times. I found out that, like Mrs Syvret and myself, she can no longer sing Hymn 916 because it upsets her too much As she said: "People who have no one away, do not understand how we feel." I wonder how my dear Alfred has got on today in his Manse and in a new Circuit where he will not know anyone. I hope he has not been too lonely. It really is so terribly disappointing and upsetting that we are not together to begin this new Methodist year in the ministry.

*Sept. 4th.*    I took Margaret to an interview with Miss Barton, Headmistress of the Girls' College, who is staying at Mr Stapleton's farm (Sands) at St. Brelade. What a job we had to find it, for the Germans are everywhere on the place. They have a huge farm building with cattle, sheep and pigs where the drive once was, and all around the house and garden and fields are huge camou-flaged tanks. What a place! Miss Barton asked many questions of Margaret, and was satisfied, because she accepted her as a pupil next term! Afterwards, I had to go and see Mr S's heifers and pass my opinion on them! I felt how ignorant I was really, but I did know which was the best one! Margaret and I managed to wheel our bicycles through a field of oat stumps, etc. and found our way out of that 'maze'. Afternoon I went to La Pompe to take them some grapes. They had friends in the drawing-room so I had a cup of tea with them. We discussed the news, whether the Germans will surrender and so on. From today there is no more gas, so some people cannot cook. It is an awful situ-ation for people in town. People are allowed to take one dish only to be baked in a Baker's oven. That is all they have cooked, in one day, unless they can find enough wood to make sone kind of fire. Some will have a long way to go to take their dish – and how to keep it warm on the way back? There are some cases of Scarlet Fever at Millbrook Nursing Home. I hope it won't spread further, as things are serious enough already.

*Left: Occupation Bread, often mouldy and containing foreign bodies.*
*Below: People going to baking ovens when there was no fuel for private houses.*

War news is very good: Brussels has been liberated. I wish one could hear the wireless. Herbert and John hear from that station in Normandy with the crystal set, and last night I listened for a moment and happened to hear the Hymn, 'Guide me O Thou Great Jehovah.' Even that was lovely to hear, though it made one feel so very lonely of England. They cannot imagine, I am sure, what it is to be cut off from the outside world, like we are.

*Sept. 5th.*　　British or American planes have visited us several times today and been shot at and an incendiary bomb is said to have dropped at the Airport. We heard the plane dive. Tonight a force of them has passed, probably on the return journey from Brest. The States of Jersey have prepared a report from all the Departments of Essential Commodities, showing how serious the state of things is for the civilian population, with regard to food, medical supplies, soap etc, and sent this report to the German Commandant. So we wait to see if anything will come of it.

*Sept. 6th.*　　Alice told us that there was trouble amongst German soldiers at Ville au Bas, St. Ouen, supposed to be because they haven't enough food, and some were seen with their hands tied. Joyce had come back with a copy of the Bailiff's report sent to the Commandant – things are pretty bad. The Germans say they can hold this state of siege until January 31st, but the Island Government has heard this with 'unfeigned dismay' and believe it is impossible to go on so long without serious consequences to the health of the population. The Bailiff ends his report with a threat. The whole thing is well-prepared and well-written, and one feels thankful that our Bailiff is doing his best for us all, but I fear it won't have much effect upon the German Commandant.

*Sept. 7th.*　　I feel very thankful to God for good news today – the BBC has announced that the danger of V1s and V2s is over; the battle of London has been won. One has heard that many anti-aircraft guns (which have shot down a large percentage of V1s) are manned by women. How brave they are and yet how sad that women should have to do such things. Will these women ever settle down to home-life again and will they have lost their sweetness and womanliness. Sometimes one fears what women will be like when the war is over!

Went to town. Called at Walkers and had dinner at Montpelier. Took a pie and carrageen pudding with me to help Mrs Du Feu a little, as cooking is so difficult for them now. Went to Local Preachers' Meeting at Grove Place. Called at Rev. Fell's; Ed. de Gruchy was with me and Mr Fell showed us a Hymn he has composed for 'Peace Day.' Mr L Herivel has written a tune for it and all choirs are to practise it at once so that we shall all be quite ready when our great Thanksgiving meetings will be held. May that day be soon! In town I've been sad, as usual, to see the long queues of people waiting for their skim milk. It is so cold today too. Mrs Fell was in a queue and Rev. Ward and Rev. Clark in another. Again at dinner-time people have to fetch their dish from the Baker's oven. People are going to suffer; how can people wash with no soap and no hot water, how cook or keep warm without fuel? Hot water is now being sold in some places in town, at 3d a quart. People are being told to bring their tea-pots. Roger came for tea and Herbert showed him the crystal-set John has made. Roger has made one too; he told us that a Miss B. (I've often seen her but did not know her name) was in prison all last winter for throwing horse-dung at the Germans! They came and teased her one day, and she took up a forkful and threw it at them! So, six months imprisonment.

*Sept. 10th. SUNDAY.*     Went to Sunday School to give out recitations to the children, then cycled on to preach at Six Roads. It was their Harvest and they had taken great pains to decorate their chapel. I was very impressed! Preached at Bethesda tonight. Kath has felt poorly all day. I do not like her to be ill. I feel anxious as she works too hard for her strength. There is a rumour today that several American parachutists have been dropped during the night. Anyway, the Germans have been searching for something or someone. Houses at St. John's and outbuildings have been well searched, and Mrs Syvret saw soldiers searching the fields at Val de la Mare, with guns in their hands. I must find a hiding-place for several things in case we are searched. How lovely it will be to be free again, to talk about anything to anyone, and not to have anything to hide. Mrs Vautier, Betty's mother, told me she had hidden her camera in a tin of dried beans! When I knocked at her door, she thought it was the Germans, because her sister had just phoned to warn her that they had just been to search her place.

*Sept. 11th.*     Kath better. I am glad. Scrubbed potatoes. Some people have been imprisoned for having a wireless. One of them, Mr Ed. Le Quesne and one Russian escapee were captured at St John's yesterday. Joyce told us an amusing story tonight. The States of Jersey are now selling sea-water to the townsfolk for cooking, as there is no salt to be had. They have dépôts at different places in town, one of them being Brighton Road School yard. And last week the schoolchildren went and bathed in this tank of sea-water! So the States had to throw it all away!
It is six years ago that my dear Alfred went away, oh, Black Monday that it was. And I'm finding it so difficult to be brave, and to keep away the tears tonight. I must not look back, but believe that it must have been God's will that things should turn out thus.

*Sept. 12th.*     More leaflets dropped. The Germans pick them up as quickly as possible and are said to be annoyed – the Officers, I suppose. Apparently, the leaflets are having some effect; soldiers are said to be becoming troublesome and some have had to be disarmed. Dad went to La Rocque to take grapes to poor Cousin Sophie who fractured her other thigh and is very ill at a Nursing Home, but he did not see her. He had taken his sandwiches and ate them at Mr P Crill and they gave him some of their dinner too. They told Dad about thefts taking place in their part of the Island also. One woman had her fowls stolen, went to the German officer and told him his men had stolen them. All she got was, "Madam, those fowls were yours; now, they are ours, and we are hungry." Another woman, a Mrs L., had her rabbits stolen and a man came into her yard and told her he had just met a German with a sack on his back. Whereupon Mrs L. got on her cycle, caught up the German and began trying to make him understand that she knew he had her rabbits in his sack. She was afraid to do anything when her servant appeared on the scene, also on her cycle. This gave Mrs L. courage, and she suddenly pulled the sack off the soldier's shoulders, slung it on her own and cycled off! The German was too surprised to say anything. Plucky woman!

*Sept. 13th.*    Alice helped me all morning to wash potato pulp. We finished pulp after dinner, and she went on washing the flour whilst I went to town, as Elsie specially wanted me to go to her Local Preachers' Public Recognition Service She felt I should be there to represent Alfred. It happens to be exactly six years ago today that Alfred's Valedictory Service took place in London, prior to his sailing for Africa. There was Sacrament for Elsie, family and friends, and as we rose from our knees the words which Rev. South uttered filled me with fresh hope and comfort: 'Now unto him who is able to do exceeding abundantly above all that we ask or think.' Yes, God is able to restore my dear Alfred's love and joy. On my way back, the sun was just setting, a lovely red ball as I turned at West Park. What a lovely sight! How beautiful Jersey is still! Esme Blampied has been imprisoned by the Germans for having picked up leaflets and then spread them in the roads. It comes as a shock that one of our Bethlehem girls is in prison. Leaflets are dropped every night now.

*Sept. 14th. SUNDAY.*    Reggie here for tea, with his fiancée, Monica Valpy. We were quite charmed with her! Phyllis Le Brun rang to invite me to go the their Harvest Service at St. Ouen's Church tonight. She thought it would cheer me up! Sweet of her to think of it. I decided to go, especially as Beryl Jordan had been asked to sing. I don't think I had been to Church of England service in Jersey before and I enjoyed it very much – the Harvest hymns, the Anthem by the 'gowned' choir, the duet by Beryl J. and Eileen Marett, the sermon by Rev. Killen, who spoke in poetic language; all appealed to me. I sat near Mrs Syvret who helped me to find the places in the Prayer Book. It really has done me good to go.

*Sept. 15th.* A German Officer went to see the damage at Uncle Ernest's cottage today, and in talking about the war he said: "If Germany Kaput, me Kaput, you Kaput because," and he made Uncle understand, "Bolsheviks would shoot Uncle," (and he pointed his pistol at Uncle!) "and take and destroy his home!" I suppose the Germans believe this and perhaps are pleased to think it too. If they can't destroy England they probably hope the Bolsheviks will!

*Picking up RAF leaflets.*

*Sept. 16th.* Put all my potato flour out to dry. Tonight the leaflet plane came earlier than usual, as we were having supper. I went to the back door and listened to it. The sky was full of stars and the plane sounded fairly low. Then we heard the usual pop as the casket of leaflets opened. One loves to feel that a friendly plane is near! Last Sunday, several men tried to escape to France but were caught, and are in prison. One was 59 and had travelled all over the world, yet the poor man was very sea-sick and could not do his share of the rowing. They were on floats, tied together, and when the wind changed they were blown back to Jersey and captured. So that was the end of their brave attempt.

*Sept. 17th. SUNDAY.* Went to help Lucille at Sunday school, then came back to help at home. After dinner and washing-up went back to Bethlehem for Anniversary practice. Got back at 5 o'clock, fed rabbits, brought in flour, had tea, then cycled off to preach at St. Ouen's, without having time to read over my sermon at all. I hate going off to preach in such a rush but it's been like that these last months. The leaflet plane passed over just as I finished my prayers at 11.45pm. The pops were quite close. One feels as though 'Father Christmas' had just come and one had to wait till morning before looking to see what he has brought!

*Sept. 19th.*   Dad's 60th Birthday. What a pity one gets old so soon. I feel sad that Dad and Mother are already 60 – they seem so very much younger than that. God has blessed us in giving us such good parents and such a lovely happy home. I hope we will never disappoint our parents. Joan Syvret came to watch Laurence extract the honey from his hive. Margaret also here for tea. We all spent the afternoon in the kitchen. Laurence, Herbert, Kathleen, Christine and Joan helping with the honey, and myself sifting my flour. I have 28 pounds out of 208 pounds potatoes – quite a record.

*Sept. 20th.*   Léa came and we picked a small basketful of lovely blackberries, went back with her to have tea. She kindly gave me a piece of German soap out of her little stock of seven pieces, and she is going to type out the whole of the Bailiff's memorandum for me. Rev. and Mrs Struthers came again for a bottle of milk, etc. They are always so hopeful, so one is glad to see them. They told us that nine boys had attempted to escape to France last night, but their boat struck a rock and two were drowned. The others, including Rev. Killen's son, are in hospital. Léa told me she knows of others who have made plans to escape to France. Also, that not long ago a Dutchman succeeded in getting away with his girl. They used to have a pleasure trip every day around Havre des Pas and one day cruised a little further than usual and were away before the Germans realised. It is not surprising that people who have an adventurous spirit try to get away now that the Allies are so close. The German Commandant has a warning on the *Evening Post* saying that further attempts at escape will be considered as espionage and severely punished. So he wants to make sure that we know he is still boss here!

*Sept. 21st.*   In the night I couldn't sleep, thinking and worrying about my poor Alfred. This trial is so hard. I try not to speak about it, and no one knows how difficult I find it to keep cheerful and how sad and heart-broken I feel at times, and getting no news makes one imagine all sorts of things. The Allans here for dinner and tea. It gives them pleasure to come. Mr A. told us of a conversation he had had with a German soldier who spoke English. Mr A. asked what he thought of the war and the soldier said:
"We're beaten, of course."
When asked what he meant to do after the war, he said, "I'm courting now."
"A German girl?" asked Mr A.
"No, an English girl here in Jersey, who comes from Lancashire."
He then said that after the war he meant to go to Canada and try to get naturalised by promising to be a good citizen of that country!

*Sept. 22nd.*   Hundreds of leaflets were dropped over town last night, they were hanging from trees and roofs of houses. Though they are for the Germans, people are thrilled and glad that the RAF come over every night. It does make us feel less lonely! Monica Blampied was at the Practice at Bethlehem tonight. She told us that her sister Esme has been sentenced to three months' imprisonment and will probably go in next week. Monica is very upset, but she says that Esme is not worried. They had found hundreds of leaflets in their fields, and Esme took about five dozen in her bicycle basket, and let them fall in the road on her way to the shop at Carrefour Selous. A German soldier saw her and took her to the Officer at Le Couvent. They kept her there, guarded, from 10.30am to 5.30pm without food. They allowed Monica to take her a coat, as she was just in her pinafore. Then they drove her to prison, kept her there for two nights, then set her free until her trial today. They also searched the Blampied's house and took away a sackful of leaflets which the girls had kept for lighting the fire. But they did not find the camera and other leaflets which Monica had hidden elsewhere! It is believed that some of the boys who tried to escape have arrived in France – perhaps none were drowned after all.

*Sept. 23rd.*   Heard that Mr M., the baker from St. Peter's Valley, is in prison because his sons, aged 12 and 15, hoisted up the Union Jack on a flag-pole he had. The Germans, some living in his house, pulled it down and hoisted up the Swastika, then the boys took that down! The prison is becoming overcrowded.

*Sept. 24th. SUNDAY.*   After Sunday School, I cycled back to take the service at Philadelphie. Afterwards, Mr Le Rossignol told me I had preached a wonderful sermon (I don't think so!) but there was one little point he wanted to discuss. I was able to explain it, to his satisfaction, fortunately! However, it is very good for me to be criticised; it makes me realise how very careful one must be about each point and how sure and clear one must be in one's own mind, concerning the things one is preaching about. Criticism is good when it is not unkindly given but given, as in this case, in a spirit of helpfulness.

*Sept. 25th.*   A friend came to see Mother. She told Mother how upset she has been about her niece's fiancé, whom she loved as a son. We had heard about it some time ago. Totally unexpectedly, the niece had a message telling her that he had married someone else, over in England. I suppose he got tired of waiting, as one reason he gave was the length of the separation. But I feel so sad for that girl, and she is so young to be disillusioned; that man has shattered the faith of a really good girl.

*Sept. 26th.* It is Alfred's Birthday. He is 33. We are not together, and I've no news of him. No good crying even if I feel like it. I can't expect God to alter things just for me! So many people are suffering in one way and another, and I must be content to have my share, and try not to complain.

Went to town, called at Miss B. and she gave me some of Uncle Gordon's pears. What a shocking state his house and garden are in, though the Germans haven't been, which is almost a miracle. Went to Montpelier. Mother had made a little blackberry and apple pudding which I brought for Alfred's folk and Laurence had sent them some honey. The food situation is getting bad and the fuel question is acute. Alfred's Mother is so good, she actually gave me a piece of soap which she had made with tallow which Elsie managed to buy. I hated to take it because Alfred's folk have been without soap for months, but it gave his mother pleasure to give it. Went to see Joy. Hit a curb on my way and fell, bicycle and all and scattered the contents of my basket on the pavement, but I was not hurt. Went with Joy to take her dish to the Baker's oven. Thefts continue everywhere. Mr H Du Val has had 42 head of poultry (all he possessed) stolen, and Constable Du Val all his grapes; Mr.Vibert two tarpaulins, and others, apples and pears. Joyce heard on the crystal set that the prize for the best novel of the year had been awarded to a Miss Elizabeth Goudge for a book on the Channel Islands. Wouldn't we like to read it! However, I think that probably a more interesting book could be written when all this is over! With tears, I pray for my fiancé tonight. May we be reconciled and reunited, long before his next Birthday.

*Sept. 27th.* Alice and I washed potato-pulp all day until I was absolutely done up! But it had to be done – we must have food.

*Sept. 28th.* Washed potato flour and put it on dishes. Sad to hear how terribly our soldiers have suffered at Arnhem.

*Sept. 30th.* Put out all my dishes of potato flour to dry as weather had not been fine enough this week. Spent all evening making the programmes for our three Sunday School Anniversary services tomorrow,which kept my mind well occupied.

*October 1st. SUNDAY.* Bethlehem Sunday School Anniversary, and we've had three very good services, with better congregations than we've had for years. Rev Scott this morning. I played the piano for all the Children's Hymns and solos and Uncle Ernest joined in with the harmonium for the congregational hymns. It was a rush to get there in time for each service but we managed! Mrs Syvret and Joan came to tea and joined us at two services. I've felt more hopeful and cheerful today. Calais has surrendered. Last night Mr F. had a 70-pound pig stolen, it having been killed first with an iron bar.

*Oct. 2nd.*     Fine and sunny so able, at last, to get all my potato flour dry. Afternoon I spent a full two hours at les Potirons with Lucille, preparing the Programme for tomorrow. All sorts of rumours are flying round! Chiefly, that women and children are going to be evacuated, to Spain, Geneva. Supposed to be so that the Americans can bomb the Island until the Germans give up. These rumours may have arisen on account of the evacuation of civilians at Calais, who knows?

*Oct. 3rd.*     We concluded our Anniversary services tonight. Had to start at 5.30 as we have no black-out in the chapel. Again, so many people came that extra chairs had to be put in the aisles. I thank God that everything has gone so well – if all goes as I hope this will be my last Anniversary at Bethlehem, and it will be a happy memory to have. It was a joy to train the children and to see them tonight. I was kept busy all the time, playing the piano and prompting for all the recitations, but I enjoyed it. How sweet are all the boys and girls and what a pleasure it was to watch them. I pray for them all, and ask God to bless them and keep them on the right path.

*Oct. 4th.*     Two of Mother's friends came and Mrs P. got me down in the dumps. She was so depressing about the situation, said the Germans will never surrender, and they will definitely be here at Christmas. My heart sank. To think of another Christmas under these conditions and without news of Alfred is more than unbearable.

*Oct. 5th.*     After crying myself to sleep last night, silly as it is, first thing that happened as I was preparing breakfast was Herbert coming in with the news that all his ducks, 22 of them (all except two), had been stolen in the night. I felt awful – poor Herbert, after all the trouble he has taken to rear them, and the young ones were almost ready to lay. It is cruel and maddening. One feels murderous towards all Germans! We heard no sound and the dogs did not even bark. It was a windy night though, and I loved watching those ducks, always so noisy, quacking away in the back field. How we've missed them today, though I would get annoyed with them for dipping their beaks in my potato flour water sometimes, I'd love to have them doing it now. Poor ducks, where are they now? Laurence is mad and says we have done our best to help others all the time, and we seem to be punished for it!
I know all sorts of bitter things come to one's mind at times, but when one thinks of the thousands who are suffering much more than ourselves during this war, one realises that it is very wrong to complain, hard though we may find things. The Germans don't care if we starve, as long as they have plenty. No use reporting thefts. The boys had not heard it, but people say that, in answer to a question about the Channel Islands in the House of Commons, Mr Churchill said that a demand for surrender had been refused, but the

1.

*German:* "Pourquoi si maigre?"
[Why are you so thin?]
*Jerseyman:* "C'est de votre faute."
[It's your fault.]

2.

Thieves at night – 22 ducks, etc.

3.

Enjoying the spoils.

civilian population were not suffering undue hardships. We had heard a rumour that the Germans had been asked to surrender and evidently it was true. To think that if they had been willing to give in, we would have been free now. A German Officer had told Uncle Edward that a Canadian Colonel had been to Guernsey to try and get a surrender – maybe that was true after all.

*Oct. 6th.*     The Germans have been to Dad's cottage in the lane and removed two windows and their frames. I suppose they will take away all the wood-work as they've done elsewhere in unoccupied houses. In Uncle Edward's cottage they've even broken the oven, out of sheer malice, and removed the floors. They love to destroy! Busy with housework all day. Grandpa not very well and giving us trouble. I found him lying under the bed tonight, instead of in it, and I don't think he knew, poor Grandpa. It is so sad, as well as trying. I don't know what to do to keep cheerful. Hope of release soon has left us now. We felt so hopeful at the time of the Invasion, and when Cherbourg fell. Our spirits are at their lowest ebb – mine are, at any rate! What helps is to tell God just how badly I feel, because I know He understands.

*Oct. 7th.*     Mr Robert had a pig stolen during the night, in a sty just beneath their bedroom windows. Madeleine Luce heard a noise and rang the big bell to give the alarm, but it was too late, and M. saw two Germans carrying away the pig between them.

*Oct. 8th.*     Preached at Bethlehem morning and at Philadelphie evening.

*Oct. 9th.*     Today I thought: If only I could escape from the Island, as some have done. But I can't row, I can't swim, I know nothing about seafaring and I know nobody who could take me. And it's all selfish as I have others to think of beside myself. It is just that this separation from Alfred and anxiety about him is enough to drive me desperate. Then Joyce brought back a scrap of news that cheered me. Someone heard on the BBC that a certain Commander W. has been relieved of his post so as to reorganise the Channel Islands Airways Service, which service will begin to operate on the very day the Islands are released. It is lovely to know that in England they are thinking of us and that travelling will be possible as soon as we are free. People have often told me that we would not be able to travel for months. I feel like going to the Airways and booking my passage now!

*Oct. 10th.*     Francis took a big load of apples to town this afternoon for differ-ent friends. I polished Dolly's harness for the occasion! Uncle Ernest went with him. They left at 2pm and returned at 7pm. They took some to Alfred's folk, Howells, Walkers, Wards, and other friends. There are lots and lots of apples this year, and how thankful we are to have something to give. Everybody wants sweet apples, as there is no sugar for cooking. I'm glad that load has gone as I was so afraid they would get stolen. How our grapes were not stolen is a miracle! I went to Parish Hall to pay rates for Dad and Grandpa. It was amusing to see all the gentlemen sitting at their little tables! They hope to be paid in English money next year, no more 'beastly marks', as everyone says!

*Oct. 11th.*     Very stormy, windy day, but Joyce and I cycled out to La Rocque to see poor Cousin Sophie. She looks so frail but was pleased to see us. We went to her house, Langmead, where Mrs Toomer was pleased to be able to give us a piece of pie and a cup of (Occupation) tea. Had dinner at Montpelier. Joyce went on to the Office and I stayed writing a letter to Alfred because Elsie has heard of someone who intends to try to escape soon and is willing to take letters. It is risky, but I simply could not miss this opportunity of sending a word to my poor lonely Alfred. I hardly knew what to write, but assured him of my undying love, and I enclosed a photo. I took my letter and Elsie's to her friend, who is seeing to letting the right person have them. We do not know who it is, but I told her to tell them of my gratitude if they can do this for me. Not knowing where Alfred is, I addressed the letter c/o The Methodist Society, London.
I called to see Joy. We discussed the possibility of trying to escape. She says Emily's father would be willing to row us three over to France. But, in talking things over, we decided that it would be very foolish to risk doing such a thing, especially as we cannot believe that the Occupation will last much longer. Mother is not strong now and it would be wicked of me to do anything to upset her. Tonight I wrote out practically a whole sermon as I sat in the breakfast-room with the others. It is on the text: 'Remember Lot's wife', and I am preparing specially for Young People's Day. I wondered how I would find time to make this new sermon, but it is wonderful how God gives me thoughts.

*Oct. 12th.*     Rough weather still. Francis took apples to 13 different homes at St. Ouen's. We have heard that some young men who tried to escape this week were seen and shot at by a German guard; one was shot dead and the others are in prison. What a tragic ending. Maybe it will discourage others from trying. My letter to Alfred may not go after all but I would not want anyone to risk their lives for my sake. And I must try not to worry about the letter. I would not like it to get into the wrong hands. How awful it would be if I got my parents into trouble.

*Oct. 13th.*     I finished typing out my sermon this afternoon and evening. It took me three hours to get it right! Ruth R. came and was in a very doleful mood – they have nothing to put on their bread and sometimes haven't the courage to eat it she said. They are amongst those who have no electric light. Her husband tells her he would escape if he had a chance and she could go to live at her Mother's. Fancy, thinking of leaving his wife and children like that, in these hard times. He says he is fed-up with everything. There now seems no hope of release before Christmas so I must accustom myself to the thought otherwise it will be a terrible disappointment again.

*Oct. 14th.*    The Germans have been stopping everybody on their way to town and taking their parcels. Joyce was ever so lucky. She had one pound of butter in four separate packets, but we had taken the precaution of getting her to hide them in her clothes, not in her basket, except one piece which was hidden inside the sleeve of her cardigan. She was stopped by a German at West Park, who said: "Have no-ting against you. I am looking for Black-market." He half lifted her cardigan, but did not notice anything. So she passed alright!

Of course, had he found the butter, Joyce could not have proved that it was only meant for friends. In any case, we are not supposed to have any spare butter – it would have meant trouble. Lots of people have to go to College House tomorrow. Mr P Du Feu had nothing in his basket, just his mac., so

when he was stopped, he shook it out, and said:
"There you are, I've got nothing."
Whereupon the German said:
"You very wicked man. College House tomorrow morning."
How they hate to be cheeked! And he took away his Identity card.
Three soldiers came sneaking round the yard today, said they wanted apples, but I fear they had a good look at the place where the fowls were settling down to roost. We can't think of a safer place for them. I feel so angry with the Germans for stopping people. It will be so risky to take things to one's friends now. However, I am determined that Alfred's people shall still have their half-pound butter and bottle of milk every week as usual. I'll find a way of hiding it as I cycle to town! We had a scare – Rev. Scott came to tell us that one of our cows had fallen on the German railway track and couldn't get up again. The boys found that it was so and Dad phoned the Vet. Then they got the cow on a board, which they had placed on a hay-ladder, and then got Dolly the mare to drag her home! The boys looked so miserable, with several sympathetic neighbours bringing up the rear. But the cow, one of our best ones, looked quite pleased with herself, sitting there like a queen on a sleigh! Then when we'd had all that trouble and the Vet. arrived, she suddenly stood up, perfectly all right! We were all very thankful!

*Oct. 15th. SUNDAY.*       Young People's Day; at Bethlehem morning. Irene de la Perrelle gave a special address and to my joy, afterwards, ten of our young people came forward and asked for a Decision card. God bless them all and help them to keep to their promise. Peter Crill and Evie were here for dinner. Went down to Bethesda for 3 o'clock. Joyce came with me and sang a solo, appropriate for this special day, 'Come Today.' I preached a very serious sermon on the hardening effects of sin (remember Lot's wife). Four girls signed Decision cards afterwards which made me glad. Joyce and I had tea at Mrs Syvret's. It was nice being there. Joan showed us photos of her father, ships and so on. How I pray that Capt. Syvret may return safely after the war to his loving wife and daughter. Tonight I feel disturbed in my mind. Peter has told Herbert that he is making plans to escape, so at once I thought of asking him to take a letter for Alfred. I want to do all I can for Alfred yet am afraid to get my folk in danger. I did not yet speak to Peter about it.

*Oct. 16th.*    Irene here washing. Poor Granny and Grandpa are giving us much trouble. What a care they are and so difficult. I hate Mother to have so much worry and it is so very sad for Dad to see his dear parents like that.

*Oct. 17th.*    I've been trying, ever since Sunday, to prepare a letter for Alfred, and praying earnestly for guidance. I am so afraid to say the wrong thing, Something that Alfred might misunderstand perhaps. This fear of making a mistake has become almost an obsession with me. It has arisen because, though I prayed for guidance in 1940, I waited a day or two too long and got 'caught' here (though I will never know for sure that I could have got away, in any case).

*Oct. 18th.* Very stormy. Alice told us that Dr. Shone has been deprived by the Germans of his job as representative of the Red Cross because he gave a note, which had been sent with a cake, for the American prisoners here. He was seen doing it! I spent most of the afternoon in my bedroom typing out a letter for Alfred and have not told Mother what I was typing. I feel quite bewildered. Then the thought comes: Will Alfred think that I ought to have tried to escape? Will he think that I don't love him enough because I haven't?

*Oct. 19th.* Léa called and asked to see me alone. It was to tell me that someone she knows is hoping to escape and was willing to take a letter, but I must write it tonight. It is kind of Léa to think of me and I must take every opportunity that comes to get in touch with Alfred. Léa brought me the Bailiff's Memo. which she has typed out for me. How shall I repay all her kindness? I went to town, had dinner at the Misses Alexandre. We were all going to a Women's Missionary meeting at Grove Place but I told them I would arrive late as I had to go on a 'secret journey' first. I cycled on to Samares to see Mrs Crill, who received me very kindly (I had been rather afraid to ask). She called Peter, who said he was willing to take a letter for Alfred. Mrs C. gave me a cup of tea and a piece of cake, which was so kind. Her mother came in and I stayed awhile. Mrs C. is so brave to let Peter go, when her other two sons are away already, and Peter wants to join up also. Peter said he would let me know when to take him the letter as he isn't quite ready yet, also the weather is too bad to take the risk. Mrs C. gave me three sheets of thin Air Mail paper and an envelope so that I could write a long letter.
I cycled back to town quickly and got to Grove Place just in time for the last item, the play by the Grove Place Circuit. Everyone said it was very impressive, but I'm afraid I saw and heard very little as I felt strange and bewildered, yet very relieved to have seen 'Cousin Olive' and to have a chance to write a really long letter to Alfred. Mother thinks I was at the meeting all the afternoon, but I can't tell her where I've been, because Cousin O. told me not to tell Mother that Peter was going – she knows it would worry Mother. Wrote a short letter to Alfred for Léa's friend to take; I don't know who these other people are who hope to escape but I hope something will reach Alfred and be of help to him.

*Oct. 20th.* Cleaned rabbit hutches. Joan brought us a nice lot of winkles yesterday and we had some for supper tonight again. Mrs Syvret had gathered them at La Pulente in spite of the stormy weather.

*Oct. 21st.* Dad went to a meeting of the Agricultural Committee in town and brought back the news that the Germans have forbidden farmers to grow any wheat or oats at all next year. The 570 tons of wheat which the States of Jersey had put aside for sowing the Germans have already taken for themselves. They say the farmers must grow cabbages and cauliflower. I suppose they know they won't be here by next Harvest so they don't care about us now or then.

*Oct. 22nd. SUNDAY.* Went to Bethlehem. Spoke to the children at Sunday School and reminded them of what had been said last Sunday; Joyce came and sang her solo. I feel very happy about our children all this time. They have been impressed, I am sure, and I hope they will continue to feel that desire to serve Jesus Christ. I must do all I can to help them. Mr and Mrs Le Rossignol had dinner with us. Mother had asked them specially so that they might share in the little bit of extra that we had. (We had veal, having somehow 'smuggled' a calf!) I was occupied all afternoon, washing dishes and dairy cans, feeding rabbits, bringing in grandparents' clothes etc.

*Oct. 23rd.* Rain and cold. Irene doing washing but could not dry anything. We heated big brick oven, where we used to bake bread, and baked apples, potatoes and pies. Mrs Syvret came afternoon and we spoke about the letter I am writing to Alfred, and I thought she might like me to get a message sent to her husband through Alfred. Poor Mrs S. – she is so anxious about her husband, and longs for news, yet dreads what she might hear. The fact that she and I have our loved one away binds us together. Her husband is always in danger on the sea, and my fiancé could be in danger on land; we don't know where either of them are. And we both worry because we think they are blaming us for the separation, and we cannot explain anything. She brought us another piece of pre-war soap and a few pieces of pre-war chocolate. She is much too kind.

*Oct. 24th.* Kath's Birthday. She and mother and I celebrated by having a cup of 'real tea' during the afternoon, with a little cake Christine had made. Weather very rough and wet. I went to tea at La Pompe and Miss Ethel and I went to the Guild business meeting at Bethlehem. They appointed me as Vice-President, to act in Rev. Scott's place when he is unable to go. Our next Session promises to be very interesting and everyone seems keen.

*Oct. 25th.* Weather better and we managed to dry all Monday's washing. Oliver Mourant says the Germans at College House are getting jittery and he thinks there is something in the wind!

*Oct. 27th.* We have heard that some young men escaped last night. I hope they got across safely. We heard a plane hovering over today, which is unusual now. I wonder what it was doing. I went alone in the wash-house after tea to stir the sugar-beet syrup. As I sat there in the dark, near the fire, stirring, I talked to God aloud, telling Him all that troubles me, especially those letters for Alfred.

*Oct. 28th. SUNDAY.* Stayed in morning doing dishes, Grandparents' bedroom, etc.; lots always to be done! Afternoon went to preach at St. Ouen's chapel and Herbert came with me. Phyllis Le Brun came with the Syvrets as she had wanted to hear me preach. Congregation 74. Singing good and, after service, people stayed to practise Rev. Fell's hymn.

*Oct. 30th.* Irene here washing. It was so windy. I had a cold job at the clothes line! Spent most of my day there and preparing potatoes for tomorrow's big dinner. Irene heated the brick oven and Christine baked her pies etc. and got her soup ready. Just before supper I managed to scribble a few notes for my address at the Guild Meeting tomorrow. We heard a plane flying low tonight, there was heavy shooting and I saw a very big flash. Mr A. who arrived then, said it had dropped flares over the Airport. Quite a change to hear a plane these days!

*Oct. 31st.* An interesting day! Mr Farrell's threshing-machine here threshing our wheat and oats. We used to take our wheat and oats to his place, but as we had so much Dad thought it best to have the machine here. All the morning we women (Mother, Kath, Christine and myself) also Irene and Alice, were preparing the meal, arranging the tables etc. We'd borrowed a load of chairs from Philadelphie chapel (used at concerts in the Parish) and cups (used at Sunday School treats and teas), also borrowed boilers and tins and dishes from various neighbours. We gave dinner to 38 men; half sat in the breakfast-room and the others in the kitchen, including the German inspector. We were very upset when we heard that a German inspector was being sent to farms where threshing was going on and at first said we would not give him a meal! But in the end we had to do like everybody else, and we decided to carry on quietly, as though he wasn't there, so things went all right. Dad sat by him, and he ate everything we gave him and said nothing. I offered him a second helping, which he declined. The dinner consisted of vegetable soup. Poor Christine cried over her soup because she found out that it tasted sour, so she put in two jars of sugar-beet syrup, to try and improve it. I told her it was quite all right and tasted like tomato soup. And it was funny, because all the men thought it was tomato soup, though there wasn't one tomato in it! And they found it good! As one said: "Well, I'd never tasted tomato soup before!" I think the cause of the trouble was that Christine had prepared her parsnips last week, thinking we'd be threshing yesterday, and probably they had fermented and caused the sour taste! Well, after that nice thick soup came baked potatoes, beans and hash (made of rabbit and secretly kept veal) with a layer of potatoes on top and plenty of gravy. Lastly, apple pie and potato flour pudding, a cup of sugar-beet 'tea', also sweet cider. A fine dinner for occupation-time! We had put vases of Chrysanthemums on the tables! After all these men had dined, we women ate what was left, and enjoyed it. So, altogether, we were 46 persons dining at Homestead today! (That includes the grandparents upstairs).

At the threshing, Dad and the boys managed to get a good number of sacks of corn for ourselves when the German inspector's back was turned! We believe that he deliberately turned away to let us have some sacks, as a 'Thank You' to us for having given him a good meal and treated him kindly. After all, he was only doing his duty, poor fellow, and he wasn't at all arrogant like some are. He was evidently satisfied with things and said that Dad was a 'good' farmer! He managed to make us understand that he had not liked it at another farm, where all he was given to eat was two potatoes! I went to see the machine at work, it was so interesting.

Alice and Irene did the washing-up as I had to get to Bethlehem for 3.30pm to preside at a Cradle roll meeting. Had tea at Evie's with Lucille and Miss Ethel, then we went to Bethlehem for our Wesley Guild opening night. As Vice-President, I had to take the chair and give a talk on the Aims of the Guild, our responsibility, etc. We had several items, then enrolment of members, then we all sang 'One Heart, One Way.' With such a bewildering, busy day, I don't know how I managed to collect my thoughts to speak at those two meetings! So at end of day, I thank God, and ask Him to bless and keep my dear Alfred.

*November 1st.* Threshing-machine still in our back field, threshing for our neighbours. More and more houses being searched, supposedly for black-market stuff, but, in reality, Germans seeing what they can find for themselves. We don't know where to hide the wheat we managed to get yesterday, our own, of course. Fancy stealing our own property! We've heard that the plane which crashed last night was an American, and some of the crew were killed. It makes us very sad and angry because the Germans shot at a machine which they knew perfectly well was in distress and trying to land. Not the first time they've done that.

*Nov. 2nd.* Called at Emily's. It was her Birthday and I had nothing to give her but a few eating-apples, two pears and a small bottle of milk. I found her and Joy cooking a rabbit, which Emily had fattened, so for once they were going to have a good meal. Went on to Montpelier. I feel so sad to see how little food they have. All they had for dinner was potatoes (cooked at the Baker's oven) and a few very small pieces of carrot. The pudding consisted of oatmeal and milk and perhaps a little potato flour. I wonder if Alfred worries about his people. Lack of fuel is a great trial for townsfolk. One sees people 'wooding'. I even saw Rev. Fell with a big branch of fir tree on his bicycle.

How far does one branch go!
Called at Mrs Bunting – Margaret was just going off with her bicycle, loaded with old tins, to get some tar, as it is said there won't be any more after this week, people have been using it for fuel, mixed with saw-dust. Went to tell Mrs Ward about the letter which I've written for Peter to take. She rather disturbed my mind, though, by asking me if I'd asked Peter to take me with him. I would have thought that she would have tried to prevent me, had I proposed to do anything so rash, but apparently she does not think it so risky as all that! What about those who've already drowned or been shot trying to escape! However, she told me it would be wrong to do a thing like that against my Mother's wishes. She asked me if I'd prayed about it. Of course, I have. In any case, Peter has enough to worry about without taking on board a woman who can't even swim and who isn't as brave as he is either. It would have been wrong to ask him, even if I'd thought of it. And surely Alfred would not want me to do anything so risky. It seems that something is always cropping up to torment me more! But when Rev. Ward came in, his prayer helped me.

*Nov. 3rd.* Backward with work through having been to town yeaterday. Things getting worse. The Germans have taken large stocks of our butter and oatmeal, and are asking for 50 shirts from each parish! The German 'wheat' inspector told Uncle Ernest that the Commandant, Heine, was 'bad'.

*Nov. 4th.* No cheering news this week, not locally at any rate. A man aged 42 has killed his wife, aged 30, and hanged himself afterwards because she went with the Germans. It is said that there will be many more such tragic happenings. Residences, supposed to be pro-German, have been tarred. And a man was found placing a large quantity of dynamite to blow up a certain shop because the owner has always sold at black-market prices, and now only sells to the Germans. Horrid man – I went to the shop once and found him much too familiar.

*Nov. 5th. SUNDAY.* Went to Bethlehem morning. Spoke to the children about William Tyndale – wish I had time to read more about these wonderful men. Rev. Fell was our preacher. I had brought a bag of potatoes and some apples and a scrap of butter for him to take home. Preached at Tabor afternoon. Mr Benest played the harmonium as there was no electric power for his organ. People are very indignant about the plane the Germans shot down on Tuesday night. We've heard that it was a transport plane taking twelve men on leave. It was in distress and trying to land, had all its lights on and threw out landing lights, yet the beasts shot at it and all the men were killed except the pilot. The plane fell into the sea and some bodies have been recovered. The wounded pilot is said to be furious and to have told the Germans that they will be punished for it. One feels so sad, and for the families of those men who were expecting them home. I think that most of the planes shot down here, if not all, have been some that were in trouble already.

*Nov. 6th.*    Peter told Joyce to tell me to send him my letter tomorrow, so evidently he is hoping to escape soon. Joan called to show us a baby, Michael Vautier, seven-months-old – the sweetest-tempered baby ever! I loved holding him in my arms. Poor Mr John Trachy has had all his fat rabbits stolen – he was keeping them for friends at Christmas. It is a shame.

*Nov. 7th.*    Pouring rain all day. Cycled to town; just as I arrived a ship's siren went. Schmettow, the Commandant in Guernsey, is supposed to have arrived for meetings with the Commandant here. Wish they were planning to surrender! Went to Montpelier for dinner, and Joyce. In spite of the rain Elsie came all the way back with me, to fetch a few pounds of wheat. It was blowing hard too. I don't think Peter and his friends will be able to attempt to go just yet – strange what bad weather we've had for so long. I called at Crill's office and gave a few shillings in silver to Mr C for Peter. I only had 3s.6d of my own, so my sisters gave me another 4 shillings. Now I have no English silver coins at all. However, I expect Alfred will have some! How strange it will be to be using silver again after all these horrid paper marks!

*Nov. 9th.*    No rain but very strong cold wind. I spent all day trying to get Monday's washing dry, what a job putting it out in that cold wind; washing dishes, peeling potatoes for dinner and tea and for tomorrow. Also cleaned rabbits and attended to Granny. Dad heated the brick oven and we baked potatoes and apples.

*Nov. 10th.*    Mrs S. Le B. and Beryl came and brought us four small cooking-bowls, one small tin of black boot-polish, some pepper and lentils, all of which they had in their 'secret hoard' in the shop. What lovely presents! How we appreciated them! I feel anxious because of the dreadful V2s which Hitler is sending over England – the danger was not over, after all.
We've heard that Schmettow is here to try and make Heine willing to surrender because in Guernsey the population is very badly off. One had heard that Schmettow would be willing to surrender, but not Heine, the Commandant here. Thieves have come again, for Dad has discovered that a good and large waterbutt has disappeared. We were remarking today that we all feel better in health and much less tired than some months ago, and we put it down to the sugar-beet syrup, which we've been making again lately, and eating it on our bread and drinking it with milk. I'm sure that is what has given us fresh energy. But what a job it is to make. Poor Herbert has so much trouble.

*Nov. 11th.*    Our grandparents are getting to be a great trial now – so much washing, and we can't get things really clean without soap. It is so sad. And young people are dying every day. This week, the husband of someone we know has died of TB aged only 37. Also, we are sad to hear of a few farmers who are selling foodstuffs at high prices to the Germans, whilst their own countrymen are near starvation. The love of money is, indeed, the root of all evil. More thieving; this time 12 boxes of potatoes have been taken from our big shed and Dad's axe and wood-splitter from the wood-shed. I'm afraid the rest of my rabbits will get stolen. Joyce says four more young men escaped last night. There is said to have been an important meeting between the two Commandants, but no surrender.

*November 12th. SUNDAY.*       Someone told Dad that the Germans now say they can hold out until April. It makes me feel sort of desperate. If only I could have a scrap of news of Alfred. It is the suspense of not knowing how he is feeling – at times I feel lonely and comfortless, which is stupid, with all the family here around me. My turn to stay in this morning. Grandpa fell again – we had to call the boys to help him. It frightened Mother. Evie here for dinner. Went to service at Bethlehem this afternoon. Watch followed us, and during the first hymn walked up the aisle to the choir, jumped up, putting his fore-paws on the bookrest opposite me! And he was all wet too! When Joyce tried to take him out, he just flopped down heavily and refused to move. So he sat in the choir under our feet during the prayer, then during the second hymn, he decided he'd had enough and walked away down the aisle and Joyce took him out!

*Nov. 13th.*       Peter Crill and his friends got away on Saturday night, but as yet no one knows if they got to France safely. Why must I be tormented with the thought that when Alfred gets my letter he will think I should have tried to escape, rather then send a letter. There will be no peace of mind for me until this wretched occupation is over! There's a notice on the *Evening Post* to the effect that the German Authorities have made arrangements to send an Appeal from our Bailiff, to Switzerland, letting the Red Cross know the state of things. But though the Bailiff has prepared his message, we cannot trust the Germans to see it through. This is the second attempt and, as far as we know, the Red Cross never received the first appeal. I have found fresh strength in praying tonight, and am going to bed with these words in my mind: 'For in Thee, O Lord, do I hope: Thou wilt hear, O Lord , my God.' Psalm 38 v. 15.

*Nov. 14th.*       Grandpa cannot help himself since he fell and poor Dad had to get up twice to help him, and he and Granny made a lot of noise in the night talking loudly. And more washing to be done this morning. Elsie came to fetch some sugar-beets and had dinner. She is very happy that my letter to Alfred has gone. Perhaps tomorrow, or even today, he might receive it. Surely he will be glad to have such recent news. Went to Wesley Guild tonight. Several of our members read papers they had written about their jobs: a postman, a stall-holder in the market, a butcher, a housekeeper, two bee-keepers, a village carpenter, and a farmer. The last, by Francis, was exceptionally good. I felt proud of my brother! Very sad news today: four men who attempted to escape have been drowned, their boat smashed to bits by the rough sea and rocks. Two bodies have been washed up at La Saline. It is said that they had shouted for help, but the Germans would not help and others could not go on account of the mines. I feel anxious for Peter but hope all is well. Germans now threatening reprisals on the population, if others try to escape again. There is a notice on the *Evening Post* that we can send Red Cross Messages again. I haven't much hope that they will get very far – what we want is release.

*Nov. 15th.*   One never knows what is going to happen from one moment to another, even in one's own household. We thought the doctor should see Grandpa, and he was expected when I left for town, about noon. When Joyce and I returned at 6 o'clock we were greeted with the news that a trained nurse was coming, as poor Grandpa has broken his thigh and, of course, Mother and Dad do not want to send him to a Nursing Home. Poor Grandpa, he will never walk again. I feel so sad, also sorry not to have been more sympathetic since he fell. The nurse arrived at 7.45pm in the Ambulance. Just as the front door bell rang, the light went out, unexpectedly, as it often does nowadays, and there we were greeting her in the Hall with an inch-long candle! So tonight Kath and I have been preparing my bedroom for Nurse to sleep in and making up a bed for me in my three sisters' bedroom. Tomorrow we shall make more permanent arrangements.

We all feel so strange tonight and the boys have spent their evening beside the hearth in the boulangerie (bakehouse) whilst Nurse sat with Dad and Mother in the breakfast-room. Well, with 12 of us in the house we were enough already. We won't be so private as before but we shall have to get used to it. One never imagined such a thing would happen. I hope it won't make Mother ill again. Fortunately Alice was here but, had I known, I would not have been to town. Joyce and I had dinner at Montpelier, then I went to Samares to see Mrs Crill. (She says I must call her Olive). I am getting to like her so much and I used to be rather afraid of her! She told me the very good news that they know that Peter has arrived safely in France. I thank God. She told me about the escape. Peter's boat was in a garage at Samares, and he got a furniture removal van to take it down to Gorey on Saturday after working hours. He had to give his bicycle (so precious these days) as a bribe to the driver. There were two boats: Peter's (12 foot) equipped with oars, sail and motor, also canvas covering one end. There were two others with Peter and they had enough food for three days. Peter had 25 letters, the Bailiff's memorandum and a letter of introduction to the BBC. He hoped to get Sandy MacPherson to play a tune. It helps to feel that over in England they will get reliable information through Peter. The other boat was larger and manned by an experienced man who used to be sent to Granville as buyer for the States of Jersey. Both boats left at 8.10pm on Saturday, making for Granville. There wasn't a German in sight, but on the beach were 27 civilians to see them off. Whether the guards were bribed or not, Mrs Crill couldn't say, but Peter and his friends had filled their pockets with Reichmarks, just in case. I expect it depends who the guards are – some may turn a blind eye. One does not know.

*Nov. 16th.* All day we've been preparing the dining-room, to put Grandpa and the nurse in there. Dad had such a job finding suitable beds and fixing them. Now the hall is full of furniture. And we did not know what to do with the nurse whilst we were preparing! So Kath lit a fire in the dining-room, and she sat there and read her novel whilst we worked! When all was ready she phoned the ambulance; the men arrived with their stretcher and carried poor Grandpa downstairs. He suffered in being lifted but bore it well. Uncle Ernest came. In the midst of all this, I heated the brick oven and we baked apples, potatoes and pies, including one for Mrs Laffoley. Granny is alone now, and we don't like to see her alone, but she did not seem to notice when the men took Grandpa away from her side. The nurse is not very approachable – or lovable! She does not seem grateful that I lent her my bed. She says she's been frozen all night and had never spent such an awful night as in that bed and she's got tonsillitis and so on! Oh dear, what shall we do with her. At meals, I feel like laughing out loud, for no one speaks and she doesn't see a joke! It is awful! However, I expect she feels strange here and maybe things will improve when she gets settled. I am very pleased to be back in my own bedroom tonight.

*Nov. 17th.* Things improving now that Nurse is settled, as she stays by the fire in the bedroom. I take her breakfast in bed so we are alone for one meal in the day, at least! Poor Grandpa seems to suffer very much and I feel very sad to see him so. He does not like his nurse much, he told Uncle (in Jersey French) that he wouldn't like her for his wife! She was in the room! She says she does not understand Jersey-French – I wonder? Dad and the boys have been very busy all day making holes in the ground in the greenhouse and elsewhere to hide wheat, oats and potatoes because farmers have been warned that the Germans are coming to take what we have. So we must hide, not only for our own sakes but so that the Germans have as little as possible, for the less they have the sooner this Occupation will be over. But our problem is how hide and where hide. My tortoiseshell doe had a litter of rabbits at last! It is months since I'd had any little ones.

*Nov. 18th.* Full of work! Cleaning, preparing Granny's room and so on. We put Granny in my bedroom. Mrs Laffoley lent us a small bed for her and she seems quite happy in my little room. I must sleep on a stretcher in the girls' room until Granny's room is ready for me. Cleaned my rabbits this afternoon. Grandpa seems frail and has slept all day. Tonight he is talking strangely. Nurse is 'thawing' somewhat! I was trying to, prepare for Sunday School tomorrow but the electricity failed twice and also I feel too tired to do it properly. We've had such a week! Laundries are closing down as there is no more fuel. The latest saying is that whilst there is one tree standing and one cow left in a field, the Germans will hold out! Farmers are all busy trying to hide their foodstuffs.

*Nov. 19th. SUNDAY.*      Went to Bethlehem morning. Gave the talk to the children in Sunday School, and then I had to take the service in chapel because the preacher did not turn up. I had some notes with me, fortunately, but still I felt very unprepared and hardly know how I went through the service, after our upsetting week too! Nurse went out for dinner and tea today. Francis and I went to tea at the Alexandres – Norman is such a nice boy. It was pouring with rain on our way back – an awful ride, with only one small light between us, and so many potholes. I was glad to be back safely.

*Nov. 20th.*      Irene here washing but too wet to dry. We have all been terribly busy all day – somehow work seems to increase. I spent my whole day washing dishes, peeling potatoes, cleaning, seeing to clothes etc. And Dad and the boys have again spent their whole day hiding things. Dr. Shone came and found Grandpa better and is not sure that his thigh is broken, after all. But I don't find Grandpa well at all. Mr F Jehan, carpenter, here today, starting to do the bedroom for me.

Mr Averil, farmer, told us today of how someone had sent an anonymous letter to the Germans, and they came to search his place. They turned out every drawer in his niece's bedroom and they took all his wheat except one barrel. He had an unregistered pig and they tried to make him say where he had got it. His reply was: "I was born under the British Flag, and soon will be under it again, and I'd rather be put against that wall and shot, than tell you where I got it!"  To go before the Gestapo at Les Niemes, he put on his oldest cap, back to front, and his dirty working clothes, making himself look as awful and untidy as possible! They had taken two pounds of butter, which they had found, and they offered to give it back, so he said: "I want to ask you one question: did your soldiers have clean hands when they poked my butter?" Also, his wife, seeing that they left one barrel of wheat, said: "Oh, how kind of you, thank you so much, God bless you!" This made them angry, they hate sarcasm! Their reply: "Enough of that – prison!"

*Nov. 21st.*      Mr B., neighbour, came early to warn us to expect the Germans, as they had been to his house. He was white as a sheet, he is so nervous! Not quite knowing what to do, we began feverishly hiding things. I saw Dad digging a hole in the garden, where he hid a biscuit tin containing a piece of veal and a piece of pork (which had been given to us, Mr H Du Val, returning kindness for kindness). I hid my camera, diaries, Bailiff's memo. and RAF leaflets in some bushes; other things, including John's crystal set, in Granny's bed and others in Grandpa's bed. However, after our scare the Germans have not come today and we've fetched our things into the house again!

We had plenty visitors this afternoon. Tonight Joyce and I went to Home Missions meeting at Bethlehem. Rev. Scott spoke about Samuel Chadwick and Uncle John, who was presiding, was pleased to be able to tell us that his Birthday was on the same day as S. Chadwick's. Rev. Scott had to hurry up with his address, for once, as we only had light for one hour; we had to disperse in the dark!

*Nov. 22nd.*   Doctor came and said Grandpa must be X-rayed. After dinner we saw two Germans come into the yard and they held out a form to Dad. They had come to 'take stock'. They did not search, they went where Dad showed them what they wanted to see. In the attic, there were five barrels of wheat and we are only allowed to keep 3. They also allow us one barrel of potatoes per head – that wouldn't last us long either. These soldiers appear afraid of the Gestapo. They told Dad they could not leave us more because, "Gestapo come!" So we must expect them. On the *Evening Post,* there is a notice that in response to the Bailiff's broadcast appeal a fortnight ago, we are to receive Red Cross parcels, food, medical supplies and soap. Will those parcels come? What we long for is release rather than parcels. One has a lurking fear that the Germans will only stay longer if we get help from the Red Cross.

*Nov. 23rd.*   Dr. Warrington came and took an X-ray of Grandpa's leg. Dad and the boys still very busy digging holes to hide things. What a job! We heated the big brick oven this afternoon. I called at two farms to see if people had an army blanket or two to spare for the American prisoners here, who are in the damp and cold at the Fort, and Miss Messervy wants to make sleeping bags for them.

*Nov. 24th.*   Same depressing wet weather – even indoors everything seems damp. All Monday's washing is still in the wash-house waiting to be dried. This morning I washed all the things from Grandpa's bed, etc. with my new soap-substitute – wood-ash – and I found it answers very well indeed. I boiled the wood-ash for about ten minutes and then soaked the bits of blanket and sheets, etc. in that water and washed later. Nurse is as usual – somehow she is not at all like us, we seem to have nothing in common. I don't feel I would like her for my nurse if I were ill! She has tied Grandpa's feet and hands to stop him fidgeting and it seems cruel to us. Today he is mumbling and groaning and hardly knows us. It is pitiful to see him lying thus. I fear he is rapidly getting worse. The X-ray has revealed a broken thigh and there is nothing to be done. Poor Papa, I wish he did not suffer so. He had fallen so often that we did not realise that he was badly hurt.

*Nov. 25th.*     I find poor Grandpa getting rapidly worse. We heard him calling out in the night, and he clutches at the bedclothes, and calls upon God to have pity, "O God, my Father," he cries. I helped Nurse when she washed him today, as Dad had gone to town and I was horrified to see a bedsore as large as a saucer at his back. It is horrible. I had never seen one before, and to think that it has got so big just in these few days. Poor Papa, no wonder he suffers. It is pitiful to hear him when one moves him. I nearly wept before Nurse whilst I was holding him, whilst she washed his poor back. And he has gone so thin. I think Papa is dying. People are so kind. Joyce brought back two large pieces of soap – real pre-war soap – sent to Mother by Miss Marie Hacquoil. She must have heard that we had no soap.

*Nov. 26th.*     Our dear Papa passed away peacefully this afternoon. We are so relieved he died peacefully. He had been quiet since last evening, gradually going into a deeper and deeper sleep, and just breathed his last quietly. Mother and Dad were there with Nurse. This morning, I went in first, as usual, with Nurse's breakfast, and Papa's eyes were closed. I spoke to him and said 'It's Nan' and I know he heard me, for he opened his eyes just for moment. I took his hands but they were cold and no longer gripped mine. When I went in later, he could no longer hear me speak. I kissed his brow, but he knew it not. Seeing him so bad, we did not want Nurse to touch him for washing him, so we phoned Dr. Shone, and though doctors do not usually go on Sundays now, he managed to come. Dad told Dr. Shone that he had always hoped that Grandpa would live to see the end of the war, and the doctor said: "He'll see it before us."
I'm sorry now for the times I've felt impatient with Papa. It was not his fault that he gave trouble lately, and I should have realised it more. The only way I can make up for it is by living the best life I can, and trying to be as good a Christian as Grandpa was. People say I am the most like Grandpa in character and I am glad and proud if this is truly so. How thankful one should be to have Christian grandparents and parents. How much we owe to them we can never measure. What would I have been had I not been brought up in a Christian home, I dare not think! For I have as much evil in me as anybody else, but I've had a better chance to develop the good than many others have had. Alice and Hilda came to see Grandpa but were just too late. They were very sad, and poor Uncle Ernest burst into tears when he came. Nurse asked me for some flowers, and I gave her a purple and a white Crysanthemum and she put

the little bunch in Grandpa's folded hands. Nurse seems nicer somehow, and this morning she was very kind, for she offered to wash Granny for me. So she gave her a blanket bath and cut her hair. Poor Granny, we have not told her about Grandpa. She spoke of going down to see him, but quickly forgot and spoke of something else. I feel sad to see her alone. I must be very kind to her. Poor Granny, she likes my bedroom.

*Nov. 27th.*   All feeling very sad. Mr Maillard, the undertaker, came to arrange with Dad and Uncle for the funeral. I am so sorry for my dear Dad. On top of his sorrow, many other things worry him. He had his head in his hands at dinner and Mother asked what was troubling him. He said he saw no improvement in the situation and he's heard that the Germans are not allowing us to keep any calves at all after December. They've taken 26 tons of butter for themselves, out of 30 tons which our States had put by for the civilian population. I hope Dad won't be ill. He has suffered so much to see his father suffer and there's been all the worry of hiding things.

*Nov. 28th.*   Pouring rain all day. So sad and strange indoors with the blinds down all day. The much-talked-about Red Cross ship was supposed to arrive today but it has not! I feel so anxious at times about Alfred. Herbert tells me that Hitler's V1s and V2s still go every day over England – many houses have been destroyed and more civilians killed or injured than soldiers at the front.

*Nov. 29th.*   All day in the wash-house. Alice did not come as J P was ill but the copper was lit so I carried on, and Joyce came later to help me. I had soaked the washing in wood-ash, and put a bag of wood-ash in the copper – that was the only 'soap' I had today to do all that big wash! We worked all day, with hardly time to eat our dinner; yet darkness fell and we had not finished. Dad came and washed the trousers for me and helped us to empty all the tins. I've had to leave quite a lot of things from Grandpa's bed.
Mr Maillard came and we all went to see Grandpa. He looks lovely in his coffin. Somehow, he looks much better and more himself than he had looked during the past months and I don't feel upset to look at him. Dear Papa, I've already forgotten all about the work and worry he had given us lately, and I remember all that he has been to us, his good life, and especially how he was always thankful for everything. If ever a man counted his blessings, Grandpa did. On his lips, the words 'Thank you' were ever-ready, to the very end. He even said 'Thank you' when the Nurse tied his poor hands. Uncle came tonight. He and Dad are taking so much trouble to make sure that Grandpa's funeral is as he would have wished it to be.

*Nov. 30th.*   This afternoon our dear Papa was laid to rest in St. Mary's cemetery. Joyce came with me whilst Kath and Christine stayed to help Mother give

243

'tea' to those who came in. I went to look at Grandpa several times and felt sad that I shall never look upon his face again. The coaches arrived just after 2 pm. It was nice to see dear Rev. Ward – it is so long since he came into our house. And Alfred's father. Our wreath, 'from all his loved ones at Homestead,' was really lovely – a big cross made of white Dahlias, bunches of violets and a few orchids. Miss Silvey, whom Grandpa was fond of, had made it, and taken special pains, I am sure. I was able to see her afterwards and to thank her. I arranged a spray of my Chrysanthemums: 'from his loving wife' to be buried with the coffin.

Joyce and me walked to Bethlehem with Mrs Averty, then sat with Auntie Edith. The Chapel was full (apart from the gallery) and we had a lovely service conducted by Rev. Ward, who gave such a fine tribute to Grandpa in simple and straightforward language. What made one happy was to know that every word was true: Grandpa's love of home, and his influence there and as Constable of the Parish for six years during the war, his 60 years as a Methodist local preacher, his help to his widowed sisters and so on. And we felt the sympathy of everyone. Some had cycled from the other end of the Island and others would have come, had there been means of transport, but not one bus goes on a Thursday, and not one taxi or cab to be got! Mr Maillard had managed to get four coaches. As the cortège left the chapel, the choir sang the French hymn 'Sainte Cité' which Grandpa was so fond of. The coffin was carried by the bearers from the chapel to the Church cemetery, all the mourners walking behind. It was an impressive procession. Elsie came to the service – so good of her. I wish our dear Alfred could have been there. He was fond of Grandpa and I'm sad he won't see him again. Tonight Uncle Ernest came and we were all sitting round the poor little fire in the breakfast-room during the half-hour without light. We all thank God that Grandpa died here at Homestead and not at a Nursing Home. How terribly we would have regretted it had we sent him away, as the doctor suggested.

> I have fought the good fight
> I have finished my course
> I have kept the faith.

These words are true of Grandpa, and Dad had them printed below the notice of his death on the *Evening Post*. We rejoice that Grandpa has 'entered into the Joy of his Lord.'

*December 1st.*      Another month – will it bring us change, one sees no hope of it at all. Everything seems gloomy and sad. Dad phoned Rev. Ward to thank him for the way he had spoken at Grandpa's funeral. Dad told him that when he was young he had said to himself: "I want to be to my father what I would wish my son to be to me." Well, Dad has been always so good to his father,

and certainly has absolutely nothing to reproach himself about.
We have no more salt, not even to boil the winkles that Mrs Syvret has sent us. Herbert has managed to borrow a pound to carry on with, until we make some more. We've already used up the 14 pounds we'd made from sea-water. Francis has been to town with the van and hoped to bring back a canful of sea-water, but the tank at the dépôt was empty. Also, there are no more stamps at the Post Office.

*Dec. 2nd.* We have received many cards and kind letters of sympathy from people who knew and admired Grandpa. Pastor Hanks has written Dad a really lovely letter. The local news are more depressing than ever. From now on, all our calves are to be killed. We've heard also that people are going to have only a quarter of a pint milk a day instead of half a pint and one day a week with no milk at all, and no butter after this month. There's a notice on the *Evening Post* that the Germans are going to take our potatoes, wheat, oats and sugar-beet and we are not allowed to dispose of any of these things. Only what we've hidden is safe. It is such a pity we could not hide our seed potatoes. Dad is upset, because he had no idea they meant to take those as well. Two brothers have been drowned this week, whilst attempting to escape. Their companion was caught. Tonight, I had a fit of rebelliousness and anger against God, for this anxiety about Alfred is too terrible to bear – time goes on, no change, no news. It is enough to drive one crazy. Is it possible that I must spend yet another Christmas without Alfred – the seventh since we parted? So I told God all about my wicked rebellious thoughts and asked for forgiveness, new strength and courage. And God answered, because as soon as I got up from my knees, that mood had passed!

*Dec. 3rd. SUNDAY.* Did not go out at all, as I have a bad cold. Tonight read the story of Joseph from the Bible, intending to make a sermon showing how God can bring good out of evil. After reading, I had no ideas yet. Went to light the fire under the kettle on the big hearth. Sat there in front of it, read from a chapter headed Man from the book *Outline of Theology*. Then the light went out as usual. As I sat there alone, in the dark, except for the flickering of the wood fire, I prayed for Alfred and for guidance for my sermon. Light came back, and just as suddenly came clear thoughts for my sermon! Got supper, took up Granny's, had mine, poured out for the others, and at the same time wrote out the outline for my sermon. That is how thoughts come, and it is wonderful how God guides me!

*Dec. 4th.* Plenty work! Put all the washing to soak in wood-ash water. Mother washed the flannels. I put them out and they fairly dried in the strong wind. Had four visitors this afternoon but I was too busy to see them. John told us that a soldier told Capt. Roberts yesterday that if the Commandant does not surrender by January they will shoot their officers. People say the soldiers haven't enough food. Tonight I painted a birthday card for Joy. It is strange to be crowded in the girls' bedroom, and it isn't quite so easy to pray as when I was alone in my room.

*Dec. 5th.* Spent the whole day from after breakfast washing the clothes, with Kath helping me when she could. I put a bagful of egg-shells to boil with the clothes – they say it whitens and I have nothing else, no soap-powder or soap. I find the wood-ash very good for soaking but not so successful in the copper, probably because I don't know what quantity to use. I wanted to finish early as Mrs Syvret was coming, but I had two copperfuls left over from last week and didn't finish till 4.35pm. What a day! However, I quickly fed the rabbits, rushed in to change, and was able to see Mrs S. for ten minutes. Just when we need her most, Irene cannot come as her husband is ill, poor Irene. The Germans have begun collecting the wheat and oats from the farms and at some places have taken the fowls. So, the boys have been busy making a hiding place for our fowls. I fear they won't lay much 'up there' after being loose in the farmyard. But what can one do? We got sea-water from La Pulente today to make salt. My tortoiseshell doe is not doing very well and I am disappointed. She has only four little ones left, having squashed two, one of which Herbert had to kill, and the other I found dead.

*Dec. 6th.* Spent most of day running to and from the clothes line in the back field; got some things dry between the showers. Mother cleared the cupboards of Grandpa's things. We miss him and Dad is still sad that Grandpa did not see the end of the war, and we all wish he could have been with us for Christmas. Dad has been making salt today. Manual workers are to have their bread ration reduced to four pounds four ounces per week, as we are all alike now. Also people with cattle are not to be given any butter ration from next week. Yet, we are not supposed to make butter! Mother has given half a pound of our butter ration every week to Alfred's people, and we don't want them to be without. Mrs Le Brun phoned – she believes in the Red Cross ship, says it is coming on Saturday! We had quite given up hope!

*Dec. 7th.* Went to Quarterly Meeting at Grove Place. Reggie Jeune argued with Rev. Ward about the singing of the National Anthem in our chapels! I noticed ever so many people with old prams, boxes on wheels, etc. going to see if they could find any wood lying about. If it wasn't so sad, it would be funny to see crowds of people around a fallen tree – sawing, tearing, pulling off the branches. People are mad for wood. It is pathetic, really, to see the poor townsfolk. I really don't know how they live. I had a bag of apples and gave them to children that I saw on the road – nearly all of them were carting home their findings of wood, some had such cold pinched faces. Their faces lit up

246

when they saw an apple! How lovely it is in these days to have something to give!

I went to see Mrs Ward and found her trying to cook a sort of oatmeal biscuit on a fire so small that I could hardly see it. It is awful that people have no fire to warm themselves, and not enough to cook properly. There are so many in need that one can only help them a little. Dad told me that one cow out of every three is being slaughtered. We have 15 so that means sending five to the butcher. We've already sent four. It is very worrying, as we've spent years building up our herd of pedigree cattle. Things get worse and worse, and no sign of the Germans going. Tonight, went to a YLU meeting at Bethlehem. Enid Le Feuvre spoke on the work done in various Children's homes in the Island, then Mr Ph. Le Feuvre gave such a fine appreciation of Grandpa (who had been President of the YLU branch at St. Mary's since it began in 1902). He mentioned especially Grandpa's cheeriness, his approachability and his enormous energy. He asked us all to stand for a minute in silence. Then he said he had good news to tell us. He had just heard from the Bailiff, who had been told by the German Commandant that the Red Cross ship was on its way to us, having left Lisbon last night. Everybody clapped!

*Dec. 8th.*     Rain and hail, very cold. I began typing out my sermon on 'God meant it for good,' and it helped to strengthen my own faith!

*Cooking difficulties*

*Dec. 10th. SUNDAY.*      Joyce's 23rd Birthday. I preached at Philadelphie morning. This sermon, made in such a short time, has helped me tremendously. I wonder if it has helped anyone in my congregation as much! Service in the schoolroom as they are fortunate enough to be able to light two wood fires there. Went to Bethlehem evening. Rev. Scott had a 'memorial service' and preached well on 'Let me die the death of a righteous man' and also he paid a fine tribute to Grandpa. Tonight I wrote to Uncle Gordon in case he is still in Germany. The Red Cross ship is supposed to take letters when it comes. Rev. Scott told us that he had preached to the American prisoners at the Fort this morning – all very nice fellows. They introduced themselves to him, and how Rev. Scott would have liked to tell them some news, but he could not, with the German guard there all the time.

*Dec. 13th.*      There's a notice on the *Evening Post* telling us that the Red Cross ship has not left yet! Will it ever come?

*Dec. 15th.*      Spent any spare moment in starting to make little books of Bible pictures to give my Sunday School scholars. Dad took a sackful of vegetables and apples to the Town Hall in response to the Appeal. I received another letter from the Secretary Mr Jackman, giving me details. Scores, even hundreds, of aged and infirm people in and around town, are being given small parcels of beans, apples, or an egg, jar of sugar-beet syrup, matches, wood and having their wood chopped.

*Dec. 16th.*      Busy tonight sticking my little picture-books, such a bother when the light goes out though. Mrs Syvret says that she's heard that thousands of letters are waiting at Lisbon for the Channel Islands. We both feel in suspense, having been so long without news. One longs to hear, and yet one is afraid.

*Dec. 17th. SUNDAY.*      Went to Sunday School. Mr Boxall came to give a special Christmas talk to the children. Pastor Hanks preached a very good sermon, as always. He has a special gift and makes us see things. He came back this way, so that we might give him some milk and apples to take back, but he would not stay to dinner.

*Dec. 18th.*      In the wash-house all day with Kath helping. Ellen Amy called afternoon and came into the wash-house with an apron on and kindly helped for an hour. I was so pleased. She washed the men's working-trousers for me, which I find so heavy to handle. If I were as big as she is, I might not find the work so hard! People now think the Red Cross ship is coming on Saturday. We shall see!

*Dec. 19th.*      Mother in bed with a bad cold, so did not go to town as I intended. Saw to getting clothes dry, etc. Started painting the words of a Prayer on a card to give to Alfred's parents, which I think they will find helpful. Went to Guild at Bethlehem tonight for the usual week-night service. Guilders had brought gifts of foodstuffs to be sent to Miss Le Breton's Home for the Aged and to Mrs Ward for distribution amongst the needy in town. The response was very good; someone had even thought of bringing wood. Tonight I feel in a bad mood, fed up with state of things, I've even stamped my foot in anger and frustration!

*Dec. 20th.*    Went to town. Called at several places with a little milk, butter or eggs (all carefully hidden as I cycle to town). Misery everywhere. Feel down-hearted to see how people suffer especially through lack of fuel. Even if they had more food, they could not cook it. Most people keep their overcoats or dressing-gowns on all day to keep warm. The Germans are laughing at us about the Red Cross ship – now they say it is leaving today! A fortnight ago the Commandant told the Bailiff that it had left! Had dinner at Montpelier. The journey back from town tires me. It is the hills – whichever way I come back there is a long hill to walk up, pushing the bike.

*Dec. 21st.*    We had to take two fowls to the Parish Hall for the Germans to eat at Christmas. It is awful, when so many Jersey folk will be without a Christmas dinner. But it is best to let them have what they want otherwise they will take it by force, and maybe punish us too.

*Dec. 22nd.*    Alice and Miss Marcus here. I went to town. Called at Rev. Fell's to give them some cheese Mother had made. Mrs Fell insisted on giving me a few tablespoonfuls of soap-powder and I know she needs it herself. But she says she can manage till the Red Cross ship comes. She'd just had a letter from Guernsey which she read to me. Her friend had sent her one teaspoonful of bi-carbonate of soda in her envelope which was in exchange for two teaspoon-fuls of real tea Mrs F. had sent her! I went to Town Hall to take beans for the Friendship League. Place was crowded with poor people and one woman would not let me pass. "You will not pass, I will not let you," she said. I felt very indignant and told her I was taking something for the poor townsfolk, and if she did not let me pass, she wouldn't have any! I managed to push my way past. It was only later that I realised that probably the poor woman thought I was trying to take her place in the queue!
And no wonder they are 'fed-up' of being in queues in the cold. Joy told me that there were hundreds waiting for tar this morning (and as it was cold, the tar only trickled out of the tap) with little carts, prams, also horses and carts. One old woman had come all the way from Grouville. It meant hours of waiting. I tried to find Christmas presents in a town of boarded-up shops, or shops with second-hand things. I bought a few books, not as clean as one

would wish though! It is amusing – one buys other folk's cast-off goods and they buy ours! Oh, what a Christmas! I'm sure people in England couldn't even imagine what it is like here: nothing, nothing in the shops!

A little boy asked me to give him tuppence to buy an empty tin he had seen in a window – a tiny, and not too clean tin! He wanted it to put his Mother's Christmas present in (two cheap rings). He went into the shop, so pleased. I gave him an apple that I had, poor little fellow. I was late, and Joy offered me some dinner. It was kind of Mrs Walker and Joy to share their few potatoes and carrots with me but I know it gave them pleasure to do so. Their char-woman had had her baking-tin with her dinner stolen from the baker's oven. So, there are kind people, but also mean people, some helping to make things easier for others, others making things more difficult. Called at Alexandre's, then at the Skyrmes. Miss S. was so pleased with the scrap of cheese I brought, for they were at the end of their food today. I wished I'd had milk for them, but I'd already given away what I had brought. Miss S. is so good and sweet. She cheered me so! She said, "I know it will be good news for you, Nan, when it comes." God bless the Skyrmes and all our good Christian friends. Tonight I finished painting my few Christmas cards but I've not finished the little books for the children yet.

*Dec. 23rd.* Very busy, housework etc. Mrs Pepin and Mrs Le Brun came. Laurence had a cock for Mrs P. Elsie came because we wanted to give her some wood, to help their fire on Christmas Day. We spoke of Alfred and I felt cheered because she feels as I do, that all this must be for a good purpose, for we have always done what we felt was best and cannot really reproach ourselves. We sent a bagful to the Wards, which I packed – a little bantam-cock, which Laurence prepared for their Christmas dinner, potatoes, beans, a bottle of milk, a quarter pound of butter and a few Rouget apples. How I wish they could have dined with us but there is no transport.

*Dec. 24th. SUNDAY.* Preached at Bethlehem this morning, but only got there two minutes before service was due to begin because Granny had got into trouble and I had half-an-hour's work in her bedroom before I could leave – what a rush. Luckily for me, the children were late coming out of Sunday School. Lovely sunny day, and Christmassy, everything white with frost. I had taken a bunch of Christmas roses for Miss Clara and for Evie. But when I gave them to Evie, it made her cry. What a fool I am. I meant to give her pleasure, but it only reminded her of the loss of her Mother. She said to Kath afterwards: "I don't know why you've given me these when Ma isn't here to see them." I feel upset to have been so foolish. Reggie and his fiancée came to tea and stayed till 10.45pm. Curfew being extended to midnight tonight. I do like Monica and think Reggie is very fortunate! We were glad they were here, we also had Mr and Mrs Vibert.

*Dec. 25th. CHRISTMAS DAY.* Lovely sunny, cold, nippy, frosty weather – exhilarating and refreshing after the rain and damp of the past months. Joyce was the only one of us girls who had time to go to service, for yesterday being Sunday, we did not want to prepare the veg. etc for today. Laurence had fattened a fine cock and, though we were 14 for dinner, we have some left for tomorrow. Mr O Mourant and the Watson-Allans were here for dinner and tea. This afternoon I went out on my bicycle. I knew Mrs Syvret would be finding it hard, as I am, so I felt I must go and see her. So, about 4 o'clock, when my work was done, I cycled down Jubilee Hill with bunches of Christmas Roses for my friends. (They've done very well this year, without being covered). The hillsides were still white with frost, the air exhilarating, the sun was down below, over the sea. I was glad I had been as Mrs S. was feeling so 'down' today. She told me that when she got up, she just sat down and cried. And she didn't have the courage to light a fire in her sitting-room. So I found them in the kitchen – her sister, with her children, Enid and little Arthur, were there. Mrs Syvret made me a cup of 'tea'. Then she walked up the hill with me, and we talked of our loved ones, and the hope of news by the Red Cross ship. She had trouble to walk, being bruised by knocking into a German motor-bike yesterday.

Called at Phyllis Le Brun and saw her Granny in bed. Rev. and Mrs Norman were there, also feeling sad, because their son is away. Then I visited 'Auntie' Florrie Pirouet and Alice and Hilda. It did me good to go out and everyone seemed pleased to see me! Tonight, after our visitors had gone, we spent our evening quietly, reading by the fireside. We thought of Grandpa. John had cried this morning because Grandpa was not with us for Christmas, but we know he is better where he is. I dreaded this day, but it helped me to go out, and I've been well occupied all day, so that I've not wept in secret as I think I've done every Christmas since parting from Alfred! I've read the copy of the letter I sent him through Peter and feel that it will have helped him. I wonder how he spent this day. Someone from his Methodist flock will have invited him, I know. For the first time ever, we've had no Christmas pudding – nothing with which to make one!

*Dec. 26th.* Mrs Syvret and Joan were here for about two hours tonight. We were glad to have them to talk to as the light was out for most of the evening, and we couldn't have done anything. I put all washing to soak for tomorrow. Weather is frosty, everything still white. Tonight, the moonlight and starlight were so lovely. I looked out, and longed for my darling Alfred and for a walk with him in that lovely moonlight. I felt ready to cry and it was really hard not to, especially seeing Christine and Raymond together in the sitting-room.

*Dec. 27th.* In the wash-house all day with Kath helping. Red Cross ship is supposed to have arrived in Guernsey. Our Bailiff has left for Guernsey to meet the Red Cross Officials – all sorts of rumours are going round.

*Dec. 28th.*    There was a meeting at the Parish Hall today about the Red Cross parcels if and when they come! Each Parish must arrange for them to be fetched from town. Dad was there and there was an awful row between the Constable and Mr X. The latter had offered to fetch parcels with his van, but when the Constable read out his list, Mr X. was not on it. When he asked why, the Constable told him bluntly, "Because I don't want you." My orders are to choose my men and I don't want you." Then ensued a terrible row, Mr X saying that the Constable ought to have a swastika stamped on his forehead and so on! The Constable ordered Centenier E. to show him the door, which order Mr X. ignored. It looks as though the Constable knows something about Mr X. and feels that he doesn't deserve the honour. It might be that he's had dealings with the Germans. We don't know, but what a pity to row over the Red Cross parcels!

*Dec. 30th.*    The Red Cross ship has arrived! One can hardly believe it after all the disappointments. Mrs Syvret phoned at 4.45pm to say she could see it in the St. Ouen's Bay. I ran to the top of the field, but was too late to see it. My feelings are mixed – within the next few days we might have news; will it be good? One moment I'm full of hope, next, full of fears! I've not been good this morning. Kath wanted me to move into the bedroom, which is now ready for me, and I did not want the bother today as I felt I had enough to do otherwise. So I grumbled and was angry with Kath and moved my bed angrily. Then I was very sorry and ashamed, for Kath is so good and she even lit a fire this afternoon to warm the bedroom for me.

*Dec. 31st. SUNDAY.*        Just as we were getting ready to go to Sunday School, Dad happened to phone the Vet and the telephone operator told him (quickly, in Jersey-French (though we are only supposed to speak in English on the phone) that if we had anything to hide, to hide it at once for the Germans were searching all the houses in St. Peter's. In no time they were here. I saw three on bicycles enter the back yard. What an escape we had – John was only just hiding the crystal set, when they were at the door! Two marched upstairs at once, opened various cupboards, but only peeped into Mother's and Granny's bedrooms when they saw that they were occupied. We all had to show our Identity Cards. They did not search minutely here, but they did in some houses. No one knows what they were looking for. It must have been a person or persons. All the people going into Philadelphie chapel were stopped for Identity cards. Joyce and I were late for Sunday School.
This afternoon I preached at St. Ouen's; congregation 58. Herbert came with me. Looking back over the past year, I realise how God has helped me to bear what I thought I could never have borne, another year without Alfred, and in

suspense, months without news. I've had many moments of doubt and despair, but God has always lifted me in answer to my prayers. Tonight I look forward to 1945, believing it will bring us deliverance and peace, and reunion with loved ones.

*Mother in bed when Germans searched all houses in St. Peter*
*one Sunday morning.*

Pre-Occupation scenes at Homestead,
our Jersey farm;
Left: Christine (front) and
Kathleen picking blackcurrants;
Below: Jersey cows;
Opposite: Harvesting Jersey
Royal potatoes.
Top: The Le Ruez family at work;
Bottom: The author (right) and sister
Kath picking up potatoes.

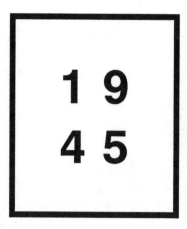

# 1 9 4 5

*January 1st.* First thing we heard was of the thefts of two cows in the night. Mr C Le Gresley had a one-and-a-half-year-old heifer taken and Mr Vallois a two-year-old. He got up, but the Germans pointed their bayonets at him. He got the German police and all he got was, "And they didn't leave you a piece!" They went away laughing to themselves; no doubt they will feast on the heifer themselves. These thefts are no doubt organised and we can only expect more. The Germans don't like us to be having Red Cross parcels and not themselves! Francis went to La Pulente this morning to fetch sea-water for salt-making. Went to town, took bottle of milk to the Fells, and found Mrs F. trying to make a pudding with macaroni and water. When I got to Montpelier, 'Father' was just back from the bakehouse and the dinner was cold – on New Year's day too! The potatoes and gravy were cold, and the stewed rabbit too (it was their Christmas present from Mr Howells).

Alfred's Mother was very pleased with the Evening prayer I had written out for her. Took some milk to the Walkers then went to Uncle Gordon's garden and got as much wood as I could possibly carry and hold on my bike, and brought it to Montpelier so that today, at least, Alfred's folk could have a fire worth calling a fire. Mrs B., the neighbour, was all right and gave me two lovely pieces after I'd given her a scrap of butter and cheese! Later, I went alone with 'Father' up Mount Bingham, where we had a view of the Red Cross ship, the *Vega*. (I felt sad when, looking over the wall, I saw Algerian prisoners in their bare, cold camp-yard, surrounded by barbed wire). I enjoyed that walk with 'Father' and picked up any odd bits of wood that I came across. Elsie says that people in town have got 'wooditis'; I think I've got it too! How glad I was that Alfred's people were able to have a good fire tonight, and they did enjoy it. There's enough wood left over for several days. We had dinner and tea in the sitting-room, where the fire was, and tonight we played Lexicon and Halma.

*Jan. 2nd.*     Breakfast at Montpelier, visited a few friends then went to Red Cross Office to take a Message for Alfred but they would not take it, as I had sent one in November and they are only allowed to send one thousand this month. The Red Cross ship is apparently not taking messages or letters back and I am very sad about it. Worse still, we may not have any news at all. People at the Red Cross Bureau have heard no news, but I will go on hoping till the end of the week, anyway.

Things are so discouraging everywhere. People faint for lack of proper food, many die suddenly of heart failure and one woman was shot last week by German soldiers when she went downstairs one night, and has died. So, I have not found much to cheer me in town. Felt tired when I got back, and did not go to Guild tonight. It is because I am tired, I suppose, that I'm feeling discouraged and hopeless tonight. It seems as if I shall never hear good news of Alfred again. I've read on the *Evening Post* that there are letters from prisoners in Germany which have come in the *Vega* but no mention of any others.

*Jan. 3rd.*     Woke up feeling more discouraged than ever – I'm so disappointed that there will be no letter or message from Alfred. Alice came and helped me with the washing. We finished much earlier than usual. I fed my rabbits and got ready to go to La Pompe. Kath, Joyce and I went for tea and Francis came afterwards. We had such a pleasant evening with the Arthurs. We played Chequers quietly by a lovely warm fire, not the usual Occupation fire tonight. And we had a cup of real tea before leaving for home. Coming back in the dark, it was pelting with rain and we got soaked. But what lovely people the Arthurs are!

*Jan. 4th.*     I went into the back yard about 8.20am to see Francis going off with the van to help fetch the Red Cross parcels in town. It was not yet fully light, the moon was shining and a bitterly cold wind was blowing. Constable Du Val, Ed Le Feuvre, Mr Priaulx and Mr Maillard went in our van. 'Dolly' went well and they arrived first in town. After having loaded at Martland's store, the 14 vans lined up and left for St. Peter's. Francis was proud to be leading the convoy! The parcels were dropped at the country shops and Herbert fetched our eleven in the hand-cart this afternoon. (If only Grandpa had been here he would still have appreciated these parcels). After tea we opened two, and the rest tonight. How wonderful all the things are! It brings tears to one's eyes. One feels so grateful to all who've had a share in the making-up and the delivering of all these good things for us. What have we done to deserve it! The parcels are almost alike, though some have soap and others have none. We are particularly delighted to have found tea in all but one. This food has come just in time. What rejoicing there must have been in many homes today, especially in town. Only those who have come near to starvation or even reached it know just what these lovely parcels mean. Here are the contents of mine: Cabin biscuits, 5 ounces chocolate, quarter pound tea, fine sugar, 7 ounces Atlas raisins, 6 ounces prunes, 4 ounces cheese, 1 ounce mixed pepper and salt, 1 tin (10½ ounces ham) Kam, 1 tin Cap (12 ounces corned beef),1 tin Marmalade (12 ounce), 1 tin butter (16 ounce), 1 tin Klim (16 ounces powdered milk), 1 tin salmon (7 ounces), 1 tin sardines (3½ ounces) and 1 tablet toilet soap.

Mrs Syvret and Joan here to tea. We enjoyed their company so much. The *Vega* has gone back today, sailing straight for Lisbon. Will she bring news next time? Mrs Syvret told us that Adèle Martret now sleeps in her stable because the Germans milk her cows at night. Some nights ago she chased them, barefoot, with a fork! She is in danger of being shot. Mr Vallois showed us the scar caused by a bayonet when he tried to stop the soldiers from stealing his heifers. It is no good trying to stop them.

*Jan. 6th.*     Washed my hair with the little piece of red soap Mrs Fell had given me. All the talk is about Red Cross parcels. People are so thrilled and grateful. Only a few grumble because perhaps there was no soap or tea in their own particular parcel – they ought to be ashamed of themselves to grumble! We all feel so thankful for everything. Why, even before the war, we would never have thought of buying so much all at once, and we've got more tins of food in the house now, from those parcels, than we've ever had in the house before! It seems extravagant, somehow, each of us that big parcel to oneself. Edward Le Feuvre and Mr W Priaulx came to collect for the Red Cross. We all gave something in memory of Grandpa, and we shall have opportunity of giving again. People say that in a three hour Conference with the Red Cross Commission, our Bailiff told them everything (the Germans being present) and how we could have managed without help if the Germans had not stolen our food and stocks. He even spoke of "if I am alive next time you (the Red Cross) come." He was brave enough to speak out, not fearing the consequences. I suppose the Bailiff is fed-up now. He's had so much to put up with that he can keep silence no longer, even if it means being shot. But I don't think the Germans would do it now. Harold S. is in prison for 18 months for having said to a German soldier, "Why don't you shoot your officer?" It happened some weeks ago, then, this week, he was called to College House. As he did not return, his father went to town to look for him and eventually found him in Gloucester Street prison.

*Jan. 7th. SUNDAY.* This first Sunday of 1945 has not been a very cheeerful one and we feel sad and upset tonight. We meant to eat a little of our Red Cross chocolate but did not do so, as we would not have enjoyed it. Because a plane was shot down before our eyes about 5pm and, so far, we have not heard if the pilot or other occupants were able to escape. Why did it come here at all? Mother and the others saw it through the window, as it came down in flames after the Germans had shot it through many times. Kathleen cried and all were very upset and Mother was frightened also of the shooting. Joyce and I were with Auntie Edith and Margaret just past St Mary's church – we heard no plane, but suddenly, this terrific shooting began and I saw balls of fire rushing through the sky. We all took shelter under the nearest bushes and only came out when the shooting was over. I felt that a plane had been shot down. The weather is stormy and cold; perhaps the pilot had lost his bearings. I preached at Six Roads chapel this morning; congregation 40, including 24 children. There will have been prayers of thanksgiving for the parcels in all our chapels today.

*Jan. 8th.*      Hail and snow, but our hearts are lighter because the pilot of the plane was saved, thank God. He parachuted and fell into the sea, whilst his plane fell on waste ground at La Moye. He steered away from houses before jumping. Two American prisoners have escaped from the Fort, and we are warned that if we shelter them, the penalty is death. One is called Capt. Clark and the other Lieut. Haas. Mother has been in bed all morning – she had not slept after yesterday's upset. Dad and Kath are in bed with bad colds so I had four breakfasts to take upstairs. Joyce stayed away all day from the office so as to help me. Fortunately, Irene turned up to do the washing and I only had to prepare for her and to put out and bring in the clothes, between showers!
Mrs Le Feuvre came with Edward's wife and baby girl. She told us that it was high time the Island had help for we only have flour for five weeks. She said that the Bailiff told the Germans (in front of the Red Cross representatives) that they were but a gang of thieves and robbers! I have exchanged my tin of marmalade for one of apple and grape, from Mrs Laffoley, as they had no marmalade in their parcels. We had cabin biscuits with milk and real sugar for supper – what a treat! It seems that one is having too many good things all at once – real tea every day for tea and after dinner! Granny is so noisy and restless at night. I got up twice to see to her, then I had trouble to go to sleep again, worrying about Alfred and lack of news.

*Jan. 9th.*      Kath still in bed. No news to cheer one up. Germans taking more bicycles and things, and generally making things harder for us. The American pilot who was shot down is at hospital, his foot was hurt. A young Jerseyman went to his rescue on a raft but was unable to help, owing to rough seas, so finally the lifeboat went out, but he had already been on the rocks for two hours. We hear that the pilot was short of petrol, and thought he was over the Isle of Wight and signalled that he was going to land. We would like to give the American prisoners something from our parcels but we are not allowed. Wulf, the Chief of the German police is said to have been sent to prison by the Commandant because Dr. Hanna made a fuss when Wulf opened a tin of Kam with his dirty knife, to make sure there was nothing hidden inside. (Martha Messervy was there and saw him do it). Then Wulf wanted to put the tin back like that in the parcel. Even the Red Cross parcels they must open!

*Jan. 10th.* Alice helped me to sweep bedrooms, etc. Kath still in bed. From today, there is no electricity except in the evening, and even then it is cut off for the usual two half-hours and goes off entirely at 10.30pm. It is so awkward in the mornings. I had the three breakfast trays for upstairs to get ready so had to use a candle and we've only a few left. It is nearly 9 o'clock before one can see to do one's work. We heated the big oven this afternoon. By a new German order, we are not to be allowed to keep more than one dog. We don't know what to do. Watch belongs to Francis and Vicky to Laurence and both are such fine dogs. The Germans are mad because we've had parcels and they will only hatch more ways of annoying us whilst they can. Joyce, Herbert and I had tea at the Le Brocqs at the Stores. They gave us some pre-war tinned ham – it had kept perfectly. What a treat! Edward let me have a bottle of ink. I am so glad of it as one can't buy any anywhere and we've just about run dry of what we had. I feel less down-hearted tonight and have been thanking God for my blessings. And especially for the Power of Christ to save and forgive.

*Jan. 11th.* Cold and freezing, hail lying on the ground. Kath got up after-noon. John has told me that Mrs Le B. the widow, has been sentenced to over two months' imprisonment. The Germans searched her house and found RAF leaflets and 1½ hundred-weight of corn, most of which the poor woman and her daughters had painstakingly gleaned. Her house was searched because her brother-in-law, who sleeps there, had tried to send a letter to his wife in Eng-land through a bargeman who intended to escape. Then he was caught, and the letter found on him. (What if Peter had been caught and my letter to Alfred found and Homestead thoroughly searched!) German soldiers are supposed to be angry because the parcels we've received show that the Allies have plenty food, and they've been led to believe that England and her Allies are starving! It has snowed heavily tonight. It makes one anxious about the townsfolk. Alfred's father in that cold Office all day, and his Mother with her hands full of chilblains and no fire to keep herself warm.

*Jan. 12th.* Snow has turned into rain and it's been a cold, wet, slushy day. I've felt wicked and irritable all day, perhaps because I don't feel too well, have a cold coming. Hope it won't be bad, because I don't know who would do the work. Kath isn't well yet and Christine has enough to cope with trying to keep the wood-fire burning under the cooking pots etc. Mr O Mourant today shook hands with young De la Haye of St. Brelade's who tried to rescue the American pilot on Sunday. This boy saw the man land on the rocks about a quarter mile from shore. He swam out with a float. He got the American on to it, but after having gone about ten yards the float broke because the Ameri-can was so big and heavy. The boy managed to swim back to the rock, holding up the American. He then swam back to shore and found a German fussing more over the fact that he had lost a ring, than trying to go to the rescue of the stranded man. The Germans had no boat at St. Brelade's and the pilot had been on that rock for two hours, cold and wet, before they finally arrived with the lifeboat. The boy had gone to bed, quite exhausted. That American has had a miraculous escape, for he could neither swim nor float. He was on his way from London to Paris when one of his engines failed, and his plane could not rise, when it was shot at. More and more tales of thefts of cattle and potatoes etc. The second lot of Red Cross parcels appears to have been tampered with – maybe there won't be enough to go round.

*Jan. 13th.* It froze hard in the night. Thankful I've been well enough to get up and work! So many rooms to sweep and tidy. Mother helped me with the bedrooms. Kath got up afternoon and prepared vegetables. Plenty new Orders tonight: No more butter ration for anybody after this week, and milk for everybody, invalids included, only four days a week. The Germans are annoyed that we've had parcels and so are taking our rations. At times I am so afraid that Alfred's people may not be able to stand the cold. Elsie told me on the phone that they've burned their scullery table to make a fire. People are reduced to burning their furniture now.

*Jan. 14th. SUNDAY.* Not well enough to go out today. Kath much better and got up for dinner. Have been very busy all day until now 4pm but I won't be left long in peace! I hear the clatter of dairy cans already, so must set to and wash them. I'm feeling irritable, tired of trying to be brave and cheerful when my heart is so anxious, heavy and sad. I know this mood will pass when I get on top of things again, but just now I feel at the end of my tether. The St. Mary's farmers have now had an Order to send 20 loads of seed potatoes tomorrow morning for shipment to Guernsey. The Germans are pretending that it is for the civilian population there. They will take away everything from us and say that we are being fed by the Red Cross!
*10.30pm.* I feel much better, my despondent thoughts have gone! I began to feel better when I read again parts of the letter I sent to Alfred through Peter. Then I read ten pages from the chapter on 'Christ' in the book of theology which helped me a lot. Then Herbert told me that the war news was good. Let me be more patient and trustful!

*Jan. 15th.* Irene here, lots of washing but too damp to put anything out, and there is still some from last week, waiting to be dried. Mother in bed with a bad cold. Mine improving but not well enough to go to Mrs Syvret's for tea, very disappointed. Local news getting worse: more theft, more imprisonments. A girl has been imprisoned for three weeks because she tried to send a letter to her brother in England through an escapee who was caught. Many imprisoned for having wheat (some, gleaned with much trouble). Houses are being searched again. Dad found soldiers sawing the beams in his cottage in the lane. They are actually felling good telephone poles for firewood and many people cannot use the phone. Town is said to be cut off entirely, except for doctors, etc.

There was a riot at Westmount on Sunday. Scores of people went with saws and axes to chop down trees. When a tree falls, women and children dive for the branches, a proper scramble. The Germans came and tried to stop them, took away their tools and the wood they had got and they even got the Bailiff, the Attorney-General, the Constable and Centenier of St Helier to come and quieten the people. People are so cold and hungry. The Germans take what they want; they are even cutting down lovely old trees in people's gardens. Francis has been to town to take a load of potatoes for Uncle Ernest who has to obey the 'St. Mary's order'. There were scores of vans and carts there, he said, unloading into the stores. (We know who will eat those potatoes!). Today there were soldiers by the dozen, digging away in farmers' fields for carrots, left-over potatoes and turnips. They must be hard up for food.

*Jan. 16th.*    The baker told me that if the Red Cross ship does not come by the end of January there will be no bread at all. There is only enough flour left for a fortnight. Joyce and I went to Guild at Bethlehem tonight. The subject was 'When Peace comes' and three of us read papers we had written on that subject. Stephen B. recited from 'Hiawatha' and Rev. Scott spoke also, and I had asked Mrs Le Herissier to read from 1 Peter 3 v. 8-17. Such a profitable evening but a pity there was so little time – the light came on at 8.15pm and went out at 9 o'clock, just as I was in the middle of making an appeal for the Friendship League for money to buy wood for the poor and aged. I was much impressed when two boys, both brought up at the Home for Boys and now working on farms, gave me 5 marks between them (10s.8d.).

*Jan. 17th.*    Feel really upset by another Order: no one is allowed to go 'wooding' any more, not even on their own property. Whatever are people going to do to cook and keep warm. Tons of seed potatoes are still having to be taken to town. Things seem to have got worse since the *Vega* came. I wrote to Joy as her phone is not usable whilst ours still is, don't know why.

*Jan. 19th.*    Last night was one of the stormiest we've ever had – the wind was terrific. There is no more fuel left for smithies, so if we want our horses shod, we'll have to go to the German smithies – they will allow our smiths to work there if they wish.

*Jan. 20th.*    The Germans had a meeting with the Constables of all the Parishes yesterday about wood. They will allow no one to use any wood that is lying anywhere, not even on their own property, not even branches already cut, and they will take all they want from any farm or field. They want an enormous amount – to last them until August, they say. We hope they'll be gone long before that, liars and thieves that they are! Our Constable also expects them to take all saws and axes from farms for their own use. One German officer sneeringly observed that next time the Red Cross ship came it might bring us coal. May it be our turn to laugh soon! I feel bitter against them these days, for the suffering they cause. Some men were cutting and loading their own wood (before the latest order) and the Germans were watching them. When the load was ready, they forced the farmer to drive his cart to their own Headquarters at St. Ouen's. He could do nothing about it.

*Jan. 21st. SUNDAY.* My turn to stay in morning. Preached at Tabor this afternoon. I was glad to see Léa there. She told me that one letter I'd sent through her in November had gone for sure. The boy who took it escaped about the same time as Peter. Another she had tried to send she gave back to me. I was relieved, because I didn't like to feel it was still in a stranger's hands, especially as several persons have been imprisoned lately when such letters have been found in their possession. Mr Vibert had sixty boxes of potatoes stolen last night. He reported it to the German police who told him they couldn't be bothered to listen to him as they had been up all night! So he knows who had his potatoes. During the week, Francis received an anonymous letter insinuating that he (and all our family) was cruel to animals, and expressing surprise that 'good church-going people' like the Le Ruez should be so, and that he (so the writer is a man!) would like to see Francis' horse walk, once in a while! A stupid letter, and it must be someone who is jealous. Dolly is certainly not cruelly treated. Why, Francis has a job to keep her still, she so enjoys trotting! I feel very angry that Francis, who is so good, should be the victim of this annoyance! Read another ten pages of Clarke's theology, what a splendid book it is.

*Jan. 22nd.* Went to town. Called at Fells with a drop of milk and a scrap of cheese which dear Mother makes. Found Mr Fell very downhearted. He said, "Oh well, there is one thing we can still do, that is, die, and yet that is hard nowadays. It is too expensive, undertakers are so costly." He finished up by laughing when he said that there was one comfort, at any rate, one could not feel worse than one felt! Had dinner with Alfred's people. His poor mother's hands are in a dreadful state, and she said that yesterday she was so down that she did nothing at all.
Afternoon I spoke at Wesley Sisterhood. About 35 ladies present, such a friendly atmosphere. Mrs Walker presided. I hope my talk on Genesis 50 v. 20 proved helpful. Heard that the electric light will be completely cut off after next Thursday. Called to see Phyllis Le Brun at the bank. How lovely she

looked – a sight for sad tired souls, so bright and young and full of life! May all her life be beautiful! Cycled back with Joyce. Felt awfully chilly all evening. I expect I'd got too heated up cycling. I always do! Dad and the boys have been trying to hide our wood so that the Germans don't get it.

*Jan. 23rd.*    Mr Arthur Querée had a five-month-old calf stolen last night. It was a fine calf, from 'my' cow Tiny Louise which Dad had sold to him, and his only calf. Oh, those wicked Germans! Some days ago they stole a sow who had 13 day-old piglets and of course they've all died. A German soldier told Uncle Ernest today that the war will be finished in eight days, he thinks, because Russia, England and America are crushing Germany! He will be jolly glad because he wants to see his wife again. He said it was all Hitler's fault that war had come, but he must not be caught saying it. Evidently, that soldier is not a real Nazi! Went to the 'Ladies Evening' at Guild tonight. I had to preside though I did not expect it, but I am prepared to be pounced upon for such things now when others back out! We cannot hold any more week-night meetings now as there is to be no more light. It is a pity our Guild must close down.

*Jan. 25th.*    Went to Sunday School Council meeting at Grove Place. We decided to hold our Convention on May 24th, if conditions have not changed. But, in view of the way things are going, we decided to have another Council at the end of March, when we hope we'll know better what to decide – dare one hope for the Occupation to be over by Easter? Called at Town Hall and left 112½ marks for the Friendship League, the result of my appeal at our Guild. I had not dared hope for such a splendid result. Went to the Wards and took them a scrap of butter, milk, cheese and potatoes. It was over a month since I'd been able to go; it helped me to speak to Mrs Ward. They both have awful chilblains on their hands and nothing to be done about it. Had dinner with Mrs Walker and Joy. How things have changed for them! Felt so sad to see their miserable little fire, in an old paint-tin, on which they boil (or try to!) water for drinks and washing of dishes etc. Things are most difficult, and tar all over the place in the grate and on the mat. The ration of potatoes they get is very poor – small, and often many bad ones. I don't know how they live. I took little parcels and bottles today, as usual, hidden in my coat and basket, and am so thankful I was not stopped and searched. I was afraid of it when I left! On my way home, I went to Millbrook Nursing home to see Mrs F Du Feu who has had an operation. She asked me to read St. John ch. 14 , and then I prayed with her. She told me how God had helped her, for she had so dreaded the operation.

*Jan. 26th.*    Dr. Shone came as Granny has bronchitis. Everything is snowed-up tonight, inches deep. I have just been out on the lawn, and the house looks lovely – all the windows are snowed-up and everything covered. How beautiful it all looks: the whiteness makes it seem light instead of dark. I wish Alfred were here and we could go out now, and walk in that lovely snow. No electricity today. Most folk now just have to go to bed when it gets dark – nothing else to do, with no heat or light. Uncle Ernest has sent us a little paraffin which he had stored, so we've lit a small lamp to see to have supper and to wash the tea and supper dishes.

*Jan. 27th.*  Herbert and John went out last night and made a snowman in the gateway of the 'Little Field' but today it has nearly all melted away. It is freezing tonight. The sun came out and it has been a lovely day, though one can't enjoy the sunshine much when one is indoors all day doing housework. Yet one must be thankful to have work to do, and the strength to do it. From today, there is to be no *Evening Post*. Not much loss really! Elsie phoned and said they had to go to bed at 7 o'clock last night – no light, no wood to make a fire. The Germans have shot Jack Le M.'s pedigree Airedale dog, for no reason whatever. They were shooting Lapwings and the dog was near the clothes-line and they deliberately shot him between the forelegs. He got as far as the yard, then died, poor beast. It is the Germans who are beasts!

*Jan. 28th. SUNDAY.*  Very cold, much snow still lying about frozen, making roads dangerous. Only three children at Sunday School, the smallest number I've ever seen. But the children have no good footwear or clothes, and there's no heating anywhere. So I gave the Scripture Lesson to three scholars and five teachers! We decided to have no Sunday school during February as it is so very cold, worse than any other time during the whole Occupation. Went to service this afternoon. How cold our feet were! Tonight we just sat in the dark by the fireside – and how blessed we are to have a fire at all. I find it hard not to be able to read when there is time. However, I thought about what I had read on my return this afternoon, from Clarke's *Theology*. I have found this book so enlightening on things which puzzled me about Christ.

*Jan. 30th.*  Weather less cold, with rain most of the day – roads still very slippery, so did not go to town, nor did Joyce. Busy all day. Tidied drawers in my bedroom. My hands got frozen, had to wear gloves to do the sweeping. Herbert tells me it is fearfully cold in England also. I hope my Alfred is all right. I wonder when the *Vega* is coming again and will there be news of our loved ones?

*February 2nd.*  Busy with household tasks. Was much amused when Willie Laffoley came and asked me if it was true that I wanted their rabbit's head as they were killing their last one but he thought I might be offended if he brought it! By and by, along comes Edward, his brother and, with a nice bow,

265

he said, "A present from Willie" and presented me with the rabbit's head on a plate! They don't eat it, fancy! Only two pounds of bread each next week, and the next, and then no more. However we all hope the Red Cross will come again soon. We were in the dark this evening, as usual now. I find it very frustrating. I'd like to read or do some mending, and one can do nothing! However we have much to be thankful for and must not complain.

*Feb. 3rd.*     Feel very sad at all the suffering going on in Europe – the German women and child refugees trying to flee from the Russians, for example.

*Feb. 4th. SUNDAY.* My turn at home this morning. Afternoon preached at Bethesda. Joyce and I had tea at Mrs Syvret afterwards and Mrs S. and I had a nice chat as we washed up. Herbert joined us and we three cycled back together – very difficult in the rain and dark, with only one light between us.

*Feb. 5th.*     The Germans are commandeering turnips; the farmers must take in loads and loads for the soldiers. I think the farmers would refuse if it were not that it would get our Constables into trouble – it is so difficult to know what to do and the Germans would get what they want, in any case. They've been taking stock of everything on farms. One hears that all the German Marines here have escaped. Hundreds of loaves have been stolen by them from the bakers lately – perhaps it was to take with them. Also, the Gestapo is supposed to have feared the marines and not dared interfere. The *Vega* is reported to have left Lisbon with parcels, but without flour.

*Feb. 6th.*     There is a message from our Bailiff on the *Evening Post,* saying that, unless help comes, the bread ration will entirely cease after February 10th.

*Feb. 7th.*     Took some milk and some of Mother's cheese to the Fells and Wards. They are making the best of things. Mrs Ward's eyes were shining with hope. She said: "I'm sure you'll be seeing Alfred soon now." Had dinner at Montpelier. 'Mother's' hands seemed much better today. Went to see Cousin Sophie; she is very frail now, and her mind not too clear. Mrs T. is having a difficult time looking after her. Francis went with Dolly and the van to fetch another lot of Red Cross parcels from town. When I got home ours had already come from the shop and we opened them after tea – such excitement opening them! We are so pleased with everything. Only four of ours had soap this time and some of the cheese had gone stone hard! I expect some of these parcels have been packed for a long time. On my way to town I had met all the St. Peter's vans coming up the hill with the cases of parcels. Tears of emotion came to my eyes. We really have so much to be thankful for.

*Feb. 8th.*     Housework, cleaned rabbit hutches, cleared up and tidied old papers, books etc. I am clearing up and arranging things in the hope of being with Alfred soon, and going to live in England. I do not know what the next months have in store for me, but I hope and trust that God will restore my dear Alfred to himself and to me. We've heard that several soldiers tried to escape to France to give themselves up, but were caught, and shot by the Gestapo.

*Feb. 9th.* The *Vega*, which was to arrive today, is delayed in Guernsey, some say because the Germans did not want the cranes to be used for unloading. Farmers have been told to be at the pier Tuesday instead of tomorrow.

*Feb. 10th.* Many soldiers are said to be ill with dysentery, malnutrition and TB and that their doctor wants the Commandant to surrender because of this but he will not, though some soldiers are said to have died. A boy of nine has been killed by a fall of sand in an Air-raid shelter in the Parade. The poor little fellow was in search of firewood for his parents, and hacked away at a support, and was buried alive – a tragic happening.

*Feb. 11th. SUNDAY.* Pouring with rain all morning. Went to Bethlehem and to Philadelphie afternoon, where Mrs Ward was preaching. She preached on Isaiah 55 and it helped me tremendously. I heard tonight that over 500 people were killed and more than a thousand injured by enemy action over southern England last month. It worries me a lot. What an invention of the devil those V1s and V2s are. If only war would end.

*Feb. 12th.* Went to town. Called at Miss Morin, Fells, Walkers, Alexandres, Miss Ching and Buntings with milk, butter etc. Thank goodness I was not stopped, with all my hidden bottles of milk and bits of butter. Dinner with Alfred's folk, then went to Women's Work Intercession meeting at Wesley Chapel. Mrs Walker presided and we had a most inspiring meeting. There was a strong sense of God's presence and of us being all one. There were several spontaneous prayers. We prayed for our missionaries overseas, especially those known to us personally, for their converts, we remembered our King and Country, all those serving in the Forces and prayed also for our so-called 'enemies.' About 55 women present. They are all so nice to me. I told them about Mother not being able to go out all this time. Cycled back with Joyce. News tonight that the *Vega* has arrived!

*Feb. 13th.* Francis left about 8.15am with Dolly and the van to help unload and deliver the Red Cross supplies. The Vega had not yet arrived when they got to town. It was 10.30 when she entered the harbour and it was unloaded this afternoon. Francis says that it was a lovely sight – the farm-horses were harnessed to trolleys. There were 37 of them lined up on the pier. (Farmers and horses were from St. Peter's, St. John's and Grouville). Dolly was rather frightened of the unfamiliar noises, like the cranes, and she stood up on her hind legs several times! (Or, was she happy to be fetching Red Cross supplies!) One German soldier was put on each trolley and F. says he felt sorry for those soldiers. No one spoke to them and they looked – as many of the rank and file do – dull and harmless, reminding one of sheep. There are parcels for the Algerian prisoners this time, also parcels of clothing.

*Feb. 14th.*    We forgot it was Pancake day yesterday; soon it will be Easter. What will, or will not, happen before Easter? Weather foggy and damp and none of this week's washing has been put out yet. Went down Jubilee Hill to meet Mrs Syvret as she wanted to give us a share of a small conger she'd had given. We saw Mrs Le Sueur, whom I wanted to meet because she is at the Telephone Exchange and her voice always sounds so charming!

*Feb. 15th.*    A lovely sunny day – what a change, so I've spent a good deal of time at the clothes line. How lovely to feel the warm sun. Francis had to go to help finish unloading the *Vega* this morning. He says there are many cases of medical supplies.  There is a message from our Bailiff on the *Evening Post* informing us that the *Vega* must go back to fetch flour, which is waiting at Lisbon, and it is hoped that it will reach us by the second week in March. The *Vega* has brought oil for the cranes next time, so until then we must manage the best we can. Mr and Mrs Le Brun came. He told us that some men in town were planning to burn down German Stores if no flour came. So, thank God, it is coming, because there might be awful trouble here. It wouldn't do to get the Germans annoyed, armed as they all are, and we defenceless.

*Feb. 16th.*    Foggy all day. Went to Plaisance Nursing Home at St. Laurence to see Cousin Sylvia Le Brocq and Miss Nellie Ahier. I also peeped around the open door of another bedroom, and saw my teacher of long ago, Miss Rowe, sitting up reading in bed with a cat on her lap. What a picture – with an unpleasant look on her face! She won't see people, so I dared not let her know that I was there!

*Feb. 17th.*    Had a lot of trouble with the washing. Put out all last Monday's sheets etc. but nothing dried – drizzle kept coming and going. I felt fed-up with the washing. Today is the last day of bread delivery for there is no more flour. As it was, the bread has not been very nice lately. I even found a whole label and string in one loaf, a hat-pin in another and droppings of mice! It seemed as if our poor bakers were sweeping the last remnants of flour from the floor! I am disappointed that there has been no news brought by the *Vega*; it is strange that it can't bring us Red Cross messages. Herbert went to Philadelphie to pump the organ for Doreen Egré's wedding, the girl who had had the accident near us.

*Feb. 18th.* Preached at Bethlehem this morning. Congregation 30 including nine children. Enid took the afternoon service and brought four girls to read lessons, sing etc. and she spoke mostly about the hymns she had chosen, seven of them! Tonight we sat in the dark by our little fire – we are fortunate to have a fire to sit by.

*Feb. 19th.* Well, today brought unexpected news because the *Vega* had brought news from Germany after all. I've had two letters from Mr Rodd and two from Uncle Gordon, written last November. Both had heard from Alfred but I don't know when. From what they say, he is still feeling the same. They don't say that he sends his love to me, but that he is *earnestly and impatiently longing for reunion when he hopes all will be well.* But surely it rests with him. I am in despair: all my loving messages don't seem to have done much good. Of course I've no idea if he's had the letters sent through the escapees. Uncle says Alfred is living in Hampshire, apparently in or near Southampton. So he is in a dangerous area, which makes me more anxious. I am feeling very tired of this suspense, but I go on loving and praying. Then, there is very sad news for poor Uncle Edward. Mother is so upset and does not know how to tell him, for his elder son, Peter, has been killed in an accident whilst training in the Air Force. Uncle was so proud of him, and he must have grown into a handsome young man. Oh dear, sad news all the time. And I had thought that maybe Uncle Gordon and others in that camp had been sent back to England. Uncle seems discouraged now and says that he has got so hardened to things that happenings no longer move him. Mr Rodd seems less cheerful than he was, and seems anxious about friends in the Channel Islands. Well, it is no good crying, which is all I feel like doing. I've found myself kneeling by my bed trying to pray, but even that was difficult. Words from Psalm 42 come to me: *My tears have been my meat day and night, while they continually say unto me, Where is thy God?* Joan came with baby Michael Vibert again. How lovely he is, and when I saw his happy baby face and heard him 'crowing' I longed for the day when I hope Alfred and I will have a lovely baby of our own.

*Feb. 20th.* Went to the Wards and told them about the news from Alfred. Mrs Ward cheered me wonderfully. She said it was good news and I must take heart. She is sure all will be well when Alfred sees me. Mr Ward said: "We men are strange, you know!" Mrs Ward then told me how, long ago, when they were engaged, Mr Ward had got quite a wrong idea into his head and though she did her best to explain it away in letters (for they too were separated, though in England) it was no use. So she left it, and when they saw each other again the misunderstanding vanished immediately. So she said that Alfred was not the only 'dogged' one. I was so glad she had told me this, it did help!
Went on to have dinner with Mrs Crill (Olive!) and her Mother. I had such a

nice time. She showed me her house, and her sons' rooms (little knowing the bad news in store for her, and she told me how much she missed Peter.) Called at Montpelier and had a chat with Alfred's Mother. She is pleased with the news about Alfred and she told me again, with tears in her eyes, how very wonderful her son is really and how happy he will make me. I told her that my one great desire was to make him happy.

Cycled home with Joyce and she told me the tragic news that Mrs Crill's eldest son, Jack, who was in the Forces, was killed last July. Apparently about two thousand messages have come through the Red Cross. How terribly sad we all feel for the Crills. Mother is very upset. One wonders what other bad news there are in store for some people. It must have been terrible for Peter to get this news on arrival in England, and he went away so excited, full of hope and the spirit of adventure. Our hearts are heavy tonight.

*Feb. 21st.* Mother had a message from Uncle Bert, dated October 1944, but he gives no fresh news, not even the name of Adèle's baby.

*Feb. 22nd.* Granny is 88-years-old today. It is Evie's Birthday too, so Kath and Joyce went to see her. Germany is being dreadfully bombed; how one longs for the war to be over. Dad has been making salt today – the boys fetched sea-water yesterday.

*Feb. 23rd.* I had a very stale Red Cross message from Alfred, dated 3rd March 1944. It's taken a year to reach me! He tells me to keep smiling and sends me much love, so he wasn't feeling too bad then. But I so want less stale news from him. Scores of houses in town have been tarred with the Swastika and are in an awful mess. It is supposed to have been done by the German Marines out of spite perhaps, or for want of something to do. In some streets every house has been tarred, and it is so difficult to remove. Doctor Lewis came to see Mother. He told us that the doctors are terribly disappointed with the Medical supplies brought by the *Vega*. They are mostly pills which we certainly don't need: Slimming tablets (and we are starving!), sea sickness pills (and we can't travel), little liver pills, and so on! It is very strange. People are dying for lack of necessary drugs and medicines, and that is what the Red Cross sends us. There must have been a mistake or neglect somewhere.

*Feb. 24th.* I made toffee with sugar-beet syrup, Klim and butter, to give Elsie for her Birthday tomorrow. Joan has had a message from her father but it is a year old too! The baker brought us each a one pound loaf for this week. As we did not expect any at all; it was very welcome.

*Feb. 25th. SUNDAY.* Cycled to town in time for 11 o'clock service at Wesley. Sat with Elsie. I wonder if Alfred has remembered that it is his sister's birthday. Dined at Montpelier. Had brought a pie, a milk pudding and a cake, for it is so difficult for them to cook anything. Alfred's Mother is always so grateful for any little thing that we do. As always, I enjoyed being with them. Visited a few friends and then cycled home. I met plenty German soldiers all the way going to town, to the Pictures, I suppose! Poor Uncle Edward was here when I got back. He's had no news from Auntie Hazel, so knows no more about Peter's death. Some say that copies of the *Daily Mail* were found smuggled amongst medical supplies brought by the *Vega*.

*Feb. 26th.*    Went to Phyllis Le Brun to take two young rabbits I had promised her, as they had had theirs stolen. Last night they had all their fowls stolen. Tonight, I wrote to Uncle Gordon, hoping he is still safe, for I really am almost afraid of what may have happened to them all in those camps. I also wrote out a Red Cross message for Uncle Bert. We are only allowd ten words now! I am so sorry I can't send one to Alfred, but only one per household is allowed, and Mother wanted to send to Uncle. I wonder what news the *Vega* will bring on her next visit?

*Feb. 27th.*    I wrote a letter of sympathy to Mrs Crill. I've been feeling that I must write, though Mother had done so, on behalf of us all, but it is so hard to know what to say. How can anything comfort people who are going through such sorrow as Mr and Mrs Crill? And one realises not only their own personal loss, but the loss to our Island of a man of high and noble character, such as Jersey is so sorely in need of. Rev. South had a Message from someone at Southampton, probably sent in November which says *Du Feu here*. It cheers me to know that he was safe then, and I like to think that he is near now, though in another sense so far! If only I could see him!

*March 1st.*    Went to Local Preachers' Meeting at Grove 3pm. 12 men present and two women (May Luce and me). Rather a lively meeting, lasting an hour and three-quarters, at the end of which Jurat Gallichan said he felt better, for he'd got things off his chest that had been there for a long time! I am rather getting to admire him! We agreed on most things today! I dared to say that it would be a good thing if our ministers took a holiday and went round to hear every preacher that they've got on the plan, turning up unexpectedly, to which 'Brother' Gallichan said, "I heartily agree with what Miss Le Ruez has just said!"
I've been thinking of Alfred and wondering how he gets on presiding over meetings like this one. The war news is good, but things can't end too soon. Some people fear there will be trouble when flour comes. The sailors are getting troublesome – one hears that they tried to set fire to Martland's store where the Red Cross parcels are stored. They are responsible for the Swastikas. I saw a huge one on a wall with ENGLAND FOR EVER written underneath,

all tarred. The Germans wanted the States of Jersey to remove it, but they refused!

*March 2nd.* Herbert's 21st Birthday – fancy, the youngest of us already 21. We have no presents to give him, but Christine made him some toffee. It isn't everybody who can do that; we can, by using sugar-beet syrup, which, with difficulty and very hard work, we make. Mr E P Ahier came to fetch some corn we had offered him, to help at this time when there is no flour. Our little store is hidden in a big bin underground in the greenhouse. I started preparing an address for a Sisterhood but did not finish as there was no light. By telephone we got the order to advance clocks by one hour tonight – German orders! One hears all kinds of rumours. Schmettow, the Commandant in Guernsey and other high officials are said to have gone back to Germany. If so, is it to make their escape whilst there is still time? Anti-Nazi leaflets have been distributed amongst the soldiers here (don't know by whom) urging them to surrender and to shoot their officers! It is not likely that things are going too well with the German Command here, especially as the soldiers complain of lack of food, the naval men, especially.

*March 3rd.* Laurence's Birthday. Lovely sunny day, but cold. I took advantage of the sun by washing my hair and drying it in the sun. I wonder if Alfred will like my hair as he used to. It has much improved since those days.

*March 4th. SUNDAY.* My turn at home morning. Preached at St. Ouen's afternoon. (Text: Genesis 50 v. 20). Herbert came with me. Congregation 70. Singing and music very good, but I wish the choir-girls didn't whisper so, especially at the beginning of my sermon! Mrs Pipon and Betty Du Feu sang a very sweet duet 'Sunshine and Shadow.' Francis went to 'Auntie' Florrie's tonight. Apparently 'young' John had appreciated my sermon. I used to think he didn't listen, but I must have misjudged him. Dad went to see Uncle Ernest tonight, as he isn't well. The Frenchman who comes every Sunday for food, showed Mother his well-groomed, freshly-cut, parted-in-the-middle hair, and said,
"J'ai eu mes cheveux cringés, c'est pour faire plaisir aux jeunes filles."
"Oh", said Mother, "avez vous une jeune fille, donc?"
"Non" he replied, "mais c'est la votre qui me plait!" (meaning Joyce!)

*March 5th.* Herbert told me that the Germans have renewed their flying bomb attacks on England, having built more launching sites, also that they are going again widespread over England, with planes. It makes me feel so anxious about Alfred. It seems that every time one has felt that things were improving, something happens to depress one again. It takes away one's courage. I must write out my sisterhood address but I've hardly the heart to do so.

*March 6th.* Francis went again, with other farmers, to fetch Red Cross parcels from the store in town, all from New Zealand, this time we had ours this afternoon. Some have got damp, and the chocolate is somewhat *passé*, but we welcome everything!

*March 7th.* Alice here, as usual on Wednesdays – wouldn't we miss her if she didn't come! I went to give my talk (Subject: Passers-by) to the sisterhood at Aquila Road. Over 40 present. They are all such nice women. I think those Sisterhoods do a tremendous amount of good. Mrs Fell presided.

Last week called at Rev. and Mrs Fell and left 12 pounds of wheat (which I had carried tied round my waist, hidden under my coat) not knowing how much in need they were. Their door was open, but they were not in. Everything looked so cold and bare. I hesitated about leaving the corn in case Germans walked in and took it. Finally, I did decide to leave it. Today, Mrs Fell told me that that morning, on waking, she had looked at her husband and said: There's no food left, not a scrap of flour even, what shall we do? Who can we ask to help us? To which her husband had replied, "Don't worry, my dear, the Lord will provide." They had then knelt to say their prayers, as was their custom. Then, as there was no breakfast, they had gone out to visit their neighbours. On their return, the first thing they saw was a bag of corn on their kitchen table! "The Lord had provided!" (through my father who had given me the corn!) The Fells then made a little fire with a few sticks and managed to boil some of the corn for their breakfast. Wonderful how God uses us to answer other people's prayers!

People in town have been expecting trouble when the *Vega* arrives again, but it has started already. This morning, the Palace Hotel was blown up – explosions were going on all day. The Germans pretend it is an accident, but everyone believes it is the work of their Marines. We don't know how many officers and men were killed, but Joyce saw many German ambulances on their way to hospital. No civilians have been injured but many houses have had windows blown out. Uncle is not sending Leslie and Margaret to school tomorrow – the windows at College were broken. Will the Germans be forced to surrender at last? Their men look ill and thin, no wonder they are fed-up. Alfred's Mother fell down 15 stairs in the dark last night. She says she is all right, but I feel anxious as she is not strong enough to have shocks like that. It is surprising that more accidents have not happened in the dark.

*March 8th.* Joyce and I went to Plaisance Nursing home and we even saw old Miss Rowe. She made herself charming, but we know, and so do the staff, that she isn't always so! She couldn't believe it was me, says I've changed so much. Well, it is a while since I was a 12-year-old school-girl! Everyone was so grateful for the small gifts of food Mother had sent. Miss R. the Matron had managed to get two loaves in exchange for some of the Red Cross cigarettes. It is high time flour came. Mrs Simon came to fetch two rabbits I had promised her, as they've had all theirs stolen.

*March 9th.*   I spent a long time in prayer last night, chiefly for Alfred, but also because I am sad to see how some people have lowered their moral standards, how cheap and vulgar they are, how they mock at sacred things, at the Church, at love and marriage. It is one of the results of war and occupation, I suppose. This afternoon, I was cutting off old flower heads from the hydrangeas, when Mrs Syvret phoned to say that she could see the Red Cross ship in the bay, so, thank God, the flour has come! But, what news has the *Vega* brought?

We've been to the Concert given to raise money for the Red Cross, but we didn't enjoy it very much, there wasn't one item that could be said to be at all uplifting. The acting was very good so a pity it was wasted on rather 'cheap' stuff. The tone of these concerts needs to be raised. Early this morning we heard heavy shelling, and wondered what was on. John heard on his crystal set that the Germans had made a Commando raid on Granville on a considerable scale, and that there were prisoners on both sides. Presumably, the raid was made from the Channel Islands. We know it was from here, and unfortunately, the Germans have brought an American ship into harbour which they captured and it has German prisoners on it! We don't like to think that the raid was made from here. No doubt the sailors were given this to do, so as to keep them busy and so prevent more trouble. Mr W Priaulx told me that the Germans went in the night, and shot his sow in the jaw. They meant to kill her and take her away, but they were disturbed and went away.

*March 10th.*  Housework, as usual. Lovely sunshine. Francis carting manure. He has already carted a hundred loads on different fields, and has about 50 more, then it must all be spread. We are well to have a strong mare. Dad not only takes out of his fields, but he puts in. So, in life, we must give to the world, if we are to receive! A German came to Dad in the field today and offered free petrol to plough his land. Dad refused – said he had made his arrangements to plough with horses. The Germans are offering free petrol and boots to farmers. We will have none of their offers. I wonder why they are doing it? Looked over my sermon tonight and prepared my Sunday School talk, whilst it was still light.

*March 11th. SUNDAY.*   Went to Sunday school, then cycled on to Les Frères to take the service. One man said: "Well spoken." Well, if I can do anything to raise people's ideals, then I am thankful, and I did speak very frankly this morning and very seriously. We had quite a thrill tonight about 11pm (10 o'clock in England) when John called from his bedroom, that Channel Island refugees were broadcasting hymns. We all rushed and sat on the bed, the eight of us having turns at the two earphones, and heard our fellow-islanders in England singing hymns from Westminster chapel, London. It was wonderful, and tears came to my eyes, especially when they sang, 'Holy Father in Thy mercy, hear our anxious prayer,' One speaker said: "We sing this hymn with a peculiar depth of feeling." How it helps to know that they pray for us, and to think that they were gathered together in London, where flying bombs go over.

*March 12th.* Mr Mourant called, says there are Red Cross messages in. Poor Oliver, he is anxious about Helier, his son. One awaits these messages with mixed feelings. Everywhere there are complaints that Germans are digging up potatoes as soon as they are planted. One doesn't know what to do. Dad phoned the Department of Agriculture but they have no help or advice to offer. We had lovely real white bread for tea, which the baker brought, made from flour brought by the *Vega.* It is wonderful – we gazed at it!

*March 13th.* Have been to town. Dined at Montpelier. Feel very disturbed in my mind again. Elsie said that a Hospital ship is coming and sick folk, and a friend or relative to accompany them, will be taken away. Alfred's folk have thought that I might have a chance of getting away thus. But I am not sure that the Hospital ship is going to England at all. I want to do what is best. I've told Alfred's people to find out all they can.

*March 14th.* Very foggy. Mrs Syvret's Birthday so I went down to see her for a few minutes. I had painted her a card and made some toffees with sugar beet and Red Cross sugar. Mother made her some doughnuts as we've had a ration of oil. Joyce heard that 4,000 messages have come.

*March 15th.* The baker has brought some more white loaves, this time made with Red Cross yeast. They are really lovely and we are to have four pounds of bread each a week! After being in suspense all day, waiting for the postman, he hasn't come at all. Roger de Faye has come and told us that people over 70 will be allowed to go on the hospital ship when it comes. I am bothered and bewildered and I can hardly eat with worry. Would there be a chance of my going to accompany one of these older people? There seems no hope of the Germans giving up here, none whatever, and I feel at the end of my tether. I want to get to Alfred. Day by day, week by week, month by month, year by year, I've been doing my best to be cheerful, brave and patient, but oh, how hard it is at times. I've been remembering how happy Alfred was with me and how he used to say: "Nan, you put new life into me." No wonder he has got so terribly lonely and depressed. He has needed me, and I wasn't there. Christine has seen her fiancé three times today. There, I'm crying, I knew I would! Francis has been ormering with Raymond at L'Etacq; they caught 24. What delicious stew we'll have! The Germans are making much propaganda out of their raid on Granville.

*March 16th.* Last night, I had trouble to sleep, then I was helped by words from my Daily Readings:

> *Love divine has seen and counted*
> *Every tear it caused to fall*
> *And the storm which Love appointed*
> *Was its choicest gift of all*

I pray that one day I may see that it was so.

The postman came about noon, and Mother called that there were messages for me. I felt afraid to open them, and yet thankful that Alfred was alive to send them. Then I read: *Don't worry. I am well, but very lonely because I am loyal to you,* sent on November 8th. Then one sent on November 1st: *I still love you but waiting is hard. Never mind. Soon over, Love.* He tells me not to worry, so I must try not to do so. Alfred's folk have had news. He says that he is well and happy in his job and that he is in charge of Methodist Central Hall. That is good news and it shows that he is getting on well, but where is he? Uncle said he was no longer at Matlock.

Here, the Germans are acting as though they mean to stay for ever, giving petrol and oats to farmers (those who are foolish enough to accept!) so that they may profit from our crops later on. Also, it is a kind of propaganda to keep up the morale of their troops, which we begin to see is getting very low – when one sees the fuss they are making about the Granville raid, big headlines etc! According to their account, the port is completely destroyed and unusable; none of us believe it! How different I feel from last night. I ought not to let myself get so down.

*March 18th. SUNDAY.* Took the service at Bethesda afternoon. Herbert came with me and we had tea at Mrs Syvret afterwards. Found preaching hard today, as though I wasn't doing any good. Felt disheartened and sad later to hear about another girl having a 'German baby'; it is happening too often. Enjoyed being at the Syvrets. We went for a long walk. What changes along the Five Mile Road! The Germans can't have much to eat. We saw some stones and ashes in a field where they had been cooking limpets – there was a huge pile of shells nearby!

This morning I suddenly had a wonderful feeling that God was watching over Alfred and myself, hearing all our prayers, having compassion over our mistakes and helping us through all the time, because He knows we trust Him. I felt reassured somehow, and my worries dropped away.

*March 19th.* Joyce tells us that a German garage in town containing ammunition, petrol, lorries and tanks has been burnt out; people believe it to be sabotage again. More anti-Nazi leaflets are said to have been distributed amongst the troops to try and put them against the Admiral who is here now, and a soldier is supposed to have said that a revolution is brewing amongst them here. Last night Francis went with Mr S Maillard to keep guard at Marrett's bakery. Guards with no weapons and the potential thieves are armed!

*March 20th.* Had tea at Lucille's and we went to the Overseas missionary meeting at Bethlehem. Evie, meaning to cheer me, said, "Well, perhaps you'll be with Alfred by September!"
"September,'" I said, "I'll go mad if I can't be with him before!"

*March 21st.* Cycled to town with Mrs Syvret and Phyllis le Brun, whom I had invited to come with me, to the Women's Work Quarterly meeting at Aquila Road. About a hundred women present. A very good meeting. Mrs Mylne spoke about the Nosu people of China. Spoke to many friends afterwards. I find myself wondering why Mrs Syvret is fond of me, and says she looks forward to seeing me. Another German-occupied place has been destroyed, this time a big farm at St. Martin's. The Germans have demanded one hundred cows to ship tomorrow. They say for Guernsey, but who knows? Farmers are very upset. We just hope the British will capture the ship; wish we could tell them about it! I've sent Alfred a Red Cross message, only ten words allowed now.

*March 22nd.* I wrote to Uncle Gordon, in case he is still in the German camp.

*March 25th. SUNDAY.*    Preached at Tabor this morning. The organist was 15 minutes late, which did not please me, as he had no good reason! How stupid I was not to begin the service without him!
After dinner, and feeding my rabbits, went to Bethlehem for our Flower and Egg service, as we had last year. The children sang a hymn as they marched round the chapel with their flowers and decorated baskets. We also had some tins of Klim and condensed milk (from Red Cross parcels) and a little butter, flour, beans and a few apples. There were 165 people there, including the children. Miss C Arthur received the flowers and Pastor Hanks the baskets of eggs. He also preached a very good sermon on Jesus' last word on the Cross. Mrs Syvret and Joan came to tea, also Reggie Jeune and Monica. Mrs Syvret doesn't seem too well. I'm sure she is worrying about her husband. This has been quite a tiring day, and Granny has given me plenty work in her bedroom tonight, on top of everything!

*March 26th.* Went to Bethlehem afternoon, where Miss Ethel, Lucille, Evie and I arranged and packed the eggs etc. in lots. We had 124 eggs given, which is splendid, considering that so many people have had their fowls stolen. Evie and I went on to Plaisance home, carefully carrying eggs on our bicycles, which we gave, with flowers, to the old ladies there. We saw Miss Rowe again, and Miss Nellie Ahier, who says she is so well looked after and couldn't think of anything to complain about. Then, Cousin Sylvia, who first closed the door of her room, and began to run down the place including Miss Renouf herself! Cousin S. is such a character. How she made me laugh, I really couldn't help it! She says Mr Mourant would like her to go on the Hospital ship, if it comes. I offered to go with her, if it was sure to go straight to England. But even the doctors don't seem to know anything about it – one must wait and see, hoping the war will end and that I'll be able to rush across to Alfred by plane! I got back after 7 o'clock feeling very tired, and wishing Alfred were there to take me in his arms!

*March 27th.* Housework morning. Afternoon went with Lucille and Doreen Le Maistre to distribute more eggs for the gift service. On my bicycle I carried 63 eggs, 2 tins condensed milk, bags of apples, flowers (also 3 bottles of milk and two tins of Mother's cheese for our own friends). Thank goodness the Germans did not stop us! We took 24 eggs, 3 tins milk, 1 tin butter, 3 boxes beans, and flour to the Friendship League, c/o Town Hall, where we were told that they help five hundred families and that we have places in town more slummy than at Liverpool – proper hovels. Then we took 30 eggs, 2 tins milk, apples and flowers to Mrs Ward, and 24 eggs,1 tin Klim, 1 piece soap, apples and flowers to Rest Haven. We saw 13 women there, mostly in bed. One poor soul has an obsession that she has lost God and will go to the devil. She looked terrified, so Lucille told her that I was a preacher and would pray for her. It was difficult and I think she was rather deaf, but it helped her for the time, and she asked us to go on praying for her.

There was an English lady, a Mrs Stokes, who has been a Maternity nurse on the Indian mission field and later working amongst destitute women in America. She came to England to visit relatives, and found herself here when the Germans came. She went three times to the boats to try and evacuate, but was sent back every time. It is hard that she should have been 'caught' here when she meant to go back to work in America. She is at Rest Haven because she cracked her knee. Those Homes give me the creeps and I wouldn't like to see Granny there. It is very sad for old people who have no relatives to look after them to have to go to those places, with all sorts of others, some who are quite 'strange'. The Germans have found a crystal set at E Pallot's and at his brother's – they had received a letter – one feels very bitter against these traitors. Of course, the Germans searched for other things and discovered his stock of 12 barrels of potatoes, and three of wheat. I don't know how they intend to punish him, but he doesn't worry. It is said that there are 160 people on the waiting list for prison!

*March 28th.* We've had another batch of Red Cross parcels. How lovely again!

We know that events in Europe are moving swiftly. After all these dreadful years, it is difficult to believe that the war is coming to an end. I feel excited already at the thought of seeing Alfred – it seems too good to be true. Mrs Ward told me to begin, quite quietly, to get ready, so tonight I've been looking at my small stock of books and discarding what I don't want to take away with me. The Germans have held a big meeting at the Forum, and told their soldiers to hold out here and to fight to the last, even if the war is over elsewhere. However, I'm not worrying. We are in God's hands. He has brought us through so far, and we must trust Him for the future.

*March 29th.* Mother's Birthday, and we had nothing to give her. I tried to make sweets with Klim, sugar-beet syrup, and milk coffee, but they didn't turn out very well! Some of us had turns with the ear-phones to listen to a programme for Channel Islanders at 11am. Lord Justice du Parcq spoke, also a Channel Islander, a schoolmaster and a soldier, and girls sang. We heard how wonderfully kind Britishers, Canadians and Americans have been to our refugees. The *Vega* was mentioned and statements made by the Government concerning Red Cross supplies. We were also given to understand that most of the escapees had arrived safely. It was lovely to hear and to know how much people on the other side have been thinking of us. Internees who had been deported have again arrived in England – surely Uncle has got there by now. Miss W Arthur here for tea, and she, with Herbert, Joyce and myself, went to see a Passion Play by the choir of St. Ouen's Church at the Parish Hall. It was very good. Phyllis took the part of Pilate's wife. Rev. Norman gave a short talk.

*March 30th. GOOD FRIDAY.*    Fine day. Everything fresh after the rain. I preached at Philadelphie on 'The Seven Words on the Cross.' Congregation 41, better than usual on a Good Friday. The junior choir sang 'There is a green hill.' I took half a dozen of Laurence's duck eggs to Madeleine Luce to take to the American prisoners here (for their Easter). There are now 48, as 27 were captured on the Granville raid. Two of them, poor fellows, were brought back, still in their pyjamas and slippers, and Martha M. had an awful job to find clothes for them. Madeleine L. is quite excited about the Channel Island broadcast yesterday. Of course, I didn't tell her I had heard it myself.

*April 1st. SUNDAY.*    We began holding services again in the evening today. I preached at Bethesda at 6.30pm. Only 17 present, including two children. Not one man! I feel physically tired all this time as if I hadn't the courage to cycle to town tomorrow and yet I want to see Alfred's folk. And I hate to be told that I am pale, and every time I go to town someone is sure to say so. Why can't they keep those nasty remarks to themselves. It certainly doesn't help to make me feel better.

*April 2nd.*　　Mr Mourant here for dinner. I left at 4pm for town. It began to rain and continued all evening. Mr and Mrs Slade were at Montpelier for the night. They and Alfred's parents went to Grove Place and Elsie and I stayed in. There was no fire and it was not too warm, and so dull with the rain outside. I realise how much people in town have suffered through lack of fuel. (We have never been without a fire in the evenings, even if a very poor one!) For cooking, they only have that tin 'pot' (I think an old paint-pot) and Alfred's father had been to the Stores to try to get something to burn. He got four small barrels and brought them back all the way on his shoulders. But that won't last long, so they were burning a wash-stand. I must ask Dad to try and take them some kind of wood: old potato boxes, perhaps, because I feel awful to see what a plight they are in. Margaret Bunting told me that they had been spending one guinea a week on old barrels for fuel. I saw people everywhere carting these home from the Stores. One woman even had two small barrels in the pram with a tiny baby! It is pitiful, and soon the Stores will have nothing more. People now have tea and coffee from the Red Cross, but they have trouble to heat water to make these beverages, quite apart from heating water for washing dishes and clothes. I've heard of some who were given an egg and had no means of cooking it. Margaret Bunting told me I would not see Alfred this year. She thinks that even if we were released, we would not be able to travel to and fro for months, I don't want to believe that! I am still hoping to be married by my next Birthday in July. There is a rumour that the Channel Islands are being kept for Hitler, and that he is coming to live here! Some people are stupid enough to think this is possible!

*April 3rd.*　　Breakfast and dinner at Montpelier. Joyce joined me, and we went to La Rocque to see Cousin Sophie. Found her very frail. It was sad to see her – she used to be so bright and full of fun; old age and illness are sad. Called at Mrs Crill. We did not mention her sorrow, but as I kissed her I knew we were both thinking and she knew I felt for her. In town, I went to get weighed, I was so surprised that I weighed so much that I went back to the Market to ask the man at the King's Weights if his machine was right! So he weighed me again, and it was right. I have never weighed so much before: 7 stones 9 pounds (107 pounds). My normal weight being a hundred pounds. Well, I'm glad I've improved. It must be the Red Cross parcels – the lovely cheese, perhaps!
I bought some clothes pegs, not very good ones, at one mark for 13. People, seeing them in my basket, asked me where I had got them! Some months ago, Laurens told me they could not get wood to make any, so I was surprised to see these today. Came back with Joyce. Found the long cycle ride so tiring – the wind was strong and it was cold and dusty. I felt parched, and would have given much for a drink of water. If only one could get a cup of tea or something in town. Where are the days when we popped in to Gaudin's for a cup

of tea and a cake when we felt tired or thirsty! Next time I go to town I'll take a bottle of water with me.

*April 4th.* There was a theft of 68 loaves form Mr Amy's bakery last night, whilst John M. and John P. and two other men were on guard! They are very upset – they found the Germans squeezing the loaves through the bars of a small window, but they didn't catch them! They got the German Gendarmerie, but of course they did nothing, merely said that their soldiers were hungry. Last week, whilst the Parish hall at St. Ouen's was being prepared for the Passion Play, a German soldier walked in and played the British national anthem. The Jersey boys there began to sing it and the soldier gave them a nice smile, before re-joining three comrades outside!

*April 5th.* Yesterday and today I did about an hour's gardening, hadn't had time to do any for months! The tulips are starting to bloom already. Those at the end of the avenue have been picked, no doubt by the Germans, and the Polyanthus, Wallflowers and Forget-me-nots are in bloom. The rain has done good and the flowers look so fresh. I love Spring flowers.

*April 6th.* Began typing out a sermon – did it in Granny's room this afternoon where it was sunny, and continued tonight.

*April 7th.* Busy with housework, sweeping bedrooms, etc. In spare time, tried to finish my sermon on, 'Blessed is the man that keepeth the Sabbath.' This subject is so important and I am not getting on very quickly. Granny wasn't too well today. Poor Granny, I feel I want to be very kind and patient with her. It is so sad to be old and to get 'strange', and I wish I had been kinder to Grandpa and not minded when he went and poked things in my bedroom – he liked to go there because it was sunny.

*April 8th.* Went to Bethlehem morning. Mr Huelin preached – he is over 80-years-old. After dinner and washing-up, I fed my rabbits, then the same Frenchman came and I had to give him milk and talk to him, and he bothered me. As soon as I had got rid of him I began to try to finish my sermon. It worried me and I could not get on as I would have liked.
Helped to prepare tea. Uncle Edward here. He looked quite smart in a suit Mrs R. from Samarés Manor, had given him, when she saw that he was almost in rags, and he apologised to her. Mother had already given him all she could spare. Preached at Bethlehem tonight. Though I've worked so hard on this sermon, I felt nervous and not in my usual form. I wanted this service to be of real help and blessing to my congregation. It is so important that people should realise the value of Sunday. Uncle Ernest was at chapel again, the first time since his illness. The *Vega* has entered harbour again this afternoon. What news does it bring?

*April 10th.* The Germans can't have much to eat. They went to one of our neighbours when he was planting potatoes, and they wanted to cut off the bottom half of them before he planted them, so as to have that to eat. They no longer dare dig them up or they would be severely punished, so they walk over the planted fields and take up all the bad ones that the farmers have thrown away.

*April 11th.* Alice here as usual. Heavy thunderstorm, sharp, short and sudden. Cleared up and we had a fine afternoon. Went to town. Chain of my bicycle broke on Beaumont Hill; left it at Berry's Garage and Enid Simon kindly lent me hers. So was late arriving at Wesley, where Margaret Bunting had invited me to a programme by the High School. Only saw part of her class performance. Went on to tea at Beechvale, Sion, where I had been invited, with other friends and we all went with the Luce family to Sion chapel where May was being publicly recognised as a Local preacher. There were a hundred people present and it was an inspiring service. My part was to give the Dedicatory prayer after May had given her account of her conversion and call to preach.

*April 12th.* Well, I've received a Red Cross message from Alfred, but it is very stale, sent on March 28th 1944 – over a year ago. So, there's no point in worrying about it. He thanks me for a message, but I've no idea which one. It is strange that so few messages come via the Red Cross ship, and that they are so stale. It can't be the fault of the Red Cross. Went to a sacred concert at Philadelphie tonight. (Collection for Red Cross came to £43.) A very inspiring evening. The scenes from the Life of Christ were particularly good, and reverently done. The girls Vibert and Herbert were taking part. Mrs Vibert sang and Laurence and Christine sang a duet, for the first time. I felt how much good a concert of this type can do and it is a shame that so many concerts held lately are rather second-rate because, deep-down, I know people do appreciate good stuff, and it should be given to them. Herbert tells me that many V2 bomb sites have been captured by our men in Holland, and had these sites not been bombed all the time, the Germans would have been able to send over 2,000 of these dreadful things per day over London.

*April 13th.* It has come as a shock to hear that President Roosevelt has died suddenly. Mr Churchill must feel it a lot. Dr. and Mrs S. from St Brelade's came to see the cattle. He does not think the Germans here will give up. Seven of them have been shot for being anti-Nazi. One, who was a guard at Grève de Lecq, tried to escape in a boat, lost his way, and had to return, only to be shot. So the Nazis here are as brutal and unrelenting as ever, but many of their soldiers are tired of it all. Dr. S. said that a young German NCO, whom he often saw, has also been shot. He had made plans to escape and one of his companions betrayed him. Joyce has heard too, that the Germans shot a Russian worker, and that they did what they've done before – carried the coffin in front of their victim as they marched him to his death. How callous they are.

*April 14th.*   I have received another message, over a year old, from Alfred, in which he says that his loneliness was becoming impossible. Had I not had more recent messages, which showed he was bearing up better and telling me not to worry, I would have been pretty desperate over this. As it is, it upsets me that he has to suffer so much, and I just pray that it won't be long now before we are reunited.

*April 15th. SUNDAY.*     Felt sad and without courage on waking, but asked God's help and especially that He would be with Alfred today. I preached at Six Roads. To the children, I gave a talk about President Roosevelt and we sang, 'Now praise we great and famous men' as a tribute to his memory. Congregation 30 children and 18 adults. When I got back, Dad told me that Irene de la Perrelle, who was preaching at Philadelphie, had chosen the same hymn. Then I met Mrs Laffoley and Edward, who said that Rev. Cassap at the Church had also spoken about Mr Roosevelt and compared his death to that of Moses, who saw the Promised Land but never set foot on it. A very good illustration, I think. We had the same hymn tonight at Bethlehem. Uncle had suggested it to the preacher and he said a few words himself about Mr Roosevelt.

*April 16th.*   Lovely day. People out in summer frocks! Went to town. Saw Mr Le Brun, who told me there is a rumour that we are to be attacked and released this weekend. The Germans are supposed to expect it. Anyway, we have begun to hear heavy bombing and explosions again, for the British or Americans are attacking places still holding out on the French coast, with a view of clearing out all those pockets of resistance. I wonder when our turn will come. Mr Le Brun says that the Germans would surrender here if they were offered a good dinner! They are starving. Two have been shot dead for stealing potatoes in a field at St. John's. Such are the orders now, and the guards don't hesitate to shoot on the spot, and at their own men. They are a cruel and callous lot. I feel that one can believe all the atrocity stories about them, having seen what we've seen here. One soldier has been to Westfield and told Uncle that as soon as the British land, he will shoot his officer and then put up his hands. Many talk like that now.

I called to see a few people to ask if they could help with a few items for a Concert I want to organise to raise money for the Red Cross. (A 'high-class' concert, because we've had neither the talent nor the training to do anything worthwhile amongst ourselves at Bethlehem.) The result was that the young people from Aquila Road chapel will do half the Concert for me, and I am so grateful. Rev. and Mrs Fell understood exactly what I had in mind and got in touch with Mrs Lobb. Joy, Emily and Elsie will give items too. So I feel quite pleased though rather nervous, as I've not had the responsibility for such a concert before.

*April 17th.*   Another lovely warm day. We've not had such a lovely Spring since 1940 when the Germans came. Today I heard the cuckoo for the first time this year. There has been the sound of heavy bombing all day. The Germans expect the British – they've been practising at their heavy guns. One came for food. Dad gave him a cup of milk and he had to be content with that. He was very thin, and looked very dull. He said they had lost the war and had no money in Germany to rebuild houses and no wood. He put the blame on 'Les Capitalists' of England and America who made war so as to give work to their unemployed. When Hitler came into power, in 1933, there were thousands of unemployed in Germany and by 1936 he had found work for all – peace-time work. And it was only when Hitler saw that war was coming that he got his people to work for war! So, this German is steeped in Hitler's propaganda, a real Nazi! He spoke in 'good' French, and ended by saying that it wasn't war itself that was bad, but it was the aftermath. Poor fellow, he has nothing much to look forward to, I suppose. He comes from Nuremburg, and the last he heard of his wife was that she was in the Hartz mountains. Dad listened but spoke little – it is best to be wise. Someone told a German soldier that rumour had it that when the British came, the Commandant here would resist, to which he replied: "He will fight alone, when Berlin is finished we fight no more."

*April 18th.*   We went to Bethlehem for the Men's Evening. Francis gave a short paper on President Roosevelt, Hedley L. on the founder of the Red Cross. The hymns were accompanied by Clifford on the harmonium, with one finger, and Walter Querée with his concertina. The men enjoyed themselves and we enjoyed ourselves too – all so nice and homely. Francis went to fetch more parcels. We had seven from New Zealand and four from Canada. The N.Z's are not in perfect condition, but what pleasure we have in receiving them.

*April 19th.*   I began preparing a poster to put in the porch at chapel when we have a collection for the Red Cross. The Bethesda people had a Concert at Philadelphie and raised £50 for the Red Cross. I found it very good. Stanley Le Ruez recited a composition of his, entitled, 'What the Occupation has taught me,' which was very amusing! A plane came tonight and, we think, took photographs; are the British coming at last? Curfew extended to 11 o'clock tonight on account of Hitler's Birthday tomorrow!

*April 20th.*   People in the Military Zones have been turned out by the Germans. A Spaniard who comes occasionally for food, told us that the British are expected this week-end, and as soon as they land the German anti-Nazis will kill the Nazis and then give themselves up. The Germans have been quiet, even though it is Hitler's Birthday. The Commandant did take the salute in the Square, and the band played and soldiers sang. I continued to work on my poster. Tonight, Margaret, Dorothy and Joan Toy came to sing to Mother, and they enjoyed coming with me to see the farmyard, and the flowers in the garden.

*German Field Police.*

*April 21st.*    Well, seven years ago Alfred and I became engaged – all those long years have passed and I dare not look back on the last 6½ years. It is too awful to think that we've not been able to be together. No, I must not look back, but surely now there is good reason to look forward with great hope. And I feel that I love my Alfred very much, as always. This week the weather has been glorious, just like mid-summer. It is said that we have not had such weather in Spring for 40 years. I've been several times fetching rabbit-food on the railway tracks. Yesterday when I was weeding on the one near the Laffoleys, I remembered how last summer I was there doing the same thing and all the time thinking and worrying about Alfred's messages. The countryside is beginning to look lovely with all the fresh leaves on the trees. And the Spring flowers are in bloom in the garden. Yet in Europe war is still raging with dreadful things happening, and now danger of epidemics. Rev. Killen, we're told, was sent for by the Commandant, who told him that he didn't much like sending a clergyman to prison, so he let him go free. Rev. Killen was due to go to prison when a vacancy occurred for having been found to have a wireless. Either this Commandant is not too bad, or he is afraid of the British when they come!

*April 22nd. SUNDAY.*    No milk for civilians today. The Germans have taken it all. Things get worse. The Admiral in Guernsey (who held out for so long at Cesembre) has sent drastic orders to the Commandant here, who, one hears, would like to resign, as he does not want to carry them out. It is said that whoever disobeys will be sent the the Concentration camp in Alderney. We have been discussing the 'cow and milk' question all day, but no one knows what to do. In any case, the Germans will get what they want!. The end of the war seems near (the Russians are not far from the centre of Berlin) and yet, in these poor little islands, things are daily getting worse, and it seems as if it was going on for ever. We really feel at the end of our tether. Farmers are having a terribly worrying time and it does not help that some folk in town don't realise it at all and blame us for lots of things. Yet they would not like to have our responsibilities, nor to have to work as hard as we do! Much colder today — back to warmer clothes.

*April 23rd.* Francis and I went in the van to La Pompe — it is years since I'd been in our horse-drawn van and I enjoyed it. We went because the Arthurs are moving to Les Ruettes and wanted to give Christine and I (for our bottom drawer) some calico which had been bought for them in 1915! We called at Westfield and I thought what lovely cows Uncle has — real Jersey beauties! Today we had a ration of candles, toilet and household soap brought by the *Vega*. We feel quite rich with these lovely things — we needed them so badly!

*April 24th.* Went to town. Called at Wards which cheered me again, said they were sure all would be well between Alfred and me. Went to Fells. Mrs F. read some of her husband's poems to me. It is only since the Occupation that he has discovered that he can write poetry. If he goes on, he will soon have the life story of Christ in poetry. I took a message for Alfred to the Red Cross Office. Had dinner at Montpelier. I could see Alfred's Mother was feeling depressed and discouraged, so I tried to cheer her. Someone had been last night and told her about all the atrocities the Germans have committed in the concentration camps and said there was going to be terrible street-fighting here, and so on, so 'Mother' could not sleep last night. I felt too tired and worried to go to a meeting at Bethlehem tonight, and it was late, so I just fed my rabbits and worked on my poster. I've felt awful all evening, because I heard in town that any woman can easily get away on the ship that is coming to evacuate invalids, as women will not be examined by German doctors. I don't know if this is true, but I'm again troubled and unsettled. If it is true, then I ought to try and get to Alfred that way. But where is the boat taking sick people? And is it worth it, supposing we are to be released soon? I'm so afraid to make a mistake. Mother reminds me that I did what I felt was right in 1940, after much thought and prayer, and I must believe it was for the best. I know Mother is right, but I have this awful fear of doing the wrong thing and of causing Alfred to misunderstand again.
We are all so worried about the milk. Dad has received a stiff letter signed by TJB saying that the Germans have threatened to take 750 cows per month if

farmers don't send more milk. (At that rate, in a few months' time, there will be no cows left). As it is, the milk is chiefly for the Germans; if only more could get to the Jersey people. We take risks all the time, trying to squeeze little amounts to give to people in town, and to make little amounts of butter by shaking cream in a bottle. Oh dear, what can we do now?

*April 25th.* Sunny but cold wind. Rev. Fell has come to fetch a few potatoes etc. Things are very serious in town. No potatoes. He had to do his best to hide them under his coat – he hung about ten pounds in a bag around his neck. It isn't only him that would be in serious trouble if he was caught with them, but us. I worked on my poster again tonight, after fetching rabbit food. War news encouraging – Berlin is surrounded by the Russians. A German soldier, yesterday, seemed highly delighted, as he told Francis that Hitler was in Berlin and so were the Russians!

*April 26th.* A year ago it was the Girls' League Rally at Grove Place, as it has been today. I thought then that I might be married by now, but here we are still under Occupation, and the Germans doing exactly what they were doing that day practising with their heavy artillery!
The weather was lovely today. Joan and Audrey were with me and we enjoyed the cycle ride, except when we got near town where Germans were firing heavy guns from Westmount. The shells whizzed over our heads and dropped with a great splash into the sea. I've always hated guns! We had a good Rally, and tea, having brought our sandwiches. Thanks to the Red Cross we did have sandwiches to eat! We went into the chapel to look at the 'Red Cross posters' painted by Oswald le Breton and Doreen Lucas. At tea-time we put questions to our visitors – nurses form the Crèche, the hospital and Home for Girls. So we thought of many different kinds of 'service' today. It has been a most helpful afternoon. I thought how lovely Grove Place Chapel is. Somehow I love it. We've had some wonderful meetings there before the Occupation. I took a bottle of milk to the Misses A. But it is very risky. I hear that there is a notice up in Tanguy's Dairy to the effect that if anyone is found with milk they will be taken to the concentration camp in Alderney. A German threat, I suppose, but one can't be too careful these days.

*April 27th.* Good news: Mussolini has been captured by patriots and the Americans and Russians have met – we are not supposed to know! Usual jobs today – washing dishes, doing vegetables, cleaning my bedroom and Granny's, cleaning out rabbits, fetching rabbit food, washing my overalls etc. and worked at my poster. Mother suggested that I should go and see Dr. Lewis to ask him if there was a chance of my getting to England on the Hospital ship. He believes that the Occupation will be over before the ship comes. However, he will see Dr. McKinstry tomorrow and 'phone me at once if there is a chance. He says that crowds of applications have poured in from people who are not ill at all. My mind is at ease now. I'm glad I saw Doctor about it. I feel willing to go if there is a chance, for I long to get to Alfred and have all this suspense over. At the same time, I'd be sorry to miss the day when the British and Americans take over. For Mother's sake too, I hope the Occupation will end first, because she would be so anxious if I went off like that, not knowing what would happen to me.

One of our bulls got swollen tonight and Francis only just saved it by plunging his little 'sword', as I call it, into its side so that the gas came out of its body. I went to see the exact spot where it had been done! Afterwards Francis went to Bethesda to read his paper on Roosevelt. Our men from Bethlehem were visiting Bethesda.

*April 28th* Christine's 26th Birthday – how the years roll on! The war seems to be nearing the end at last. Things are cracking in Germany. What about the poor little Channel Islands? We wait, alternately hoping and fearing. We've been patient for so long, that we can remain so a little longer! A man and his wife, aged 61, have been brutally murdered in Guernsey by German soldiers who were seeking food. And this week a Jersey woman was shot for having harboured a German deserter.

*April 29th.* Stormy and cold, as if Winter had returned. But people are excited and telling each other the news (there are crystal sets everywhere!) We are moving rapidly towards the end, thank God. Mussolini is dead, shot by patriots, and Hitler is reported dead of a stroke, or suffering from haemorrhage of the brain. His end will come, if it hasn't come already. At Bethlehem, Rev. Skyrme preached and thanked God for the dawn that is breaking at last. Elsie here for tea; she preached at Bethlehem tonight. Uncle John was very taken up with her, says she is a model for all lady Local preachers! He heard every word. She speaks so slowly and distinctly. (Whilst I'm still trying to master my fault of speaking too fast.) I am still thinking about a sermon for next Sunday. It is difficult, with things so uncertain. What shall I preach? How can I best get God's message across?

*April 30th. SUNDAY.* Sun, rain, hail, snow, wind! Last night, as I was going off to sleep, thoughts for a sermon began to take shape in my mind and all morning, as I've been going about my usual household tasks, I've been thinking and trying to work it out. But work is needed to arrange my thoughts in order and in the fewest words I know – it will come in time. People are expecting some very important news, some even say the war may end tomorrow. We shall believe when we see!

*May 1st.* A thin covering of snow on the ground when we woke, with frost on top. But the snow has saved the potatoes from being badly frozen. At 5.30am I got up to see to Granny, and Mother called to tell me that the Russian flag was flying at the Reichstag and Post office in Berlin, and that the war was nearly over. I feel nothing yet – one must not hope too much, as there may be some resistance yet. Things seem very quiet here in the country. I have not seen one German soldier today. I wonder if they've been told the news, and what they feel like. Last night I met one, picking sorrel from the hedges, and they came yesterday to beg for food. They keep stealing and eating cats and dogs! And, lately, they've entered people's bedrooms and stolen Red Cross parcels.

At tea-time, I was mad when I discovered that someone had entered the calf-stable and stolen three of my rabbits – the best ones, of course – my lovely fat buck and my best doe. Worst of all, she had little ones in the nest and now they will die. But what can I do? Nothing! After all the trouble I take to look after those rabbits, and this is the second time the fat ones are stolen.

*11pm.* I've put the poor little bunnies in a basket, and given them milk and water with a tiny salt spoon, but I doubt that I can rear them as they are only a week old and still have their eyes closed. I left them on the hearth, where there had been a fire. John has just told us the Germans have announced that Hitler has died in Berlin. I suppose he is dead, but whether it has just happened, or whether he has been dead some time, one does not know! Well, all things are in God's hands, and I will lay myself down to sleep and not worry.

*May 2nd.*    I've finished my Red Cross Poster at last! Alice here and Irene has been spring-cleaning the drawing-room. Great news tonight: North Italy has surrendered unconditionally and John says that Berlin is completely finished now. One can hardly believe it. I don't know how to prepare for next Sunday, not knowing what further exciting events may take place before I preach again. I pray for guidance. And how is my darling Alfred feeling now, I wonder?

*May 3rd.*    Joyce and I have been to the Le Seelleurs at Cloverley, St. Martin's, for dinner and tea. I did enjoy the cycle ride through the countryside which is so lovely, green and fresh at this time. We only took three-quarters of an hour on the way. It was so nice to see the Le Seelleurs and we talked about Methodist affairs, as usual!

Miracles are happening: the Germans have actually surrendered at Hamburg. One can't believe it – so unexpected. Here, one is at times hopeful, at times, not so. The Germans put a notice on the *Evening Post* saying that the British have asked their garrison at Alderney to surrender and they replied: 'Out of the question!' It is said that they will never surrender in the Channel Islands but one wonders, after Hamburg!

My eight motherless rabbits are still alive. It takes me nearly an hour feed them with milk and water. Tonight I began writing notes for my sermon. I think my text will be, 'The Power that worketh in us.' I don't expect any change in the situation here by Sunday now, so can carry on with my preparation.

*May 4th.*    I am really perplexed. I've not done any more work on that sermon, because I don't know if I'll have to prepare something different. People are saying that we shall be under the British flag by Sunday. John has heard that the German Commandant has told our Bailiff that they will surrender at noon tomorrow. Anyway, flagpoles are going up everywhere, and people have been buying flags like mad. (Where have they come from?) Some bakers were even delivering bread today instead of tomorrow, so as to be free to celebrate and so on. As for me, I feel calm, not wanting or daring to believe such good news yet, for I can't bear any more disappointment! And I shall not feel really happy and at peace until I hear from Alfred. The Frenchman has come and told us that the Germans are clearing up the Airport and removing mines, as they must give up by the 10th!

After feeding my poor little rabbits, having supper, and getting ready for bed, thoughts came to me for a more appropriate sermon, the text being 'Beware lest thou forget' and in spite of the lateness of the hour, I was thinking of writing notes when John came to tell me that he had heard on the English news that the Channel Islands were still occupied. Of course we still are! Rev. Ward and Rev. Fell have written to all the chapels to make ready at once for Thanksgiving services. People in town are getting excited and talking openly about the news, no longer fearing. I wonder what will have happened a week hence. I pray for all who are in suspense about their loved ones, because there will be sorrow as well as joy when news comes.

*May 5th.*    5.15pm. A few minutes ago, I was having my bath, when Mother called from below: "Nan, they've surrendered, they've surrendered!" No. I just can't take it in yet – we are to be free at last and, please God, I may see my beloved Alfred soon. It is too wonderful! John was just back from town. He had seen Joyce and she told him the news which, she said, is not official yet. Dad had come back earlier and knew nothing of it. There have been rumours all day. Dad and John had been to town to get Red Cross boots and had to queue for ages, until afternoon, to get them. Everything was quiet, Germans about as usual, though rumour said they were confined to barracks. Crowds of people had gathered in the Square, having heard rumours of a Proclamation, but dispersed again. Two Germans came here, asking for potatoes. We sent them away, as usual, but not unkindly. So, things seem quiet, but now they are going to get exciting.

Last night, after midnight, I wrote out an outline for my sermon, having finally decided to preach on Deut. 6. v. 12. ('Beware, lest thou forget'). All day, I've been so busy doing the usual jobs in the house, that I've only had 20 minutes,

so far, to work at it. But I know for certain now that the right text has been given to me. Never before have I been so much at the last minute making a sermon. But God helps us when we do our best and pray for his guidance.
*11.15pm.*      Things are very quiet. Nothing has been said on the News and we are beginning to wonder if what we've heard is true. Joyce says it was Mr Mourant who told her. The Bailiff has been at College House instead of being at the Sitting of the States, so the Commandant must have had something to discuss with him. After washing the tea-things, I've been all evening making my sermon, and finished it at last. I'm not sure what hymns to have. I sent my list to Jurat Brée, and he said I might find it necessary to change them. I wish there wasn't so much work to do, so that I could have gone to bed early tonight, because my head is tired after all that thinking and I feel quite bewildered. John says that a German officer has said that the Americans are expected here anytime within the next three days! I must pray and get to bed for tomorrow will be a busy and tiring day, and I shall need extra strength to get through it. (I must not look tired and ill when Alfred sees me again, so I must not overdo it now). In town, people have been buying red, white and blue garlands (probably left over from Coronation Day and brought out now by the shops!) and going through town with them, and the Germans said nothing. One man had a van-load!

*May 6th. SUNDAY.*      At Bethlehem morning. Mr Tom Renouf preached on 'And a bright cloud overshadowed them.' Very appropriate, I thought! Things are extremely quiet everywhere. We met one German only, cycling along. There is no official news about surrender. I suppose it is true, but people at Bethlehem didn't seem at all excited. And, of course, at the back of some people's minds, is the dread of getting bad news of loved ones. A Notice was given out about Thanksgiving Services which will be held as soon as we are freed. Francis and I cycled to town afternoon. Weather fine and wind going down. Everything peaceful, countryside lovely, and on the sea-front people were sitting on the wall or taking walks. Germans in helmets were still on guard at several fortifications, others strolling about, some with civilians, but most of them looking very dull. Saw one naval officer near Snow Hill who was still swaggering, his sword dangling and swinging as he moved his arms! We had tea with Alfred's folk and the Howells, then we went on to La Rocque chapel. Old Mr Gilbert showed us where to put our cycles, spoke to us awhile, and Francis sat with him. Jurat Brée arrived in the vestry at 6.15 and gave me a very warm welcome, and prayed for me and for the service. I felt my great responsibility as I mounted the pulpit and began to wonder if I had the right message for today after all. (Mr Brée had told me in the vestry that everything one has heard these days is rumour and not to be believed!) Congregation 65, singing very good, not dull and slow, therefore helpful. I felt that people here were alive and all so attentive. Afterwards, many thanked me and shook me warmly by the hand – Mrs O Brée especially was charming. They all hoped I would go again. Yet I myself felt dissatisfied and disappointed in myself, especially with regard to the prayers. I couldn't think as I wished, and forgot things I should have prayed for. Mr Brée, who is a little deaf, told me, very kindly, that when I spoke too fast, he did not catch what I said. I feel really discouraged about my preaching today. I did try to speak more slowly, and did not succeed. Francis said that I went awfully fast at times! And I did not realise it at all. How can I improve? I liked the folk at La Rocque and wish I had been planned there before.

Called at Montpelier and 'Mother' gave us a cup of tea. How good and kind she is, and how grateful for everything. How splendid and uncomplaining Alfred's folk have been all through these difficult days. Would that there were more like them. I thank God for them. How unhappy I would be if my 'husband's' parents were not the kind I could get on with. But we have so much in common, especially our faith. We cycled back by Old Beaumont Hill, and I made Francis stop to look at the splendid view of St. Aubin's Bay. How beautiful everything looked: the sea was like a mirror; Elizabeth Castle and St. Aubin's Fort had a background of thundery clouds, and just below us green fields, trees and a cluster of houses. I thought of next time I shall look from that spot, when, please God, 'Beautiful Jersey' will be free again. Tonight, I felt very conscious of my sinfulness and prayed for forgiveness for myself, and for Alfred.

*May 7th.*     Today at Reims the Germans have signed the terms of unconditional surrender on all fronts. So the war in Europe is over at last! We've been many times to the crystal set in John's bedroom, as Mr Churchill was to make a statement, but learned that it will be tomorrow and the King will speak also. Tomorrow is Victory Day and we expect to be freed. It would be awful if in England they were celebrating Victory and Peace and we were still under the Germans. All day we've felt alternately hopeful and downcast. Rumours flying, as usual! Some said the Airport had been cleared, then guns placed there again, as the Germans intended to fight because they were furious that some people had been seen with Union Jacks already. A German officer told the Viberts that the Admiral from Guernsey arrived last night in a destroyer and was not pleased that preparations for surrender were going on. But tonight I am at last beginning to feel certain that we shall be liberated soon. I expect to hear and see British or American planes early tomorrow, so that we may also celebrate Victory Day! Herbert has seen an Officer dressed all in white, looking very smart, not far from the Airport, carrying what looked like a huge white flag. And the Germans have set free all political prisoners here. The Royal Square and Howard Davis Park have been wired off (is it for a Proclamation by the Bailiff?) and the States cars have been ordered to be quite ready (to go to the Airport, I imagine). Mr W Le Brun has been to his office and prepared everything for the arrival of the first mailboat. So, I can believe at last! But it seems that I cannot feel really excited or happy, or like celebrating until I've heard from Alfred. That matters more than anything to me. (Am I selfish?) When will we get news, I wonder? It has been warm and sultry today. Irene has been here washing. I've done the usual jobs, dish-washing, preparing vegetables for dinner, putting out the clothes, seeing to Granny, washed my hair, and fetched rabbit-food on the track tonight. Everything fresh, lovely and peaceful. One of the cats rushed in and killed one of my tiny rabbits as I was giving them milk – how awful it was to see the poor thing suffer and die in a minute or so. I felt like killing the cat! I told Christine that that cat must not have a red white and blue ribbon tomorrow! The two German Inspectors who've been coming regularly about the milk came tonight and told Francis that it was the last time, and that they were going to 'la misère'. One can't help feeling sorry for them, going back to a smashed-up and occupied homeland and having lost the war! I wonder what Alfred feels like tonight? Only a fortnight ago I felt so downhearted, and could not see the end for a long time. So it seems like a miracle that we might see each other soon! All Glory and Praise and Thanks be to God Who 'has done exceeding abundantly above all that we asked or thought.'

*May 8th. VICTORY DAY!*     The war in Europe is over!
*10.30am.*     I am beginning to feel a bit excited. We've had a restless night. Granny was making such a noise that I didn't sleep much. And when I awoke, instead of feeling excited and happy, I felt sad and depressed! I thought of Mother and was anxious that she is no stronger. And I thought of this lovely home that I must soon leave. I felt that I could have been better towards my parents and brothers and sisters than I have been; then I felt anxious about Alfred and wondered if he was feeling better. There was the sound of thunder rolling in the distance, and rain falling against the window. The thunder increased as we were getting up, and there was a terrific crash right overhead, and Joyce saw a ball of fire. After all, it wasn't the sound of American planes, as I had expected to hear, first thing!
At 9 o'clock, when Herbert returned from taking the milk to the depot, he said that the Bailiff had phoned Constable Du Val to tell him that the Union Jack will be hoisted on all the States' buildings at 3pm today. At last! I think I must go to town to see what is happening. So far, everything is quiet and peaceful here in the country. We can't celebrate until the Americans (who are supposed to be expected at noon!) come. Our flags are waiting. It is wonderful to feel that we need not hide things any more. I no longer need worry about hiding this diary, for instance. John is getting a wireless set out from its hiding place, my camera has been removed from Granny's bed, and so on!
I've just listened to the news on the crystal set, and in England, America and Europe, there is the wildest rejoicing, but the Channel Islands have not been

mentioned. I wonder what our friends in England are thinking. Laurence and Kath are putting down the stair-carpet (after the spring-cleaning of the hall). Christine is cooking the dinner, Dad and the other boys are working on the farm and I'm going to clean my bedroom and do the potatoes. Mother is washing Granny (my usual job). So we are busy with our tasks, and asking ourselves if we are to be released today!

*11.30pm.*      Cycled to town afternoon. Went to the Square with Elsie. At 3 o'clock Mr Churchill's statement was broadcast, but we only caught the end of it. I was so disappointed not to have heard him when he mentioned the Channel Islands, because he called us 'our dear Channel islands!' We'll never forget that! After his speech, our Bailiff, high up on the Court House, hoisted the Union Jack, followed by Mr Ned Le Quesne with the Stars and Stripes. Then, flag after flag went up everywhere. People cheered and sang the National Anthem. How everyone cheered again, when the Bailiff announced that he had been informed that a flotilla of British cruisers and destroyers were approaching the Channel Islands, bringing a British 'commission'. How wonderful it was to hear that; we had wondered how they would first come. The Bailiff said he did not know when they would take us over.

Francis, Joyce, Elsie and I went up on the Fort, where we had a lovely view (from behind Mr. Mourant's office) of the town and all the flags. As we stood there, we saw flags going up on Victoria College. On to Mount Bingham we saw the Algerian and Morrocan prisoners hoisting up the French flag at their camp, and Monsieur Dubras making a speech to them preparatory to their release. (The Germans were making an awful noise shooting or exploding things in the harbour.) We saw a few American prisoners still in their camp at South Hill. We went to Grove Place where a short service was going on, but we arrived just as Rev. Ward was pronouncing the Benediction! There was a huge flag draping the pulpit! All churches and chapels were open for prayer. All the chruch bells were ringing – how lovely it was to hear them! The English news were being relayed in Halkett Place, yes, the News! We saw people carting wireless sets about, hidden for so long. Old cars and motor-cycles have appeared from nowhere. What strange scenes, we felt as if we were in a dream.

Had tea at Montpelier. On our way home, Joyce and I were hoping to see the British rounding Noirmont Point; they were not in sight but we could see 'specks' on the horizon. Nearer home, we heard the Germans blowing up mines at the Airport and, now and again, firing a few startling shots from their guns! When we got home, Evie and Eunice were there, and the girls Vibert and Raymond, all hoping to hear the King's Speech at 9 o'clock, but we were disappointed – not one of the three wireless sets would work, though Ed. Laffoley and John have been working hard on them all day – they've been hidden and out of use for too long! So we only had the crystal set, and as so many people were here we had to let them listen. And Mother, Kath and I heard nothing! I fed my little rabbits and wished I was listening to the King! His speech was being relayed in town – if only I'd been there! As no one was bothering about curfew, we all went to bed late. The electric light had come on again, and we were washing up the dishes happily, in this lovely light, when it suddenly went out, so we had to resort to our lamp and candles again. I wrote a letter to Alfred before dinner and posted it in town. Elsie said some people had done this, but, as we've heard nothing yet about letters it may well be returned to me! And I feel so strange and bewildered that I didn't even know how to write. It is wonderful to feel free and to have no fear of being searched any more. It is strange to be celebrating Victory and having all the Union Jacks up, with the Germans still here. One can't help feeling sorry for walking beneath our flags, most looking on in grim silence. I did see a few smiling. The Bailiff appealed to us all to keep calm and people have behaved extremely well. There have been no wild scenes of excitement, probably because the Germans are still here, and though it has been Victory Day in England, the British have not yet taken us over – we still wait to celebrate Liberation.

*May 9th. LIBERATION DAY* – at last!
*11am.* The sun is coming out, though there are plenty clouds about yet. I was so tired yesterday that I've slept very well. Joan has phoned to say she can see one British ship in St. Ouen's Bay. No planes have come yet. I expect the Germans were not prepared for surrender! Constable Du Val told Francis that at 11 o'clock yesterday morning they were still talking about fighting. It is hard for them to surrender!
*Later.* It has been such an exciting day, and so wonderful! The British Tommies have arrived at last. And I realise how very very thankful we must be to God that we have been freed without bloodshed. It is a miracle, and God's doing. The Commandant of the Channel Islands was still refusing, all day yesterday, to surrender, and it was only at the very last minute that he gave in (one minute after midnight). We were wondering what was the best time to go to town, when at about 1.40pm we heard the sound of planes. We rushed out and there were British planes roaring past, quite low. At that moment, for the first time, I really began to feel excited! The British have come at last, I thought. We waved, and I am sure that the pilots saw us and our Union Jacks flying from several places. The planes did not land but roared overhead several times during the day and evening, throwing out coloured lights. In town, how people cheered and cheered them as they passed over. This was our first sign of the arrival of the British!
Joyce, Joan Syvret, Herbert and I rushed off to town on our bicycles whilst the others (not poor Mother though) went in Mr Vibert's lorry. We had all heard that there was going to be a ceremony in the Royal Square as soon as the British commission had landed, so we left our cycles at Mr Mourant's office and made straight for the Square. We went into an office and sat near a win-

dow and waited expectantly. The Square was crowded. We waited and waited and nothing happened. By and by we learnt that we had missed everything. The British officers had landed from the destroyer, arriving in the harbour in a small boat. Our Bailiff, with the German Commandant and his staff, had gone out to the destroyer in a small boat to sign the surrender and had been given a tremendous welcome by the crowd that had gathered on the pier and Weighbridge. Then a British officer had made a lovely speech from the balcony of the Pomme d'Or, said how proud they were to release us, how splendid we had been to stick it for five years, and how they did not come before because it would have meant bombing us to smithereens. Only a few men were with him but he said others were coming. So we heard about it all from the girls who were lucky enough to go to the right place! We'd been in the Square for three hours, all to no purpose! We were disappointed! In Hill St we saw a crowd of boys and girls mobbing a 'Jerrybag'. They ran after her like mad. I don't know if they caught her. We were told that she was trying to shake hands with a Tommy when someone recognised her as a 'friend' of the 'Jerries' and began hitting her with an umbrella. I expect there will be many more such incidents.

We went to have tea at Montpelier and came back to town, hoping to be more fortunate. We saw Kath, Leslie and Margaret who had come in the lorry, but, unfortunately, we lost them when we went to put away our bicycles! There was such a crowd on the piers and Weighbridge. We did not know exactly where to go to see anything. We must have been guided to the right spot, for we went along to the North pier, and just as we got near the cranes there was a British boat just arriving and crowded with British Tommies, our first sight of them. Tears of joy and emotion welled up in our eyes. The crowd was terrific, but I managed to stand several inches higher, on the bottom of a crane, and had a lovely view. How we cheered and cheered! The soldiers began landing immediately, and as they passed, in single file through the crowds, all who could manage it shook them by the hand and said how pleased we were to see them. I shook hands with many and how we all smiled! The soldiers kissed the children and gave out sweets, chocolate and cigarettes. How wonderful to be there, I'll never forget. We stood alongside the boat and many people crowded onto it and chatted to the soldiers. One started calling out for the boys from La Moye. I felt so thankful for their Mother's sake. Don, Ed, and Jim Le Boutillier were all safe. Then I realised that the soldier who was shouting out the good news was a Jerseyman I knew: John Fiott. I saw one soldier sitting happily with his arms around four girls of different ages – reunited – it must have been their father. Joan was very keen to speak to one of the Naval Officers that we could see down on the boat. She so wanted to find out if he had any news of her father. Then the Officer came off the boat and Joan asked me to ask him for her. So I plucked up courage and asked him if he knew Capt. Syvret, and explained about Joan. How charming he was and such a

*Sub. Lt. Cooper,*
*Liberation Day.*

handsome young man too, with lovely teeth! He stopped at once but said he did not know Capt. Syvret. He told us he wanted to look at a German boat that was lying nearby, hoping to get a Nazi flag to put under his Union Jack! As he stood looking at the German boat (the German sailors were still sitting about on it, playing cards) we went back to ask his name. He told us it was Cooper and that he came from from Blackpool. Then we had a lovely long conversation with him. How kind of him to speak to us for so long, just to us four. He told us many interesting things – that the German in command of the Channel Islands would not surrender. On Victory Day he had not surrendered. This officer and his men were waiting at Plymouth and wondered why they could not leave before. (I realise again that only by a miracle have we been saved from terrible things). I asked him what would have happened if the Commandant had refused to give in, and he said we would have been bombed and shelled with heavy guns. He told us his ship was an assault boat, such as they used to invade, to smash defences and land troops. He said the Germans were no good as sailors and that often British ships had come, especially one Naval officer called Higgins, or Higginson, anyway, a man with the DSO several times over, an 'amazing fellow' he told us, near to the Channel Islands at times only five miles off the Jersey coast, to try and draw the German ships out to sea, but they never succeeded. However, they enjoyed their little game with the Germans and caused them confusion. He asked if we heard the shore batteries when the Germans shot at them! I should think we did, and we wondered what was happening – now we know! He told us about the horrors in German camps; this has obviously made him dislike the Germans intensely. He wanted to know when we knew that the Germans had surrendered and how we knew. Did they suddenly lay down all their arms? We told him we didn't know it for certain until just then, when the British had landed. He hoped to stay in Jersey for a month but he expected to have to leave immediately. He had never been to Jersey, though he knew it well on his chart. He amused me when he asked our opinion of the Americans, not realising that we just had a few prisoners here, and had not spoken to them. He said the Americans had stolen all their girls! He is not married (so he told us) because he cannot love his ship, and a wife, then, he has been away so long and with such short leaves.

I can't think why he spoke to us for so long, we insignificant beings in all that crowd. And when we shook hands, he held mine tightly and put his other one over it. I expect he was 'touched' to see the joy in everybody's eyes and to realise what this day meant to us all. Joan was so thrilled and could have stayed near that boat for ever, I think! I was so glad, for her sake, that we had been so fortunate to arrive in time, and she was so pleased that this sailor spoke to us. She is so interested in naval men and ships because of her father, whom I fervently hope is safe and well. I'm glad, for her sake, that I dared speak to this Naval Officer. Well, we stayed so long on the pier that we only got home at 11pm. But, Herbert being with us, it was all right, and there were no disturbances or wild excitement anywhere. It is really surprising, but one has trouble to take in the fact of release and freedom. It is so strange, with the Germans still about everywhere, unarmed, of course, looking on, mostly silently and grimly. Ah, they are no longer arrogant and swaggering!

The weather has been cloudy and mostly dull, and very warm, with a lovely sky tonight; fireworks here and there. Alice was here today. She told us that a farmer who had dealt with the Germans had been trying to get a turn at ringing the St. Ouen's church bells, but P's father had refused to allow it and they nearly fought over it! I suppose the 'Jerry-bags' and others who have traded with the Germans are not feeling as happy as other people today! Well, how much there is to thank God for tonight! By the time we had chatted over the day's events with Dad and Mother, had supper and washed-up, it was very late, and past 1am before I've finally got into bed. All my life I will re-member one of the first things Naval Officer Cooper said, and it was what I liked best of all in the whole of our conversation. He said:

"I have never yet been so touched as today. I've been there at the Liberation of other countries in West Europe but I've not been so very touched as today, in liberating my own people. It is a privilege to be the first to come, we all wanted to be first!"

He said this so sincerely. It is lovely of them to talk of liberating us as a 'privilege!'

What a *wonderful* day! But how much more wonderful will be the day when I see my Alfred again. That is what I live and long for!

# Postscript

The days that followed Liberation Day were most exciting. Crowds flocked to St. Helier to watch more and more British soldiers and sailors land. Huge tank-landing craft coming up to the beach at St. Aubin's Bay disgorged lorry-loads of food and clothing for us. And hundreds of German prisoners marched along the beach and up the ramps of those same boats, to be swallowed up inside and shipped out of our sight.

Yet amidst the excitement of it all there were many Islanders, like myself, whose minds could not rest until we had received news of loved ones. It was three weeks later, on May 31st, that my fiancé's parents and myself had letters from Alfred. Though he and I would have things to explain to each other, I now knew for certain that all would be well between us.

As travel restrictions made it impossible for Alfred to come over to Jersey, he had arranged that as soon as I could get to England myself I would stay with friends of his until we got to know each other again. Then we would go to Jersey to be married, with Rev. W J Ward officiating. I thought this was an excellent plan!

I applied immediately for a travel permit but it was not until July 3rd that I was able to cross the Channel which had separated us for so long – and at last we met on Southampton docks. I can still picture him as I saw him from the boat, wearing a mac!

We applied for a permit to get to Jersey; meanwhile I was kindly given hospitality by Rev. and Mrs George Ridge and Mr and Mrs Higginbotham. Weeks went by and we could not get the permit. Finally, in desperation, we went in person to the Home Office in London. In spite of our pleading to be allowed to go to Jersey, even for one day for our wedding, we were refused permission. This was a terrible disappointment to us and to our families.

The kind friends who had looked after me arranged a reception at their home and we were married on October 13th at Swaythling Methodist Hall, with Rev. Ridge 'giving me away'. A cousin of my husband's, Alan Du Feu, who was in the RAF, acted as best man, and three bridesmaids materialised at the last minute – no time for new frocks! One was Lydie Le Brun, a friend and distant relation who was working in London, and two sweet little girls, daughters of the friends who had taken me into their homes in my time of need. About four hundred people, members of my husband's churches in town and country, were there to wish us well.

The irony of it all was that on the last day of our honeymoon, as we left the hotel, we saw the headline on the morning paper: RESTRICTIONS TO THE CHANNEL ISLANDS LIFTED.

One of the happiest days of my life occurred the following Christmas when Alfred

*Above: Nan Du Feu, née Le Ruez, in her garden
at Spalding, Lincolnshire, May 1994.
Opposite above: Marriage in October 1945;
Opposite below: At Launceston, Cornwall, after
Alfred had officiated at a wedding, 1965;*

and I arrived in Jersey on Christmas morning, and both our families were reunited as we shared Christmas dinner together at Homestead.

In August 1947 our first son, David John, was born, whilst Alfred was still stationed at Southampton. In 1948 we moved to Radstock in Somerset, where two more sons were born, Christopher Robin and Peter Henry; in 1954 we went to Tywardreath in Cornwall, where John Francis, our fourth son was born. In 1957 we moved to St. Austell when Alfred became Superintendent of that Circuit. By 1963 we were in Launceston, and in 1967 we had moved up to Spalding in Lincolnshire. In 1972 back to Cornwall, to serve at Carbis Bay and St. Ives. In 1976 Alfred was due to retire and we bought a little bungalow at Spalding. However, on hearing that a part-time minister was required for a year at Higham Ferrers in Northamptonshire he offered himself, because he loved his work and was not keen to retire until he had done forty years. So we went there and this was followed by another two years of part-time minstry at Lincoln.

In 1979 we at last settled permanently in our bungalow, both of us continuing to find much joy in sharing in the life of the Methodist and other Churches, including preaching on Sundays.

Sadly, Alfred died very suddenly, in 1985, after only six years retirement together, and six months before we would have celebrated our fortieth Wedding Anniversary.

My sons and their families are a great joy and blessing to me. They are scattered between Scotland and Jersey. I have nine grandchildren, three of whom Alfred did not live to see: three girls and six boys.

After my husband died, I found a little note which he had left for me, in which he said: 'Thankyou for sharing your life with me. I shall look forward to the time when we meet again in the Home on High.'

> *Many waters cannot quench Love,*
> *Neither can the floods drown it.*

Song of Solomon.

*Nan Du Feu*
*July 1994*

*Other titles from SEAFLOWER BOOKS on the Channel Islands are as follows:*

## JERSEY RAMBLES
by John Le Dain
This book describes the routes of 28 rambles, from easy twenty-minute strolls to longer, more demanding rambles.
All aspects of the Jersey landscape are included here, from the rugged and magnificent north coast to the gentler charms of the island's well-wooded, south-sloping valleys.
*128 pages; Pen & ink drawings plus 28 maps, Price £4.95*

## THE JERSEY LILY
by Sonia Hillsdon
Born Emilie Le Breton in Jersey in 1853, married to Edward Langtry at the age of twenty, Lillie Langtry was destined to be universally known as 'The Jersey Lily', the most beautiful woman in the world.
*128 pages; fully illustrated; Price £4.95*
'This book is thorough, well-written and entertaining.' – *The Jersey Society in London Bulletin.*

## JERSEY: NOT QUITE BRITISH
by David Le Feuvre
This book is about an island, its history, its culture and its people. The author outlines events which helped to form the special character of the men and women who were Jersey's original inhabitants.
'This is gripping reading, colourful, proud and sad. It is not only an enlightening and entertaining work, but also an important one, whose author has done Jersey an enduring service by vividly conveying and recording the true nature of what is lost.' – *Jersey Evening Post.*
*160 pages; illustrated; Price £5.95*

## JERSEY IN LONDON
by Brian Ahier Read
In 1895 a lone Jerseyman in London arranged a meeting with friends from Jersey who worked in the city. *Jersey in London* tells the story of how that small group of expatriates grew into a flourishing organisation. Its members have included some of the most eminent Jersey people of the century. For the Jersey historian this book offers a unique insight into a hitherto little known aspect of real Jersey folk and members of some well-known local families.
*192 pages; illustrated; fully indexed; Price £6.95*

## LIFE ON SARK

by Jennifer Cochrane

What is it really like to live in a small island community? Most holiday-makers to Sark are day visitors during the summer season – the impression they gain is very different to the reality of the winter months and the rest of the year.

This well informed and fondly written book is guaranteed to delight anyone intrigued by this island gem, which is perhaps the Channel Island with the greatest mystique.

*128 pages; 42 black & white photographs; 12 pencil drawings; map; Price £4.95*

*SEAFLOWER BOOKS are published in paperback and are reasonably priced, though their design and presentation is of a high standard with good quality illustrations integrated into the text. We intend that our list will build into a body of work to represent the best writing about the real Channel Islands, in a format and at a price which will be accessible to the greatest number of readers. Comments and suggestions from readers are always welcome.*

*SEAFLOWER BOOKS may be obtained through local bookshops or direct from the publishers, post-free, on receipt of net price, at:*

*1 The Shambles, Bradford on Avon, Wiltshire, BA15 1JS*
*Tel/ Fax 0225 863595*

*SEAFLOWER BOOKS is an imprint of Ex Libris Press which publishes a range of books on the themes of history, countryside, walking guides, biography and literature. Please ask for our free, illustrated list.*